Backtracking

By Fred K. Gray

October 13, 1924 – December 18, 2022

At age 91, Fred began writing his memoir.

Backtracking by Fred Gray

Photos courtesy of the Johnson County Library
Cover illustration and design by Steve Rzasa
Book layout by Steve Rzasa
Edited by Nancy Tabb, Jonette Goraj, and Dolly Fraley

Published by the Johnson County Library
Copyright © 2023 by the Johnson County Library

International Standard Book Number: 9798218315979

Dedicated to all the people named in this book, past and present,
none of whom were aware they were contributing.
Please forgive me — if appropriate.
Above all, this is dedicated to the people of Johnson County.

Fred or Freddy
(however you know me)

TABLE OF CONTENTS

INTRODUCTION

Mr. Gray began visiting me in the Johnson County Library Local History Room when I started working there as the Research Librarian in 2016. If I noticed him walk by without stopping to chat with me, I would find him in "his" chair, reading *The Wall Street Journal*, in the library's reading room. Neither of us could hear very well, so I sat on the floor in front of him to visit. I called him Mr. Gray, but others knew him as Fred or Freddie. He called himself Fred K. Gray. One time I asked him what the "K" stood for, and he explained he was named after his uncle, Karl Hepp.

Often, he would stop at the library with the name of a person, place or thing and ask if I could locate any information about his current research subject. Without my knowing what he was up to, he asked to read the files of John "Posey" Ryan, John Winchester, and Steve Muschel. He asked for vintage photos of Buffalo, Wyoming, and shared with me amazing family photos, as well as photos taken by the Army photographer on Canton Island in the South Pacific Ocean, where he was stationed during World War II. Mr. Gray claimed he was stationed there where he would be safer because of his valuable typing skills learned at Johnson County High School. Very few men took typing in those days.

I had the pleasure of recording two interviews with Mr. Gray for the library archives. I learned of his childhood antics and school years in Buffalo. He told of his time on Canton Island and explained each memory immortalized in the photos. He told of working for the Highway Department and owning and living at Trailside in the Bighorn Mountains. He and his wife, Patricia, raised five children: Carrie, Stephen, Robin, Anthony, and Randy. With his permission, I shared his interview and photos with *The Buffalo Bulletin*. When he saw his face on the front cover of the newspaper, he was tickled and stopped by to thank us for making him famous. He gave us a big grin with a mischievous twinkle in his eye. He, of course, had already become famous in Buffalo for walking five miles every day no matter the weather, still spry at 98 years old.

Mr. Gray was one of my go-to people whenever I had a history mystery to solve. He could answer most things off the top of his head, saving me hours of research. We shared a lot of laughs as he explained things, like how the train between Buffalo and Clearmont, Wyoming, got from the depot to the roundhouse. I often saw him walking in his old neighborhood, most likely backtracking. I realize that he was teaching me so much about Johnson County in Wyoming history as he was "waltzing on memories" to write his story–this book.

Previously, several notebooks of his wonderful manuscript were printed and given to family and friends. He donated one to our Local History Room. This book was not his first experience with publishing a book because he had published his half-brother's, Claude Gray's, life story in *Never a Dull Moment*. As Jonette Goraj, Dolly Fraley and I read Mr. Gray's precious memories, we were convinced *Backtracking* needed to be published too so it could be shared with a much wider audience. Like an answered prayer, one day an anonymous donor offered to pay publishing expenses, confirming our feelings that this book was meant to be.

Without many talented people this book would not have been possible, and I thank them all from the bottom of my heart. Among them are Fred K. Gray's family, who graciously allowed us to share his story. Jonette Goraj and Dolly Fraley, both volunteers in the Local History Room, truly got the job done. They kept me motivated and organized, did all the computer work of preparing the manuscript, and offered terrific advice. Bill Goraj image-edited the photos that had been donated to the library by Mr. Gray–most of them found in an envelope labeled "For Backtracking"–and had sneak peeks at the manuscript as Jonette edited it. Thanks to Steve Rzasa for making the book publishing world easy for us to navigate. To Lindsey Belliveau, Johnson County Library Director, thanks for the support and encouragement you gave us along the way. Dan Fraley, thank you for sharing Dolly with us as she transcribed histories all of these years. And thank you to my husband, Dozier Tabb, for loving me through it all and for listening to one more funny story again and again. Of course, thank you to our anonymous donor. Above all, thank you, Mr. Gray, for writing your memories for us all to enjoy.

Fred K. Gray left this world December 18, 2022, at his home on Burritt Avenue in Buffalo, Wyoming. His house was located right next door to his grandparents' house, where he was born 98 years earlier. His life had come full circle.

Nancy Tabb
Local History Librarian
Johnson County Library
Buffalo, Wyoming

PREFACE

I have always been a collector of "stuff"–maybe an inheritance from my grandfather, Chris Hepp. I also have a habit of writing down something funny or an unusual incident and then dropping it into a box or drawer to be forgotten. Years later, when I would come upon it, it would jog my memory back to the circumstances of why, when and where it took place. I don't even remember when I started the practice because the notes weren't dated.

They were usually typed because it was easier to think about what I was going to say using a pen or pencil, plus my handwriting is a thing to behold and unreadable. I once had a friend, Corkey Howells, who didn't have to be concerned about public relations, tell me words to the effect that it looked like the scrawl doctors use to write prescriptions.

Several years after I retired, I ran out of something to do, and a couple of my kids suggested that I ought to write down some of the things that had happened in the "olden days," so I started gathering up some of my old notes and adding some new ones. It turned into quite a job. Many times I wondered why I was wasting my time.

One thing that really helped was that I had saved all my income tax records dating back to the first one I had filed after graduating from high school in 1942, so it was easy to pinpoint employers, business ventures, etc., and the people connected with them some 70 years later. Memories before that time were a little iffy, but that was offset by the fact that the vast majority of people who could contradict me had taken up residence in Willow Grove Cemetery.

Like all storytellers–even the ones that won't admit it–I know I've gotten some of my wires crossed. It would be impossible to remember all the incidents verbatim, but I've tried to point them in the general direction and time period they occurred to get the main point across and then fill in the blanks. I have also tried to put them in some semblance of order, but that didn't work out too well because my train of thought wandered all over the map.

In 2014, with the help of a very dear friend, Margaret Smith, I published a book, *Never a Dull Moment*, from notes written by my half-brother, Claude Gray, and was so glad I did. His upbringing and mine were polar opposites, just as mine and my children's are. I enjoyed his recollections, no end, and hope someday my children and grandchildren may say the same about my book.

Fred Gray

*Fred Gray and the house where he was born,
726 N. Burritt Ave., Buffalo, Wyoming*

PART I

Growing up in Buffalo, Wyoming

My family moved down on the east side of Clear Creek across from the railroad tracks on Bozeman Avenue (Charles Street at that time) in 1929 when I was five. It was during the Depression, and Prohibition was on in full swing. There were several people who made and sold bootleg beer in the neighborhood, so our single street acquired the name of "Bootlegger Alley." It was only two blocks long and was crowded between Clear Creek and the railroad tracks to the west with a big hill to the east, so it was more or less isolated from the rest of town. It was a dead-end street, and the only way in or out was to the south where it followed Clear Creek for several blocks with no houses on either side. Cars were scarce, so all the foot traffic back and forth to town was across a swinging footbridge that ended up at the railroad tracks. From there, it was another couple blocks to Main Street.

About half of the men who lived along the street were immigrants who made their living as coal miners. They walked to work to a Wyoming Railroad mine about a mile to the east. I can still remember seeing them filing single file up and over the big hill, carrying their lunchboxes. Some of the names I remember were Lager, Rossman, Kostenbauer, Abrams, Piercy, and Pichlmaier on the east side of the street and Connor, Patch, Osborn, and Gray on the west.

There were a number of children in the neighborhood who were in and out of the houses as if they were their own home with two exceptions. Those kids were not allowed out of their fenced yards or to associate with any of the rest of us at any time or in any way even to visit when we walked by their yards. I got to thinking about it in later years. The two homes where the kids were locked up had the most tragic consequences in their adult lives. I guess the rest of us grew up street smart and were better prepared for the future.

Most of the homes along the street were saturated with the smell of malt on the inside because of the large vats of beer, fermenting behind the coal burning kitchen stoves, but we paid no attention to them. We were used to it in our own homes and accepted it as completely natural. The main house involved with selling it was the Lager family–Albert and Marie. They didn't have any children of their own but were raising two girls, Gail and Mary Armstrong.

I never knew what the connection was or what had happened to their mother, but their father was at the Lager's home a lot. He was a World War I veteran and had been exposed to mustard gas during the fighting. He had a severe cough that would double him up at times and completely disable him. He may have been living at the Soldiers' and Sailors' Home, later renamed Veterans' Home of Wyoming, which was limited to veterans only. I think his only income, if any, would have been a very meager veteran's pension.

The Lagers were never bothered by the law for selling bootleg beer because some of their best customers were on the police force. Mrs. Lager and her neighbor, Mrs. Rossman, spoke mostly German. We couldn't understand them very well. They were really unique to us kids because they both smoked corncob pipes, and we had never seen a woman smoke before.

There were some cottonwood trees in the Lager's backyard, and the two women had an old two-door car body, sitting under the trees that they used for a patio. It didn't have a chassis, windows or frontend and was just a shell that sat on the ground. The whole inside was gutted except for the backseat where they sat, smoked and gossiped in German. They peddled a lot of homebrew out of it. If someone wanted hard liquor, there was a little door under the seat that opened to get to the bottle. It was supposed to be a secret, but every kid in the neighborhood knew about it.

Mr. Lager never worked for a living, and I saw more $20 bills in their cupboard than I knew existed in the whole world. One time, he took me fishing out to Lake DeSmet in his old car. When we got back, he was drunk, and his wife lit into him with both feet for driving drunk with me in the vehicle. That was the first and last time I ever went anywhere with him.

One family that lived just across the street to the north had an adopted daughter, Helen, who the whole neighborhood talked about. She was kept locked up in the yard and wasn't even permitted to visit with any of us kids through the gate. If they caught her, she disappeared into the house. She eventually married a local man named Albert Benton and worked as a cook in some of the local restaurants.

Mr. and Mrs. Rossman–his name was Andy–built a greenhouse at some point and sold produce and plants to local people. It was separate from the house. I don't know how many customers ever saw the inside of their home. I know I never did. I would suppose Andy had his crock of homemade beer, brewing behind the stove, unless he was a teetotaler, but I'm pretty sure they never got into the business of selling it.

Years later after I was married, my wife, Patricia [Davis], and I built a house in the same neighborhood. One day when I and the three oldest kids were heading home, we saw Mr. Rossman, lying in the grass across the street from his house with a rifle across his chest. The kids were excited and wanted to stop, but I knew what had happened, so I told them he was probably just resting. I dropped them off at home and drove up to the sheriff's office and reported it. By the time we got back a few minutes later, the three of them were standing over him examining the body–so much for protecting your children from unpleasant circumstances like a suicide.

§ § §

The first person I ever hated, besides being deathly afraid of her, was my first grade teacher, Miss McEachran. This was in 1930. Of all the people who I ever felt were mismatched for the profession they were in, she was one of the worst. But this opinion is coming from a person who didn't like arithmetic and didn't have the foggiest notion how two apples plus two apples was the same as four apples. There were four or five of my classmates–all boys–who were in the same boat trying to figure it out.

In the afternoon after the rest of the class had been dismissed, she would line us up facing the blackboard with a piece of chalk in our hand. We weren't allowed to turn around. She would give us the apple problem. Sometimes she used oranges to mix us up. The first one to write the correct answer on the blackboard was allowed to leave the room. It was just like musical chairs, and there were never any ties.

She would then walk down the line and pull each remaining boy's hair and slap his face. We could hear her footsteps coming down the row. We would just close our eyes and grit our teeth, waiting for the hammer to fall. I wanted to quit school, but my mother wouldn't let me. My sister, Edith, who was good at arithmetic, had Miss McEachran for a teacher three years before me and liked her. She agreed with Mother, so I had to stay until I graduated the following spring.

The next teacher on my bad list was Miss Brown. What I remember most about her was that she would stand inside the door of the boy's bathroom at recess when we used the toilet. Some of us were still using outhouses at home and weren't used to the ones that flushed. It was hard to use the bathroom when she was in the room. She also made us use the sink to wash our hands–something our mother had been preaching to us since day-one without much success.

I think the reason she was in there was because the janitor had complained. We boys didn't like him, and I don't think some of the parents did either because he was always giving candy and dolls to some of his favorite girls on the playground. My older sister, Edith, was hired as the school secretary by Mr. Kuiper, the principal, when she graduated from high school. She tried to tell him the janitor had some problems but was never able to get the message across. And this was in the days when you didn't need a reason to fire somebody.

4

Miss McKeag had a combined class of third and fourth graders when I started third grade. The first morning she had us write the names of our parents down on a sheet of paper and turn them in at her desk. When she checked mine, she noticed I had written "Mrs. Fred Gray" for the name of my mother, so in a very nice way–because all the other kids were listening– she asked me her first name, and I insisted that's what it was. She told me to talk it over with my mother when I went home for lunch and see her when I got back to school.

When I got back, I told her Mother said it was Elsie. If she would have just asked me what my aunts called her when they were visiting, I would have gotten it right the first time. I had the unique experience of being the only kid in the third grade that didn't know their mother's name. But she was a real nice teacher and I liked her. Later on, she married a man named Carl Kaltenbach.

As it turned out, that was not my only problem with names in the third grade. On Valentine's Day, each classroom had a big cardboard box decorated with red hearts and a slot cut in the top so you could send cards to anybody you wanted and nobody else would know who sent it. In the afternoon someone was picked to open the box and pass out the Valentines to the ones with their name on the envelope.

There was one girl in school who was the most beautiful one in my class, and I figured when we were old enough, we would get married and live happily ever after like the prince and princess did in the storybooks. Her name was Mary Dixon. My problem was that I didn't know how to spell her name on the Valentine, and this was a really serious problem. As everyone knows, there are 26 letters in the alphabet, and hers had nine that were all different. I was having trouble enough memorizing all of them at one time anyway. The odds of getting all the ones in her name in the right order were not good, and I didn't want her to get the idea I was a dummy. I don't remember how I solved the problem, but everything turned out okay in the end because I married a girl name Patricia, who was a lot prettier, and I even knew how to spell her name.

In the fifth grade my teacher was Vee Cooper, who later married one of the Seney twins. She had a habit of tapping kids, including me, on the head with a ruler when she was upset which, as I remember, was quite often.

In the sixth grade I had Miss Lane and have no idea how old she was, but she had taught all of my older sisters. She was very tiny and strict but sincerely interested in each of her student's progress. I think I was one of her pets because she let me answer the door when a parent would knock on it while visiting our class. It was a very prestigious job, and I even got to escort them to a seat. She had been teaching for a long, long time. I heard a teacher tell someone that Miss Lane was standing on the bank to greet

Columbus when he came sailing up Clear Creek.

In the seventh grade I had Miss Moe, and I was sure glad because the other seventh grade class was taught by Mr. Dan Ahern. Every kid–without exception–was afraid of the man, and I think some of the teachers were intimidated by him too. He had spent a number of years in the Army and ran his class like a Marine boot camp. He grew up on a ranch on Powder River and was hard as nails. He never used first names for the members of his class. Each student was addressed as Mr. or Miss. Then he added their last names. He was the school disciplinarian, and all the teachers used his services.

The kid that screwed up knew he had an appointment with the paddle the next morning at a specified time to give him all night to think about it. The teachers would open their classroom door at the appointed hour so we could all hear the unfortunate kid crying after each whack from the empty room that had been set aside for that purpose. The number of hits was determined by the severity of the offense, and the whole procedure was very effective in pointing the rest of us down the straight and narrow path. He was still teaching–and paddling–25 years later when my kids had classes under him, but times have changed and the paddle has long since disappeared into history.

One year he started an after school boy's organization he named the Big Horn Trailers. Most of the boys in my class joined, but there were some of us who got involved because of peer pressure and intimidation. At one basketball session he became annoyed at one of the kids and threw the ball at him but missed. I was in the line of fire. It hit the side of my head, and I went down for the count like a chunk of lead. I sure didn't like that guy.

Merida Maggard was my eighth grade teacher, and I think he was also the principal at the time. He was a nice guy but had a habit of telling jokes in class that went way over our head. I remember one about President Roosevelt, who had been in office as far back as any of us kids could remember. According to Mr. Maggard, when President Roosevelt died and went to heaven, there was some kind of mix up because he thought he was God. None of us kids were able to make the connection.

My freshman class was a new experience and had homerooms with classes in separate rooms. My homeroom teacher was Marjorie Davis. She told jokes by asking us a question first. One example I remember: Do you know what a honeymoon salad is? Lettuce alone. She had quite a bunch of them, and we thought they were pretty dumb but laughed anyway so she wouldn't get discouraged. She was a rather large lady and sometimes wore short dresses with cowboy boots–kind of different. She later married Dale Young, and they purchased the Mansion House on North Main Street, remodeled it, and furnished it with antiques. I think it was mostly her idea

6

and design, and she did a super job.

I remember two new teachers, Mr. Maul and Miss Perkins, who started during my freshman year. Mr. Maul taught Civics classes and got off to a bad start because, as everyone knows, Civics is a pretty boring topic. He lectured by roaming around the room while spouting statistics. One day, he was in the back of the room working his way forward when he came up behind a big kid named George Hibler, who had fallen asleep at his desk. He rapped George on top of his head with his pointing stick, and George woke up and came off his seat like a coiled rattlesnake. He hung one on Mr. Maul's chin, who dropped to the floor like a sack of wheat. George walked straight out of the room and out of the building without bothering to stop at the principal's office to get official notice that he was expelled. I think he may have been a senior at the time. I don't remember if they ever let him come back and finish school, but, knowing George, it probably wouldn't have made much difference one way or the other.

Miss Perkins taught Algebra. I've already mentioned my experience with arithmetic in the first grade, and I hadn't made much headway with any type of math since then. We had to have two credits to graduate, and I wanted to get it over with, so I signed up for Algebra I. My sister, Edith, was a senior taking Algebra II. She was the only reason I made it. I put on the performance of my life and treated Miss Perkins like she was Queen of the Universe for the entire year. Edith helped on the daily work, and I scraped bottom on the tests and squeaked through. Miss Perkins gave me a passing grade at the end of the year. I was home free for math credits.

Mrs. Bess "Ma" Muir taught Literature, and it was a snap. She was one in a million and took a personal interest in every student she taught which was a bunch. She was there for many, many years and taught some of her students' children before she retired. We had one kid in class, Kenneth Namphedt, whom she never gave up on but never made much headway either. Literature for him was like math to me. I remember one time he walked to the front of the room and handed an essay to Mrs. Muir for review, and it was so bad she started crying.

I knew her husband, Dave. He was the polar opposite. He talked with a Scottish brogue, and every third sentence ended in profanity. They had a homestead down on Powder River, and when they sold it, he got into the guiding business with a string of packhorses. He headquartered out of Lucasta Camp, which had a few tourist cabins that had been constructed in the 1920s in the Bighorn Mountains about 12 miles west of Buffalo on Highway 16. At the time Dave was there, Anne Baker owned the cabins, and Walt Cortner was working for him. I think later on Walt took over the business from Dave. They guided guests in the Cloud Peak Wilderness area on hunting and fishing trips.

While in high school, I liked Biology but had a lot of problems with Chemistry. A friend, Walt Hushbeck, helped me out. I tried to return the favor with anything connected to spelling something correctly, but it was a chore for both of us. Miss Fae Baird, later Buster Eschrich's wife, was the typing teacher. I really liked it, so I took it for the two years it was available. She had two daily classes totaling about 40 or so girls and four boys, including myself, that I remember. Of all the subjects I took in high school, typing was the one that helped the most after graduating.

I never liked anything at all connected to organized sports and never participated in any unless I couldn't figure out a way to get out of it. Hunting and fishing were my prime interests.

We had an hour to get home, eat and back to school. Some of us had to run to make it. There were no school busses. When country kids reached high school age, their parents would have to board them in town or make other arrangements. Even the kids in Kaycee had to come to Buffalo after they finished eighth grade.

World War II started in my senior year, and from then on practically every boy was drafted soon after graduation. A few even quit school to enlist. Of my high school classmates about a dozen were KIAs–killed in action.

§ § §

At some point every summer, rubber gun fights would take center stage. It was usually between buddies who would take up sides, but sometimes it would spread out into warfare with neighborhoods against each other.

During the 1930s before the age of tubeless tires, all tires had tubes made out of real rubber. I think synthetic substitutes started to appear during World War II when the sources for natural rubber dried up and had to be replaced with something else. The synthetic tubes were inferior to the real thing for our purpose because they wouldn't stretch as far and lacked springiness. You had to look around and find the right size tube so when you sliced it into bands, they would stretch out to the right length. Truck tubes were worthless because they were too thick and heavy. We sliced the bands into widths of about a half to three quarters of an inch wide.

We made pistols out of laths with the barrel length determined by how far the band would stretch so it could be looped over the end of the barrel. The longer the better because it would carry further. The pistol grip was any width you wanted depending on how many clothespins (triggers) were going to be nailed to it–anywhere from one, a single shot, to four or five. If it was too wide, it was hard to handle, and you had to use both hands to manage it, especially if someone was charging you.

The clothespins were lined up in a row and nailed to the backend of the pistol grip. To load them you would clamp one end of the band in the clothespin and stretch it over the end of the barrel and so on down the line to the last clothespin. If you wanted a really long barrel with a lot of mass, you could knot two bands together to lengthen them out, but it was a lot harder to handle. If you used more than one clothespin, the knots would stack up on top of each other when they were loaded, so it was best to go with a single shot and carry an extra shorter gun in your belt. The only thing you had to remember when you started firing was that the top band had to be fired first so the bands wouldn't jam up making the gun useless.

The longer bands meant more mass when they were fired–kind of like a shotgun–and would really sting if you got hit in the face at close range. It was considered unethical to aim for the face, but if you got in a real bind, ethics went out the window, and you could holler foul. This was after you had taken the hit. Your enemy would just claim he made a mistake and apologize, which is exactly what you would do if the situation was reversed.

If you had a gun with four or five clothespins and somebody charged you and got within about 10 feet, you could fire it machine gun style unless you got mixed up and pressed the wrong clothespin. Then it would jam, and you were dead meat, and your only option was a fast retreat with your back taking all the damage from your enemy. It wasn't so bad if you had a heavy jacket on for protection, but a light shirt didn't provide much. If you wanted a really long barrel with a lot of mass, you could knot two bands together to lengthen them out, but it was a lot harder to handle. If you used more than one clothespin, the knots would stack up on top of each other when they were loaded, so it was best to go with a single shot and carry an extra shorter gun in your belt.

§ § §

Thinking about the rubber gun battles brings to mind a girl, Diana, who lived on North Main Street. She was a tomboy and tough as nails. She was sort of one of the unspoken leaders in her gang of mostly boys, and nobody crossed her. Being an outsider, I wouldn't ever consider it even though I was a little older than she was. Her neighborhood was mostly Basque kids, and they would invade our territory at times. Those guys were all my classmates and some of them very good friends, but the brotherhood of neighbors was a pretty strong factor in grade school, so feelings could temporarily take second place when push came to shove at the rubber gun fights. But all animosity was forgotten when the last invader disappeared around the corner until the next gunfight. Diana had a relative we called Corky. He was bigger than she was. Given a choice, I would rather have fought him than her.

Two more girls I gave a wide berth to in spite of being older were the Danny Anderson children. Both of them had red hair and tempers to match. One of them became a pastor in adult life and led a church in Kaycee [Wyoming]. The other married a very good friend and schoolmate of mine, Bob Kerr.

One time, I spotted a couple of rabbits that had taken up residence under a brush pile on what I thought was the Anderson property several hundred yards from their house. I did my damndest to capture them while keeping an eye out for the girls but was never able to catch them. They were both white with black spots and would have made a great addition to my rabbit family until somebody rustled my whole herd one night.

In later years before either of us were married, Bob and I decided to try working on an oil rig that was drilling a well south of Buffalo. We were working the midnight to eight shift, and the driller showed up drunk every night we were there. New hands on an oil rig with a drunken driller for a boss is a great way to commit suicide, so we both quit a few nights later.

§ § §

A few years ago, I read a book devoted to health and hygiene issues that brought to mind an incident the City of Buffalo practiced all through my grade school years. The book was about research concerning the problems associated with foodborne illnesses and how to avoid the most serious ones that can sometimes end in death.

For example, it explained how some of the deadliest strains of Salmonella can reside in the ovaries of a chicken and be passed on to the person who eats the eggs and how the big commercial farms that use manure for fertilizer–and family-sized ones for that matter–have to get the temperature up to 165° in the compost heaps to kill the deadly pathogens that might be present. Things were a little simpler when I was growing up in the 1930s.

Through those years our family lived on Bozeman Avenue. Our house was about two or three blocks up the creek from the present-day county yard but on the south side of the creek. The area between the creek and Highway 16 was mostly swamp and cattails with only two houses along the highway. Wyoming Railroad had built tracks through the middle of the swamp with one spur going to the roundhouse north of the highway and the mainline continuing up Clear Creek to the depot. It also had a spur to the wool house that sat on the same lots the Family Dollar Store presently occupies. It was used every spring to store the sacks of wool hauled in by ranchers until the railroad could transport it to Clearmont [Wyoming].

The City built a sewage plant on the west side of the swamp to take care of the homes toward Main Street. It was a series of concrete channels or chutes about 3 or 4 feet high and maybe 4 feet wide, as I remember, with no cover. It was sort of like a maze used to train rats. The sewage was piped directly into the chutes where it spread out and the liquids slowly evaporated. If it couldn't evaporate fast enough, a pipe crossed under the railroad tracks to take the excess to Clear Creek. At various times, city workers had to get in the thing and shovel the settlings out with scoop shovels into the back of a truck. I assume they wore rubber boots. The smell was horrible after they had broken the crust.

One of the city employees was our next-door neighbor, Art Osborn, and his wife, Mamie. They always had a big garden and sometimes shared the produce with my family–six girls and two boys. My mother always had a big garden too. One year, Art decided to consolidate his work and garden, so he used a truckload of the "fertilizer" on his garden plot and plowed it under. I guess it saved hauling manure from somebody's barn like most other people did if they had something to haul it with.

My mother was furious because there was only a woven wire fence between us and them, and it didn't do much to stop the odor. It permeated the neighborhood for weeks. I don't remember if she accepted any produce from Art that year or not, but I kind of doubt it.

I mentioned that the pipe from those settling basins emptied directly into Clear Creek. Lots of times my buddies and I saw raw sewage floating down the creek. The outlet was about 300 feet above the tie boom, which was our favorite fishing hole along with many other people in town. It put a lot of fried trout on their dinner table, including ours.

I don't recall ever discussing this particular detail with Mother, but I thought a lot about it after I got into high school and hygiene classes.

§ § §

In 1934 when I was 10 years old, someone gave me a gold watch chain with a locket attached that most of the men wore on the front of their suits or vests. Mother wouldn't let me take it out of the house to play with because she said I'd just lose it, but I kept pestering her and she finally gave in. A short time later, of course, I lost it, and she was pretty upset. I remember at the time a man named Oscar Nelson was building a little cabin in our backyard. My father had rented a ranch from him for many years, and they had become good friends.

It was during Prohibition, and Oscar and a partner, Big George, went into the bootlegging business. They were busted several times, and in 1935 Oscar went completely broke and the bank foreclosed on his ranch. He was destitute, and my father let him build a little cabin on the back of our lot to live in. I don't remember what he looked like, but he must have been a short man because the ceiling wasn't much over 6 feet high, and the top of the door was only a few inches below that. My father would have had to stoop to get through the door.

In 1949, several years after I got home from World War II, I decided to tear out the wood floor of the cabin and put in a concrete pad, which would result in an extra 2 feet of headroom. When I pried up the last stringer that had supported the floor, I was staring at my gold watch chain, hanging on the inside of the wall. One end was caught in the mortar that Oscar had applied after I had stuffed the chain between the logs.

I took it in the house and returned it to my mother for safekeeping until she figured I was mature enough to handle the responsibility myself. Of course, I took the opportunity to remind her that I had kept my promise about not losing it some 15 years before, but she wasn't at all impressed.

In the years before I tore the floor out, the cabin was used for our chicken house, which was a big mistake. With the wood floor and the north end a couple feet off the ground, it was an icebox in winter. I can still remember the chickens huddled on their roosts with their combs turned black from being frozen. The only windows on the south weren't glass but were covered with a transparent fabric of some kind. It was tough but brittle, and wire netting had been nailed over the inside to protect it from shattering when the chickens flew into it. There was a small enclosed yard for them to walk around in, and during winter it was usually warmer outside than in the house. The daily egg production at that time of year must have been close to zero.

I can remember thinking at one time that there must be a fortune in the egg selling business, so I raised a few broods of chicks with setting hens– about 10 or so eggs to a hen. Aunt Rosy (Olson) gave me my first one, so I honored her by naming it after her. My brother-in-law, Joe Bilbao, was working as a butcher for a grocery store at the time, Table Supply, located just north of present-day First National Bank. He rummaged around in the back of the store that was wall-to-wall junk and found an old hand crank coffee grinder that I used to grind wheat to make it digestible for the baby chicks. I know I never broke even on the deal after paying for the wheat, probably because my mother was my only customer, and there was a limit to what the market would bear.

The next use of the chicken house was as a storage shed for hay and pellets when I got into raising rabbits. They were a losing proposition too. I had a little homemade trailer hitched to my bike, and I cut hay along the highway east of town with a pair of old sheep shears. I'd haul it home and spread it out on the roof to cure before storing it in the chicken house.

I got out of the rabbit business one night when someone stole all of them. This nighttime rabbit rustling had been going on for some time, and I was halfway expecting it, but there wasn't anything I could do about it. A friend of mine, Coolidge Staggs, got cleaned out a couple of nights before I did. He was down checking my extra pens at daylight the next morning before I was even out of bed just to make sure he hadn't been double-crossed. In the rabbit business you learn not to trust anyone–even your friends.

I tried to narrow the list of suspect rabbit rustlers into who I figured was the most likely one and came up with a classmate named Bob Mitten. After thinking it over for several months, I convinced myself that he was the guilty rabbit thief, but I never accused him because I knew he would just deny it. However, I never forgot it, and when we had our 30-year class reunion, I decided to get it off my mind. I spotted him in a corner of the room and asked him pointblank if he had rustled my rabbits.

He denied it and finally convinced me that he really and truly didn't do it. I've been thinking about it ever since and am now quite sure it was my friend Coolidge. He was just replacing his that had been stolen, so it wasn't like he was mad at me or something. Under the same circumstances I might have done the same thing myself if I had thought I could get away with it.

The chicken house saga had one more final episode–to date, that is. A man named Frank Bybee came into possession of my mother's house a number of years later. He and his wife owned it for a few years and then built a new home on Upper Clear Creek Road southwest of town. Before he sold the place, he jacked up the chicken house and moved it to his new property and made it into a garage. Several years after that, the new owner of my mother's property, Hilton Balinger, built a brand-new cabin on the same foundation with real glass windows and electric lights instead of kerosene lanterns. So we're back to square one and proof that what goes around comes around even if it's only a lowly chicken house. I like to think of it as coming home to roost, so to speak.

§ § §

During the 1930s era Depression, millions of men were thrown out of work, and many of them resorted to hitching a ride on the railroad in a boxcar, asking for handouts and trying to find jobs. They were called hobos, and their method of travel was termed riding the rails. Buffalo was off the main route, but we still got quite a number of them in the summer months. The ones that arrived in town had to wait until the next day to hitch a ride back to Clearmont on the train, so they camped overnight in what they called jungles. Two of these were a short distance from our house–one on our side of the creek to the north and another across the creek to the south. We could see their campfires flickering along the creek all summer long. Mother was always a little leery of them, but they never caused any problems. When it rained, they would crowd into our chicken house for shelter. She said they never stole any eggs or chickens that she was aware of. That was a big plus in their favor because they were limited to what they could carry and had to panhandle food from the people and merchants where they were camped. They didn't have any money and cooked what they were given over their campfires in coffee cans or any other utensils they could find.

It was almost a daily routine in the summertime for one or more to knock on our backdoor and ask for a handout. Mother would make them a fried egg sandwich with coffee to go along with it, and they would sit on the lawn and eat while us kids would gather around the inside house windows to watch. One year, one of them asked her for a needle and some black thread, which she gave him. When the women in the neighborhood got to comparing notes, they found he had visited every home and asked for the same thing. They had no idea why, but he must have had quite a supply of needles and black thread when he left town.

In addition to the hobos, there was always a caravan of gypsies that arrived every summer for an extended stay. They would set up their camp in the bend of Clear Creek behind the depot. They had a well-deserved reputation for stealing anything they could lay their hands on. When the situation got out of control enough for the police to interfere, they would be escorted out of town.

They were very skilled operators. Several of them would arrive at a business at the same time when only one clerk was on duty. One of them would engage his attention while the rest of them would scatter through the store and help themselves. They were short change artists. If they actually paid for something, they would confuse the clerk so badly he wouldn't be able to figure out how much money he had lost without checking the complete contents of the cash register after they had left the store. One of my classmates owned a grocery store in town in later years. Several gypsies created a disturbance inside the building to get everybody's attention while another rifled the cash box to the tune of $8,000.

The gypsies wore very colorful clothes and lots of jewelry. They loved music, and we could hear and see them dancing around their campfires in the evening. Ralph Johnson lived on Lobban Avenue directly across the street from the present Buffalo Bulletin office, and their camp was practically in his backyard.

14

Many years later we were reminiscing about the gypsy camp, and Ralph said once when he was in grade school, he went over and visited them. His mother found out about it and told him gypsies stole little boys like him, so that was the last time he did it. Then he laughed and said one of the gypsy girls was the most beautiful person he had ever seen with her colorful clothes and jewelry up and down her arms and around her neck. He said if he could have been sure that she was the one that stole him, he probably wouldn't have put up much of a fuss.

When I was in grade school with the hobos, gypsies and all the other bad guys I'd ever heard about, it was always spooky going home by myself after dark. The streetlights and sidewalk ended at the same place. From there you had to cross the railroad tracks and the swinging bridge over Clear Creek. The end of the bridge had steep concrete steps about 6 feet high to go down before you hit the next streetlight. It was in a bunch of trees and didn't put out much light even when it had a bulb in it, which wasn't very often. The creek was a favorite playground for boys with slingshots and BB guns, and glass bulbs made a great target.

From the light pole I had to walk up a narrow dirt path with a high board fence on both sides to get to the alley behind my house, and it was dark as Hades. I was always afraid someone would reach out and grab me. I did a lot of thinking about that and figured the best thing to do was vary my walking routine and throw them off balance–who or whatever they were–so I picked a spot about half way across the bridge that I could see in the dark. After that, when I started home, I'd just amble along and whistle or sing like I didn't have a care in the world. The instant I hit my spot, it was warp speed ahead.

There were six or eight steps off the bridge, but as fast as I was moving, I could grab the rail and only touch once before hitting the ground. Then it was up the path like the devil himself was right behind me. It was lucky I never met anyone head on because the path wasn't wide enough for two, and they would have been drilled by a 90-pound bullet.

Incidentally, about 20 years later I was walking home from work one day, and at the place where I had always started burning up shoe leather, I met the prettiest girl I had ever seen. I said "hello" and had to step to the side to let her pass. I didn't have the faintest idea who she was or where she came from, but I found out and a couple years later I married her. Her name was Patricia Davis.

Patricia Davis

§ § §

When I was a third grader at the school on Fort Street, I had a friend,

15

Jim Maxwell, whose father was the pastor of the Methodist Church directly across the street. I can't recall Jim having any brothers or sisters. One day, he invited me to have dinner at the parsonage, which was next door to the church. I got permission from my mother, and when the four of us sat down at the table–his parents, Jim and me–it was a totally new experience for me. It was the first time I had ever been exposed to someone saying grace, and hardly anybody spoke during the meal. I have often wondered what Jim's father thought of the renegade his son had chosen for a friend. That may have been a deciding factor in his transfer to another church.

Everything was orderly with nothing in the house out of place, and I was very uncomfortable. I was used to living in a small three-bedroom home with six sisters and a brother. Mealtimes were noisy with Mother trying to keep order and food on the table at the same time. My father was a fulltime cowboy working seven days a week. When he got a chance to come to town, it was on horseback because we didn't own a car. My mother was raised on a ranch where all the work was done with horses, and she never learned to drive anything except a team.

A couple years later, a close friend, Walt Hushbeck, invited me to his Sunday school class at the Congregational Church under slightly different circumstances. The boys and girls were having a race to see who could recruit the most members for their class with the losers furnishing ice cream and cake for the winners. The race was pretty close up to the last Sunday. The boys decided to nail things down, so they invited every boy in town to a free party to enjoy all the ice cream and cake they could eat. The girls were treating. Walt recruited me, and when I got there, it was standing room only with mostly Catholics filling the building. I think that was the last time anybody suggested a race to bolster attendance.

The pastor of the Congregational Church at that time was Mr. Ollis, who had a son named Leslie. I don't know for sure, but I think he was in his late teens or early twenties in age. Leslie started a boys club that was very successful and drew in a lot of outsiders, including me, for as long as it lasted. I think Leslie's dad may have had something to do with its demise after he found out what was going on at the meetings.

They started every Wednesday evening at 7:00. There was a room in the basement of the church with bench seats all around the perimeter, and it had one door but no windows. Us boys would fill the seats, and Leslie would shut the door and turn out the lights. Then he would tell us ghost stories that I think he made up as he went along because none of us had ever heard of ones like he told us, and I never knew a boy that didn't like ghost stories. The weirder, the better, and we were never disappointed.

His were extra special because they were so gory and full of blood and mayhem described down to the last detail. The murderer or murderess never used a gun. It was always a machete or a hatchet or a pointed rock–the duller the better. The victims were always young boys our age, and the maniac who killed them never got caught. Leslie always left them running loose in some small town exactly like Buffalo. We all sat there in the dark like petrified rocks.

I recall one story in particular where the murderer killed a bunch of kids like us with a hatchet and hung them on meat hooks in his meat locker. The guy butchered hogs for a living, so he had a lot of experience. I very specifically remember Leslie saying the guy had never been apprehended by the police.

Walt's brother, Elgin, always came to the story hour with us. That night when we left the church and started home, we walked in a triangle so we could cover all directions. To do it, one of us had to walk backwards. Streetlights were a lot farther apart in those days than they are now, and most of our way home was in pretty dim light. Four blocks from the church I had to split off from Walt and Elgin to get home. I only had two blocks to run, and it was all downhill, so it didn't take very long.

We had an agreement that they would wait where I peeled off until I reached my screen door and hollered so they would know I was safe. I never thought about it at the time, but 30 years later I asked Walt what he and Elgin would have done if I hadn't hollered. He laughed and pitched it right back to me. He wanted to know what I would have done if he was the one who hadn't hollered back. I got the point. We had been close friends for many years, and he always had the knack of pinning me in a corner with no way out.

We graduated from Buffalo High School in 1942 a few months after Japan bombed Pearl Harbor. Walt enlisted in the Army following graduation and was in the D-Day Invasion and in Europe until the war ended. After he came home, he enrolled at the University of Wyoming under the GI Bill and received an Engineering degree.

New car production had ceased when the war started. Even used cars were hard to come by. For transportation between Buffalo and Laramie, Walt bought an old 1930 something Dodge four-door sedan with suicide doors–the ones with the rear door hinges on the wrong side. That old Dodge took a beating, and most of his friends had a hand in the process.

We were going up the mountain one day, and his cousin, Elgin Young, was in the backseat. He noticed one of the doors wasn't completely latched, so he opened it while we were still moving. The wind caught it and almost sucked him out of the car. It was like trying to hang onto an umbrella during a hurricane. The door slammed into the back fender and broke the hinges. Walt really chewed him out for pulling such a crazy stunt.

We took it to a dance at Lodore in Story [Wyoming] one night, and I drove it home. I'd had a couple beers too many, high centered it on a rock in the parking lot, and punched a hole in the gas tank although we didn't realize it at the time. We got about a half mile before we ran out of gas, so we parked it off the shoulder of the road, and everybody hitched a ride home. The next morning we got a can of gas and caught a ride back to where we had left it the night before. We plugged the hole in the tank with a potato and drove it home.

Because cars were so scarce and most of the local university students were low on money, Walt always had a carload of kids on the trips back and forth to Laramie during holiday breaks. It was slow going because the roads were narrow and the asphalt ended at the shoulder, which made for a touchy situation, especially during a blizzard. At times they were stranded between towns and quite often took turns driving.

On one trip coming to Buffalo with a carload of kids, Kathleen Houston was behind the wheel. It was after dark, and coming through the Midwest oil field, she was blinded by an oncoming car's headlights on a sharp curve. They hit head on. Luckily, no one was killed or seriously injured. Walt had a heck of a time finding enough parts to put it back together.

The final blow was a year or so later when a friend in Laramie, H.B. Hurst, borrowed it. He was on campus, driving on what he thought was the main drag but was actually on a dead end street. He had too much beer under his belt and came to a halt in a bunch of trees when the street ended. Nobody was killed, but the Dodge was totaled.

Every single time that car was wrecked, somebody besides Walt was in the driver's seat. I can't remember him ever having a fender bender himself. He moved from Buffalo after he graduated, and he and his wife raised five boys and a girl. I never asked him about the cars and kids problems while they were growing up. It wasn't necessary because my wife and I had five of our own for examples.

§ § §

A number of years after I retired from the Wyoming Highway Department, I started working parttime for an auto salvage company that I had an interest in, Mr. R's Auto Salvage. I did most of the hauling of wrecked vehicles that we bought in the area plus any scrap iron that we then loaded into the cars which were crushed and shipped to a firm in Colorado.

One time, we purchased a dozen or so old vehicles that had accumulated through the years on an abandoned homestead quite some distance out in the boonies south of Clearmont. I was loading the wrecks on the truck and filling them with the scrap iron that was scattered around the place when I picked up an old rusty children's pedal car from the Montgomery Ward & Company era of the 1930s and was instantly reminded of the first car I ever stole some 50 or so years before.

I was in about fourth grade, and we lived along Clear Creek on Bozeman Avenue. There was a large deserted area along the creek that people were dumping trash in that is the present site of the New Dawn Trailer Court. I was spying on two high school boys, Tony Goryl and Kyle Grant, who had stolen a beautiful bright red pedal car from someone and were hiding it in an old upright piece of culvert that was being used for a burn barrel. After they left, I waded the creek and stole it from them.

I dragged it along the creek about a block to the north where we lived and hid it under a pile of brush. I didn't dare use it around the house or anyplace else for that matter until I thought of an excuse for how it was acquired that would get past my mother. I couldn't come up with anything plausible, and a couple of weeks later word came down through the network of heavy-duty grade school criminals that the original stealers knew who had it, and someone was going to get the hell beat out of them if it wasn't returned immediately if not sooner. I was too dumb to realize that if they really knew, they would have come directly to me, but I wasn't about to risk a thrashing, so I took it back to the burn barrel.

I took the rusty old pedal car from the homestead, polished it up, and had it painted a bright candy apple red. I set it in my living room under a glass top as a reminder of the failed car theft part of my career that Mother was never aware of.

§ § §

I had known a kid named Walt Hushbeck since we were in the fourth grade. His folks had a homestead about 15 miles southeast of town in the Wallows country. There were a few places in that area where seams of coal were showing up on the side of a cut bank, and the homesteaders started mining them for personal use. Trees for firewood were nonexistent in the area between the Bighorn Mountains and Powder River which was a full day's trip with the old cars of that period. Walt's father had been killed in a mining accident at one of the diggings, leaving behind his wife, three boys and a girl, Tom, Margaret, Elgin, and Walt, so his mother had to move to Buffalo to support the family.

Walt told me when they made the move to town, he was in the fourth grade and his mother wanted to familiarize the kids with the neighborhood, so she gathered them up and drove around their house for several blocks in every direction. They had been raised country style and weren't used to big city life–all 1,500 of us. I lived on Bozeman Avenue along Clear Creek, and their house was on top of the hill several blocks to the east.

When she drove along the road by the creek, there was a kid sitting on a log fishing and smoking a cigarette. Walt said she told him to stay away from that boy. It was me, of course, and we later became lifelong friends. Sneaking a cigarette when I got out of sight of the house was just one of the minor things I did to make life miserable for my mother during the growing up years.

I remember once when the family was getting ready to take a trip. There were eight of us kids. My father was working on a ranch several miles from town, and we didn't own a car, so the only time we got outside the city limits was when someone who didn't know any better asked us. And they never did it a second time. It must have been quite a chore for my mother to get everybody ready to go on time and together.

I had received a new shirt for a birthday gift, and Mother told me to be careful and stay away from everything dirty until it was time to leave. I wandered down along the creek and found several 50-gallon barrels of liquid roof asphalt in an old building, belonging to the Wyoming Railroad Company. They didn't have any lids on them and were the consistency of thick molasses. It was fun to dip sticks in them and stir the black goop around. Just before I headed back for the house, I shot a rock into one of the barrels with a slingshot, and it splashed back and covered the whole front of my shirt. I can only imagine what Mother thought when she saw what I had done. I can't even remember if I got a spanking or not.

Thinking about that incident with the barrels of asphalt brings to mind another one. The lumberyards used to get barrels of roofing tar in the solid state and then build fires with old tires to heat it up to liquid form before they used it. There were two lumberyards located just across Fort Street from the grade school to the northeast, Buffalo Lumber Company and Pioneer. On the way to school we would cut through their storage yards and break off pieces of tar to use for chewing gum. It tasted like unsweetened licorice smeared with gasoline and had to be sucked on for a while before it was chewable. For some reason it didn't stick to our teeth or put us in the hospital.

Unless we forgot, we spit it out before entering the classroom because the teachers were united in their hatred of chewing gum and could spot a chewer from clear across the room even when you kept your lips closed. In an emergency it was either swallowed or stuck to the underside of your desk because if they caught you, it meant staying in after school, which was cruel and inhuman punishment, especially if it was during marble season.

Another couple things besides chewing tar that made for some uncomfortable situations–I was given to temper tantrums and afraid of the dark, and the two weren't compatible. My sisters knew I had a short fuse

20

and would tease me about something until it ignited. I would stomp out of the house into the night with Mother hollering at me to come back in, but as soon as the door shut and I was on the outside, I would slow down because I knew she would be right behind me. Sometimes, if she was a little late, I'd have to go into slow motion mode until she caught up because I wasn't about to get outside the yard fence. There were all kinds of monsters lurking behind the trees, and they were all afraid of her but not me. Usually, I would only get a light spanking, and she always used the flat of her hand, so it didn't hurt although I always pretended it did.

§ § §

Experimental smoking was an annual outdoor fad among us kids that usually coincided with the first warm days of spring several weeks before school let out. Getting the proper ingredients was difficult, but we were pretty inventive, meaning that if we used tobacco, we had to steal it. Factory packaged cigarettes were called tailor made and cost about 15¢ a pack, which prohibited their use by anyone except maybe the men who worked in town at the local businesses. The men who worked on ranches, coal mines, etc. used roll your own Bull Durham at a nickel a bag. Ranch hands were short of cash during the Depression and drought years of the 1930s and only made $1 a day when they could get a job. They worked for only room and board during the winter months when the work slowed down.

Bull Durham was packaged in small cloth bags with drawstrings to close it, and cigarette papers were attached to the back. It was fascinating to watch an old cowboy who had smoked all his life and had the skill roll a cigarette that looked like it was factory made.

If he was right-handed, he would hold the cigarette paper with his left hand. By depressing his forefinger the full length of the paper, it would form a trough that he would fill with tobacco. Then he would bite down on one of the strings and pull on the other one with his right hand to close the sack, which was placed in his shirt pocket. After smoothing out the Bull Durham, he would lick one edge of the paper so it would stick to the other side and bond together. It looked exactly like a tailor made. To light it, he would use a stick match that he lit with a flick of his thumbnail with the same hand that was holding it. He did all this on horseback and carrying on a conversation while his horse was ambling along at a fast walk, paying no attention because he had seen it happen countless times before.

When I got through rolling mine, all the tobacco was in a lump in the middle of the paper, and I had to twist both ends to keep the tobacco from spilling out. When I lit it, quite often the paper would flare up and singe my eyebrows. In later years, they came out with cigarette paper with glue along one edge like an envelope. It was stamped Riz La Cross or something like that on the package, which I assumed was French or Italian or whatever. Anyway, it was a great improvement over spit in keeping the cigarette from coming apart while you were puffing on it.

Somewhere along the way, someone invented a hand operated cigarette roller, and you could make enough at a time to last a week. I think this is when women got interested in smoking, and they could smoke in the privacy of their own homes because it hadn't been accepted culturally yet.

A couple of times a summer, carnivals would arrive in town and set up by the ballpark next to the swimming pool. We could buy little clay pipes for a few cents each or win them as a prize at one of their games. The only problem was that the hole through the stem was too big. If you puffed too hard, you would suck ashes into your mouth. Golden Grain, Duke's Mixture and Bull Durham were ground way too fine, so Velvet and Prince Albert cans of pipe tobacco were the product of choice if somebody knew a place they could swipe some from. On a ranch it was the hired men's bunkhouse.

If tobacco wasn't available, ripened corn silk on the tops of roasting ears would work, but that was limited to late fall. Also, it burned pretty fast, and you had to keep filling your pipe bowl. We generally ended up smoking coffee because every household had it, and it was easy to get some out of the house without anyone noticing. It was terribly bitter, and we tried to get the coarsest grind we could find to keep the hot coals out of our mouths when we puffed too hard.

I remember my mother only caught me smoking once. We lived on Bozeman Avenue on the east side of the creek, and we had a shortcut walking path to town across a swinging footbridge located directly behind what is presently Michelena Automotive. The old bridge abutments are still there because the new footbridge was built 100 yards downstream by the Centennial walking path. When I was about 10 or 11 years old, Mother sent me to town for a few groceries. When I got out of sight of the house, I rolled a cigarette and lit up. She forgot something on her list and ran to catch me just as I started across the bridge. She hollered at me, but the sound of the water covered up her voice, and she was right behind me before I heard her. I was taking a drag on my cigarette and yanked it out of my mouth and gave it a heave without looking back. It was 30 feet to the water, and the damned thing came apart and trailed sparks the whole way down. It seemed like it took a week to get there. She never said a word–just smiled, handed me the list, and headed back for the house, which was a lot worse than getting bawled out.

I always considered myself super smart when it came to hiding things from my mother and my aunts, who I knew wouldn't approve. I loved chocolate Hershey bars and had convinced myself that eating a small square of chocolate would eliminate the smell of cigarettes on my breath. The bars were a nickel apiece and four or five times bigger than they are now.

One time, I forgot about my eyebrows. I stayed with my cousins on my uncle's ranch on Rock Creek every chance I got. The three boys were more like brothers than cousins. They had a '34 four-door VS Ford that my uncle always drove with his wife in the passenger seat, and one boy was allowed to sit by her next to the door. Whenever we went anywhere, there were two gates to open before we got to the county road. To avoid all arguments about who had to open them, we had a rule–front seat opens gates. The opener was allowed to ride on the running board between gates, and my aunt would roll down the window and hold his waist to keep him from falling off. On one of my turns, I was riding on the running board and stuck my head through the window. She noticed I didn't have any eyebrows left from my last Bull Durham cigarette encounter. I tried to suck my head back out, but I was too late and she really chewed me out. There wasn't a sound from the backseat.

§ § §

The smoking fad would pretty much end with the arrival of cold weather when it became more difficult to find a place indoors to smoke. Spit wads were a perennial favorite. The name was derived from the practice of spitting on the paper before rolling it into ammo to give it more wallop and improve the accuracy. We used rubber bands to fire them. It usually started out at school until the teachers cracked down. Then it would shift to the Saturday matinee at the Bison Theater.

The best material that didn't require any spit came from all of the major cigarette manufacturers. I can remember a few of them–Kools, Old Gold, Wings, Dominos, Chesterfields, Lucky Strike, and Camels. They were packaged on the inside with a sort of heavy tin foil to keep them fresh. By folding the tin foil into small flat rectangles, they were super accurate and would carry the full length of the theater seats.

We would pick a seat as far back from the screen as we could. When they dimmed the lights, we'd pick out women with big fluffy hair for targets. When our bullets hit, they would grab their hair and turn around thinking someone sitting right behind them had done it. We hadn't stopped to consider that we could easily have put somebody's eye out. One year, someone started cutting bobby pins in half and shaped them into a V-shape, but that was as bad as a BB gun, and the police stepped in.

One time that I still remember very distinctly, I had prepared for the matinee by putting a row of rubber bands over my left shirtsleeve and covering them up with my sweater. When I went in, I got a seat way in the back, and when the lights dimmed, I pulled up my sweater sleeve and got some pre-made ammo out of my pocket. Before I could even get a shot off, somebody tapped me on the shoulder, and I saw a hand palm up just under my chin. It was the usher, Ruth Frieze. Without a word being spoken, she confiscated my entire stock of rubber bands. Five cents went up in smoke in less than a minute.

In a way though, I got off lucky because she could have kicked me out without even giving the dime back that I'd paid for a ticket. That was the end of my rubber band career because she knew me. If they had caught me again, they would have barred me from even getting into the Saturday afternoon cowboy movies, which would have been almost as bad as dying.

My first remembrance of a movie was in the silent film era. A man named Max Hughes sat at a piano off to the left side of the screen but down level with the seats. He provided the background music. I suppose he would have had to practice with a private showing beforehand to know when the chases between the cowboys and Indians would start and stop. Cowboy films were the only ones I ever went to, and there was one standard feature that never changed. The good guys always wore white hats and the villains wore black. We knew who was who in the first five minutes without anybody having to tell us. I still think of that today when I see a cowboy in a black hat.

Nobody was ever killed except maybe for the Indians, and they would just hit the dirt and lie still, so you knew they were goners without even thinking about it. The white hat guys were always just winged, a superficial shot to the shoulder or arm, and would have a sling to support their arm appear out of nowhere–sometimes before the fight was even over. If it was the end of the movie, the black hats would have theirs on while getting on the wagon to go to jail. The hero would shed his from the morning fight by the time he rode off into the sunset with the heroine looking wistfully at him, but she had to keep her mouth shut because we wanted him to keep moving. Every once in a while after the fight, they would get the sling on the wrong arm, but that didn't matter. Minor things like those were of no importance.

One thing that did matter with absolutely no exceptions–the heroes, Tom Mix, Buck Jones, Gene Autry, Roy Rogers, weren't allowed to kiss the girls under any circumstances. As close as she could get was the other side of his guitar, or we got nervous. Roy Rogers and Dale Evans were two that we kept a close watch on. When we heard they were married, we didn't believe it. When we found out it was true, we figured they kept it a secret to keep from being fired and hoped they would ship her off to China and get somebody else to fill in.

Animal rights groups weren't on the horizon yet, and the horses were treated pretty badly. When the cowboy stuntmen forced them to fall on a dead run, it was for real. I found out later that some of them were down for the count with broken legs and had to be shot. The cowboys and Indians had a pretty rough trip too, but I don't suppose they were shot to put them out of their misery.

There was one lady that lived up on north Carrington Avenue that was different from most other women. I think her name was Myra. She was one of the few women in the county that wore men's clothing. She was built pretty husky, wore her hair short, and talked just like a man. I think the only movies she saw were the cowboy ones that I liked, so I saw her fairly often.

During the movie, she would get just as wrapped up in it as us kids and carried away like it was actually happening. To stretch the movie out, sometimes the good guy would get the drop on the black hat one in a gunfight and being the compassionate type, wouldn't hurt him and turn him loose. Ten minutes later the villain would double cross him. In one movie this had happened several times, and in a suspenseful moment when the tables were turned in favor of the hero and he had his revolver trained on the bad guy, this lady couldn't stand it any longer and shouted out, "Shoot the son-of-a-bitch!" To this very day, I can remember I didn't even think it was funny because I actually agreed with her.

Another odd incident comes to mind that could only happen in a small town theater. Sometimes while the projectionist was showing the movie, he would stop the reel and flash a handwritten note or something or other on the screen. One of the members of a large family, Joe Olson, was a neighbor who trapped anything that wandered into his traps, muskrat, mink, and even skunk. Sometimes during the Saturday afternoon matinee, the movie would go blank and a note would appear on the screen, "Will the person who smells like skunk, please leave the theater," and Joe would get up and leave.

During this same time period in the 1930s, there was a barbershop in the south end of the theater next to the lobby. The barber's name was Al Hillard. At very special times like a birthday, my mother or one of my sisters would take me in for a haircut. He charged 25¢ but would always give me a dime back when he finished. When you sat down in the chair, I always started out low, and he would jack it up and wrap a sheet around me. I can still remember the feel of the hand-operated clippers when the cool metal went around my ears and back of my neck. I would sit as still as a statue and savor the experience. The icing on the cake was when he finished and sprinkled a liberal amount of the most wonderful smelling lotion on the top of my head and rub it in. I think these were the only times I ever got my hair combed.

In later years, the barbershop was eliminated, the lobby was remodeled, and an electric popcorn popper was added. The smell of the melted butter was straight from heaven, and a foot-high sack only cost a dime. Candy bars were a nickel. The tickets were 10¢ for grade schoolers and a quarter for the high school kids. I was small for my age and got in for a dime up to my sophomore year. I had a sheepskin collared coat and would pull it up around my ears and shrink down as much as possible when I laid my dime down. Thinking back, as small as Buffalo was, they surely knew how old I was and just didn't say anything.

I knew of one small elderly lady who made her own tickets, and they accepted them until she died. She was living on a very limited income, and I suppose the theater owner, Tom Villnave, was just being charitable because it was a town joke until she passed away.

In about the sixth grade, we boys began to notice that there seemed to be something different about the girls in our class besides having long hair and wearing dresses. It was even fun to stand around and visit with them, which was a drastic switch for most of us, but we didn't like doing it with a teacher hovering over our heads like they did at school. The two best places were the swimming pool and the theater. Dating one in grade school was unheard of, and we wouldn't have known how to go about asking anyway. The extra 10¢ for a ticket and another for the popcorn was prohibitive even if you shared one bag, so we would casually mention the fact out in the lobby that we were going to sit in row so and so–any place but the first two or three rows of seats, which is where all the little twerps sat, quite often our little brothers and sisters, who we were forced to take with us–hoping to be given a free bag of popcorn after the movie started.

I remember a time when my oldest sister, Beulah, had a date to go to a dance at City Hall. The dance floor was on the second story and level with the courthouse lawn. It was torn down some years later and is presently the City Hall parking lot. She and her date were going to the show first, so Mother let me go to the theater with her. She was supposed to bring me home before they went to the dance. At that time, there were two showings of the same movie every night. The first one would start at about 7:30, and since they always had a cartoon and coming attractions, it would be about midnight before the second show was over.

I came out to the lobby after the first show but couldn't find my sister because she had forgotten about me and went to the dance. I didn't have any way of contacting my mother, so I went back inside and watched the show again. It finally ended about midnight, and they turned off the lights and locked the doors, so I didn't have any choice but to start for home. We didn't have a phone, and there wasn't any place to call from even if we did.

We lived several blocks from the theater on the other side of the creek and railroad tracks. The path home was a spooky one after dark because there was only one streetlight. Among other things it, was during the Depression of the 1930s, and hobos would ride the train into town and camp along the creek fairly close to our house. They always had campfires flickering in the dark.

I started for home, but the farther I got from the streetlights, the more my courage evaporated, and when Mrs. Myer's dogs started howling, I went back up to the end of the sidewalk and sat down. I was still there when Mother came looking for me early in the morning. There was a mix up in communication. She thought I'd gone to the dance with my sister until she came home without me. It was a long night for a 10 year old.

I remember one other time when things didn't go too well at the theater. Word got out that someone had parked a truckload of peaches in the alley between the creek and the building next to the theater. It only had a canvas flap over the end of it, and peaches were available simply by reaching in and helping yourself. My cousin, Gene White, and I heard about it before we went into the matinee and filled the inside of our shirts with peaches. Our bodies warmed them up, and the fuzz turned into something resembling poison ivy, only worse. The itching got so bad we couldn't even stay to see the end of the movie and had to go home and take a bath to relieve it. I have never eaten a peach since that time that the incident doesn't come to mind, so I suppose there's a lesson in there somewhere.

§　§　§

When I was a freshman in high school, I got the idea of replacing our old coal house, which was in bad shape and ready to fall down. Remember, this was in the days when there wasn't any money beyond barely enough to put food on the table, so its final construction costs would have to equal zero.

There was some trash in the alley behind our house. In addition to some old boards, there was an old door and a solid piece of an old roof. It was about 6x10 feet in size with linoleum nailed on top to take the place of shingles. And it was pretty dang heavy. I had never built anything bigger than a rabbit hutch before this, so I figured on jacking the roof up, temporarily nailing the door in place, and building the walls around it. It seemed fairly simple, but I really didn't plan any farther ahead than getting the door and roof dragged across the alley. Things picked up after that.

My first problem was getting the roof jacked up about 6 feet off the ground and getting it to stay there while I got the door and walls built around it. I only concentrated on one thing at a time. I was able to get the roof off the ground with a crowbar and propped up with blocks on all four corners for the first 18 inches or so. Then I was able to slide under the roof on my stomach and lift a corner by arching my back and sliding pieces of boards under it to hold it while I moved to another corner. This worked great up to about 3 feet. I was under the roof working on a corner when the whole damned thing went sideways and flattened me face down in the dirt. I was completely immobilized and could barely get enough air to breathe.

My mother was in the house and happened to see the thing go and came running and screaming. There wasn't anybody else around to help, and I know it sounds terribly unappreciative to say, especially about my own mother, but I remember thinking, "Why doesn't that woman quiet down?"

I don't remember exactly how I got out from under that roof. I suppose she used the crowbar, or maybe she was so frightened–my face was so jammed in the dirt and I couldn't speak–that she had the extra strength to lift it up enough for me to slide out. I don't remember how I ever got that roof jacked up high enough to finish the thing. I didn't have any help because nobody would be stupid enough to construct a building from the top down. Anyway, I finally finished, and it was big enough to hold several tons of coal. The linoleum must have been of pretty good quality because the roof didn't leak.

§ § §

The county jail was located in the west end of the courthouse where the records room is presently situated when I was going to grade school. The schoolhouses, three of them at the time, were directly across Adams Street to the west. The Bomber Mountain complex is now in this area.

The only windows in the jailhouse faced west and were covered with iron grates on the outside of the building. I was never on the inside of the place, but they must have had windows covering the grates that could be opened for ventilation because the prisoners could talk through the bars to people on the lawn outside.

Sometimes when we were walking back and forth to school, the inmates would call out to us, and we would stop and visit with them, but if the sheriff heard them talking, he would come out the back door and run us off. We were quite impressed with their criminal status, and it made us feel important when they would notice us as long as we had a steel grate between them and us. Transients used some pretty raw language, but most of the time the men were local and just spending a few days in the can for getting drunk or stealing something.

Ordinarily, they wouldn't have had anything to do with small fry grade schoolers unless they were bullying us, but they wanted someone to talk to and pass messages to their friends. They also needed cigarettes, which cost 10¢ or 15¢ a pack, so they would hand the change through the grates, and we would push the cigarettes back through one at a time. The bars were too close together for the whole pack. If they had asked for hacksaw blades, we would have furnished them also.

I remember once when a Buffalo guy and a couple buddies got the bright idea of making some easy money by going into the extortion racket. They sent some anonymous letters to a well to do local person demanding cash or else. The cops were able to trace the letter to the typewriter they had used and locked them up.

§ § §

Thinking about that part of my life brings back a lot of memories concerning my growing up period in Buffalo from the mid-1920s through the '30s and up until World War II started in 1941. It was a very impressionable part of my life. Sometimes I'll be visiting with someone in my age bracket, and we'll try thinking back over the locations of the dozens of businesses that came and went along Main Street during that time frame. For any history buffs that may be reading this, I'll put in my two cents worth, but don't bet the ranch because I'm looking at 70 or 80 years in the rearview mirror.

Virginia (Sheridan) Milnichak, six years my senior, is my go-to for factual information about early-day Buffalo when my memory stalls. She is one of the funniest persons I've ever met and without a doubt blessed with the sharpest memory.

Bert Pratt's secondhand store that I remember in the 1930s was just across Main Street from the City Hall parking lot and is presently the site of The Office retail store. Incidentally, the parking lot was originally the old City Hall before it was demolished, a two-story structure with a dancehall on the top floor. Bert's building was built on the old Myers Hotel lot after it was torn down.

A while back, I ran onto an old Buffalo news item, dated September 2, 1926, that mentioned Bert Pratt had taken over Hoshaw Furniture. Virginia told me it was located just south of the present-day alley entrance on Main Street of American National Bank. This is the same location in the 1930s as the Table Supply grocery store, owned by Ralph Perry, who later moved it up on Fort Street and is now the IGA.

I don't know if Bert purchased Hoshaw Furniture and operated it at that location or just bought the inventory and moved it up on North Main Street. The news article was very complimentary and commended him for "many improvements in the business ventures he has invested in," notably for "going after business on a cash basis since starting up in a small way in a secondhand store." It said he had added a good "harness and hardware" area in conjunction with a well-stocked furniture store–a classic example of an old-time general store minus the groceries. I thought the reference to a cash basis was especially telling. Evidently, credit was a well-established business hazard to be avoided even in early day Buffalo.

Bert's secondhand store on North Main's had next door neighbors to the north that were a couple of small shops owned by Otto Hart and Joe Sarantha. Otto sold candy. I especially remember his homemade taffy. He boiled the ingredients–mostly sugar, I think–then cooled it down enough to hang it over a hook above his head. Then he would pull it up and down until it was the right consistency resembling a stiff rope, which he cut into chunks and sold. He worked that taffy barehanded after smearing butter on his hands. He also chewed tobacco, which required turning his head quite often to spit. Another of his sidelines was plowing gardens for locals with a couple of mules. I remember people wondering if he washed his hands in between occupations. He kept his mules in an old red barn just south of Clear Creek on Lobban Avenue, and it is still standing. It has outlasted the mules and taffy and Otto by 90 years and counting although it could use some new shingles and a fresh coat of red paint to see it through the next century.

Mr. Gibbany took over Otto's candy shop in later years and added popcorn to the menu. He was so persnickety about cleanliness his store would have put every woman's house in Buffalo to shame when it came to spotlessness. My sisters always referred to him as Mr. Clean because they couldn't think of a higher adjective to describe him. I remember him as being exceedingly quiet and polite when he was waiting on customers and wearing a white uniform that was changed every day.

Next door to Otto Hart was Joe Sarantha's shoe repair shop. In those days, it was a good business to be in. Shoes were well made and made to last. It was a lot cheaper to put on half soles and new heels than buy new ones. His shop was very small and always smelled of leather and shoe polish. He had a very pronounced Italian accent and was difficult for me to understand at times.

Virginia told me about an experience she had with Joe and some of his repair work when she was secretary for the county agent, Pete Jensen, whose office was on the second floor of the Post Office. She received her weekly paycheck one Saturday, so she splurged and bought a new pair of high-heeled shoes. They were leather with blue fabric and really uptown, especially for Buffalo, which wasn't exactly the fashion capitol of the West at the time. She dropped them off at Joe's to have him put leather caps on the heels to cut down on the wear and tear. I think Buffalo's Main Street was still gravel at the time and hard on shoes.

Joe's shop was so small he only had room for a few shelves, so he put up some overhead wires to hang the shoes on when he finished working on them. To keep the shoes in their proper pairs, he would tie the shoelaces together and drape them over the wire until the customer picked them up. When Virginia stopped by to pick up her new high heels, they were also hanging on the wire, but with no laces to work with Joe improvised and punched a hole in the side of each shoe, ran a cord through the holes, and tied them together so they wouldn't get mixed up with the others on the line.

I told Virginia sometimes it helps to have an inventive nature, but she said there are limits to ingenuity, and it doesn't extend to punching holes in brand-new, eight dollar, blue fabric high-heeled shoes. Realizing the futility of convincing her of Joe's resourcefulness when working with laceless footwear, I gave up, and we moved on to a different topic.

Next door north of the shoe shop was the Welfare Office. I remember when it opened during President Roosevelt's first term in office. They remodeled the interior and filled the whole room with shelves that were crammed with different size cans of food. I could see through the window that a lot of them were gallon-size and all had plain solid white labels with large black letters specifying the contents. The feds didn't have to be concerned with attractive packaging to lure customers in. With the drought, the dust storms and the Depression taking place all at the same time, people that were using the products couldn't care less what the cans looked like.

One day, I was walking down the alley behind the store and saw men unloading boxes of canned food and large bolts of fabric. I always wondered what the cloth was for and 80 years later found out. As usual, Virginia had the answer. She told me in 1935 her mother was hired by the government to teach women how to sew and held sewing classes in her living room. The women were paid for the clothing they turned out, which was then given to welfare recipients. From what I can remember, the Welfare Office must have had one of the longest runs as the same tenant of any building on Main Street.

The business next to it was Miss Conroy's Hat Shop. Virginia told me she loved to go in with her mother because the hats were so pretty. In those days, all well-dressed women wore hats when they went shopping. She said a lot of the hats Miss Conroy ordered were the plain Jane variety, and she decorated them herself with artificial flowers, ribbons, feathers, and other doodads. She was very talented and artistic, and Virginia said she had a very good business. I had always heard of her being addressed as Miss Conroy, and Virginia told me she never married.

The next shop north of Miss Conroy's was Mr. Reed's candy store. It was the last building for almost a block at that point in time. The present-day Chamber of Commerce was an empty lot that extended north past the Main and Fort Street intersection to the two-story brick building that is still standing. I don't remember who first occupied it, but in later years it was Johnson County Title Company. The empty lot eventually had a gas station named Victory built on part of it that was owned by Jack Meldrum and remodeled into a liquor store by Ray Thorburn after that. It presently has several office buildings on it. North of the brick building was Neil Waugh's Chevy garage, now Coldwell Banker. Then came the Stevens brothers' gas station [Reimann Oil Company] on the corner of Benteen and Main Street. Claude Gray, a half-brother and 25 years my senior, told me it was originally owned by Gus Schlicht, who was the first person to sell gas in Buffalo back in the early 1900s. He stored it in 50-gallon drums and pumped out whatever you wanted into 5-gallon cans. Just across Benteen was Tarrant & Wiley's service station, presently Kum & Go.

The lot later became the site of Moon's restaurant when a railroad car was hauled in and outfitted with stools and a kitchen. It was pretty snug inside, but people managed. I remember it better as Stone's restaurant after it was purchased by the family of one of my classmates, Slug (A.C.) Stone. It was the last commercial building on North Main on the east side of the street for the next block until it reached Bert Pratt's original secondhand store. It's the Big Horn Motel today.

Thinking about Reed's candy store brings back a lot of memories. It seemed to change owners on a fairly frequent basis. Fennis, Bob Inkster, Johnny Chrisler come to mind. I was a steady customer, and Mr. Reed charged me a penny for large sacks of broken stick candy remnants–red and white stripes like a barber pole–that would last for several days. A penny's worth of hard candy would fill a small sack, and if you were willing to settle for all broken pieces, which I always did, you would get half again as much. Those pennies were the down payment on a lot of tooth trips to my dentist, Dr. S.E. Crouter, on South Main Street. His office always reeked of something that smelled like disinfectant, and I dreaded going into the place. Once, I fainted just after opening the door.

After getting me trapped in his dental chair, which was way too big for an 80-pounder, he would ask nonstop questions without waiting for an answer while my mouth was full of his hands, pliers and an electric drill that's whine drove me up a wall. With my mouth full of smelly mouthwash that he squirted over, around and between my teeth, I could only gurgle an unintelligible reply when he stopped long enough to grab another instrument. The only thing his toolbox seemed to lack was a hammer. He always gave me a nickel when he finished remodeling my mouth to make sure I had enough money to keep Mr. Reed in business by sucking on his stick candy, which guaranteed a return trip to his office in six months to plug more holes in my teeth. It took a while to make the connection.

South of Mr. Reed's candy store near the end of the block was the Bison Theater, my introduction to the silent movie era. Virginia told me the theater owner, Tom Villnave, loaned her and her partner, Mollie (Martin) Evans, $2,600 in the early 1940s to open up a women's clothing store, The Suzanne Shop, with no collateral. This was a huge sum in those days, but his confidence paid off because it was a very successful business venture. Tom and his wife even escorted Virginia and Mollie to the Denver Market Show and introduced them to the business world.

Next to the theater and last building north of Clear Creek was the Swan & Tate Saloon, later the Buffalo Bar and presently Margo's Pottery & Fine Arts. The first building south of the creek was an old two-story frame structure with rental offices. The renter I remember best was Mimi, who had a beauty shop on the second floor. I think she was of Hungarian ancestry with a very pronounced accent, and if she had a last name, I never heard it. She was well-liked but a real town character who always wore the clothes of her native country, bright colored full skirts with petticoats under them that made them bouncy and flare out at the bottom. They had ruffles all around the bottom edges that ended up a few inches above her ankles, and I never saw her when she didn't have a little apron tied around her waist. You could recognize her coming down the street from a block away, and if the wind was from the right direction, the smell of the perfume she used advertised her presence long before she was close enough to speak to. She wasn't married, but Virginia told me she had a boyfriend who helped out at her shop with things like cleaning up and washing her customer's hair before they got their perms.

Virginia told me she had a real odd experience in the place once. She was in high school and stopped on the way home to get a perm. Mimi's boyfriend washed her hair and then disappeared downstairs somewhere. Mimi took over and hooked her up to electric curlers that hung by their cords from the ceiling and then left the building to find her boyfriend. She was still sitting there long after dark when her mother showed up looking for her. Virginia had been able to switch off the juice to the curlers but couldn't unhook herself from the contraption or get to the telephone. She said Mimi never mentioned the incident the next time she went in the place. I asked her what she would have looked like if she hadn't been able to shut off the electricity to the curlers, and she said she didn't know but probably something that resembled a scorched fuzzy headed monk minus the beard.

Mimi's shop building was connected to Central Garage. This location became the Ben Franklin Variety Store. It, in turn, was torched by a lady arsonist in the late '80s and purchased by the City that morphed it into Crazy Woman Square.

Virginia told me another interesting story that could only happen in a small town like Buffalo when she was the owner of a shop on South Main Street that sold all sorts of fabric. It was directly south of Seney's Drug Store. One Thanksgiving, Charlie Taylor, who owned a little horse ranch three or four miles south of town, invited a friend to dinner. There was an argument of some kind, and the invited guest shot Charlie. It didn't kill him but didn't do him any good either. The shooter was tried, convicted and sentenced to a term in the county jail.

From time to time, some of Virginia's customers had problems with their sewing machines, and there was no place in town to get them repaired. She found out that a prisoner was a competent sewing machine repairman, so she paid a visit to the jailhouse and asked him if he would be willing to work on them if something could be worked out with the sheriff. The sheriff was a little reluctant to turn his prisoner loose because he felt shooting someone was a rather serious offense, but Virginia was very persuasive, so they cut a deal.

The sheriff set aside a small room for his prisoner to work in, the customers dropped off their broken machines at Virginia's fabric shop, and she hauled them up to the jailhouse. She was also responsible for collecting the money due the inmate for his labors. Everything worked out perfectly. The prisoner served his time, all the ladies got their machines repaired, and the sheriff kept his public relations reputation intact. He was even reelected to another term—no doubt with the help of the ladies with the broken sewing machines, who were all of voting age, which, I suppose, was something the sheriff had already given some thought to.

Thinking about the sheriff, Virginia told me another story concerning the town marshal, John Erhart. She was working as a clerk in one of the stores when a guy came in and spent quite a while just wandering around looking at the merchandise but didn't purchase anything. He was a pretty husky guy, and she suspected he may have stolen something but didn't accost him because a person couldn't be accused of shoplifting until after they left the premises. So she called the police station just after he left the store. The marshal, a slender medium-height fellow, showed up a few minutes later, and she could see him talking to the guy across the street. A short time later, the marshal came into the store, and Virginia asked him if he had searched the guy. He said, "Gosh, no! He was a big man!" As she was talking, I knew that under similar circumstances I would have done exactly as he did.

The telephone exchange was located a block west of Main Street on Angus Street. In those days, they had individual telephone operators that put you through to the person you were calling. You would lift your phone off the hook, and the local operator would say, "Number please." Gladys Ross was the telephone supervisor at the time, and she also filled in at the switchboard when the other girls were on lunchbreak or vacation.

One afternoon, Virginia called her dentist, Dr. [H.J.] Long, to get an appointment. The phone rang several times, but nobody answered. Finally, Gladys cut in and asked her if she was having tooth problems. Virginia said she was, and Gladys told her she had bumped into Dr. Long at the Post Office that morning, and he said he was on his way to Sheridan to pick up some supplies. He told her if anyone called his office and didn't get an answer, to tell them he would be back later in the day. Gladys told Virginia she would keep ringing his office at intervals and when he answered, tell him to call her right away, which he did–personalized service in a one-horse town.

As a side note, Dr. Long was a character in his own right. He was well liked and spent more time visiting with his patients sitting in the dental chair than working on their teeth. He was a pack rat collector of any and everything who never threw anything away, and his house, garage and yard showed it. Once he told me that when he took a pickup load of junk to the city dump that he always came back with more than he took. Whenever somebody needed an odd part for something they were trying to build or repair, he was the go-to guy, and he never charged anything for the item or his advice.

§ § §

One transition that took place in Buffalo during my lifetime that wasn't even noticeable while it was going on was the number of gas stations along Main Street. At present, there is only one, the Kum & Go convenience store on the north side of Benteen Street, where it intersects Main Street. At one time, there were over a dozen. The function has also flipped from full-service to self-service. Originally, when you pulled in to gas up, you got your windshield washed and oil level checked without even asking. Lots of the station attendants would even check your tire pressure without being asked. If you want it done now, you do it yourself, and if you don't know how to do it, there's no one there to ask.

South Side Garage, where the Buffalo Theater now sits, had a single pump in front of the building. A Standard Oil station was directly across Main from the First Northern Bank and is a parking lot at present. The grease rack was outside and a difficult place for oil changes and grease jobs in the wintertime, but the company refused to put a roof over it. Joe Goryl, who rented it in 1946, told me gas sold for 12¢ a gallon, and he received 2¢

for pumping it.

Joe told me an interesting story about Tom Guinan's son and another young man, Dode Olson. They took the motor out of a Model A Ford, remounted it in the rearend of the vehicle with the fan pointing backwards, and replaced the fan with an airplane propeller. On their trial run they got going too fast, and the front end of the Ford came off the ground. They got it shut down before they wrecked and took it back to the shop to think things over. I asked Joe if anyone got their head decapitated with the propeller, and he said if they did, he didn't remember it.

North of the Courthouse across Fort Street on the corner was the Grease Spot. The driveway cut diagonally across the lot and was accessed from North Main Street but reentered Fort Street on the south. It had a nice native rock water fountain in the front that was stocked with fish in the summer months. John W. Stevenson, a taxidermist, was the proprietor in 1929. On one wall, just for a joke, he had hung a mounted sheep with a man's face on it. It became too controversial, and local opinion soon had it removed. When the building was demolished, Pioneer Lumber Company built a new structure on the site. Later on, the County purchased the property and built the present parking lot.

Thinking about the Grease Spot and the taxidermist, I recall another story that Virginia told me. At that period of time, she lived in the 300 block on North Main Street, and the Stevenson family lived in the next block north. The two families were very good friends. One day, we were discussing the olden days, and she remembered in 1927 John had mounted a jackalope–a jackrabbit with deer antlers added–and had it displayed in the Grease Spot along with a number of other animals, birds and fish. She remembered it in particular because she had to walk by the Grease Spot on her way to grade school and thought it was a real animal.

Many years later, the City of Douglas [Wyoming] saw an opportunity to capitalize on the idea, and it has since become an icon for the town. She has often wondered if John Stevenson was the first person to actually think of the joke and put deer antlers on a jackrabbit. If so, Buffalo missed the boat as far as a tourist attraction was concerned.

On the west side of Main Street was a station owned by Slim Still. His first name was Leroy. He was a tall, lanky individual. In all the years I knew him, I never once saw him smile. I don't remember ever visiting with him when something wasn't wrong. My brother worked for him while he was going to high school. Slim later bought the Log Cabin Camp on old Highway 87 just north of French Creek from Claude Byler. It was a first-generation tourist motel–quite primitive. I don't remember any gas pumps.

Claude was somewhat of a local character himself. He had the reputation of dreaming up all sorts of inventions of one kind or another. I remember one in particular. During World War I, there was a lot of trench warfare, and Claude came up with the idea of some kind of bulldozer-looking thing that would run along the top of the German trenches and fill them full of dirt before the German soldiers had a chance to crawl out. It may have looked pretty good on paper, but I can think of a few things that might not work out so well on the ground. The war probably ended before he talked some general into trying it out.

A block north on Main from Slim's station on the west side where North Wyoming Insurance is now located was the Tip Top gas station and store. Ted Pringle owned it in the 1930s when I remember it. Virginia told me her father, W.K. Sheridan, owned it in the 1920s when he worked for the Wyoming Railroad in Buffalo. She told me that she and a grade school friend, Irene Gray, obtained some cans of tuna fish and crackers from her mother, who was running the store, and took them back across Main Street, where she lived at the time. They made them into sandwiches and sold them for a penny apiece. They built up a thriving business until her mother withdrew her financial support. Shortly after, the partnership went broke.

The Tip Top station also had several one-room cabins that they rented to overnight visitors. Virginia told me one summer when she was about 10 years old, Mrs. Pringle hired her to help clean the cabins. The agreed upon wage was 10¢ per hour payable daily. The first day she worked, Mrs. Pringle said she had earned a total of 10½¢, so she rounded it off to 10¢. Virginia thought it should be rounded off to 11¢, so after going home and discussing the disagreement with her mother, she quit.

On Highway 16 on Fort Street west of Main Street, I can recall at least four stations. Most of them were short lived because the majority of tourist traffic from the Black Hills to Yellowstone National Park was from east to west, and most tourists were already gassed up by the time they hit Fort Street.

The one exception was Alabam's Polka Dot Spot, a gas station and store, that was built by Ned "Alabam" Deloney and outlasted the rest of them. The pumps were removed a number of years ago, but the store continued on.

Alabam's Polka Dot Spot

A gas station on the south side of Benteen Street, where it intersects with Main Street, had the longest history of any of them and is the one I remember most vividly. According to my half-brother, Claude Gray, who was 25 years older than I, it was originally owned by Gus Schlicht, who was the first person to sell gas in Buffalo. He pumped it out of 50-gallon barrels into a bucket and poured it into your gas tank with a funnel. Claude told me he personally remembered our dad buying gas there in 1912 for his Model T Ford.

My first memory of it was in about 1930 when I started school and walked by it every day all the way up through high school. It was owned by Frank and Ed Stevens. In later years, it was acquired by Carl Reimann, who passed it on to his son, Richard, who in turn passed it to his son, Steve. Steve eventually leased it to another operator in 2012. Currently, it is no longer in business. Gas prices have increased substantially from what Gus Schlicht charged for it–about 10¢ a gallon.

The principal reason I remember it was because of the toilets. It had two of them. The one inside consisted of a stool in the back of the building where they stored oil, tires, parts, etc. and was only used by the employees and men customers. It was covered with grease, and I don't think it had ever been cleaned since it was first installed. The one used for women and tourists had an entrance on the northside of the building and was cleaner, but it wasn't hard to tell that it was still a man-maintained facility. It had a single ceiling light bulb–about 40 watts–with a string hanging down to turn it on and off with no light shade. It was a small room with only a stool and sink that had hot and cold water faucets, but they both ran cold water and had brown stains on the porcelain because they dripped all the time. When there was soap, it was a partial bar on the top of the sink, and the whole room smelled of disinfectant. The door had a frosted glass window for privacy and was always left ajar unless someone was inside using it. One day, I found out why.

My mother had drilled into me to never use a public toilet, schools excepted, because they all had germs on them, and under the right circumstances they could kill me. I wasn't quite sure what germs were or looked like, but I knew it wasn't good, so I always obeyed her instructions, but sometimes things do happen.

I was a second grader and headed for home one day and realized I wasn't going to make it in time. The door was ajar, so I knew it was empty, but when I went in and tried to shut it, it wouldn't close, so I slammed it and locked it from the inside. After I had finished, I tried to open the door, but it was wedged in so tight I couldn't budge it. I panicked. I was afraid to holler for help because I didn't have permission to be in there. My mother had no idea of where to look, so I'd probably die before she found me.

I have no idea how long I was trapped in that room before finally getting enough strength to get the door open. When I finally did, I shot for home. It was the first and last time I was ever in the place. I don't remember even mentioning the incident to my mother. Many years later I was walking by the place when they were demolishing the building with a backhoe in preparation for a new structure. I stopped to watch, and it was a great feeling to see that door reduced to a few splinters.

§ § §

For several years in the late 1930s, the Johnson County Sportsman's Association declared a war on predators, and it worked just as effectively as the future federal government's war on poverty, drugs or whatever. The idea was that if we eliminated all the undesirable species in the county, we would end up with a bonanza of fish, ducks and pheasants. It didn't quite work out that way, and in a couple of years, they wised up and eliminated the program.

They paid 3¢ apiece for magpies, a nickel for crows, and a larger amount for skunks, hawks and other varmints. As I recall, kingfishers topped the list at 50¢ each, which was a fortune to us kids. I spent many hours trying to sneak up on them and get a shot but always came up with a blank. Besides the cash they paid us, they had prizes for the top three finishers. They were usually .22 rifles, fishing poles or ammo.

With prizes and money like that up for grabs, it didn't take us kids very long to figure out our odds of winning could be increased tremendously by pooling our resources under one name. A classmate, Chuck Marton, and I partnered up. We also figured out one more way to increase our winnings that the sponsors had overlooked. We did not share this information with our competitors for obvious reasons.

We had to turn in the feet of each crow or magpie we shot to collect the money, but under the rules of the contest their eggs were also included. So we got a 12-dozen egg carton and filled it with packing. Then we took it along with our guns on our weekend hunting trips and used the packing to protect the eggs until we could get them home and turn them into the guy paying for them, which in this case was the game warden who, theoretically, knew how to separate the real feet and eggs from the fakes.

I don't know if either Chuck or I had ever heard about the folly of killing the goose that laid the golden egg, but if we did, we figured it should apply to magpies also. When we robbed their nests, we found out they would lay more eggs for two more times before giving up or moving to a new location. We collected their eggs week by week but knew we had to get the egg layer coming off the nest the third time to maximize our profits, so we carried a .410 shotgun along with the egg crate.

I remember one year we won a bamboo fishing pole that had been donated by Seney's Drug Store. At a class reunion some 30 years later, we were reminiscing about the magpie era, but neither of us could remember how we split the fishing pole between us. Evidently, whatever method we used was equitable to both of us because we stayed friends for the rest of our lives.

§ § §

My granddaughter [Heather Gray Largent] and I were visiting one day and got onto the subject of sports. Her two oldest children were in college, and the two youngest boys were in the seventh and tenth grades. They had all been and still were active in school sports. Later, I got to thinking what a radical difference there was between their activities and the ones I grew up with.

Their sports were completely organized and monitored by adults with paid referees, interpreting the dozens of pages of rules and instructions that attempted to cover every conceivable situation that might arise. If a dispute arose over one that had been overlooked, it would be added to the main text shortly thereafter. In my grade school era, we adapted also, but it was by consensus even though we had never heard the word or would have known what it meant if we had. If we tried something and it didn't work, we tried something else because all we were concerned with was getting the results we expected. The only two exceptions I can think of were school football and basketball, and they were limited to boys only. Girl's organized sports activities were years in the future. There were no referees to settle a dispute, and if a bully insisted it was his way or the highway, either a bigger kid would intervene, or the rest of us would refuse to play with him. One or the other always worked.

My granddaughter mentioned having to pay from $80 to $150 for basketball shoes, and the sky was the limit for specially fitted made-to-order ones. We called our shoes tennis shoes even though I don't remember if there was a tennis court in town. If there was, the court was dirt because Buffalo's Main Street still had a gravel surface.

Tennis shoes were also what we used for everyday wear and cost less than a $1 a pair. They were made out of rubber and canvas with no provision for heat or moisture to dissipate, and the odor got pretty bad before they wore out. Usually, the only time we wore socks was during school hours, and the primary reason was cost. Socks weren't thrown away when they had a hole in the toe or heel because Mother repaired them. It was called darning and took a lot of time. There were eight children in my immediate family, and she had a lot of other things to do that took priority over darning our socks.

With the exception of one or two, I imagine most of our games were kid inspired and based on the fact it didn't cost much for the equipment. I remember some of them–jacks, red light green light, hopscotch, jump rope, red rover red rover, pie played with jack knives, hide and seek, fox and geese, kick the can, ring around the rosy, and Annie-Annie over. My favorite–marbles–took an initial outlay of 10¢ or 20¢ for a large sack full of marbles. Usually, they arrived as a Christmas or birthday gift. We had two separate versions to choose from–ring or nine pots.

The playing ring started with drawing a circle in the dirt anywhere from 6 feet in diameter on up. Each player dropped their dates, antes, in the middle of the ring and then lagged to determine each player's order of shooting. Lagging involved drawing two lines in the dirt about 6 to 8 feet apart and rolling your marble from one to the other. The closest got to shoot first and so on down the line.

Each shooter, in turn, knelt outside the circle and tried to knock his competitor's marbles out of the ring. Like in pool when running the table, he got to keep shooting until he missed. He also got to keep all the marbles he had knocked out of the ring. Some of the guys were so good they could launch their shooter several inches above the ground, hit a marble dead on, and knock it out of the ring while their shooter stayed inside for his next shot. The really good players would usually clear the ring, and the game was over.

I didn't like playing ring for several reasons. For one, I never acquired the skill to shoot accurately enough to be competitive. Also, I thought the game was too slow, the stakes were too small, and it would take forever to become a million marble man. As far as I was concerned, nine pots was the only game in town.

We dug nine holes a couple inches deep, three rows of three, side by side from each other in a square about 4 feet wide. We put our dates from one each to the sky is the limit in the center pot and lagged to determine the order of shooters like we did in ring. We drew another line about 8 feet back from the pots and rolled our shooters from there towards the pots.

If a shooter landed in the middle pot, he got to keep all the marbles, and the game was over. If he landed in any of the four side pockets between the corners, he got to take his date out, and the next shooter took his turn. If a shooter landed in any of the corner pots, he had to ante up another date. We used large ball bearings for shooters, measuring up to an inch and a half in diameter, that we called steelies. My favorite was made of brass, and I still have it among my keepsakes.

Usually, each game only lasted a few minutes, and marbles changed ownership rapidly, depending on how many dates we put in the center pot to start with. Game times were only limited by weather and daylight and usually ended up with one winner, like Texas hold'em, because the last two players remaining with marbles would shoot for winner take all. Then everybody would take off for home.

I amassed a hoard of a couple thousand marbles in my grade school years and would periodically count them, like King Midas and his gold stockpile. The only way I knew how to count was out loud and one at a time, so it took a while. My sisters would wait until I was almost done and start repeating some of my numbers in loud whispers just to rattle my cage. I'd get mixed up and have to start over. It would infuriate me, so the only way to stop them was to have a temper tantrum–the longer and louder the better. I was pretty good at tantrums and had been practicing ever since I was 3 or 4 months old when I found out it would get me anything I wanted from Mother. It still worked. She would intervene and make them keep their big mouths shut.

After getting into high school, marbles lost all of their importance for some reason I never fully understood at the time, and I gave my collection away to a couple of nephews. A number of years after that, I got married and found out my temper tantrums had lost all of their effectiveness too.

§ § §

During the 1930s, Mrs. Marie Myers lived at 50 North Lobban Avenue, directly south of the present Buffalo Bulletin office. She always kept a number of dogs at her house, and some of us boys sold her jackrabbits in the wintertime to feed them. She paid us 15¢ apiece unless she got overloaded. Then the price dropped to 10¢. She never bought cottontails. They were too small.

I delivered them to the front door of her living room. When she let me in, I just dumped them on the floor. The room was unheated and as cold as the temperature outside, so it kept the rabbits from spoiling until she parceled them out to the dogs. She quit buying them in March when the weather started warming up because she had no way of keeping them frozen.

She would count the rabbits and then disappear into another room and come back with the money. Her living room was as far as I got, and I never had any desire to go any farther because I could hear her dogs barking and growling in some other room, and I didn't want any part of them. They were especially noisy at 8:00 in the morning, noon and 5:00 when the laundry whistle blew. They were only a half block away from the laundry and would howl in accompaniment as long as the whistle lasted. You could hear them from any place in town and clear out in the boonies.

The laundry, Morrison's, was south of her house on the east side of the street right next to Clear Creek. A barbershop and office rentals occupy the building now. I remember when the Morrisons built it in the 1930s and put their living quarters on the second story. The creek bank at that time was just a little above the water, and they had to haul in a lot of fill material to get it level with the street. Some of it was from an old town dump nearby, and there were ashes, bottles and a lot of other junk mixed in with the dirt.

If someone ever tears the building down and digs a basement, I'd like to be standing nearby, collecting the old bottles and other Buffalo artifacts as they come out of the ground.

They did a good business handling the linens and blankets for most of the motels and hotels in town. All the wash machines and presses were operated with steam power, and the high humidity inside the building was always hot and muggy. My two oldest sisters worked there after they graduated from high school–eight to five for $1 a day and no coffee breaks. Through the years the advent of home washers and dryers and commercial pickup services gradually put them out of business. Changing times affected them like so many other businesses that had to either adapt or die.

Thinking back to Mrs. Myers and dumping the rabbits on the floor, her living room was what was called a parlor in those days. The ones that I remember all had the same characteristics. They were never used except for entertaining visitors. The drapes were always pulled to keep out light, and the windows and doors were kept shut to keep out the dust. They always had a musty smell because they never got any fresh air. All were cold, dark and uncomfortable, and some had sheets covering the chairs and davenports (couches or sofas) and were only removed when company was expected. They all had coal heating stoves but seldom had a fire going unless it was unusually cold outside. Then they would be fired up an hour or so before guests were expected. It wasn't time enough to get the room comfortable, but the main idea was to save as much money on fuel as possible.

A lot of the homes at that period of time had the bathroom door directly off the kitchen to consolidate the plumbing because there was no way to heat the crawlspace and keep the water pipes from freezing. Houses with basements had coal furnaces, and the heat gravitated up into the rooms by a single opening as close to the center of the house as you could get. Those with two stories had icebox bedrooms with inside and outside temperatures the same. Of course, thermostats hadn't come into existence yet.

I have no idea when somebody got the idea of inside outhouses, but when they did, the sewage was piped directly into Clear Creek. When our house on Bozeman Avenue moved the bathroom plumbing fixtures to the inside of the house, we walled off a portion of the kitchen. It was heated by the kitchen coal range. In extremely cold weather, the door had to be left open to keep the pipes from freezing. There was an uninsulated 30-gallon hot water tank in it that was piped through the inside of the kitchen stove and heated by convection–no fire, no hot water. It took several hours of continuous heat to get the tank even lukewarm. A reservoir on one end of the stove next to the oven heated water for doing dishes by dipping it out into a dishpan.

Mother had a rule written in stone that everyone had to have a Sunday night bath in preparation for school the next day. The hot water tank couldn't possibly put out enough hot water for the several of us that were affected, so she upped the ante by heating a washtub full on top of the stove. Rank has its privileges, so the eldest were first and on down the totem pole to the lowest common denominator in the same water with enough added from time to time to keep it warm. It would have been impossible to do it any other way. I still feel a little guilty when my electric water heater springs a leak every eight or 10 years and am annoyed if a plumber isn't immediately available to replace it.

Another person I remember who lived in the same area was Mrs. West. Her house was directly west of the depot where Powder River HVAC is presently located. She was an elderly woman, frail looking. I have no idea what she lived on unless it was a meager pension of some kind.

There was a storage area belonging to the Wyoming Railroad Company close to her home, which is presently Michelena Automotive. The railroad always had several cars of coal parked in its yard, and there was a high security fence topped out with barbwire surrounding it. It had a wide gate on the south facing the depot that most of the time was left open. The cars were loaded with coal and rounded on the top, so a lot of it would fall off and in a short time disintegrate into slack.

I think Mrs. West was probably in her 70s. When the gate was open, she would take a couple of coal buckets over to the yard, fill them with coal that had fallen off the cars, and carry them home. Sometimes, when I was on my way to or from school, I'd meet her and give her a hand with the buckets. This was during the Depression years of the 1930s, and money was almost nonexistent.

As a result of this, we became acquainted, and she would sometimes hire me on weekends or after school to do a little yardwork. She paid me 10¢ an hour, and I was thrilled to get the money. I don't remember ever making over a quarter at a time. The most frustrating part of the job was sitting there listening to her talk while she got around to counting out the money to pay me. A dime was the largest denomination of coins I remember ever receiving. Many years later, I realized she was terribly lonely and just needed someone to talk to. I don't recall ever seeing anybody visiting her.

One story I can still repeat from memory because I heard it so many times was how her chimney was built. Of the two men who worked on it, one was cross-eyed and the other was nearsighted. The chimney was brick and mortar. Evidently, one of them went up on the roof and cut a hole to run the chimney through while the other one started laying bricks on the kitchen floor. When the bottom guy got up through the ceiling into the attic,

44

the hole in the roof didn't quite match up, so he put a little jog in it to get the smoke out. That caused no end of problems, and the stove never did work properly, but she had to put up with it until the day she died. The house was eventually torn down. A man named Ray Wallace built a sheet metal shop on the property, and I told him this story so he wouldn't make the same mistake. Evidently, he followed my advice.

Mrs. West wasn't the only one picking up coal off the ground in the coal yard. We lived directly across the creek, and me and some of my older sisters did too, carrying the buckets across the bridge to our house when the gate was open. When it was closed and there wasn't any coal lying on the ground, my tomboy sister would crawl up on top of the cars and pitch it over the fence. Mother found out what she was doing and raised hell, but it didn't stop my sister. If I could have gotten over that fence, I'd have done the same thing. Our family was going through some pretty rough times.

I remember there was a large vein of coal in the bottom of the creek directly below the footbridge. When the water was low enough, I'd pry up pieces with a crowbar and pack it home. It's still there, and I think about it every time I take a memory walk down in the old neighborhood and see it shining through the water.

§ § §

I think a lot of families have stories connected to their particular histories that are verbally passed down through the generations, and one wonders how closely it resembles the one it started with. Our family was no exception. I remember one I nailed down quite by accident almost 85 years after it started.

The first book written on the subject shortly after it happened was named *Banditti of the Plains* by Asa Mercer. It was completely biased in favor of the small rancher-homesteader type and detrimental to the large cattle owners, who were known locally as cattle barons. According to my older sisters, Mother had purchased one of the original copies, and it was one of her most prized possessions.

In the early 1930s my sister, Irene, was in grade school, and her teacher asked the class if any of their parents had a copy of the book and would be willing to have the student bring it to class for some sort of project he had in mind. Mother refused Irene's request because she had heard a rumor that someone was trying to destroy all the copies, but Irene was persistent, and Mother finally consented to let her take it to school where it disappeared. Mother never forgot it. I can remember her talking about it years later after I was married and had a family.

In 2015, I acquired a photo of the 1931 eighth grade Buffalo basketball team and their coach with identification written on the back. The names were meaningless to me, but I was curious about their backgrounds, so I took it to 98-year-old Virginia, who was in grade school at that particular time period, in hopes she could help me out. Her eyesight had failed and was of no value as far as the photo was concerned, but there was nothing wrong with her memory. She remembered all of the boys and their coach. She gave me bits of information about each of her classmates, and when I mentioned the coach, she had a few comments about him, including one involving the collection of some books he had asked the class to bring in– *Banditti of the Plains*–and they had all disappeared.

§ § §

At the present time, there are attractive metal benches on the west side of the Main Street Clear Creek bridge. The original ones in the 1920s and '30s were made out of wood. As a kid, I always wondered why the east side didn't get the same treatment, but in later years I found out why. Any mayor or city councilman who suggested it would have faced the wrath of all the female members of the community.

My first recollection of them was when I was about six years old. The occupants were all men. They started gathering there when the sun came up over the horizon and began warming things up. Weather permitting, they were still there at sunset, discussing every topic under the sun like their modern counterparts do at the coffee klatches at the fast food restaurants on Hart Street. Only the name of their organization is different. They are now referred to as the Bench Sitters, courtesy of Sagebrush Sven at the Buffalo Bulletin.

The men who occupied the old benches were called the Bridge Gang, and it was not a complimentary term. They were all of the hanger-ons and misfits that the town had to offer, including the retired and unemployed. There were a few who didn't meet the criteria, but if they were sitting there, it was one size fits all. The local women detested them because if they were walking down the west side of Main Street, they would have to cross the street before reaching the benches and then cross back over in the next block after leaving the bridge. If they didn't, they knew every eye would be on them as they passed in front of the group. It was just like a reviewing stand at a parade. They were well aware whose anatomy was being scrutinized, discussed and catalogued right down to the last microscopic inch. I am frequently reminded how things have changed when I walk by the new benches on a warm summer evening and see a young couple holding hands, leaning over the rail watching the water slip under the bridge.

I don't know how many people are aware of it, but for many years motorists were permitted to make a U-turn in the center of the bridge. The State Highway Department got involved and put a stop to it. Progress had finally overtaken us–just like the Bridge Gang.

§   §   §

I think a number of people sometimes have one of those serendipitous moments in their lives when something totally unexpected arrives out of the blue. Sometimes they're not very pleasant, but in my case it was funny. It started before I was even born back in about 1910 roughly, but I never got it put together until over 50 years later.

Besides my siblings, seven of them, I had three half-brothers, who were raised around Buffalo also–Kenneth, Claude and Harold Gray. They were all at least 25 years older than I and were married with families before I was born. When I was growing up, they seemed more like uncles than brothers.

My favorite, Claude, moved to California in the latter half of his life but returned to Buffalo for visits many times when he was in his 60s and 70s. His wife also had a number of relatives still living here. When he arrived in Buffalo, we never missed a chance to exchange stories about our hometown. During the years he went to school here, I don't suppose there was much more than 1,000 people in town, and, of course, he knew every inch of it. So did every other boy in town, especially the places they were supposed to stay out of.

One time in mid-1960, he told me a story about an old building he was exploring without permission when he was in grade school. He walked by and the door was open, so he went in and looked around. He thought it had actually been built as a garage and wasn't very big, but, of course, neither were the Model T Fords of that era. It was made of logs dug back into the bank, and the roof logs was covered with dirt. The whole south end was covered with a homemade door.

All that was in it were some pieces of furniture and other junk, including a bureau with several drawers that was setting against the north wall. The drawers were full of odds and ends, including a lot of coins. He didn't remember what country had minted them, just that there were a lot of them. Many years later, on one of his trips back to Buffalo, he walked by the place, and it had all caved in. He said he always wondered if the coins were still in the building when it collapsed and everything was buried.

As he was telling me this story, something started jogging my memory, but I couldn't put it together until I asked him where the old dugout had been located. He said about halfway between the courthouse and the railroad depot. I burst out laughing and told him I didn't know what had happened in the 25-year interim, but I could set his mind at ease on one thing. The coins weren't there the last time I checked it out when I was in the sixth or seventh grade just before the whole thing collapsed.

I walked by the place hundreds of times on my way back and forth to school and always wondered what was in it, but it didn't have any windows to see inside. The full-width door on the south side was always shut, but it was so heavy it eventually sagged enough to break one hinge, and a guy my size could squeeze through the opening. I know I wasn't the only one that did it. When the other hinge finally broke, the whole south end was wide open, but nobody ever bothered to prop it back up.

All the logs were half rotten, and the bank was sifting in on the dirt floor. The roof was collapsing, and daylight showed through in many places. It had a couple feet of dirt on top of the logs which had probably been hauled out of the Bighorn Mountains, and it was pretty dim inside until your eyes became adjusted to it. Up to this time, I imagine every boy whoever attended grade school in town had been in it at one time or the other.

It still had a lot of junk in it, but anything made of wood had come apart. I distinctly remembered the old bureau Claude mentioned because it was against the bank on the north side and protected from most of the water that ruined everything else. It was partially covered with dirt, and the drawers had disintegrated, spilling all the odds and ends that most all bureaus collect on the ground. It had all been pawed through countless times, and anything of value had long since disappeared. Any coins, regardless of who minted them, would have been some of the first things to go except for some that had been stomped in the dirt and covered up through the previous years, which, no doubt, happened. It would have been too dark inside to see everything.

I thought a lot about the coins Claude mentioned and think there's a good chance they were of Chinese origin because there were several Chinese merchants in business in Buffalo even in my time, like cafes and laundries. I would find a coin in the dirt streets once in a while, but they weren't spendable for anything—more like tokens than anything else. I remember a Chinese restaurant across the street from the Courthouse and a laundry just off Fort Street on DeSmet Avenue. A Chinese man built the only three-story building on Main Street, the Idlewild, which was a hotel and cafe across Clear Creek south of the Occidental Hotel. If I remember correctly, they called him Charlie something or other. I wouldn't even attempt saying his real name.

I still walk by the old dugout quite frequently and see the sunken spot that is directly over the remains of the old bureau. If I owned the property, it would be fun to hire a backhoe and start digging. Claude passed away almost 33 years ago, but I think if he were still around, he'd like to see what's buried under there too.

§ § §

Elmer Huff was a blacksmith, I well remember, all through my school years and into the 1950s. His shop was located a half block east of North Main Street along the east side of the alley and directly behind the Reimann Oil Company. He was of medium height but very powerfully built with husky shoulders and strong arms. The business had previously been owned by his father-in-law, James Henderson.

His blacksmith shop was a big wood structure with large doors facing south that he opened when the weather was nice to let the sunlight in and the smoke out. It was usually smoky inside due to his forge, and soot from it covered everything. The interior was dark and gloomy with just a narrow path between piles of iron. A person had to be careful when threading his way through. The only lights were bare bulbs, hanging from cords scattered around the inside of the building, and they were so dirty that they didn't put out much light. The place always smelled of smoldering coal gas.

I walked by his place on the way back and forth to grade school. If the doors were open and he wasn't watching, I'd stop and look in. It was fascinating to watch him turn the forge handle with one hand to force air through the coals while handling the iron with the other. When it was red hot and glowing, he would grab it with a pair of tongs, lay it over the anvil, and beat it into shape. He had one large cone-shaped iron thing in the middle of his shop, and I always wondered what it was. Sixty years later I found out.

Dave Osmundsen has a blacksmith shop, Arrowhead Forge, on north Lobban Avenue in the same block as Elmer's used to be. (Incidentally, Dave told me that many years before he came to Buffalo, his garage had been the site of a previous blacksmith shop.) I noticed he had an identical cylindrical cone-shaped item in the middle of his shop just like Elmer's, and he told me it was called a cone mandrel. It was used for shaping iron into perfect circles. It was about 2 feet in diameter at the base and about 5 feet high. It came to a point on top and probably weighed 400 or 500 pounds.

He showed me how it was used and also asked me if I had ever heard the expression "beating the daylight out of somebody or something," which I had. He took a piece of heavy iron strap, cut it to the desired length, and then heated it in his forge until it was red hot. He hammered it into a rough circle and then pounded the two ends together until they bonded just as if he had welded them. He heated it to a cherry red, dropped it over the cone, and beat it every place where the daylight showed through. After a few applications he had a perfect circle with no daylight showing, just like a large finger ring. I couldn't help wondering how many hundreds of years these things had been used without any modifications or wearing out. "If it ain't broke, don't fix it" came to mind.

Elmer had a top reputation as a blacksmith and never had to go looking for work, but he was also one of the crankiest men I ever knew. I remember one summer after I returned from the service when I was working for a rancher who had a place on Piney Creek that we took some plowshares in to be sharpened. When we walked through the door, he looked up from what he was doing and growled at us to throw them in the corner. He would work on them when he got around to it. We needed them pretty badly so we could get back to farming but didn't dare ask him when they would be ready to be picked up. He would probably have told us to get the hell out of his shop and take our garbage with us. But he did good work, and the local farmers and ranchers kept him busy working on their machinery. I knew his son, Edwin, who was a little younger than I. He was very quiet and withdrawn, and I always wondered if his dad's personality had anything to do with it.

Elmer also built sheep wagons. They were top of the line like everything else he did. Johnson County had tens of thousands of sheep at that period of time, and the majority of them were owned by Basque people. They migrated to the United States from Spain and France, starting in about 1900. None of them spoke English when they first arrived. When I started grade school in 1930, many of my classmates had only heard their parents speak their native language and couldn't speak English either, so this was their first shot at it, but they learned fast.

These Basques needed sheep wagons to live in, and Elmer had to start from scratch. It would take months to build one even if a person was working on it fulltime, and he built his during the slack periods between other jobs, mostly in the winter months when farming was at a standstill.

I kept up with his progress looking through the open doors when I walked by. He would pull in a running gear with wood wheels and start building the chassis. In later years, he put rubber tires on them and shortened the tongue when sheep men started pulling them with pickups instead of horses. He finished the frame and the inside while it was wide open and then added the bows, ribs and canvas top last. I never heard a sheep man say Elmer had cut any corners, and he could have sold a lot more of them if he would have had the time.

In later years, he got religion and from what I heard pursued it with the same intensity that he used when hammering on hot iron. I don't know if the finished product met his specifications or not.

§ § §

Joe Bilbao was one of my favorite brothers-in-law. I had six, and I never knew a person that didn't like him. He and my sister had completely opposite personalities. She was a hard-driving dominant person who never knew the meaning of the word quit when she set her mind on something. Her husband was the direct opposite who seldom got in a hurry about anything but was a good worker and a pleasure to visit with.

He was raised in a house on South Main Street in Buffalo that mainly spoke Spanish and Basque, so he was fluent in both languages, plus English and a little French. I think school was at the lower end of his interests and served mainly as a pathway to sports. Baseball may have been his favorite, and he was good at it. He took two years of Spanish in high school, and since he had been speaking it since birth, it didn't present much of a challenge. My sister used to laugh and say he had to help the Spanish teacher out at times when a student posed a question that was beyond her ability to answer. Needless to say, I think Spanish was the only subject he bothered to be concerned about as far as grades were concerned, and that was because he didn't have to study. I saw one of his old textbooks once, and from the looks of it, the only thing it had ever been used for was doodling on the front cover. I've often wondered how he graded his teacher.

His father and mother, John and Marie, had a big two-story house with a number of small bedrooms that they rented to sheepherders when they were spending their annual vacations in Buffalo. They also furnished their meals. I remember Mrs. Bilbao as a short, heavyset, jolly person, who spoke very limited English. She always greeted me with the same words, "Hallow, Fleddy, how are you?" I would answer, "Fine," and she would say, "That's good." If I had said I had terminal cancer and would be dead next week, it would still have been, "That's good."

She was an extremely hard worker and did all the cooking, cleaning and laundry, which was considerable because there was always from one to six extra roomers to look after. She never had any help that I remember when doing dishes or laundry, and I don't recall her husband ever pitching in to help. This may have been a cultural thing as far as the Basque were concerned. She was responsible for inside the walls and he the outside.

In the mid-1930s when my sister and Joe were first married, I always tagged along to the family dinners. I had never seen such enormous piles of food stacked on one table, which was a little different from the way I had been raised. With the exception of Mrs. Bilbao and my sister, there were never any other women present. They had a large table with added leaves, and it was always full of men roomers who were all talking at the same

51

time in loud voices. I was only interested in eating and couldn't understand a word they were saying, but sometimes I would get the feeling that something was out of the ordinary and look up. They would all be looking and smiling at me. I had no idea what the joke was, but I knew I was the topic. Mrs. Bilbao never sat down to eat with us, as she was busy running back and forth from the old coal cookstove, refilling dishes. She always had lots of pies and cakes for dessert. The men were all big bread eaters. She must have spent a large part of everyday just baking bread.

One of the neat things I remember about their house was a big player piano that required coins to operate it. The piano had to have a nickel inserted before each song. The music was on rolls of thick, heavy waxed paper with holes punched in it. They were mostly accordion polka songs. The men would gather around the piano and sing along with it. It was funny watching the piano keys going up and down with no one touching them. It was a moneymaker, especially when they were celebrating a special occasion because they drank wine at every meal except breakfast from childhood on like we do milk or water. They worked hard and they partied hard.

Mrs. Bilbao's husband, John, was in direct contrast to his wife. He was a small, slender man who talked very quietly. I never heard him raise his voice at any time or become involved with any sort of the boisterous activities his countrymen did. Money was very difficult to come by during those Depression days, and he used his head instead of his hands to make ends meet. As a friend of mine, Charlie Kershner, used to put it, "I think he was work brittle."

They had a large backyard, and he bought and sold scrap metal, copper, aluminum, brass, and deer and elk hides. Also, this was during Prohibition, and he did what a lot of other people in Buffalo were doing. He made wine to sell to his roomers and all the Basque sheep men in Johnson County. A few years later, just before his son, Joe, and I were drafted into the Army, we were working on a shearing crew, and Joe delivered wine to the shearers for $1 a bottle. I never gave it a thought at the time, but he used any old bottles he could find when he bottled it. I've wondered since just how sanitary they would have been. But, of course, that was true of all the bootleggers in the whole country. I suppose the alcohol was a good disinfectant.

Every fall he bought a ton of grapes freighted in by the local railroad and fermented it in his basement in 50-gallon oak barrels. It had to be mashed to get the brew to start fermenting, so one year when I was in grade school, he asked me to help. I put on rubber boots, dumped some grapes in a washtub, and stomped on them. If I remember correctly, I think he told me he got three different qualities of wine out of them–first, second and third class runoffs. The first, of course, was the best and worth more money. I suppose the last one was used on his roomers when they were well along the road for whatever they were celebrating and couldn't tell the difference–just like a lot of bartenders do when their customers have reached the point of no return.

When I finished stomping the grapes, I was hoping for $1 or $2 in return for my help but temporarily forgot that I was working for a very astute secondhand junk dealer. He gave me a gallon of wine instead. Besides the fact I didn't drink anyway, Basques like their wine sour, and it tasted like vinegar. I don't remember what I ever did with it, but it was the first and last time I ever helped him with the grapes.

Thinking about him reminds me of a funny story that happened between him and his wife. I was in the house one day and overheard a conversation between Mrs. Bilbao and a lady friend who were visiting in the next room. Evidently, she and John had just recently had a violent disagreement about something. He had left the house, but she was still steaming about it. She and her visitor were discussing the incident in mixed Basque and English, and I heard her say, "Him thinks him big shot! Hah! Him big shit!"

Something rather interesting happened to their house many years later after they were both dead. It was on a big lot that stretched from Main Street to High Street to the west with no alley in between. The owner, Ray Wallace, decided to build a new home on the same lot, so he split the lot from north to south where the alley should have been and sold the house to the owner of the west half, Ron Mundlin. He wanted to restore it to its original condition, so he jacked it up, turned it around, and moved it across the lot facing west on High Street. Everything turned out great.

Besides my brother-in-law, Joe, the Bilbaos had a daughter named Juanita, who married a Basque sheep rancher named Arnaud Auzqui. They owned a ranch in the Clearmont area.

After getting out of high school, Joe worked for Ralph Perry, who owned the Table Supply grocery store located on South Main Street. The Table Supply always priced their groceries higher than the rest of the stores in town. I suppose the main reason was because they had charge accounts and a lot of their overhead was in the form of unpaid bills.

Joe was the butcher. Their beef was purchased locally from nearby ranchers. He had a false bottom built into his pickup to hold his butchering tools, knives, saws, and portable tripod. He would butcher the beeves right out in the pasture of the rancher whose beef they had bought. I remember that this made for some interesting situations. He carried a rifle in the pickup to knock the critter down, but with iron sights he sometimes couldn't get close enough to make a good head shot, and the wounded steer would take off for other locations on a dead run taking barbwire fences with him. Sometimes Joe would catch up with it several miles from where he started on somebody else's ranch. It actually wasn't much different than some elk hunts I've been on. I don't know what the meat tasted like after being run down and shot.

A few years later, although it was confidential, his boss financed his entry into a store of his own, Cashway Grocery & Market, which as the name implies did not include charge accounts. He had one employee, Bob Baldwin, who had been a classmate of his in school. Bob was a super good clerk, and his customer relations with the public was second to none. Ralph Perry was a very successful businessman, and with two local, well-liked men running the store, it was surprising the business only lasted a couple of years or so. Ralph, eventually, closed up his Main Street grocery and moved it up on Fort Street, where it became the IGA, operated by his son, Robert, a classmate of mine.

While Joe had the Cashway Grocery & Market, he would sometimes hire me to do little odd jobs around the store like cleaning or moving things around. One of them was getting chickens ready for sale on Saturday mornings. He would buy 10 or 12 chickens from a local rancher who would deliver them in a crate on Saturday. I had to kill them in a certain way that Joe showed me. I would take them out of the crate one at a time, fold their wings tight against their body, and hold them feet down between my knees, then stretch their neck straight up with my left hand and slit their throats with a knife and then toss them to one side to flop around and bleed to death. I had never seen a chicken killed in any way except putting their heads on a chopping block and cutting it off with an axe or shooting their heads off with a .22 rifle. Of course, by using a knife, it didn't get any sand or dirt in what was left of its neck while it was flopping around, and the head was extra weight when selling it by the pound.

After killing them I'd heat some water to scald them and pluck their feathers. Sometimes I wouldn't do a very good job on the feathers for some reason, and the black pinfeathers would have to be removed one at a time. I sure didn't like that part of it. Joe would dress them and hang them up over the meat counter by their heads to sell them. I suppose it had something to do with refrigeration because he always had to get rid of them the same day, and any leftover were sold at a discount on Saturday night before closing.

At that period of time all stores were closed on Sundays except for maybe a gas station. I don't know if it was a law or just custom, but everybody closed at 9:00 p.m. on Saturday nights except for the bars. I think they stayed open till midnight. No Sunday sales in those days.

Joe would deliver supplies to a Basque sheep man, Martin Etchhart, every Sunday through the year, blizzards excepted, and I accompanied him from about the seventh grade and on into high school. I think he did it mainly for relaxation. He had a 1938 Ford pickup, and with no gravel on any of the roads and gumbo mud, some years he would burn out a couple of clutches in a single year, which Martin paid for. This was in the days before four-wheel drive. Even with chains on, the mud would pack into the fender wells so tight that sometimes we had to take the wheel off to pry the mud out with a shovel.

Martin was an odd duck. His only contact with the outside world was with Joe. Joe always delivered a gallon of wine with the groceries, and he and Martin would converse in Spanish, I think. They could both talk in Spanish, Basque, French, and English I was told, but Martin's English was so bad I could barely understand what he said, so I can't vouch for the rest of it.

From what I remember, Joe told me Martin had come over from the Old Country as a young man and herded sheep until he built up a herd of his own. Sometime after World War I he got mixed up with the wrong woman and lost his whole outfit, so he had to start over. I met him in the late '30s, and he owned 1,500 or so breeding ewes and several sections of grazing land he had purchased from Earl Henderson in the Wallows country southeast of Buffalo. He later sold his outfit, I think, in the late '40s to Pete Bordarrampe and returned to the place of his birth.

I think there were about three sections of land involved when he purchased the property from Henderson. Joe took Martin up to the lawyer's office to sign the papers, and there was a disagreement over the price. Martin claimed it was supposed to be $2.50 per acre, and Henderson said $3. Martin paid the $3.

One Sunday morning, Joe stopped by to pick me up on the way to Martin's sheep camp. He said he had to drop the groceries off and come right back to town, so he asked my sister, Edith, if she wanted to come along for the ride. When we got there, all three of us went into the wagon, and Joe introduced her to Martin. We visited for a few minutes, and then Edith and I went out and sat in the pickup while Joe finished talking to Martin. She was a high school senior at the time. I was a freshman.

When Joe came out he was grinning from ear to ear. Martin had told him if Edith would consider marrying him, he would transfer all his sheep and land over to her. I suppose he was thinking ahead, and since he was probably 50 years older than she was, the odds were pretty good she would outlive him. My sister was not amused at the offer in any way, shape or form even when I pointed out the advantages of owning a ranch and a band of sheep debt free. That was 75 years ago. She is living in Texas now, but I never fail to bring the subject up when we're talking on the telephone. I get the impression she has never once regretted making that decision.

One time, Martin was renting some pasture on a place southeast of Clearmont. He bought a horse in Buffalo from somebody, and since Joe didn't have a hitch on his pickup to pull a trailer, he wanted me to ride it out to his camp. It turned out to be the most miserable horseback trip I ever took. The horse's name was Nightshade. He was a big, tall, leggy gelding and had the most spine jarring gait of any horse I ever rode. It didn't matter if he was walking, trotting or loping. It was like sitting on top of a trip hammer.

Joe dropped me off at the livery stable that was located just east of the present-day Crazy Woman Square. He had borrowed a saddle for me to use, but the stirrups were too long, and we couldn't get them shortened enough to do any good. After a mile or so, I was wishing I was bareback, but Joe had taken off, and I didn't have any place to leave the saddle.

From the livery barn I went down the stockyards road to the Red Hills road, then to the TW and turned left. At some point, I turned off the TW road and took off through the hills. I'm guessing it was about 25 miles to Martin's wagon. I got so saddle sore that at times I'd have to get off and walk. I wasn't used to riding that far in one trip, and it turned into a long, long day. The trip back to town in the pickup was like riding on a cloud.

§ § §

Most of the Basque men arrived in Johnson County with an agreement to work for several years as sheepherders. Practically all of them were young men who couldn't speak English. Some of them took their wages out in payment of sheep instead of money and built up herds of their own. A good share of them were working for relatives who had helped them get to America. Being unfamiliar with the language and customs of the locals put them at a distinct disadvantage, and my brother-in-law, Joe, helped many of them through the transition period.

He was born in Salt Lake City, Utah, in November 1914 to immigrant parents, John and Marie Bilbao. When he was about a year old, they returned to Bilbao, Spain, and he lived there until he graduated from eighth grade. They moved back to the United States, and he graduated from Johnson County High School in 1935. Because he was fluent in English, Spanish and Basque, he was in a unique position to help the Basque immigrants integrate into the community, especially since his parents' boarding house was a center of activity for a lot of them. Many times he acted as an interpreter in a lawyer's office when they were involved in legal transactions. Others would contact him for advice or help in personal situations involving local customs or regulations.

The summer I was 12 years old, he even helped me take a step forward in my adult education even though neither of us realized it at the time. He was working for a grocery store in town, and one Saturday morning he received a message from a sheepherder in the Bighorn Mountains. There were no telephones in the area at that time. The herder said he had to talk to Joe "muy pronto" the next day and wanted him to drive up to his camp near Hazelton and bring somebody with him to help watch the sheep. Joe had no idea what he wanted.

When we got to the wagon, the herder and Joe had a very intense conversation with a lot of arm waving, but I couldn't understand a word they were saying. Joe finally told me he had to take the herder to town for something important. I would have to keep track of the sheep while they were gone. When they got back, the herder gave me $1, and Joe told me what happened on the way home.

On the preceding Friday, the herder had a visitor, and when she left on Saturday morning, he gave her a check for $500 for something or other. Shortly after she drove off, he got to thinking that was a lot of money, so he sent word to Joe. They looked up somebody that worked for the First National Bank and stopped payment on the check before his visitor got to the bank on Monday morning. Even after he finished telling me, I still didn't understand what had happened. Five hundred dollars was more money than I thought existed in the whole world. The only thing that meant anything to me was the silver dollar in my front pocket that the herder had given me. After I got a little older, I finally figured it out.

§   §   §

My uncle, Tom White, rented a ranch on Rock Creek for many years through the 1930s drought and Depression era. I spent all the time at the ranch that my mother would let me. He treated me like he treated his three sons, who were all about my age and were more like brothers than cousins. He and Aunt Clara had a late daughter, Janice, a number of years later. The boy's names were Darrell, the oldest, then Fay and Gene. I was a year older than Gene and closer in age, so we spent a lot of time together getting into things we shouldn't have.

One summer, my aunt hired my oldest sister, Beulah, to help her with the cooking, washing and general housework, so I got to spend a lot of time on the ranch while she was there to keep an eye on me. I was probably about in the third grade.

Aunt Clara had a flock of geese that was ruled by a large ornery gander. Gene and I didn't like any part of him because if you got too close to his flock, he would hiss, spread out his wings, and come straight at you. One day, he charged us, and Gene picked up a rock and threw it at him. It hit him in the head, and he dropped like a lead balloon. My sister didn't see him do it, but she saw us standing over him, and we figured she would report us, so we told her it had drowned. A goose that can't swim is one for the books, but evidently she never told my aunt, and they baked him for Sunday dinner.

§ § §

The first prestigious job my uncle put me to doing when I was spending a few days visiting at the ranch in the middle grade school years was driving a stone boat. It was just a homemade, heavy-duty sled used for picking up rocks around the hayfield and hauling them off to be unloaded by hand into the bottom of a cutbank or washout draw. It was made out of old planks for a bed with a couple of long poles underneath for runners and pulled by a team of horses–in my particular case the gentlest ones on the ranch, Chester and Buster. It was probably one of the safest jobs on the ranch with horses, especially so for a city kid like me, and it paid well, 10¢ a day, and built up my self-esteem to no end.

I walked along side of it holding the reins and stopped at each rock that I threw on the bed. Thinking back, Chester and Buster had long ago figured out what we were doing, and my presence on the job was the most insignificant part of the whole operation. But I didn't know that then, and my wages paid the full price of admission at the theater's Saturday matinee, which only showed cowboy and Indian movies. The best part of the day was intermingling with likeminded classmate cowboys and telling them what a hell of a time I'd had managing a team of wild broncs on something that resembled a stagecoach. They never asked for, and I never volunteered any specific details regarding the operation.

§ § §

When I was still in grade school, Uncle Tom limited my duties around the ranch. During hay season, I was only allowed to drive one gentle team of horses, Chester and Buster. Us kids would even ride them back and forth to the hayfield. When they still had their harness on, we weren't even able to guide them. They were smart enough to know they had to do all our thinking for us and would just plod along at their regular gait and pay no attention to us if we tried to turn them or make them speed up.

The sulky rake and stacker were the only two pieces of machinery besides a hayrack that my uncle would let me operate. The sulky rake was a two-wheeled contraption that raked the new mown hay into windrows.

You sat on top of it and tripped a lever with your foot when it was full or to line it up with a windrow. After it was windrowed, the buck rake was used to drive up and down the windrows to pick up the hay and haul it to the stacker, where it was hoisted up and stored in haystacks. The buck rakes were horse drawn to begin with, but along in the mid-1930s farmers began remodeling old Model A Fords and Dodges to do the work, which speeded up the haying operation by several hundred percent.

The horse drawn mowers were dangerous pieces of machinery to operate, and a lot of men lost their hands and feet when they got careless or a team would run away when they were mowing. My uncle only let Darrell, the oldest, do the mowing. Even Gene and Fay weren't allowed to operate one until they got into high school, and by then they were using tractors.

With only two wheels, the sulky rakes were really hard on the horse's neck because it bounced up and down so bad on the uneven dirt, so my uncle added an extra two wheels in front, called a dolly, which took all the weight off of the horses except for the front end of the tongue. One time, I had an accident with it that would have ended up in death or a trip to the hospital if I hadn't been driving a gentle team.

The hay was high and thick, and when the mower laid it down, the sickle bar that did the cutting reached out over the top of a deep narrow gully and laid the hay down flat so the gully was invisible. Darrell, the mower driver, wasn't even aware it was there, but when I followed his first round, I had to put my left wheel over the gulley, and when it dropped down into it, it threw me off the seat and down between the wheels and rake teeth. I screamed, "Whoa," and the team stopped immediately, and I climbed back up. If it hadn't been for that old gentle team, Chester and Buster, I would probably have been dragged to death.

§ § §

There were several types of hay stackers, but the only ones I ever saw in this area were called overshot, due to the way the hay was raised off the ground and placed on the haystack. I had heard of the beaver slide that I think were used up in the Oregon area and the jayhawks in the Kansas part of the country. I suppose this is where they got the name for their football team.

With the overshot, the hay was pushed on it with a buck rake. Then a horse drawn cable would hoist it up to the men on the haystack. The team pulling the cable would have to back up after each load was dumped and start over, so the job was pretty monotonous. After the first two or three trips, the horses would know exactly where the cable was going to stop them from moving forward, so they would stop an instant before they got there, and the hay would dribble off the end of the stacker. This created a lot of extra work for the men on the haystack because they would have to move the whole load to the back of the stack with pitchforks. If a man was driving the stacker team, he would make them lean into the end of the cable and throw the hay to the back of the stack, but they knew a kid couldn't, so they wouldn't pay any attention to me.

My uncle was up on the stack and could see what was going on, so he waited until the team was on the point of slowing down and then hollered at them. They had blinders on their bridles and couldn't see behind them, so they thought he was right on their tails with a switch and jumped forward. The cable broke, but they kept going on a dead run. I was hanging onto the reins–all 80 pounds of me–and touching the ground about every 20 feet. We covered a lot of ground before I finally got them stopped and back to the stack yard. The stacker head had about a dozen 10-foot long wooden teeth to support the hay as it was rising. When the cable broke, it came back down and broke almost every one of them when it hit the ground. It took half a day to replace the teeth.

§ § §

Working in the hayfield was a hot dusty job, and there wasn't any place to take a bath. Sometimes right after work the four of us boys would jump in the Ford, and Darrell would drive us down to a deep hole on Rock Creek. It was about two miles down the county road from the ranch on the neighboring Twing property. The creek was usually pretty low at that time of year, but the pool was in the shade and really deep, so it stayed cool.

We would strip, and Gene, Darrell and I would take a run and jump off the deep end to get the shock of the cold water over with in a hurry. After a hot hayfield, it was a teeth gritting experience. Fay would start on the shallow end and wade in an inch at a time. Sometimes, the three of us would be ready to go home, and he hadn't even been under water yet, so Gene and I would speed things up by splashing water on him.

We always made sure we could get to our shoes first before taking off on a dead run, streaking out through the underbrush naked. The creek was right along the county road and had very little traffic, so no one ever saw us because if my aunt had found out about it, she would have raised holy hell. Darrell always stepped in and stopped everything, meaning me and Gene didn't get the daylights beat out of us.

§ § §

During the drought years of the 1930s, the grasshoppers and Mormon crickets were a plague. There were millions of them, and they ate everything that grew and some things that didn't. When we finished getting the hay stacked in one field and moved to another, if someone left a pitchfork leaning against the stackyard fence for a couple of days, the hoppers would completely ruin it by chewing on the wood handle. It would splinter the wood so bad it couldn't even be sanded down and reused. I think what attracted them to it was the salty perspiration that was imbedded in the wood from handling it.

Sometimes the crickets would cluster so thick on asphalt roads that if you drove slowly with the windows rolled down, it sounded like popcorn popping. The road would become so slick with smashed bodies that the wheels would slide if you hit the brakes. When the hoppers and crickets swarmed into an alfalfa field, they would eat the leaves first, and the stems would resemble the aftermath of a bad hailstorm.

§ § §

One Friday night, I had gone to the ranch to spend the weekend, and the next morning we woke up to several inches of fresh snow on the ground. Mrs. Myers was buying jackrabbits for her dogs and paying 15¢ apiece for them, so Gene and I decided to go hunting. It was a lot easier with fresh snow on the ground because if you jumped them without getting a shot, you could follow their tracks and quite often catch up with them.

We walked down Rock Creek about a half mile and crossed the fence onto the Twing property when we ran onto some fresh man tracks, so we followed them. It turned out to be somebody checking his muskrat trapline. It seemed like a golden opportunity to get something for nothing, so we picked up all the traps, crossed back over the fence to our side, and reset them along the creek. For two bright minds like us, the thought that we were leaving fresh tracks in the snow never occurred to us.

The next morning Gene and I were cleaning out the chicken house when Uncle Tom and Kenneth Twing from the neighboring ranch showed up. My uncle asked us if we might have any idea who had stolen some muskrat traps from Kenneth's brother-in-law, Billy Pichlmaier, a kid just a few years older than me and Gene. Of course, we didn't.

We visited for a few minutes, and as they were leaving, my uncle said if we thought of any suspects, it might be a good idea to tell them to return the stolen traps. After they left, we got worried that maybe they were suspecting us, so we went up to the house to get our overshoes, and Aunt Clara lit into us with both feet. Then we knew for sure. We picked up the traps and reset them on Billy's side of the fence.

§ § §

Gene, Fay and I loved to hunt rabbits, sage hens, pheasants, and other small game with .22 rifles. Guns were a fact of life for practically every kid in the county at that time, but my aunt and uncle knew it was dangerous to have all three of us hunting together, each with a rifle, so they tried to split us up in different directions when we left the house.

It didn't work because we would agree where to meet after we got out of sight of the house and come back separately when we finished hunting. I'm quite sure they were well aware of this but didn't know how to prevent us from doing it. My oldest cousin, Darrell, wouldn't do it, so we never asked him to go hunting when we did. When he was along, we had to keep in separate areas.

After Darrell got old enough to drive, we would go up and down the county road with a .22 rifle, looking for pheasants to shoot. One day, we spotted one, but it was on his side, so he stopped the car and leaned way back in the seat so I could rest the rifle on his door after he rolled the window down. The front of the barrel was resting on the window groove, and when I shot, the bullet went through the top of the door. The window was rolled down far enough that it didn't break, and I missed the pheasant. He never told me what he told his dad, and Uncle Tom never mentioned anything about it to me.

I remember one time when Gene and I had gotten ahold of some .22 shells when he was visiting me in Buffalo. We didn't have a gun to shoot them with, so we did a little experimenting. We went up to the edge of town, which at that time was just west of DeSmet Street. It was all sagebrush from thereon and a good place to hunt rabbits when I got a little older. After a few false starts, we got to laying the shells flat on a rock and hitting them with another rock to get them to fire. Accuracy was nonexistent. I've often wondered how much damage the bullet would have made if it had hit one of us. The danger would not have been anywhere near what it would have been if fired from a rifle, but I haven't been interested enough since to find out just how much.

§ § §

Even though I was a year older than he was, Gene gave me my first driving lesson. Farm kids usually got a head start in learning to drive due to having large open areas to practice in and also being required to help out with the family finances. During the Depression years of the 1930s, the drought that covered most of the country whittled away at what little income the small ranches and farms could come by, and a large part of the hired help had to be made up by the kids as they grew up and took on more responsibilities.

My first practice run took place when I was in grade school. My uncle had an old Model A Ford pickup that was used for all sorts of jobs around the ranch, like fencing. Since it was used only on the ranch proper, it wasn't even licensed even though sometimes us kids would take a chance and take it out on the county road so we could whiz along on the gravel. Of course, we never mentioned these trips to my aunt and uncle.

We had pillows stacked on the seat and in back so we could reach the steering wheel and see out the windshield. Gene was driving when we left the house on an old two-track dirt road. When we got out of sight of the house, he stopped, and I got behind the wheel. I already knew the particulars, but he went through the process again on a step-by-step basis, explaining the shifting and clutch pedal sequence. Of course, everything was a floor-mounted stick shift in those days.

Naturally, I was nervous, but I got it started and went through the shifting routine from low to second to high with a lot of gear grinding in the process and actually got it stopped in front of the first wire gate we had to go through. I was feeling a lot more confident, but when Gene got out to open the next gate, he had to cross in front of the Ford, and I forgot and let the clutch out. It was still in gear, and I darn near pushed him through the barbwire gate, but he jumped to one side, and I went on through taking all the wires with me. It was a good lesson for me, and I never forgot it. We patched up the gate, and that was one more little escapade we never mentioned to my uncle and aunt.

§ § §

I remember one other vehicle that my uncle acquired after I got into high school. It was a big old White truck. They were not a common brand in this part of the country, and the only one I remember seeing. I don't know what year it was made but would guess somewhere in the mid-1930s. It was a two-ton model with dually wheels and 3- or 4-foot sideboards for hauling grain from the threshing machine. It wasn't very fast but was heavy built and could really take a beating and still run. The biggest problem with it was that we always had trouble keeping the brakes working. Sometimes they would completely disappear, so we got into the habit of checking them before getting to a gate or some other obstacle. If it was a wide area, like a field, you could just cut another circle to get slowed down while you downshifted. Actually, we enjoyed showing off by downshifting even when we didn't have to, just to prove how cool we were. It got to be like playing a game of chicken when we knew the brakes were fading and had to downshift all the way through the gears when we were going to end up against something solid.

Gene and I rode in it a lot and took turns driving. I remember once when he really goofed. We were in a lane with a fence on both sides and there was no room for error. We were coming up to a gate with a huge cottonwood tree near one side of it. He waited too long to start downshifting and get stopped long enough for me to open the gate. His brakes faded, and he got rattled and pulled off the road and hit the tree head on. We both braced ourselves for the hit, and it only bent the front bumper on the truck. He should have gone through the gate because it was only barbwire and easy to repair.

There was only one time when I needed brakes on the thing more than anything else in the whole wide world. We were replacing some wooden teeth on a buck rake, and the old White was the only thing with a bed long enough to haul them. It was late afternoon on a Saturday. Both lumberyards in Buffalo closed at 5:00, and we had to have them for the next day. My uncle called to make sure they had them, and they said one of the men would stay late until I got there. He told me to hurry because it was about 10 or 12 miles to town from the ranch on Rock Creek.

The county road was gravel and pretty narrow. If you met someone, you both would have to slow down and ride the shoulder while passing. There was only one steep hill to go down on the way to town with an irrigation ditch piped across the road under some old bridge planks right at the bottom. I was doing about 35 or 40 miles per hour when I topped the hill and saw a half dozen hogs, crossing the road on the planks. I jammed the brake pedal clear to the floor, but nothing happened, and it was too late. I was going too fast to downshift. All but two of the hogs cleared the bridge, and they stopped in the middle and watched me coming.

I only had half a bridge open, so my right front wheel dropped off, hit the opposite bank, and bounced back up. The duallies hit next and bounced back up. I went barreling down the barrow pit before I finally got the truck stopped. The headlights were fastened to a bar that went just behind the radiator. They broke loose and flew off to one side. Like all farm trucks, it was full of assorted junk on the floor and seat of the cab. When the door flew open, it was scattered all the way from the ditch to where I finally got the truck stopped. Luckily, no windows broke.

I have no idea how long I sat in the truck shaking. I finally got out and picked up the junk and wired the headlights back on with some baling wire. I went on into town and picked up the buck rake teeth. I never mentioned the hog incident to my uncle. Evidently, we never had to use the headlights on the old White after that. I don't know if anybody even noticed they weren't working. Its eventual demise took place one fall when we were helping a neighbor, Julius Johnson, thresh and left it at his house overnight. It caught fire sometime during the night and burned completely up.

§ § §

The only time Gene and I would tolerate Fay or Darrell was when we needed a third party to participate in some kind of game we had dreamed up. Darrel was a goody two-shoes, who never did anything wrong and would report us if he caught us doing something we shouldn't. We didn't trust any part of him. Once, he told us we were both yes-men, and though we didn't quite understand what it meant, we knew it wasn't good.

Fay was almost as big as the two of us put together. He was very strong, and we considered him a bully and had to be pretty desperate to let him join us in anything at all. He was several years older than us and the principal conveyer of solid facts that concerned our puberty years. Once, he told us exactly where babies came from, but we didn't believe it. I had always been told by adults who always averted their eyes when relating it that they came from cabbage plants and just grew up differently. It seemed a lot more plausible than Fay's version.

Fay's middle name was Elmer, and it used to irritate him no end when we would put his initials together and call him FEW brains. Once in a while during the summer months when it was real hot, we would see him go into the outdoor privy, which smelled to high heaven even though people used lime to cut the odor down and eliminate flies. Gene and I would each grab a double handful of rocks and station ourselves about 10 feet in front of the door. When we would see it start to open, we would alternate hitting it with rocks, and he didn't dare come out for fear of getting hit. He would go from pleading with us to quit, to rattling the door, to the moment he would be so mad he would come busting out regardless of whether he got hit or not. We could pretty well judge when we knew he had reached his limit. We had a 10-foot head start and could outrun him, so we made ourselves scarce until he got over his temper tantrum and would pacify him by agreeing to play with him. He tried to stop us from doing this by painting the words, Beware of Fat Fay White, on the door, but it didn't do any good.

Fay was a pain in the butt when we had our horse races. He always rode a big mare we called Blue. I was on the gentlest Shetland, Billy, because I was the city cousin and didn't know much about riding. Darrell had a half-Shetland named Lindy, and Gene rode one we called Rex. Of course, Blue towered over me and Billy, so Fay would intimidate me by crowding his horse into mine and pretending he was going to stomp both of us in the dirt. If Darrell was present, he would make him quit because if push came to shove, he could whip Fay in a fight. He would also tell my aunt and uncle.

They believed everything he told them. However, in all fairness, he usually told them everything that had happened even if he was going to catch hell for what he had done. He was really odd that way.

None of us had saddles, so I would grab a fist full of mane and hang on when somebody would yell "go." Billy loved to run, but Fay was the only one with a full-size horse, so he always won. We tried to handicap him by making him start farther back, but it never worked because he usually cheated just enough to win by jumping the gun at the word "go," especially when he was the one that hollered.

Darrell was really attached to Lindy. When she got sick and died one summer, he was really broken up about it. He wouldn't even go near the place she had died, so Gene and I, in a spirit of forgiveness, volunteered to dig a hole and bury her, which hardly anybody ever bothered doing. Usually, a dead animal was just dragged away from the house far enough to keep the smell from bothering and left for the magpies to chew on. The ground was a lot harder digging the grave than we had anticipated, and our enthusiasm diminished with each shovel full. When we ran onto some angleworms, it evaporated entirely, and we ended up several feet short of what we had originally intended, so we just rolled her in and piled the dirt up over her. Then we gathered up the worms and went fishing. Darrell thanked us profusely at first because he wasn't aware of all this, and we modestly accepted his praise without saying anything. I don't remember if we caught any fish or not.

§ § §

The first deer I shot was when I was in grade school. Gene and I were hunting in the Castle Rock area on Horton's HF Bar Ranch. I was using a borrowed .25-35 rifle at the time, which was quite popular but in reality was very underpowered for an animal like a deer. A well-aimed shot at somewhat less than a 100 yards was very effective. This was in the days before telescopic sights were widely available, and I had never even seen one. With iron sights and a good rest, anything over 150 feet was pretty iffy for a clean kill. The .30-30 Winchester was the most popular gun and better than what I was carrying, but it had its limitations too. Men would even use it on elk and brag about its killing power, but for every one that was killed with it, another two or three would be wounded and get away to die later. Those were the ones they didn't talk about.

Gene and I jumped a small bunch of deer with a little 3 point buck in the group, and I shot and wounded it. I was so excited I don't even know how I hit it. The bunch ran down a small grassy draw and disappeared, and we spent the next couple of hours looking for them. The buck was pretty sick and dropped out of the bunch and lay down before we caught up with him. He was laying down in some high grass in the bottom of a little swale, and there was a big red dairy bull and a half dozen cows just on the other side from me.

Gene was walking down the bottom of the draw to spook the buck if we jumped him, and I was on the bank where I could hopefully get a shot. When he finally jumped up and started to run down the bottom of the draw, he was moving too fast for me to get a shot, and all three of us started running after him–me, Gene and the cow herd. I was slightly ahead of Gene and up on top of the draw when I heard him holler, "Look out! Here comes the bull!" I never even looked back. There was one lonely tree about 15 feet high a short distance from me, and I got to it and was so scared, I climbed to the lowest branch still hanging onto my rifle. Gene arrived on a dead run just a few feet ahead of the bull and tossed his rifle to me. I grabbed his hand and hoisted him up. I could never have done it on a practice run, but my adrenalin was at the top of the chart. We were stranded up in that tree for over two hours because the bull refused to leave. He just walked around under it and pawed the ground and grunted.

Fay was with us when we started out that morning and was driving their old '34 V-8 Ford four-door. He had taken off hunting in a different direction and finally tracked us down when he heard us shooting into the ground at the bull's heels to scare him off. It didn't even faze him, and we didn't dare kill him. Fay was parked on the top of the bank about level with me and Gene and would yell and wave his arms, but when it started for him, he would run back to the car and take off. That bank was at least 10 feet high, and the bull would have needed wings to get up on top, but Fay wasn't taking any chances. He finally had to drive to the ranch, Horton's HF Bar, and get the foreman, Greely Hughes, to come over with a small truck and get rid of the bull long enough for me and Gene to get down and into the car. Greely told us the bull was pretty mean and they had trouble with him around the ranch at times. He said if we hadn't been able to get up that tree, we would have either been killed or badly mutilated.

Later that afternoon we made sure the bull wasn't anywhere around and drove back to the last place we had seen the buck. We finally found him lying down, and I finished him off. We dressed him out and found the bullet I had originally hit him with. It was pretty deformed. I kept it for a souvenir and some 70 years later, I gave it to my son, Robin, and told him the story behind it. I sure didn't have any problems recalling all the details.

§ § §

Thinking about the Horton foreman I just mentioned, Greely Hughes was one of the last old-time cowboys that I remember. He spent several decades on the ranch. The first old-time cowboy I knew was in the late 1920s before I started school. His name was Tom Rich and was a good friend of our whole family. He had spent several years in the State penitentiary for stealing a horse or horses. I heard my mother discussing the issue with some of my aunts, and she said it didn't make any difference to her one way or the other. She still liked and trusted him, which, for me, was the top of the line as far as references go. I have a picture as about a two or three year old, sitting on his horse all by myself, hanging onto the saddle horn. I have often wondered if it was one he requisitioned after dark.

I have always had the reputation for being frugal, which is a lot better sounding word than some others I can think of. A lot of it came naturally, but most of it was worked on and refined through the years. When I was three or four years old, Tom gave me the very first silver dollar I ever owned, but Mother told me I'd just lose it, so she kept it until she figured I had matured enough to spend it wisely. I don't remember exactly when she gave it back to me, but I know it was after I had returned from the Army after World War II ended. I stuck it in a safe deposit box until I figured out what to spend it on. It is still there as of this writing, and I am now past 90 years of age.

Several years ago, a good friend told me I was so tight that I probably had the first dollar I ever made, and the thought suddenly struck me that it was true. This may have been where the concept of saving for a rainy day entered my head. Even I can tell it's been a long dry spell.

The second person with the last name Rich I became acquainted with was in the 1960s. His first name was Leon. He became one of my very best friends. When I first met him, it was in the Bighorn Mountains back in the boonies west of Buffalo Park. I had just shot a bull elk and was wondering how I was going to get the several hundred pounds of meat moved from where I was standing to my home, which was a long way off. Leon drove up with a little CJ-5 jeep and offered to haul it for me, and that was the beginning of a long friendship that lasted four decades and stretched into hundreds of hunting and fishing trips. At the time, he was working for Claude Isenberger, who had a John Deere Implement dealership in the old Buffalo Flour Mill, located along Clear Creek next to present-day Centennial Trail.

He died a few years ago, but I still remember a story he told me while he was working there. A bachelor rancher, Galen McLaughlin, who had a farm on Muddy Creek south of Buffalo, had purchased some machinery from the firm, and he called one day and said it was broken down, so Claude sent Leon out to fix it. He worked on it all morning, and shortly before noon he went to the house to tell Galen it was fixed. Galen had been cooking a pot of beans and had just sat down to eat. His table had an oilcloth cover, and he had poured a bunch of beans on it, which he was eating with a large spoon and sopping up the juice with a handful of bread. He invited Leon to sit down and eat. Leon told me he was hungry but not that hungry. He told Galen his wife was expecting him home for dinner, which wasn't true, and got out of the house. I knew he never stretched the truth in anything he said or did, so I questioned him about this. He told me that under the right circumstances, there are exceptions to every rule, and this was one of them.

§ § §

Another cowboy I remember was Charlie Kershner. Our family called him Kush, and he was a good friend. He was born in 1912. I first remember him when he was in his teens and a frequent guest at our house. He had an infectious giggle that made everyone around him laugh with him. At the time, he was working at the EW (Works) Ranch, now the Esponda Ranch, about a mile or so southeast of Buffalo. I used to walk out there with my sisters every once in a while. The thing I remember most about the trip was that they would feed me all the beefsteak and real honest to goodness cream I could eat. The cream was so thick it could almost stand up by itself, something we never experienced around our house. Charlie and the other young cowboys working there–Tommy Skurok is one I remember–were batching and doing their own cooking, and he told me they never used an oven. They fried everything, including the ribs of the beef, deer and antelope they butchered.

We were drafted into the Army at the same time and rode the bus to Denver together. I lost track of him for a number of years, and my next recollection of him was in about 1947 or '48 after I returned home from the service. I was working for my brother-in-law, Lee Duncan, who had the Hepp Ranch on Little Piney leased. They were good friends and were both excellent horsemen and had a common interest in one thing–horses–and did some rodeoing together at the local fair and rodeo. They also both loved ice cream.

One night, Lee along with my sister, Vi, and the two boys, Gary and Dennis, decided to pick up some ice cream and drive out to the Moorhead place, where Charlie and his wife, Shirley, were working. They hadn't been married very long at the time, and there weren't any telephones to tell them we were coming. The ranch was located off the TW road and 15 or 20 miles from town, as I remember.

Lee had a new Ford car, so we picked up the ice cream and headed out on the county road which wasn't even gravel at the time. It was in the spring, and we got to within several miles of the ranch before we got bogged down in the gumbo mud. It was pitch dark, and I had never been there before, but Lee told me if I stayed on the road that I couldn't get lost and that the road ended at the ranch. It was difficult walking in the mud, but after what seemed an eternity, I stumbled into some buildings that were outlined by starlight. It was after midnight, and I just started hammering on doors until Charlie answered one of them. He just laughed when I told him that he and Shirley were invited to an ice cream social somewhere between here and town.

He lit a lantern, and we went to the barn, and he harnessed a team of half broke horses to a four-wheel utility wagon. The three of us climbed on board, and we headed back for the Duncans. The horses were skittish, and the gumbo mud was a lifesaver because it slowed them down to a fast walk. When we got to the car, Lee got a chain tied onto the front end, and we hooked the wagon on the front. He got back behind the steering wheel, and Charlie started the team up, but he didn't have the wagon exactly lined up with the car, and when the horses lunged forward, the wagon turned over on its side. Luckily, Charlie was walking alongside the wagon on the opposite side, so he didn't get hurt, but the team went crazy, and he had one hell of a time getting them hooked up on the side of the wagon so he could pull it back on its wheels. All of this was done with the aid of the headlights because we didn't have a flashlight. Anyway, we finally got the car back on solid ground. The seven of us crowded in and ate the ice cream. Charlie and Shirley headed back to the ranch, and we took off for town. We got home just before daylight.

§ § §

Sometime after the ice cream party, Charlie and his wife moved to the Indian reservation in the Black Hills, and he cowboyed there for a number of years. He moved back to Buffalo sometime in the 1960s and bought a house and 5 acres just north of the fairgrounds in Buffalo. It was during the time when Interstate 90 and 25 were being constructed. He had had some experience with a survey party during his time in the service, so he went to work for the Buffalo engineers. I had already been working there for several years. We were put on the same crew, and he was a fun guy to work with. He stayed there until he reached retirement age and told me a lot of funny stories. I wish I could remember half of them.

I do recall one of his little witticisms. When our survey crew members would get to discussing some insignificant matter over the what, where, who, and why, things would start to warm up a bit with different opinions, Charlie would break in with a grin and say, "Eagles and owls and most other fowls all look like chickens to me." Everybody would laugh, and the subject was dropped.

He had driven teams of horses all his life, and he used a steering wheel the same way he handled reins–constantly turning the wheel back and forth with short jerks. His top speed when he was in a hurry was 55 miles an hour–tops. It would drive us nuts when he got behind the wheel of our survey suburban, so we crowded him out every chance we got without saying anything, especially when we were late and headed for home and had a 100 miles to go.

He told me several times that he wished he had been born a 100 years before, and he meant it. He handled a telephone like it was a stick of dynamite with a short fuse. I know of a number of times when he drove to Gillette [Wyoming] to talk face-to-face to someone just to keep from using it. He was raised the hard way under hard conditions from the age of 12 on. I used to laugh at some of his superstitions. Rattlesnakes were taken in stride, but he had a mortal fear of mice. I think he was afraid one would run up his pants leg. I know the feeling when I've had one trapped in a room, trying to pound it to death with a broom.

He told me once he and Shirley were headed somewhere, and when they got to the edge of town, she remembered they had forgotten to put in their baby's favorite blanket. The baby cried and fussed all the way to their destination and back home, but Charlie knew it was bad luck to start somewhere and have to go back, so they kept going. I didn't ask him if Shirley had any objections.

Charlie was one of the last of the old-time cowboys as I previously mentioned. I saw him ride broncs a number of times at the Johnson County Fair and Rodeo, but he never got used to riding in a competition contest and didn't scratch (spur) his horses in a way to please the judges and build up points. He was brought up having horses blow up at unexpected times, not out of a bucking chute, when the main idea was to stay in the saddle until he got control of the horse and not for the eight second rodeo ride.

He told me once a horse blew up with him in Buffalo by the library and bucked all across the Courthouse lawn and off the bank onto Main Street, scattering a group of young ladies on the sidewalk. I suggested that maybe part of the exhibition might have been a young 19-year-old cowboy showing off. He just grinned and didn't respond.

He told me about one trip to Denver he made pulling a trailer with one horse in it. He got confused out in the middle of one of those intersections with six lanes of traffic coming in from all directions. He stalled out in the middle of the intersection, and a cop materialized out of nowhere and told him to get the thing out of the way. Charlie said, "Where do you want me to go?" and the cop said, "I don't give a damn, but get it to hell out of here."

So, Charlie pulled into the first street he saw which was a one-way, and he was headed in the wrong direction. He met a car, and to avoid a head-on he slammed on his brakes. The horse in back wasn't expecting the sudden stop and turned upside down, landed on his back, and started kicking the trailer to pieces. Charlie ran around to the back, opened up the trailer gate, and the horse rolled out. He helped him get to his feet and reloaded him right side up. He didn't say how he got the rest of the way up the street, but I think it was the last time he ever went to Denver.

As I mentioned previously, he was a terrible driver and knew absolutely nothing about an automobile, having spent his entire life being interested in one thing only—horses. Like many of his generation, his first experience with driving was with a Model T Ford and the first car he ever owned.

He laughed when he told me the following story. A local rancher contacted him one day and said he needed some help rounding up some cows on his ranch. He told Charlie he had plenty of saddle horses, so it wouldn't be necessary to bring one with him. Charlie loaded up his saddle and other gear and left for the neighbor's ranch before daylight the next morning in his Model T. They ate breakfast and started out just at daylight. Charlie left his car parked in the yard. They didn't get back to the ranch until after dark, so they had supper, and Charlie went out to his car to head for home.

The Model T started fine but wouldn't move even though he tried every gear. It was dark, and they didn't have a flashlight, so the rancher crawled under the car and used some stick matches to try to find out what the problem was. He didn't have any luck, so he switched positions with Charlie, but Charlie couldn't see what was wrong either, so he ended up spending the night there. The next morning, they saw what the problem was.

Not knowing anything about a mechanical contraption, Charlie figured when he had shut the motor off, all the gears and everything else had somehow been lined up just right, and they couldn't get off of dead center in order to start moving again. He didn't have the faintest idea how to correct the problem. It turned out to be something much simpler than that. Somebody had showed up at the ranch while they were rounding up cattle and had jacked up a rear wheel and put it on blocks. If it had vibrated off that block the night before while they were under the Ford, it would have run over them. They agreed to keep the joke to themselves until they found out who the jokester was. It was a friend, Earl Murdock, who finally reached the point when his curiosity got the better of him and had to bring the subject up. I don't know if they were ever able to return the favor or not.

§ § §

Our crew got along with each other exceptionally well, but you had to be on constant lookout to keep from being the end result of a practical joke. I dished out my share, but Charlie really got to me once.

The house he bought out next to the fairgrounds had a barn and a shed or two. He had spent half his life living in various bunkhouses around the country, so he decided to start from scratch and build one just for nostalgia's sake, and he did a great job. Using old lumber and other things he scrounged up, he ended up with the real thing. Then he started looking for things to furnish it with.

I had always been interested in antiques and had a lot of junk that I had collected through the years, so I gave him an old iron bedstead. A week or so later he came to work one morning and told me he had stripped all the paint off the thing, and it was solid brass underneath.

To this very day, I can remember the sick feeling I had when he told me that. I had been hunting for one for years, and when I finally found it, I gave it away. It was all I could think about all day, and, of course, he didn't miss the opportunity to tell me several times how beautiful the thing was and how much he appreciated the gift. I was so upset I left the shop before quitting time and drove out to his bunkhouse to see the final proof of what a fool I had been–hammering the last nail in the coffin, I guess.

It was all a joke. The bed was really iron, and he sucked me in but good. When he showed up a few minutes later, he couldn't stop laughing. But I didn't care because it was the first and only time in my life when I was truly thankful to be on the butt end of a practical joke.

§ § §

Charlie was 12 years older than I was, and for the next 20 years or so the age difference was very marked. But as the years went by, the difference blurred, and he went from a funny guy to be around to a good friend that loved to laugh. I don't know if he ever finished high school. He told me he started holding down a man's job at about 12 years of age cowboying, which was not uncommon in this part of the country at that period of time.

He had a number of short pithy one liners he used to illustrate a story he was telling. A lot of them had a reference to horses. I remember a few: Never say whoa in a horse race. Take a deep seat and a tight rein. Every day will be Sunday bye and bye. Hope for the best, expect the worst, and you'll never be disappointed. Any horse will buck and any dog will bite under the right circumstances.

Cowboying as an occupation was strictly a non-married proposition.

His everyday life prohibited that. His profession demanded that he live in a common bunkhouse with other men seven days a week with hours regulated by the time of year and particular phase of workday they were engaged in. The ranch took precedent over anything else. Most of them were laid off in late fall, and the vast majority were dead broke by the time spring rolled around and the cycle began all over again.

A lot of their time was spent on the open range without even a tent for shelter. They lived out of their bedroll and had to be ready for anything after they crawled into it for the night. He laughed when he told me Shirley's first job after they were married was to halter break him. He was used to folding his clothes and putting them in a pile by the side of the bed or under the canvas bed tarp if sleeping outside in case of rain and so everything would be ready in case of a mishap in the middle of the night. Shirley was adamant. That practice had to go.

He told me that before he got married, he never wore anything but Levi overalls, and they had to be a perfect fit–period. By the time his three children were born, he wore the cheapest brand he could get, and if he could get them on, they were a fit.

I remember a story he told me about the flood in 1912 that took a lot of Buffalo's Main Street out. About half the water came down Bull Creek, which was about a mile east of town. His family was living in the flood plain at the time, and Charlie was only a few months old. His parents heard water running during the night, so his dad got up and lit a kerosene lamp. Water was coming in around the door. His dad grabbed him, the family got ready, and they all stepped out into total darkness when he opened the door. It must have been a hairy experience.

At one time, he worked for the 28 Ranch, which belonged to the Hesse family. The patriarch, F.G.S. Hesse, was English, and at mealtime he would fill all the plates from his position at the head of the table and pass them around from cowboy to cowboy until all were served. Then they would begin eating. There were no seconds, and Mr. Hesse was the only one that did any talking. When you were finished eating, you got up and left the table.

This was in direct contrast to all the other ranches in the country because mealtimes were a time to relax and share jokes and stories. Dishes of food were passed from hand to hand around the table, and each person took what he wanted.

Another English custom he said they used was when they killed a goose for the dinner table. It was hung up by the neck for several days until the entrails fell out. Then the feathers were plucked and the goose cleaned. I guess this is where the expression "the goose hangs high" originated. Charlie did admit it was very tasty, but I don't think he carried the practice over into his married life. Shirley would have had a few things to say about that.

Mr. Hesse had two boys and a girl, Fred, Jr., George and Vivienne. I have talked to quite a number of people who grew up in that period of time, and they all said she was the most beautiful girl in Johnson County. Charlie told me she had so many suitors that sometimes when haying season started, Mr. Hesse would give her $1,000 and ship her off to Cheyenne for the summer so they could get the ranch work done.

Fred Gray's High School Graduation – 1942

PART II

High School Days

I started my freshman year in high school in 1938. Athletics were mostly limited to football and basketball–boys only–for the fulltime sports. Girls' activities came under the heading of physical education as a regular class, tumbling and acrobatics, and were performed in interludes at other school functions or as a pickup game of volleyball, soft ball or a tennis match after school or weekends. The competition was all among themselves, and they didn't travel to other towns.

J.R. Strother was the assistant football coach and school principal. He was generally well liked, but I always wondered which occupation was his top priority because, like today, football was not only a sport, it was a religion. He lived and breathed football. One of my sisters who preceded me in high school by a few years told me a couple of her classmates quit school at Christmas so they would be eligible for one more year of football. I couldn't help thinking that it may have been with J.R.'s blessing.

I was never interested in any type of organized sport activities and preferred hunting and fishing. Town ended a block west of the high school, so in the wintertime I took my .22 rifle or shotgun to school and parked it in my locker until the final bell rang. It was only a five-minute walk to prime rabbit and grouse country. A kid would be arrested if he tried that today.

Freshman initiation, hazing, was mild compared to previous years. Upper class boys would haul us out of town a few miles and make us remove our pants and walk back to town. The pile of overalls would be left in the gym. Even this was discontinued a few years later when some of the jock's carried the practice past the first week of school.

Our dress code was vastly different from present-day standards. Girls had to wear dresses–no jeans–to school regardless of the weather. The only exception was once a year just before school closed for the summer when the school board authorized an official ditch day. Students were allowed to take off for a picnic or something if they could find a car to go in, usually to Ice Cave, which was five miles west of town on Clear Creek.

In that era, practically the whole student body had to walk back and forth to school morning, noon and night because school lunchrooms weren't even on the drawing board. There were only three or four cars driven from home to school, and they were all owned by teachers. During my freshman year, the only student I can remember who had a vehicle was a boy named Kenny Waugh. His dad owned the Chevy garage on the southeast corner of the intersection at Fort and Main south of the Stevens brothers' service station.

His car was about a 1932 four-door model. When he took off down the hill to the north past the swimming pool, it was always loaded with kids inside and out because some of them would be lined up on the running boards. Prosinski Park was the football field at that time and had a vertical solid-log fence about 8 feet high all around it so people would have to pay to get into the ballgames. The logs were pointed on top like a stockade and impossible to crawl over. Luckily, the double-car gates that faced the hill were lined up with the road and usually left open. The Burritt Street bridge didn't exist nor the road to it either. There was a narrow swinging bridge suspended on cables for kids to get across Clear Creek to the high school.

If it was icy or Kenny had too much speed to make the sharp right corner onto Angus to get to Main Street, he would shoot through the gates into the football field to get stopped and turned around. Sometimes I think he did it just to give all of the free riders a thrill, and I'm pretty sure it worked.

In nice weather, the boys would sprawl out on the lawn at school before the bell rang, shoot the bull, and smoke cigarettes. I had smoked intermittently for several years but never where my mother could see me. My two closest friends were not smokers, so I never smoked around them either.

One noon, when I was a sophomore, we were gathered on the lawn, and a kid named Kenny Kerr lit up a cigarette and started puffing on it. He was a real nice kid, but his folks had a little more money than most of ours, and they dressed him differently. We wore overalls, and he wore suit pants. I don't ever remember hearing him swear. He sure wasn't supposed to be smoking, and I got the impression he was just trying to break the invisible barrier between him and some of the rest of us. Evidently, it was one of his first cigarettes in public, and he was trying to be nonchalant about it, but he wasn't making the grade. He held the thing like women did in the movies of that era–two fingers straight up, forefinger and middle, and the cigarette on top with the tips of the fingers barely grasping the cigarette. All that was lacking was a plastic cigarette holder to complete the picture. And he didn't inhale, just puffed. Something about it stayed with me, and I'll be forever indebted to him because I quit smoking right then and there.

During deer season from the sixth grade on, I spent most weekends with my cousins at their ranch on Rock Creek. As kids, we hunted the entire season without licenses and would fill anybody's tag that asked us. It was during the bad Depression and years of drought, and people were hard up. Putting food on the table was their main priority, and wild game helped a lot of them over the rough spots. There was only one game warden for the entire county, and he had been raised here. He didn't bother us kids and would have had to stumble over someone he didn't know before he would have arrested them.

I remember one game warden who lived in Story, George Redman, who said ex-poachers made the best game wardens because they knew when, where and how to apprehend someone, and he was speaking from experience. In the late 1930s, my dad had a little place leased on the north fork of Crazy Woman Creek. The game warden, Dick Bandy, dropped in to visit one day about noon. Dad told him he had shot some young sage chickens that morning and was going to cook them for dinner. He invited Dick to stay, and he did.

Another time, my brother-in-law, Lee Duncan, told me he was hunting on the UM Ranch northwest of Buffalo when he came up over the top of a hill and looked down on two guys gutting a couple of deer past their limit. One of them was Art Osborn, who worked for the City, and the other was the Buffalo police chief. Lee walked down the hill toward them before they noticed him. The police chief looked up and said, "I'm just helping Art out," which was a ludicrous statement to make because he wasn't trying to be funny. He was so rattled that he said the first thing that popped into his mind without realizing how stupid it sounded. Anyway, Lee offered to help dress their deer out and finished his hunt at the same time because they gave him one of the extras.

Money was pretty scarce, so I and my two best friends, Walt Hushbeck and H.B. Hurst, worked on ranches and shearing crews from our freshman year on. One spring after school let out, H.B. and I were working on a shearing crew east of town on Crazy Woman Creek. It was in flood stage, and we thought it would be fun to float down on inner tubes.

The day before, we walked down the creek about a mile below camp and left dry clothes stashed in a hollowed-out cottonwood tree. After work the next day, we stripped down to shorts and floated downstream to where we had left our clothes. We had to be back in time for supper, so we were hurrying along side by side on a two-track dirt road when a rattlesnake came busting out on my side. It didn't have time to stop, and neither did we. It crossed just in front of my foot, and by the time it got to H.B., he was right on top of it, but his adrenalin spiked and shot him up in the air a couple feet higher than he had ever jumped before. Supper lost all its importance, and we slowed down the rest of the way.

Walt and I were locals from day-one, but H.B. had originated in Texas, and we never let him forget it. All of the many stories about how Texas was always the biggest and best of everything that had ever been created, we rubbed in every chance we got, especially on occasions when we were in mixed company at a dance or something and wanted to cut his 6 foot 3 inch

80

frame down to a normal size. The best story I remember was about a Texas hunter coming to Buffalo during elk season. He was an exceptionally huge man, and his party was camped out in the Bighorns when he had a heart attack and died. The local undertaker didn't have a casket large enough to hold the body, so they just gave him an enema and sent him home in a shoebox.

In December of 1941, the three of us were working weekends for Dave Elsom, who had a ranch south of Buffalo. We were excavating for a basement using horses, pulling a slip scraper, which was something resembling a wheelbarrow without wheels only on a much larger scale. Basically, it was just a big scoop. We were paid $4.50 each for the two days, and Dave hauled us back and forth to town.

One Sunday evening after getting home, we heard about the attack on Pearl Harbor. The next morning there was a radio and loud speaker set up in the gym, and we listened to President Roosevelt's "Day of Infamy" speech, asking Congress to declare war. This was the last time any president ever took the trouble to ask them as the Constitution specifically requires. Korea, Vietnam, Gulf Wars I and II, Iraq, Afghanistan, and counting were all renamed something else to get around the requirement. It's possible for politicians to do anything they like as long as a suitable name is dreamed up to placate the American people.

President Roosevelt was an excellent speaker, and he told us the Japanese had pulled a cowardly trick on an innocent God-fearing nation, which had done nothing to deserve it, and we believed him. It would take historians the next 50 years to discover the things he had neglected to tell us. In the next few weeks, some of the boys quit school and enlisted. Out of the 28 Johnson County men who were killed during World War II, about a dozen were classmates who had attended high school during my four years.

Between Walt, H.B. and I, Walt drew the short straw. H.B. ended up in England, and I sat out the war on an insignificant rock in the South Pacific. Walt was in the second wave during D-day and in the middle of the fight during the Battle of the Bulge. He was still slogging east when the war finally ended in Europe.

His oldest brother, Tom, was stationed in the Philippines when the Japanese bombed Pearl Harbor and was trapped along with thousands of other soldiers. They hung on for a while but finally had to surrender because there was no way to get troops from the United States to help them. It was four years later before his mother learned what had happened to him. He died on a death march on the way to a concentration camp.

After the war, Walt went to the University of Wyoming on the GI Bill and graduated with a Civil Engineer degree. He married a local girl,

Marilyn Francis, and they had six children. He was working for Texaco when his hands and face were badly burned in a chemical explosion in Anacortes, Washington, and had numerous skin grafts that extended over a long period of time. He ended his career with the company as superintendent of their refinery in Tulsa, Oklahoma and died in 1999.

H.B. spent his entire working life after the war in Nevada on road construction. After retirement, he built a home in Boulder City, Nevada. He and his wife, Birdie, had two children. He died in 2016.

§ § §

My first car was a 1927 Model T Ford that I bought from a brother-in-law for 20 bucks when I was a junior, but it was too much of a hassle to drive it to school. He towed me from Sheridan on a trip I'll never forget. Regular gas was about 15¢ a gallon and white gas a dime. It would even burn kerosene, which was cheaper yet if you got it to running first. If you couldn't find a hill to park it on and coast off to get started, it had to be cranked. Model Ts didn't come equipped with starters.

When cranking it, you didn't hold the handle like a baseball bat. You had to keep your thumb on the same side as your fingers because if it kicked back, it would break your arm, especially if you had forgotten to push the spark lever up. It was located on the left side of the steering wheel. The gas feed was a lever on the right side of the wheel. There was no accelerator on the floorboards. I still catch myself calling it a foot-feed, which brings questioning looks from guys when we're discussing cars. Old habits are hard to shake.

Antifreeze hadn't been invented yet, so in cold weather the water had to be drained out of the radiator every night and filled back up with warm water the next morning. I also had to place a pan of hot coal ashes under the transmission to heat the oil up. At these times, it was a lot easier to start if I jacked up a rear wheel and cranked it fast enough to get the wheel spinning and keep the motor going. One time, when it finally started, the vibration shook it off the jack, and it ran into the corner of the house before it stopped. I got out of the way in time, but my mother sure wasn't happy about that one.

The Ford had three foot pedals. The left one all the way down was low, the middle was reverse, and the right one was the brake. High gear was a floor mounted gearshift rod on the left knee high by the driver's door. It had a ratchet handle that you squeezed to set the lock in place. Pushed forward all the way threw it into high while pulling the handle to the rear threw it out of gear and was sort of an emergency brake. If it was parked on a hill, I had to cramp the wheel into the curb or put a rock behind the wheel to get it to hold.

It did not come with a battery. It had a coil that distributed the spark that came from the magneto, which was a large heavy circle of magnets under the car. That was what created the juice when you cranked it.

The gas tank was under the seat, which had to be removed when refueling. The gas filler tube was on the passenger side. If the hill was too steep, the Ford would run out of gas before reaching the top, and I'd have to coast backwards to the bottom, turn around, and back up the hill.

My model was equipped with a ruxel, which was a floor mounted gearshift rod by the right knee that doubled the number of gears. Forward was high, and back was low. When it was in ruxel low, it was just like driving a tractor at two miles an hour and could almost climb a wall. The tires were solid rubber, and the early Model Ts had tractor wheels that could be changed for the regular ones and used for plowing.

It had a hand-operated windshield wiper that kept me busy in a hard rain or wet snowstorm. It didn't have a speedometer, and the ignition key was a little lever mounted on the dashboard that was moved back and forth for on and off. It did have headlights, but if you speeded up the motor too fast when they were on, they would dim and burn out. My '27 was the last year the Model T was in production before Mr. Ford came out with its classy cousin–the Model A. It was as different from the Model T as a Piper Cub airplane was from a corporate jet. It even had a battery and a starter. I bought a 1930 Model A Coupe a few years after I got home from the Army.

I'll try to remember the sequence for starting the T, but I hope anybody reading this will cut me some slack because it's been 75 years since I last crawled into one. First thing was to turn the ignition lever to on, then push the spark lever all the way up, set the gas lever to where it would idle, then get out and crank it. The high lever by my left knee would be all the way back and locked. After getting it started, I'd pull the spark lever down and depress the low pedal until it got up to about 20 miles per hour. This was all the while taking a little pressure off the high lever and adjusting the gas lever on the steering wheel to fit the conditions. Then I'd push the high lever forward when it reached cruising speed, which I guessed to be about 40. As I mentioned, the middle pedal was reverse and the right one the brake, but if I had to slow down in a hurry, I'd stomp all three pedals down at the same time and skid to a stop.

I remember a couple times when I was starting it and turned the ignition switch, the dang thing backfired and startled the hell out of me. My mechanic, Joe Goryl, told me it was just a fluke with the Fords. When I had shut it off, everything was ready to fire with the pistons in the right position. The switch just activated it. Sometimes I think of this when I turn the key in my present car and it starts.

*Fred Gray's
1938 Ford Coupe*

My Model T looked like a cheesebox on a raft, so I tore the top off and made it into a bug. It didn't exactly resemble the Ford Mustang that came out in the '60s, but I thought it looked pretty snazzy, and it may have been where they got the idea. I finally sold the thing for $25, and in my senior year, 1942, bought a 1938 Ford coupe that a local guy, Jimmy Blake, had hit a cow with and smashed the front end. It took the Ford garage a long time to find enough parts to put it back together because of the war, but they finally did, and I got about a year's use out of it before I was drafted.

It was what was called a Business Coupe with a single fixed seat and a wide shelf under the rear window. I tore the shelf out and rigged up a couple of little seats to sit on. A person had to crawl over the top of the seat to get to the back, but I was the only person in my group that had a car, and teenagers are quite resilient, so nobody complained.

Gasoline was hard to get because it was rationed, but I was working on shearing crews and ranches that were considered critical to the war effort, so I didn't have any trouble getting enough gas stamps. I blew out a tire and couldn't find a new one, so I bought one on the black market from my neighbor. It was illegal for him to sell it, and the only reason he did was because he knew me. He charged me 20 bucks for it and even apologized for charging so much because it was only worth about five at the most. The tread was recapped rubber with sawdust mixed in for filler. You can imagine how many miles it would have lasted at highway speeds, but the national speed limit was 35 miles an hour, and practically everybody adhered to it. If they didn't, they were considered un-American.

*Gillette Basketball
Tournament Ticket*

Anyway, it lasted long enough to see me into the Army, and I figured I got my money's worth. On March 4, 5, and 6, 1943, I drove it to Gillette to the basketball tournament 100 miles by the old road at 35 miles an hour. It was just before I was drafted, and there were only a few boys left in Buffalo and not very many of them owned a car. So, I loaded up six girls, Billie and Peggy Hurst, Candida Michelena, Mary Jean Smith, and the Lawrence twins, May and Fay, and we went to the ballgame. I still have the ticket.

I was so jammed up against the door I could just barely reach the clutch and brake pedals. The floor mounted gearshift was out of the question, so I would push in on the clutch, and somebody else would have to shift, at times, trying to force it into reverse when we were moving forward. We stayed all three days, and the total ticket price for each of us was $1.68, which included a federal tax of 15¢ and a state tax of 3¢. A few months after that, I rented a neighbor's garage for $2 a month and put the Ford on blocks until I got home almost three years later.

§ § §

I stumbled into a rather odd situation one night in the late 1940s. There was a night club, Pop Kelly's, located on Highway 87. It was 200 or 300 yards east of the present-day turnoff to Story just before reaching Tunnel Inn when coming from Buffalo. This was before Interstate 90 over Piney Hill was even in the thinking stage and a few years before old Highway 87 past the Fetterman Monument to Sheridan was built. It has since been abandoned.

I don't know how the nightclub got its name, but I remember it was getting a reputation for serving alcohol to under age kids because members of my high school class were going there to party. It had gambling going on in a backroom that was also against the law. There were several small rental cabins connected to the place, and the owners lived in one of them. I was never in the place until after I returned home from the service in the late 1940s.

A friend of mine, Charles Riley Jones, and I had been to Sheridan one Saturday night and were headed back to Buffalo about 2:00 Sunday morning. When we reached Pop Kelly's, all the lights were still on, so we pulled in to see what was going on. At that period of time, bars were supposed to close at midnight because it was against the law to sell liquor on Sundays, but none of the nightclubs in Sheridan and Johnson Counties, which were outside the city limits, paid any attention to it. The ones in town didn't either. They just locked their front doors and turned off their overhead lights. The backdoor was left open. It was pretty dim with just bar lights, but people managed.

The bar was packed, and when we found a couple of empty stools, we each ordered a beer. A local guy I had known for many years, Jimmy Morgareidge, was tending bar, which I thought was odd because he had worked on ranches all his life and didn't know any more about mixing drinks than I did. The next surprise was the beers he served us. They were called picnic bottles with a flip wire holding the cork in and held several times more than a regular bottle of beer did. I had never seen one used for anything but large social gatherings like a barbeque. He plopped two of them down in front of us. The third eye opener was when he refused payment and said they were on the house.

He moved on down the bar waiting on customers. When somebody would order a shot of whiskey, he set the whole bottle on the bar in front of them just like in the old-time Western movies and let them wait on themselves. If they wanted a mixed drink, they received a full bottle of whatever they wanted to cut the whiskey with. It was the standard drinks are on the house routine that he used on Charles and me.

We didn't have the faintest idea what was going on, but a short time later we found out when the chatter came to an abrupt halt and we saw the bar owner standing in the connecting door to the backroom, where he had been running a poker game. He was a big heavyset guy that could probably have cleaned the room out all by himself, but he never said a word. He just stood there looking the situation over. Then he started picking up bottles scattered around the room. I guess he figured the horse was already out of the barn.

Jimmy slunk out from behind the bar like a dog that had been caught in the process of cleaning out a refrigerator when somebody left the door open. That was the end of the party, and the owner had the place to himself about two minutes later.

The next day we found out what happened. The guy's wife had been tending bar while he was in the backroom dealing a poker game. She got drunk, went out the backdoor to one of their cabins, and passed out. I don't suppose it was a very pretty scene when he woke her up and they discussed the night's event or if they thanked Jimmy for filling in.

At that period of time, orchestras were hired to play up to about midnight when the bar was supposed to shut down. Of course, it didn't, so to get them to play longer, it was common practice to take up a collection from among the crowd. One night, two guys I knew ran out of money before the night was over, so they walked around to all the booths, holding a hat upside down for people to drop money in. Then they took what they got back to the bar and spent it.

They bought me a drink, but when I found out how they paid for it, we had quite a discussion on the ethics of the transaction. They insisted they hadn't done anything wrong because nobody had asked them what the donation was for, and they didn't see any reason to volunteer the information. They just held the hat out, and people dropped money into it. It was no different than a freewill offering dropped into the collection plate at church according to them.

The nightclub had a number of lessees through the years it was in operation. A guy named Jimmy Huggins from Story and his partner, Joe Crackenberger, were two of them. One Saturday night, they were running wide open, and Allen Leath and another kid from Sheridan were bartending when the law came through the front door. Twenty-one was the legal age for drinking. Allen told me he and this other kid were only 19 at the time, so they closed the place down. The owners were fined but got to keep their liquor license.

One day sometime later, a young lady walked into the bar and asked how old a person had to be to buy a six pack. The bartender was quoted as saying if she was big enough to see over the top of the bar, she was old enough to buy beer. I don't know if she was a plant or not or whether the bartender was just joking, but the authorities nailed him for selling beer to a minor. I think the nightclub changed ownership shortly after that.

Pop Kelly's final chapter was written when the place burned to the ground. There was some controversy over how the fire got started according to the insurance agency, and I don't know what the outcome was. I do remember it certainly had a colorful history during the years it was in existence.

§ § §

In the summer of 1942, the year I graduated from high school, I was working for Dave Elsom, herding sheep up on the mountain. When we trailed down that fall, my sister, Beulah, told me that she, her husband, Willie, and son, Lynn, who was in the first grade, were going to Topeka, Kansas, to work on defense work for the government and asked if I wanted to go along. Dave told me he had plenty of help for the winter, so I went with them. Up until this time, the farthest I had ever been away from Buffalo was a trip to Midwest [Wyoming] with my cousins–a whole 70 miles from town.

When we got to Topeka, we had trouble finding a place to live because the town was full of newly arrived workers. We finally found a little two-room apartment in a house the owners had converted into several apartments with the one community bathroom located in the hallway. Ours was a tiny kitchen-dinette room with a small living room-bedroom attached and one little closet. Beulah and Willie had the bed and Lynn and I slept on cots. There was barely enough room to get between the beds. The apartment was pretty cramped, but we were lucky to even find one to rent.

Willie had a job waiting for him when we got there, but I didn't. I answered an ad in the paper, and they said to show up at a certain address at 8:00 the next morning. I had to take a city bus to get there, and I had never ridden one before, so I was pretty apprehensive about the whole process. The landlord told me the downtown bus stop was only two blocks from our apartment and would stop at the address they had given me. I sure didn't want to be late, so I got there two hours early and had the whole place to myself.

They had told me over the phone that a company bus would transport the workers to the job site. When I got there, one was parked in front of their office with the door open. I figured that had to be mine, so I checked it out. I tried all the seats and finally picked out one in the rear and sat down, waiting for someone else to show up.

After a while, I got to thinking about something I had read or heard about where someone was sitting over the rear dually wheels of a bus, and it ran over a piece of pipe lying in the road. The danged thing jammed between the wheels and came up through the bottom of the bus and cut him in half or almost. I looked out the window, and sure enough I was sitting right over the wheels, so I got up and moved. It was an hour or so later before anyone else showed up.

When we got to the construction site, everyone filed into the office to punch the time clock–the first I had ever seen–and I filled out a form for carpenter's helper. They had to show me how to punch the clock. A man said, "Follow me," and led me out to an area about the size of the Midwest oil fields where hundreds of men were working on buildings a half mile long. He led me to my boss, who handed me a shovel and pointed to a trench where a long line of men were working. He didn't say anything, but I assumed he wanted me to join the group, and I knew how to run a shovel, so I went over and got in line. By the end of the day, I learned something that stayed with me the rest of my life. If you're employed by anything connected to the federal government, they do not expect you to work. It's an option. I was sure wishing I was back in Wyoming herding sheep.

Over the next few days as I got acclimated to the job, I noticed two men carrying a couple 2x4s 16 feet long on their shoulders up one side of a long warehouse and stacking them in a pile. Then they would walk back to where they came from and pick up a couple more and return to the pile. In between trips, I noticed a couple more men picking up the 2x4s and carrying them down the other side of the building. During one of our lunchbreaks, I walked down to the end of the warehouse to figure out what was going on. They really had a system going packing those same 2x4s around and around that building. But even though they weren't walking very fast, they were working.

One of the guys on our crew drove to work in his pickup and carried a .22 rifle behind the seat. It wasn't very far from where we were working to where the tall grass would begin, and sometimes in the middle of the afternoon, he would go hunting. I noticed he always got back in time to punch the clock with the rest of us.

I found out later how these defense job contracts were given out. It was called "cost plus ten." The contractor was given 10% profit over everything he spent. Even I could see there was no way to lose any money on these jobs. The more you spent, the more you made. Packing 2x4s around and around a building began to make sense.

I had a little extra problem getting home after the company bus dropped us off at the yard. I didn't know which one or where to catch the city bus because it had a different route in the evening to get back to where I started, so I walked it every day for the three months we were there. It was 27 blocks. I truthfully rather enjoyed it because I liked to walk anyway and my job was so easy. It kind of broke up my day.

We spent Christmas there, and we were all so homesick we decided the pay wasn't worth it even though we were making 60¢ an hour–90¢ for overtime. I still have my last two days' earning stub. In fact, I framed it (16 hours regular time @ 60¢ = $9.60 minus 10¢ withholding taxes; 3½ hours overtime @ 90¢ = $3.15 minus 13¢ withholding taxes; $12.75 total minus 23¢ withholding taxes = $12.52 net amount due). All that for just two days' work ending on January 20, 1943.

I had a few days to kill before Willie quit, so I lay around the apartment with just my shorts on and read. Lynn was in school, and my sister was the only one there. She had told the landlord we would be leaving in a few days in case someone wanted to look at the apartment while we were still there. We had everything packed and ready to leave for home within 15 minutes of when Willie got home. As I mentioned previously, there was only a tiny dinette-kitchen and small living-bedroom with no partitions in between plus a 4x4 foot closet.

One afternoon, I was laying on my cot, reading when the doorbell rang. Beulah answered the door, and it was two ladies wanting to look at the apartment, so she invited them in. She couldn't see the cot I was laying on and thought I had gone down the hall to the bathroom. I was trapped, and the only place left was the little closet that we had cleaned out when we packed. I could hear them talking as they made their way to the kitchen and then the few steps to the living-bedroom area. I prayed they would bypass the closet, but they didn't. I covered my eyes with my hands, faced the wall, and heard the door open 4 feet behind me. They had all been talking, but it ceased instantly when they saw the only thing in that closet besides a couple of empty coat hangers was a man in his skimpy underwear with his back to them and hands covering his eyes. My sister was just as shocked as those two ladies were, but she recovered first and said, "This is my brother," and shut the door. What an introduction! We broke up with laughter after the women left.

My brother-in-law finished his job, and we headed for home within minutes of when he walked through the door. He was a man who always whistled to himself when he was walking or doing something he enjoyed. My sister told me later that she had noticed he hadn't once done it while we were in Topeka. She heard him whistling the first morning back in Buffalo and said it was one of the best sounds she had ever heard.

§ § §

I started working on shearing crews in the Buffalo area when I was in high school. Like almost everybody else, my first job was wrangling, which entailed getting the sheep into each individual shearer's pen. It was hard work and paid the least of any job connected to shearing–a few dollars a day and only in dry weather because sheep could not be sheared when they were wet. The shearers were paid by the number of sheep they individually sheared each day, and the wool tier and tromper were paid a few cents each for the total number of sheep sheared. The faster the crew, the more money they made, and they made very good wages when the weather cooperated.

After a sheep was sheared, the fleece had to be tied with a long paper string and carried to the wool tromper's platform about 8 feet high with a wool sack suspended from it. It was tossed up to the tromper, who would drop several fleeces into the wool sack and then jump down into it and compress them as he worked his way up to the top of the sack, where he stitched it together. Paper strings were used to tie the fleeces so they would not disintegrate while the load was being processed at the woolen mill. They were very strong and difficult to break unless they got wet. The full sacks of wool weighed at least 250 pounds each.

Being paid for each sheep he sheared, the shearer's paycheck depended a lot on how skilled he was in keeping his shears in top condition. I tried shearing a few myself but didn't like it, so I started tying fleeces for the whole crew. I didn't make as much money as they did but also didn't have any tools to buy. I also had a lot more free time after the day's work was done because I didn't have any shears to sharpen or maintain.

They were called blade shearers because they used handheld sheep shears that resembled large scissors. In later years, machine shearers moved into the country and eventually crowded them out altogether because they could shear twice as many sheep in a day. They also sheared differently by tying up each sheep while shearing it, and the blade shearers didn't. There was lots of controversy over which was the best method as far as the wool and sheep were concerned. The individual sheep men were just as biased in their opinions as the shearers were. At any rate, I was prejudiced in favor of the blade shearers and never worked around a machine crew or had them shear my sheep when I had a band of my own. All of the shears were made in England.

Most of the sheep shearers belonged to the Sheep Shearers Union and ordered all their blades and other supplies from it. I remember one item in particular with an odd name. It was called a hootenanny and was actually listed in the catalog that way. Its function was to spread the two blades apart while they were being sharpened, ordinarily twice a day, although the shearer had another three or four on standby.

It had a reverse nail point sticking out of the end, which the shearer jammed into the wood backstop several times, until he figured out the correct angle to sharpen the shears. The hootenanny had a grip on one end that permitted him to rotate it a 180 degrees and also back and forth with his left hand while turning the grinding wheel with his right. It's about like patting one's head with one hand while using a circular motion on the stomach with the other, incidentally something I was never able to master.

The 12-man crew I worked on covered Idaho, Wyoming and Montana. The crew boss was Roy Dickinson. Both he and the crew were mostly from Idaho and Utah. They spent about six months shearing and the other six working in jobs like coal or gold mines. Our meals were furnished free by the sheep ranchers. Some of the men had travel trailers to live in, and a few lived in tents. I had a camper on the back of my pickup. A few of them brought their wives with them. About our only expense was buying gas to get from one job to another. Some of us saved our money, and others were just as broke when the season ended as they were when it started because they spent what they made in the barrooms. Every job on a shearing crew was hard manual labor for eight hours a day, and it never made sense to me why some of them threw it away between jobs on a drunk and a hangover. While shearing, they were bent over all day long, and some could hardly straighten up at the end of the day. A few rigged up slings to help take the pressure off their backs, but they were mostly cumbersome affairs.

Being boarded by so many different outfits during the season, the range of satisfaction with the food ran from excellent to worse than terrible. Some of the ranches were located so far out in the boonies, where even the drinking water had to be hauled in. The cookhouse and dining area were sometimes housed in sheds. The cook would have an old woodstove for preparing meals for up to 20 men and heating water in a dishpan for washing dishes. A few places in the Basin country on the west slope of the Bighorns were so barren the ranchers had to haul in firewood for the cook. Then our next job would be located along a pretty little creek with cottonwoods on both sides. I can still remember the two most extreme examples in my years with the crew.

The worst by far was located a short distance from Mountain Home, Idaho. We were supposed to start shearing in mid-February, but the weather turned cold. It snowed, and we had to kill most of a week in town. I was sure glad I had living quarters on the back of my pickup. The shearing rules were that once you got your feet under the rancher's dinner table, he was obligated to feed everybody until all his sheep were sheared. It didn't make any difference whether it took a week or a month. All of us, of course, wanted to work every day and all day–both shearers and sheep ranchers–but if the weather didn't cooperate, it was a great help to have breakfast, dinner and supper on the house–great help to us not the rancher.

When the weather finally cleared and we pulled into the ranch, the first morning's breakfast was an experience in itself. There were two cooks, both of them young men in their early twenties. They were Basque and neither spoke English. The breakfast menu was coffee, bread without butter, and lamb fries mixed with scrambled eggs. The fries, in case you're wondering, were the testicles of young male lambs saved from their last docking operation.

We docked the lambs at about two weeks of age, depending on the weather and work schedule. Docking meant that we castrated the males, cut both male and female tails off for hygienic purposes, and cut a notch in the ear of the females to be able to ascertain their ages in succeeding years. The earmark location was changed every year. Each lamb was also vaccinated. Castration was done by cutting the tip of the scrotum off, squeezing the top of both sides of the scrotum with thumbs and forefingers, and pulling the testicles with your teeth. I personally did this many times while in the sheep business. It was not an enjoyable job. If it seems rather barbaric, other alternative methods were developed, and none of them were pain free. Many, if not most, of the big sheep ranchers still use this method. It comes down to a matter of choice, and people who like lambchops generally prefer not to think about it.

The fries were edible and used by almost all the sheep ranchers and their herders at the only time of year, spring, when they were available. The problem with the ones mixed in with the scrambled eggs on our first breakfast was that they hadn't been cooked long enough and were only half done. As the wool tier for a dozen sheep shearers, I knew I had several hours of hard labor ahead of me before the next meal, so I picked out a few pieces of egg and finished up with bread and coffee. After we finished shearing that evening, I drove the short distance into town and stocked up with enough groceries to last the rest of the job.

Fries from both lambs and calves were considered a delicacy by many folks, and some restaurants in the smaller towns featured them on their menu, using the western term Rocky Mountain oysters to describe them. When tourists placed their order, the waiter was supposed to explain what they would be getting, which often resulted in a change from what they had previously ordered. Even today the fries are still saved at docking time on some sheep ranches for afternoon barbecues. During my growing up years in the late '20s and '30s, when branding season rolled around, I remember the cowboys would throw the oysters into the branding fire for a couple minutes, break off the charred outside crust, sprinkle on a little salt, and eat them on the spot. The meat resembled the taste of fried chicken and was very rich. It didn't take very many to curb an appetite.

Many years ago I read a poem about Western oysters that stuck with me. I'll try to remember how it went. I have no idea who the author was.

"Oysters"
The sign upon the cafe wall said, "Oyster fifty cents."
"How quaint," the blue-eyed sweetheart said with some bewildermence.
"I didn't know they served such fare out here upon the plain."
"Oh, sure," her cowboy date replied, "we're really quite urbane."

She said, "I'd guess they're Chesapeake or Blue Point, don't you think?"
"No, Ma'am, they're mostly Hereford cross, and usually they're pink."
But at times I've been so cold myself what you say could all be true,
And if a man looked close enough, their points could sure be blue.

She said, "I gather them myself out on the bay alone.
I pluck them from the murky depths and smash them with a stone."
The cowboy winced to imagine her with a little calf beneath,
And said, "I always use a pocketknife and yank them with my teeth."

"Oh, my!" she said, "You animal! How crude and unrefined!
Your masculine assertiveness sends shivers up my spine!
I prefer a butcher knife too dull to really cut.
I wedge it in on either side and crack it like a nut.
I pry them out. If they resist, sometimes I use the pliers
Or even Grandpa's pruning shears if that's what it requires."

The hair stood on the cowboy's neck. His stomach did a whirl.
He'd never heard such grisly talk, especially from a girl.
"I like them fresh," the sweetheart said and laid her menu down,
Then ordered oysters for them both when the waiter came around.
Her cowboy tried his best to smile though her words stuck in his craw.
But he fainted when he heard her say, "I think I'll have mine raw."

After the oyster experience in Idaho, the direct opposite took place several months later in May after we reached Wyoming and sheared at the Elmer Tanner farm located between Ten Sleep and Worland.

Elmer had a little irrigated place. He bought lambs in the fall, wintered them on his meadows, and sold them as yearlings the following spring. He booked with our crew for a number of years, and we always looked forward to working there because the fleeces were so clean and the food was the best on our circuit.

Elmer's wife did the cooking for the outfit, which was usually around 18 or 20 men, counting the shearers, tier, tramper, and wranglers. She was a small petite lady, very quiet and gracious, who always looked like she had just stepped out of a beauty parlor because she never had a hair out of place. I guessed her age to be in her late 50s or early 60s.

Ordinarily, sheep outfits would set up tables in a separate area to feed the crews because so much dirt got tracked in. Mrs. Tanner served us in their formal dining room with linen tablecloths and napkins. The high-back chairs had cloth seats, and the silverware was lined up on each side of the hand-painted china plates. We were used to tin dishes and coffee mugs. Her little tea cups with saucers held about three teaspoons of coffee each. The handles were so small there was only room for a thumb and one finger. I really concentrated on the handle when I picked one up for fear of dropping it, and I know I had plenty of company. Dessert was served in individual dishes. If you wanted seconds, it was placed in front of you on a clean dish. Nothing was ever said, but Tanner's was the only place we all changed work clothes when we went in to eat. It just seemed like the right thing to do.

Mrs. Tanner's husband was a big jolly man who always wore striped bib overalls. He was as outgoing as his wife was reserved. He sat at the head of the table and started the plates of food around the table clockwise from man to man as his wife brought them in from the kitchen. There was a large variety of food and plenty of it. He laughed a lot and carried on the table conversation practically all by himself, which was good because most of the rest of us were afraid of saying something wrong in his wife's presence–like if you needed a word that meant the same as dammit and couldn't think of one.

Sheep in places like the Rawlins and Rock Springs areas had a lot of sand in their wool and were difficult to shear. It didn't take very many sheep to wear out a pair of shears or pit them so badly they were not useable. Also, those areas were mostly all Rambouillet, fine wool sheep, and Elmer's were clean open face ones, where the fleeces cut like butter. The shearers could shear almost 50% more sheep in a day than they would ordinarily. Out of the dozens of places we worked through the season, the Tanner's was everybody's favorite and far ahead of what was second.

In one of those what goes around comes around serendipity events that has occurred at intervals throughout my lifetime, some 60 years later I happened to strike up a conversation with a complete stranger who was visiting from out of town. Her name was Doris Ready from the Basin country, and she was doing some research work for a museum she was connected with. During our conversation, the subject turned to sheep, and I related the story of Mrs. Tanner's petiteness and the odd experience of sitting at her dining table during shearing season. I couldn't even remember Mrs. Tanner's first name. The lady started laughing and told me it was Martha. She had been raised on a farm next door to the Tanners, and her family had been good friends with them. She shared several stories about the diminutive Martha and her polar opposite husband.

Another completely unrelated instance she mentioned was that when she was a teenager in the late 1950s, she spent a couple of summers working for a wealthy family that owned Camp Comfort, our closest neighbors when we were living at Trailside. It seems like a small world at times.

§ § §

I wore heavy canvas pants to work in like a lot of the shearers did but had to remodel mine to fit the conditions. All wool tiers used a different knot when tying fleeces, and it had to be fast and one that wouldn't slip. With a crew of 12 shearers, I had to move from one to the other and wrap and tie a fleece about every 20 seconds. There were no timeouts. My legs were shorter than most tiers, so to put pressure on the string without breaking it, I came down hard on the right knee to finish the knot. This worked great unless a clump of cactus was mixed up in the wool and right under the top of my kneecap.

I sewed several layers of canvas on the front of the pant leg and shaped them as tightly as possible around my leg. I had to point my foot like a ballet dancer to get them on, but they worked perfectly and stopped the cactus. The difficult part was getting them off at the end of the day's work without help. Iron plated leotards with zippers would have worked even better.

Grabbing the occasional cactus and handling so many wool strings each day made wearing gloves a necessity, but I had to cut the middle finger out of the right one to keep it from tangling up in the knot. Skin wouldn't have lasted very long, so I taped my finger with several layers of adhesive tape, which had to be replaced two or three times a day. One thing that was no problem with any of the crew was keeping our hands soft. The lanolin in the wool grease was an excellent skin conditioner and kept the skin just as soft as if it had been soaked in hand lotion, which I guess it was. It just hadn't been bottled yet.

I don't know why, but wood ticks were never a problem throughout the shearing season. They were the cause of Rocky Mountain spotted fever, which was a very debilitating disease and took months to recover from unless you died first. Springtime was the height of their season, and ranch hands had to be especially watchful when working in tall grass or sagebrush. Doctors recommended vaccination, and I got the shot every year just to be on the safe side.

Sheep ticks were a different problem altogether. They weren't dangerous, and the bite was about the same as a mosquito bite. There weren't very many of them, and I don't remember getting chewed on very often, but I do recall how annoying they could be. Every once in a while, one would get into the top of my shoe while we were shearing and start crawling up my leg on the inside of my pants. The pants fit so tight it would have taken me 10 minutes to get them off and locate the varmint. That option was completely out of the question. The floor would have been covered with 20 or 30 fleeces, and I never would have gotten the mess cleaned up, besides having the rest of the crew on my back. The only thing I could do was wait until the miserable thing reached my belt, and it might take an hour for it to crawl that far. My job was so repetitious I didn't have to think about what I was doing, so I had plenty of time to concentrate on the route it was taking and the homecoming reception planned for it when it reached my belt buckle and I got my hands on it.

After finishing the herds in the Basin country, we moved over the mountains to the Buffalo area. At that period of time, 1940s and 1950s, there were tens of thousands of sheep in Johnson County. I knew of one other blade crew besides ours that was working on the east side of the Bighorns. There was also one machine crew that I think was from Australia. Our crew would move to Montana after finishing up the Wyoming herds, but I never went with them. It was usually around the first part of July, and I was ready for something different in the line of work.

At that time, I was being paid 2½¢ a fleece, and we sheared up to 1,500 head a day, which was around $35 plus board. Shearers were making about $50. Very few jobs around Buffalo paid even half that. The Highway Department, for example, paid $1.25 an hour, less than $10 a day, and hourly employees did not receive any perks like paid vacations or sick leave, as I was well aware of, because later on I went to work for them.

I kept a yearly tally, and we sheared in excess of a 100,000 head of sheep in a season. That translates into a lot of time bent over touching my toes, but I lucked out and never had any back problems. The shearers had to be careful at the beginning of the season and limit the number of sheep they sheared for the first week or so to keep from breaking their hand down. When that happened, they paid a very painful price for the next couple weeks to get their hand healed up by shearing a few at a time.

Our crew boss, Roy Dickinson, was from Utah and booked our herds at least a year in advance. He was in his 60s and sheared with the rest of the crew when he wasn't reassuring individual ranchers of their place on our schedule. Rain at the wrong time and place would really screw things up.

The worst situation I remember was one spring when we were shearing at the TW Ranch a few miles east of Buffalo in late May through June and into the first part of July. It was owned by two Basque men, Simon Harriet and Bernard Marton, and was one of the biggest sheep outfits in Wyoming at the time.

It rained almost every day for several weeks, and their wives were doing the cooking for a couple dozen men. It took over twice as long to finish their herds as it ordinarily would have, and we really felt sorry for the two women. I imagine the sight of the backs of our heads when we walked out the door of the cook shack for the last time was a hallelujah moment for both of them.

In cases like this, sometimes in late spring when the weather started warming up, the shearers had another concern. On hot muggy days after a period of prolonged rain, the sheep would be slow to dry, but somebody would want to push it while the wool was still damp and get back on schedule. The fumes from the freshly sheared fleeces would, at times, cause what the shearers called wool fever. The unlucky ones would be severely weakened and have badly congested lungs. Some of the older men would still be feeling its effects the following year. They were through shearing as far as this season was concerned by necessity, not by choice.

At times like this, if several of the crew refused to shear, the rest of the men wouldn't either regardless of what they thought individually. It would have been a hell of a mess otherwise because some of them would have gotten mad and quit, and the rest of the season would have been a disaster with no place to go for replacements. Even the crew boss had no authority to order them to shear. All he could do was tell them to hit the road if push came to shove because he wasn't paying them. The sheep man was. They were all more or less individual contractors who were paid a flat amount for each sheep they sheared, and the crew boss was paid by the same rancher for getting 12 men on the job.

It was up to each of them to abide by the unwritten crew rules. If they didn't, the rest of the men would see to it that they moved on. I only saw it happen once when several of the shearers got into an argument and somebody pulled a knife. Nobody got hurt, but three of them left the crew immediately. The whole altercation was along racial lines, not sheep.

As far as wool fever illness was concerned, I've often wondered if it was a type of pneumonia that was somehow triggered by the combination of moist wool and muggy weather. It only took a day or two to make its appearance after being exposed to it. That happened a long time ago, but to the best of my memory the odor was like being in a small room with the overpowering smell of ammonia present.

§ § §

I first met Dave Elsom in the fall of 1940 when I was a sophomore in high school. He was trailing his neighbor's, Earl Henderson's, sheep off the mountain, and Earl had hired me to help him. The next spring, I quit school a month early to help him lamb. Then his son, J.D., and I took the sheep to the mountain camp and stayed up there all summer. I was a month late getting back to school that fall. I repeated the same schedule the next year and also worked for him on weekends throughout the school year.

Our camp was quite isolated and mostly reachable by horseback only, so we seldom saw anybody except Dave, who brought up our supplies every 10 days or so. Their mountain camp was mostly deeded land just south of Billy Creek. It wasn't very well watered because there was only one spring in about the center of the camp, and we had to take the sheep there every day to water them.

In the two summers I was up there, I only went to Buffalo one time, and that was to a doctor because I got a rash on my face, and it swelled up pretty bad. I still remember the strange experience of being back around a lot of people and seeing things like green lawns and a swimming pool. Not having any social life wasn't any fun at that age because I had a crush on a girl that was the most beautiful person in the world, but I needed money for school clothes, and that took precedence over anything else, even beautiful women. Due to my looks with the rash, I couldn't even call her up and take her to a movie. Hot water and a bathtub was the highlight of my vacation.

Ranch and farm workers in those days were paid by the month with no time off for anything except a real emergency, like if you died. It was seven days a week, and the weather usually dictated everything you did. Board and room were furnished, but you had to supply your own bedroll, and you had to live in a bunkhouse with all the other men, which prohibited marriage in the vast majority of cases. In late fall at the end of the harvest season or livestock operation, the ranchers would have to drastically cut their workforce to a minimum, so you worked for your room and board if you were lucky. Otherwise, you got by any way you could until spring. There wasn't such a thing as unemployment compensation.

Most of the permanent employees on the sheep and cattle ranches never drew their pay unless some of it was needed for clothes, tobacco or things like that. At the end of the year, you settled up with your employer. He would deduct what you had drawn in the previous months and pay the balance in cash. Most sheepherders were only paid once a year. In late fall after the lambs had been shipped, they would take two weeks off and spend it in town. Many of them would spend their entire yearly wage on a two- or three-week drinking spree in town and go back to their camp flat broke. They used the same routine until they reached old age and were unable to work. A lot of the bartenders, merchants and rooming houses took advantage of them while they were drunk and robbed them blind. But a year later, the herder would invariably repeat his previous mistake.

The first year I went to work for Dave Elsom he hired me at $35 per month. This was more than fair because grown men were only getting $30 working in the hayfields, etc. When we settled up that fall, he paid me off at the rate of $50 per month. If this sounds rather insignificant, consider this. How would you feel if your present employer tucked a holiday cash bonus in your Christmas card that equaled almost 50% of your entire year's earnings?

Dave and his wife, Lila, had three children. J.D. was the oldest and about three years older than me. Gwen was second and then Ellis. After their parents retired, the boys bought the ranch from them, and Gwen married and moved to Wheatland. They always treated me like one of the family. I don't know why, but from day-one Dave was always Dave, but his wife was Mrs. Elsom. I lost connection with the whole family during my time in the Army and after, but Ellis and I hit it off some time after that, and we became good friends. In fact, I was best man at his first marriage. In later years, Ellis bought out his brother's interest and became sole owner of the ranch.

Since I'm on the subject of Ellis, I'll relate a couple of stories I remember about him. I was working one summer for his dad in 1952 and had gone to a dance in Buffalo on the evening of July 3rd to help celebrate the Fourth. I had to work the next day, so I planned on getting back early. Ellis decided to celebrate the Fourth too but in a little different manner.

The ranch was located about 12 miles south of Buffalo, and the house was several hundred yards off Highway 87. It was an old low log building, and the ranch road was between it and a steep vertical bank about 20 feet high that bordered the North Fork of Crazy Woman Creek. The house had only two bedrooms, and Ellis had to go through his parent's bedroom to get to his. He waited until his folks had gone to sleep, and shortly before midnight, he crawled out his window and put a stick of dynamite on a rock between the house and the ranch road. He put a long fuse on it, lit it, and ran back to his bedroom and crawled back through the window. The blast exceeded his wildest expectations. Those old logs had 50 years of accumulated dust on them, and it all rained down on the inside of the house. His parents were jarred out of bed, wondering what the hell had happened when Mr. Innocent came through the adjoining door, rubbing the sleep out of his eyes.

I was using a sheep wagon to sleep in, and Ellis was over at daylight preparing me for the breakfast meeting with his mother. She had convinced herself I had lit a large firecracker outside their bedroom window, and she didn't appreciate the joke. Of course, Dave knew it wasn't a firecracker, but it would have been useless to argue with his wife, so he didn't say anything. Ellis said he would appreciate it if I kept my mouth shut, and she went to her grave thinking I was the guilty one. I heard all the one-sided evidence against me during that 45 minute breakfast ordeal, but I offered no rebuttal. The three of us never opened our mouth except to eat. It was a long, long meal.

We always waited outside the house after breakfast, and Dave would give us our work schedule for the day. After he finished that morning, he turned away, then turned back and said, "You know, boys, if you ever happen to run onto any old dynamite lying around the ranch, it might be a good idea to bury it." Then he went back in the house. I asked Ellis later what he thought would have happened if I had been coming home and drove past that dynamite when it went off. He said it hadn't occurred to him when he put it there but supposed it would have blown my car and me off the bank into Crazy Woman Creek. Evidently, if he found any more dynamite after that suggestion from his dad, he remembered where he buried it because some 30 years later he invited me out to the ranch for a cup of coffee and a fish fry.

I wondered what he had used to catch the fish with because every time I fished that creek, I came up empty handed. In warm weather, when the irrigators farther up the creek were sucking water out of it, it was mostly trash fish, like suckers. Trout need cold water to survive. The lower and warmer the water, the less oxygen it contains. He fished it year around and caught some nice trout, but this was August, and the creek was barely running.

When I got out there, he told me he had tied a stick of dynamite on a small board, set it in the creek, lit the fuse, and then got out of the way. It floated downstream to a large pool, and when it went off, it emptied the creek. Almost all the fish he killed were suckers, but he salvaged a couple of trout, and we had enough for our fish fry.

Ellis and I both loved to hunt. I can remember the first time he invited me out to hunt pheasants. They were farming part of the ranch and had several grain fields that guaranteed a crop of birds. We walked out behind the house to a small draw with cattails growing in it—one of us on each side. He asked me if I was ready, and I said, "Ready for what?" He told me if we didn't move fast enough up that draw, the pheasants would run ahead of us, and when we got to the end of it, they would be out of shotgun range when they took to the air, so we ran up the draw, and it worked.

He used the same idea when he hunted elk. Ordinarily, when a guy spooked a herd of elk in the timber, they would take off on a dead run, crashing through the trees and sounding like a freight train out of control. Trying to sneak up on them after that was almost impossible because they knew you were behind them, and they would move along very quietly just out of rifle range. Ellis had a different tactic. When they would take off through the timber on a dead run, he would be right behind them not concerned about how much noise he was making. Quite often, they would wonder what was behind them crashing through the timber and would stop and look back, and he would get a shot at them. You had to be in top physical condition to do this, and he was. To keep in shape, he would put on a 60-pound backpack and run up and down the hills at the ranch. I could usually keep up with most guys on a fishing trip in the mountains, but he pushed me to my limit.

His wife died of lung cancer, and a couple of years later he became acquainted with a woman from the Philippines through a correspondence course. They eventually married, and a year or so later planned a cruise to Alaska. They drove to North Dakota on the way to visit some of his friends and rented a motel for the night. During the night, he had some violet seizures and died.

He was buried on the ranch, and I was one of the pallbearers who rode out in the hearse from town. After the services, we walked over to the house for the usual brunch and gathering to show respect for his family. He was well-liked in this area, and there was a huge crowd that spilled out of the house into the yard. I don't like being in large groups and small talk. I happened to look over to his gravesite about a hundred yards and saw the funeral director and sexton getting ready to finish the burial, so I walked over and offered to help. I helped lower the casket into the grave and put the plastic shroud over it. Then I scattered a couple shovels full of dirt over that as a farewell gesture. Then the backhoe finished filling the grave. It was an odd experience for me because we had been good friends, but I was glad I did.

§ § §

Dave Elsom was a great guy, and I respected him as much as any man that I have ever known. He and his wife took out homesteads in the Trabing Road area and went through some really tough times. He showed me their original homestead shack and told me they subsisted a lot of the times on jackrabbits. They finally got a small two-room house built, and that is where they raised their three children. The bedroom was in the loft that was accessed by lowering a ladder down into the living-dining room. In all the years I worked for them, I never saw the upstairs or saw them lower the stairs. The house was very small and sat on a little knoll. Two rooms, kitchen and living-dining room. It was the only thing standing above ground for quite some distance in every direction and one day was struck by lightning. The lightning bolt came down through the roof and welded a pair of scissors to the sewing machine just missing Mrs. Elsom. After that, they studded the roof with lightning rods.

The year before I went to work in the mountains, Dave hired me and my two closest friends, H.B. Hurst and Walt Hushbeck, to dig a basement next to the house that they were going to add the upper room to at a later date. They never got it finished because while I was in the Army during World War II, they bought the ranch on the North Fork of Crazy Woman Creek along Highway 87 from the McMullin family. H.B., Walt and I came out every weekend to help dig the basement by using a slip scraper and a team of horses. A slip scraper resembles a big wheelbarrow without a wheel, like a big scoop. We made $4.50 each per weekend. We finally got the hole dug and poured the concrete for the walls and floor. Of course, it had a flat roof, so we put roll roofing over it, but it leaked, so we put a layer of bentonite over that, and it still leaked. It was a miserable damp location–no heat–that we stayed in during lambing season.

The Elsom's family income depended 100% on their sheep herd except for milk, which came from a herd of goats. The goats were butchered for meat, and the milk was used for everything from ice cream to bread. I got so used to it cow's milk tasted funny because it was so flat and tasted like skim. Goat's milk is thick and creamy and rich. If I remember correctly, the cream doesn't separate from the raw milk like cow's milk does.

Lambing season lasted from about April 20th through May, and we worked from before daylight to after dark. We never finished supper before 10:00 at night and were back at the sheep corrals before daylight. We ate the rest of our meals in shifts. I remember one time H.B. lay down on the ground in the middle of the sheep and went fast asleep–mud, manure and all. In later years, I worked for a Basco sheep man, Martin Etchart, who phrased it perfectly when he was talking about the Elsom family. He said they never gave the lamp chimney time to cool off. But Martin was doing range lambing, and we were using sheds, which is the difference between night and day.

A band of sheep averaged from about 1,500 to 2,000 head. In one 24-hour period, the ewes would drop (give birth) to from 50 to 100 new lambs. If you were range lambing and a bad storm hit, there was no way to keep them alive. You lost 100% of the lambs that were born as long as the storm lasted and for a couple days after. We were shed lambing, and in bad weather we would haul the mother and newborn lamb to the shed as soon as it was born with a team of horses and a wagon.

The wagon was built with small single boxes attached to the inside top of the wagon to hold individual lambs to keep them separated and from being crushed by their mothers when the wagon was full. We would crowd about 10 mothers at a time into the wagon. As they were loaded, we stamped a number with paint on each ewe and her lamb so we could pair them up when we got to the shed. In cold wet snowy weather, it would be a mess when we got there, and if we didn't get them mothered up as soon as possible, some of the ewes would bum (abandon) their lambs. Each ewe and her lamb were put into an individual jug (pen) for a time to make sure this didn't happen. If the lamb was too cold to nurse, we would take it to the house and put it behind the coal cookstove in the kitchen to warm it up. You can imagine what a mess that made. The reason a lot of sheep men didn't shed lamb was because it was a lot more expensive and took a lot more help. Most of them didn't have the facilities anyway.

I remember one time when I was driving the wagon around, picking up the newborn, when a bad hailstorm hit without much warning. I had a gentle team, but I knew what would happen if the storm was bad enough, and it turned into the worst one I had ever experienced. I got their tugs (chains attached to their harnesses to pull the wagon) unhooked from the double trees but didn't have time to unhook the reins to separate them or unhook them from the neck yoke (a wooden bar that tied their chests together) before the hail hit. It was golf ball size. They took off on a dead run still hooked up to each other. If I hadn't gotten them loose from the wagon, it would have been a disaster.

I crawled under the wagon for protection but got hit on the head before I got there. It felt like someone hit me with a hammer, but my hat saved me from a concussion. Three of the newborn lambs had their spines broken. One of them died, but the other two lived even though they were both paralyzed from the middle of the back on down. They could only move by using their front legs to drag themselves, but their mothers raised them, and we butchered them that fall. Hard times prohibited wasting anything that could be utilized.

The lambing sheds were built at the bottom of a big hill to provide protection from the wind. A small flat dry draw was right in front of the sheds with an old plank bridge built across it about 4 feet off the ground. It didn't serve any purpose, and I always wondered why it was there. One day, I asked Dave, and he told me the story. Back in the 1920s, they had just sheared their sheep, and they were grazing about a mile from the sheds. A cold wet snow hit without warning, and he drove them to the shed for shelter. When he got there, the draw had a couple feet of water running down it, and he couldn't get them to cross it to get to the shed a mere 100 feet away. Newly sheared sheep can't handle much cold, and half his herd froze to death. He built the bridge to nowhere, and the draw had never flooded since. It was still standing when I went back there for a look over 50 years later.

§   §   §

One summer when I was working at the ranch along Highway 87, Dave and his wife decided to add another room on top of the main floor. They waited till July to start and hopefully cut down their odds of having a heavy rain while the roof was off. There were five of us–Dave, J.D., Ellis, Guy Smith, and myself. Guy was from the Mayoworth country and was related to Mrs. Elsom in some way. We all called him Uncle Guy, including me. He was a big man, probably in his 70s, wasn't too active, and shouldn't have been working on the roof, but he was. I gathered he had some carpentering experience somewhere in his background and sort of unofficially had the title of chief carpenter. I don't know if he was volunteering his expertise or got paid for it. He was a nice man and easy to get along with, but even I could tell that his prior construction experience had probably been somewhat limited.

We had torn off the roof of the old building, and it was wide open to the weather. To keep the dust and debris out of the main house, we left the ceiling up, but it was only a type of hard board a half inch thick nailed to the kitchen ceiling joists. Sheet rock hadn't been invented yet when they built the house some 50 years before. The ceiling joists were way too far apart–2 feet–and were only 2x4s that swayed when you stepped on them. A single misstep would land you on the downstairs floor, and it was only a question of who, not when, would be the one to do it. That turned out to be Uncle Guy.

Unfortunately, he straddled a 2x4 joist on the way down, and his two feet were all that were showing from below. He had presence of mind enough to support his body with his two hands and keep his private parts a quarter inch above the joist. He was positioned over the refrigerator, and a piece of the ceiling went down behind it and got caught in the fan but didn't stop it and made a hell of a racket. Mrs. Elsom was cooking on the stove next to the refrigerator, and she went ballistic. It was probably the funniest thing I ever saw in my entire life if I'd only had time to appreciate it, but Uncle Guy took our undivided attention and getting him un-straddled from that 2x4 was a big job.

We eventually got the roof on the new addition without a major rain ruining things, and only one more incident happened. I was responsible and it wasn't funny. As I mentioned, we were doing the remodeling in the middle of summer, and it was really hot. Mrs. Elsom only had an old wood and coal stove to cook with, and it would make the kitchen unbearably hot when she was preparing meals for the crew, especially the noon meal. So to cut the heat to the minimum, Dave would climb down off the roof about 11:30 and build a short hot fire out of wood for her to finish preparing dinner. She generally had something already prepared like stew or a casserole that only needed reheating and then let the stove fire burn out.

One day, I saw Dave climb down off the ladder to go start the fire, and I happened to be next to the stovepipe that we had temporarily wired to one of the rafters to hold it up. I had an empty gallon can we had been using to put old nails in, and on a whim, I put it over the top of the stovepipe. I intended to leave it for just a short time but got busy and forgot the damned thing. About 20 minutes later, I saw Dave and his wife come out of the house looking up at the chimney wondering why the stove was smoking. He didn't say anything, but she exploded. It smoked up the whole inside of the house. It was lucky for me that they were going to remodel it anyway because the smoke ruined what they had. It was just a damn fool spur of the moment thing, and I always regretted it.

When we came in for dinner, nobody said anything because we could tell she was still mad by the way she was slamming dishes around. When we sat down, she announced that she had planned an exceptionally nice dessert for supper, but some unnamed smart aleck had changed her mind, and we were going to get canned peaches instead, and she kept her word.

I can remember one other time I got crosswise of her–big time. We were all sitting at the table when the subject of water witching came up. She had a countywide reputation for doing it, and a number of people had her witch a well before they started drilling. She had a place just in front of the outside door that she used for demonstrating her talent, and she was quite proud of the gift. I made a statement to the effect that it was a bunch of baloney, and I regretted it before the last words had even left my mouth. She bounced up off that chair, grabbed my arm, and hustled me out the door to the apple orchard in back of the house. She picked out a particular forked branch and ordered me to cut it off. There was no way I was going to do anything other than exactly what she said. When we got back to the demonstration area, the whole group was waiting to watch my humiliation take place with wide smiles on their faces.

She placed my hands on the forked stick in the 10:00 and 2:00 positions, took bold of my wrists, and led me over her underground water location. It was one of the most embarrassing moments of my life, and to top it off, the place where the two forks came together started down, and I couldn't stop it. The branch was soft green wood, and I gripped it so tight the bark peeled off in my hands, but the fork didn't stop moving until it was pointed straight down.

Since that experience some 60 years ago, I have read a lot of comments on the subject, even some from the scientific community. A few of them are admitting they don't understand it. I have personally watched City water workers locate lines before digging. Some of them use a file and some a bent welding rod and it works. I compare it to acupuncture. When I first read about it in grade school, it was for laughs. Today some doctors are recommending it to their patients, and some insurance plans cover it. I still think maybe I don't believe in witching, but I don't see the point in taking unnecessary chances. If I was drilling a new water well, I'd dang sure have somebody witch the location first.

Mrs. Elsom was a good cook and cooked the things that men liked and needed when they were working hard, and there was always plenty of it. She had a big garden and canned a lot of things in the fall. I think she used a pressure cooker to cook and preserve the meat they butchered, either goat or mutton, because that's what J.D. and I used in the summers on the mountain. It was in sealed glass jars and didn't need refrigeration. I really liked it.

When something startled her, she had a one-note shriek that would bring you bolt upright. It was ear splitting and was like someone scraping their fingernails across a blackboard at the top of the octave scale. I remember one time she baked some bread that came up a loaf short after she had taken it out of the oven. She intimated that one of us had taken it but didn't have a clue as to why we would want to. Her house was always pretty cluttered, and about a week later, she moved some clothes that were stacked on the sewing machine. When she shrieked, we knew the lost loaf had reappeared.

She talked a lot at mealtime, but we were all busy eating and not interested in gabbing, so it worked out well. Her voice was soft, well-modulated, and pleasant to listen to. I remember my sister, Juanita, once called her on the phone, and she told me Mrs. Elsom had the nicest telephone voice of anyone she had ever talked to. She read quite a bit and would cut out interesting newspaper clippings and tell us about them while we were eating. She was well-versed on the latest findings of health foods and worked them into our diet. I remember once she had several plats of alfalfa sprouts growing in one window.

I don't know if she was ever a schoolteacher, but her reading and writing skills were excellent. I can remember only one exception that always used to bug me, but I wasn't dumb enough to ever bring the subject up, or maybe I was afraid she'd prove me wrong. She pronounced the word cafe with a long A, like "cayfe."

She and Dave were one of the most devoted couples I was ever around. In all the many years I worked for them, I never heard a sharp word, criticism or argument between them. I don't recall that she ever helped with any of the work with the livestock, like some of the women of that era did, but I'm sure she did when they were first married because they started from scratch. There seemed to be a general understanding between her and Dave that the house was her domain, and everything outside the walls were his. Yet, I noticed the times when Gwen, their daughter, was gone, he always helped clean up and do the dishes after supper without her saying anything. The kids all had their chores to do before and after school—milk the goats, feed the bum lambs, etc. I don't recall them ever complaining about it or their parents ever having to tell them to go do it. It was just accepted as a matter of course.

None of the family ever swore except maybe Ellis after he had completed his four-year enlistment in the Army. One time Gwen, who was out of high school by several years, had something happen at the kitchen sink while we were eating supper. She said, "What the H." She didn't say hell, just "H," which could have meant heck, but her folks weren't taking any chances, and they came up off their chairs in tandem like they were both sitting on the same rattlesnake. I never heard her ever say it again.

Dave had a little Farmall tractor that we were having trouble with. One morning we couldn't even get it to fire, so we took all the electrical and fuel components off and cleaned and checked them. We worked on it all day and put it back together the next morning. Dave got up on the seat and turned it over a few times, but nothing happened. He stared at the exhaust stack for a few seconds and then turned to me and said, "That certainly isn't very satisfactory, is it?" I thought to myself, "No, it certainly isn't. If that was my tractor, I would pulverize it with a sledgehammer and ship it back to the Farmall factory—freight collect."

Writing about the tractor brings to mind our grain harvesting operation. We used a binder to cut and tie the grain so it could be shocked, but that was eventually eliminated with the invention of the combine. The threshing machine was a dirty, dusty, earsplitting piece of equipment that nobody liked to work around. Horses were scared to death of the thing, and a lot of runaways occurred when trying to get them close enough to be able to pitch the bundles into the machine. The trucks hauling the grain to the granary didn't have hoist beds and had to be unloaded with a scoop shovel. That's what finally got to me. I was okay unloading any kind of grain except bearded barley. For some reason, that particular dust felt like thousands of tiny needles poking my skin, and I had to push the job onto Ellis because it didn't bother him.

Speaking of things poking the skin reminds me of Mrs. Elsom's Christmas cactus. She started out with just a slip of a plant, but through the years it blossomed into something that took a 30-gallon barrel to support it and used up a good portion of her living room. She was very proud of it and gave many starter slips to other people in the county, including me. That was over 50 years ago. I like indoor plants but am approaching the saturation point with her gift in my dining room and don't know where to call a halt. She died many years ago, and I have often wondered whatever happened to her original plant.

§ § §

When Wyoming was being settled in the late 1800s, hard feelings existed between sheepmen and cattlemen and lasted into the 1920s with some sheepherders being murdered and their flocks shot and scattered indiscriminately. This animosity had disappeared by the time I worked for Dave Elsom and was replaced by a friendly rivalry between them. Some cattlemen even started acquiring small herds of sheep of their own to diversify their operations. Sheep were considered by many to be better moneymakers because they had two incomes a year–wool in the spring and lambs in the fall.

Stockmen, like the Elsom family, were at the mercy of the markets when they sold their livestock and had to take what they could get. Banks and merchants carried the vast majority of ranchers throughout the year and had to be paid when the lambs, wool and cattle were sold, unless a bad storm had already put them out of business. It was one of those occupations where you always thought, "Hopefully, next year will be better," but quite often it wasn't.

There were hundreds of thousands of sheep in Johnson County in the pre-World War II era, but after that, wool substitutes started making their appearance, and today only a fraction of that number still exists.

One big drawback with sheep is their predilection for dying. It seems sometimes they don't even need a reason. They just die. A bad three- or four-day blizzard could completely wipe out bands of several thousand head. They would drift with the wind until they piled up against a barbwire fence and smothered and froze to death. Even when they found shelter in the lee of a cutbank if the storm lasted long enough, they would eventually be covered with enough snow to smother them. At times like these, their wool would slip, and we would pull it off in big handfuls to salvage what we could. It was of inferior value, but at least it was something.

Sheep men weren't the only ones to lose their herds in this manner. Cattle also perished in the same way and horses. I remember a particularly bad winter in 1949 and '50 when the moisture from the horse's nostrils froze into icicles several inches long and killed them because they couldn't breathe. Even the stockmen who avoided bankruptcy in these storms would spend the rest of their lives recovering from it.

If low prices and storms didn't put a dent in their sheep raising operations, there were always coyotes and death camas on the mountains. It was a particularly deadly plant that was dangerous in the spring when the ground was moist. After eating it, the sheep would bloat and a few hours later would be dead. The above ground part of the plant didn't bother them, but in wet weather the underground bulb would pull up with the plant and kill them after they had eaten it. When we found large patches of it, we wouldn't let the sheep graze on it until later in the summer after all the grasses had cured out.

The two summers, 1941 and '42, that J.D. Elsom and I herded their sheep in the mountains, we started trailing the sheep after shearing to their mountain camp about the second week in June and came back down about the middle of September. The times were dictated strictly upon the amount of grass that was available both spring and fall.

One job that I particularly dreaded was shoeing our horses. Because of the cost, hiring a professional horseshoer was out of the question. The only experience I ever had was watching someone else do it. We didn't have the proper tools–chief among them, the heavy leather apron that all professionals used. Our horse was tied to a tree with his halter rope. Horseshoe nails were tapered. Whenever I hammered one in, I was afraid it would turn in the wrong direction and hit a tender spot in his hoof. The horse would flinch, jerk his foot, and there was only a thin layer of denim jeans between the point of the nail and getting your leg punctured. We had to shoe them about twice a summer.

We each had our personal horse plus a spare in case something went wrong. We picketed them on ropes at night, but sometimes we would put hobbles on the extra horse, and he would stay with the others. I remember one time we were camped at a place called Hamilton Park. Our extra horse, Nipper, had a halter on, and we tied him to a log so he could move it to get to more grass. During the night, he got his front horseshoe hooked in his halter, and the next morning he was dead.

My personal horse was named Midget. I have no idea where she got her name. She was a tall, leggy bay mare, and I really liked her. She had contracted sleeping sickness at some point in her life, and when she recovered, she had a bad habit of wanting to run at certain times and was hard to control. She had one quality that used to irritate the hell out of me. We always carried slickers (raincoats) on the back of our saddles. Lots of sheepherding involves sitting down and keeping an eye on them. At these times, I would just drop the reins so she could feed, and it doesn't take a horse very long to figure out they have to turn their heads slightly to the side to keep from stepping on their reins and jerking the bit in their mouth. In fact, once they get the hang of it, they can move along at a trot with no trouble at all. When it would start to rain, I'd untie my slicker from the saddle. If I didn't hang onto the reins, she wouldn't let me get close to her after I had put it on, so I would have to take it off and drop it on the ground before she would let me catch her. By that time, I was usually soaked.

There was a logger in our camp, Dallas Knighten, who had bought some timber from the Elsoms and lived with his family in an old slab shack he had built. The school board furnished a teacher, Doris Tillman, to teach their kids, and she boarded with the Knightens. I think the Knighten family was from the Linch country.

In the evenings, sometimes we would have horse races for entertainment, and Midget could outrun all of them but one that belonged to Dallas. A few years later, I went into the sheep business for myself and bought Midget from Dave Elsom. I had rented some pasture a few miles east of Buffalo in the Red Hills. One noon, I was riding her to the wagon to get dinner, and we crossed quite some distance above a dry reservoir. The ground was cracked and looked perfectly safe, but it was only crusted mud, and she bogged down clear to her belly. I dived out of the saddle over her head as she was lunging to get out and helped as much as I could by pulling on the bridle reins. She finally got to dry ground, and we went on to the wagon. When I came out after dinner, she wasn't holding her head right, so I left her and walked back to the sheep. When I got back that evening, she was dead. I assume she had ruptured a blood vessel or something similar.

I acquired a couple more horses while I was up on the mountain with J.D. His mother had a brother, Murray Patch, who owned a place on Little Elgin Creek northwest of the Klondike Ranch. Somebody had been pasturing a little pinto mare on his place and wanted to sell her. Murray described her to me, and I bought her sight unseen for $20. A few days later, he rode up to our camp, leading her, and I had a bonus in the form of a little pinto colt that no one had known about. I named the mother Trixie and the colt Dixie.

Trixie was the first horse I ever broke. I didn't know anything about breaking a horse to ride, and, fortunately, she had never broke a rider to a horse before either, so we learned together. After she unloaded me a few times, we made a truce, and she turned into a nice little saddle pony. Just before I was drafted into the Army, I sold the pair to Dave but don't remember whether I made any money on them or not. The Elsoms owned a buckskin stud horse, and over the next few years he sired several colts from Trixie.

J.D. and I lived in a tepee and had to move it every day because we bedded the sheep down at a different bed ground every evening. The coyotes were thick, so every night just at dark we would tear strips of newspapers and walk around the herd, scattering them behind us because this seemed to deter them from entering the bed ground. If the grass was wet or it was raining, we would shoot firecrackers because the smell of burnt powder seemed to keep them out also. We didn't dare use firecrackers when it was dry because of the risk of fire. Some of the early day Basque sheepherders used to use dynamite for the same purpose.

We had several sheep dogs and several goats. We always snapped the tepee door shut at night, but after we went to sleep, the dogs would sneak in and spend the night inside too. The goats usually had their heads stuck through the flap in the morning, reminding us it was milking time. The sheep would leave the bed ground a little before daylight, and one of us would have to be at the lead and the other at the tail end to try to keep the coyotes out. Sometimes it didn't work, and they would hit the middle of the herd.

Of course, we had no means or time for cooking breakfast at that hour. Mrs. Elsom had made us small gunnysack bags to fit a Mason quart jar and a spoon. It had a small loop of rope attached to wrap around the saddle horn. The night before just at bedtime, we would fill the jar with dried pieces of bread and sprinkle a mix of sugar and cocoa over it. It might be nine or later in the morning before we had the opportunity to eat. Then we'd call a goat over, put a handful of cottonseed cake on the ground that we carried in our saddlebags, and while they were eating, we'd fill the quart jar up with milk. The excess milk was fed to our dogs. This was our breakfast and supper menu for the day and every day for the three months we were up there–no exceptions. I gained weight on it and have thought about it many times when I put a bowl of oatmeal in the microwave and hit the go button.

For the one meal a day that we cooked at noon, we took turns. There was an old slab shack left over from some logging operations with a stove and a table in it. It was located at the spring where we had to take the sheep for water every day. We had an old wood box in the spring where we kept our butter and other perishables under water. It was probably at about a 40° temperature and worked perfectly. The one whose turn to cook would leave the herd early to prepare dinner. On my day, I always cooked the same thing. Mrs. Elsom canned meat in glass jars that we kept in the spring box. While my potatoes were boiling, I had a big cast iron skillet to heat the meat up in and make gravy at the same time. The meat was already cooked, so it didn't take much time to heat it up. When J.D. showed up with the sheep, we would put a slice of homemade bread, which Mrs. Elsom sent up with Dave when he tended camp, on a plate and cover it up with the gravy, meat and mashed potatoes. For drinks, it was either goat's milk or cold spring water. The frying pan usually had a hard crust of gravy around the inside, but that was no problem because we didn't wash it anyway. Every scrap of food left over went into the skillet, and the dogs chewed on it till it shone. It might take them an hour. We just wiped it out and hung it up on the wall for tomorrow.

Taking a bath was a problem just like it was for any of the hired help working on ranches at that period of time. If you were close to a creek, it was no big deal. We weren't. The only alternative was heating some water on the wood cookstove and taking a sponge bath. We didn't do it very often and were better off for not doing so because frequent baths wash all the natural oils out of your body and the sun and wind are hard on faces and exposed skin. Present-day body lotions partially cover that aspect. I don't remember if they even existed at that period of time. Even if they did, most people, including us, didn't have the money to purchase the product anyway. Our first aid kit consisted of a jar of Vaseline that covered everything up to snakebites.

On the subject of snakes, rattlesnakes had been a problem through the years according to Dave, and he had had several close calls. I only killed two, and that was in my second season. I was riding my horse by an old uprooted tree that had been blown down by the wind, and one advertised his presence from a good 15 feet away. The other time was a lot spookier, and I can still remember the exact details.

During the late summer when the sheep were bogged down during the heat of the day, J.D. and I would take turns, riding back into the timber a mile or so along the face of the mountain and cutting pitch fence posts with an axe. We would tie a rope on it, dally it around the saddle horn, and snake it out to the park where Dave could drive to it and it load on his pickup. One day, I was hammering on a standing dead tree to fall it when I had the strangest sensation that something was wrong. It was a really hot late August afternoon, and I had my horse tied to a tree by his halter rope. My dog was sleeping, stretched out in the shade. A horse will usually notice something out of the ordinary first and throw up his head and stare straight at it. I glanced at him, but he was standing with his head down and asleep just like my dog was. But I still had that funny feeling and turned around and saw a rattlesnake crawling straight for me just a few feet away. They shed their skins several times a year and go temporarily blind. I think what happened was that it was blind and maybe hadn't eaten for a few days and was attracted to the sound of my axe working on that tree. Anyway, it sure shook me up, and I never cut another post up there without checking out what was behind me every few minutes.

Dave came up to our camp to bring what supplies we needed about every 10 days. My mother would send up clean clothes, and he would take my dirty laundry back down with him. We never had any visitors because the last mile into the camp was just an old logging road that required low gear in Dave's old Chevy pickup at three miles an hour max. It had just enough trees brushed out to squeeze through, and you had to be careful or the stumps and rocks would tear out a transmission or punch a hole in the oil pan. Most of the time, if we knew when to expect him, we would ride out to the park and pack our groceries back on our saddle horses. Four-wheel drive vehicles did not come into use until after World War II ended and Army surplus Dodge Power Wagons became available on a limited basis. After I got out of the Army, the first I remember seeing in Johnson County were owned by sheep men east of Buffalo in the gumbo mud country. They had wide tires and could grind along at two or three miles an hour. Gas mileage was terrible, but at least they could move. Two-wheel drive pickups were almost useless in the mud.

One Fourth of July, we had a surprise visit when all the members of my family and their spouses and children walked into camp, carrying a picnic lunch. The leftovers lasted for several noon meals afterward and relieved us of the chore of cooking dinner.

§ § §

I previously mentioned one of the old slab logging cabins that we used at noon for a cook shack. They looked pretty decrepit but were actually very practical for what they were used for. For one thing, they cost practically nothing to build except labor.

Loggers would set up a saw in the open and start cutting what materials they needed for a shed to cover it with and cutting boards and timbers to use in constructing their slab cabins at the same time. They built double walls of any width desired and filled it with sawdust for insulation. Lots of them were 2 feet or more in width and were easy to heat with a cookstove. Wood for fuel was free for the splitting. They didn't have electricity, so lamps and lanterns were used to light them. They could saw any size floor joists, boards and rafters they wanted, and the foundations were just flat rocks if even that. If the timber they were harvesting was judged to only last a few years before having to move the mill, they would just set the bottom log on the dirt. All it had to do was last as long as their timber sale lasted. About the only things they had to purchase were nails, windows, roll roofing, and door hinges because they made their own doors. Some of this material was salvaged from their old cabins when they moved to a new location. Some of them even put sawdust on top of their ceiling boards.

They were firetraps, and some of them burned up, but that didn't stop the practice of building them.

The Forest Service put a halt on all these building practices in the Bighorns in the following years and gradually eliminated all sawmills. Now, all logs are hauled off the mountain and processed at central locations. Even sawmills on private land have been discontinued.

While I was in the Army, J.D. was boiling some kind of paint mixture on the cookstove in our old cabin, and it exploded and burned it down. Fortunately, he wasn't hurt. I don't know what they used after that.

I have used the term bogging down in reference to the sheep we were taking care of. In hot weather, nose flies would swarm around the sheep and pester them so badly they couldn't even eat. At these times, they would crowd together as close as they could and lower their heads to the ground to keep the flies out of their nose and ears. Of course, their wool protected their bodies. This was what we called bogging down.

They would leave the bed ground just at daylight or shortly before and feed until it got hot and the flies started bothering them around 10:00 or 11:00 in the morning. They had to be watered every day unless it was raining, so we would head them toward the spring, and they would bog down until it cooled off at around 3:00 or 4:00. Then they would feed until dark. The days were long in the summer, so we didn't get much sleep. Our only opportunity to catch up on our sleep or repair something that had broken down was when they were bogged down during the heat of the day. During rainy weather, they fed from daylight to dark, and we tried to take turns taking short naps by lying down under a tree and covering up with our slickers. I could usually fall asleep almost instantly.

In late fall when the grass got short in the parks, we would force them into the timber for an overnight stay. They didn't like any part of it and would attempt to go back to the park all night long. At these times, a couple of hours before dark one of us would load up a pack horse and haul our beds and tepee a mile or so back in the timber so we had a place to sleep when we got there. We could only hold them in there a day because there wasn't any water.

One late afternoon, I had hauled our stuff in, and after unloading it, I knew it would be pitch dark when we got back with the sheep. I figured if I left my saddle there with the rest of the stuff, I would have one less thing to take care of when we got back with the sheep, so I rode back to the park bareback. This was a big mistake.

We fought the sheep every foot of the way, and when we finally got them to where I had left our beds, it was long after dark, and we found out that a bear had gotten there ahead of us. It went through our whole outfit and scattered it all over the ground. I had borrowed a saddle for the summer, and he had ripped the sheepskin lining pretty bad, I suppose because of the perspiration and salt that was caked on it. It turned into a long night.

Of course, we were terribly frightened and afraid he would return and knew the tepee was no protection, so we just laid it out flat, spread our bedrolls on top of it, and lay down with all our clothes and jacket on–never even took off our hats. If he came back, we didn't want anything to slow us down even though we didn't have any place to run. All we had was a flashlight apiece, and the sheep wouldn't settle down, so every hour or so we would each take a side and weave our way through the trees and force them back on the bed ground. J.D. had a .30-30 rifle, and I only had a .22 WRF revolver I used for blue grouse. It was way too small. I was sure glad when it got daylight.

The next morning just before noon, J.D. stayed with the sheep, and I rode back to the cabin to make a couple of sandwiches for our dinner. My dog was named Cubby, and we called her that because she was the color, shape and size of a small bear–even walked like one. She usually walked along the right side of my stirrup, keeping pace with my horse. I was going through the trees when I saw her on the trail 100 or so feet ahead of me. I thought, "How in the hell did she get up there without me seeing her?" I glanced down by my stirrup, and there she was.

I had seen my saddle ripper. He took off running, and I got a couple shots off with my revolver but missed. It was fortunate I did because a small caliber would only make him mad if I had hit him. J.D heard me shoot, and with the help of the dogs we treed him, and J.D. shot him.

It was a couple miles back to our cookshack, and we thought we would have trouble packing the bear back on a horse, but we didn't. One of our horses was a buckskin stud that was as gentle a horse as I ever rode. Most studs are hard to handle and quite often mean. I never heard of a horse that wasn't afraid of a bear, but Buck wasn't. We dressed him out and got him laid out over the saddle and tied him down with no trouble at all. When we got to the cookshack, the Knighten family helped us string him up and skin him. We all kept enough meat for a meal or two and sent the rest of the carcass down with Dave, who showed up a day or so later. Although there were bears in the canyons on both sides of our sheep range, that was the only one that ever bothered us.

Thinking about the buckskin stud, reminds me of another unusual horse that the Elsom's owned. His name was P.J. He got his name from a relative of Mrs. Elsom who sold him to them. I think the relation's name was Peter John something or other, so they just used his first two initials. He had the easiest lope of any horse I ever rode and was a pleasure to ride–just like sitting in your favorite rocking chair. He had only one drawback, and that wasn't his fault. For some reason, a saddle would cause saddle sores to develop on his shoulders after a few hours of use. The Elsoms sewed the stirrups and cinch on the undersides with several layers of heavy canvas and put an extra blanket under that, and he was good for all day and every day. The only thing about riding him was with no swells to catch you when he would stop suddenly, you had to be ready when he did. One time, I was a couple miles from the ranch house, and it got dark before I started home. I was in a hurry and got him started running down a long slope that turned out to be a lot longer than I had remembered. It was just like riding bareback with no way to slow him up. Halfway down I remembered that a few prairie dogs had showed up in that area and started digging some holes. I was sure glad when we hit bottom and he leveled off because it was pitch dark.

One other horse of the Elsoms that comes to mind was one of Gwen's and Ellis' Shetlands that they rode back and forth to school. Mrs. Elsom had a knack for coming up with unusual names, and she named the smallest one they had, Twinkle Heels, which I thought was pretty neat. She was a small dainty, little pony that always moved with short fast steps. When you watched her walk away from you, her little hoofs would kind of flip with each step and gave the impression they were twinkling, especially if there was snow on the ground. Her feet would flip little pieces to the rear with each step. Many years later, I thought of her when I saw the blinking lights that flashed on little kids shoes when they ran down a sidewalk. She would have been a sight to see with all four feet, twinkling on and off like colored confetti.

Mrs. Elsom was also responsible for naming the home ranch by the stock trail that Sue, Ellis' daughter, is using for the connecting ranch on North Fork of Crazy Woman Creek. It was in 1942 when I was working out there. She called it The Folded Hills Ranch. The way some of the hills look, they do give the impression of being folded. A friend of mine, Jim Still, was also working there. He was a few years younger than me. He would joke and call it The Folded Up Ranch but never where she could hear him. He would have been cut down right fast like a willow in front of a chainsaw. Years later after World War II ended, I found out that Jim had been drafted but didn't adjust to military life very well and was pretty depressed while in the Army. He was killed after shipping overseas.

With the exception of a hitch in the Army that Ellis left the ranch for, he and J.D. spent the rest of their time working for their parents, and when they retired, the boys took over the operation as partners. The mountain property was separate from the main ranch on Crazy Woman, and the boys owned individual parts, but it was still used for summer sheep grazing operations. They divided their duties with Ellis doing all the farming, and

J.D. took care of the sheep.

J.D. had a large family, and Ellis told me that unknown to him, his brother split the mountain acreage among his children, and they later cut it up into small parcels and sold them. Ellis was pretty depressed when he found out about it. He still owned his acreage, but it was useless as a livestock operation. He eventually bought his brother's share of the Crazy Woman Ranch.

When Ellis died suddenly and unexpectedly a number of years later, his daughter, Sue, and her husband purchased the ranch from his estate. They are currently operating it as a combination working ranch and commercial operation with a large guesthouse and cabins on Crazy Woman Creek. They offer guided tours for hunters and fishermen on both it and the mountain property.

Having had so many close personal ties to both the ranch and family through an impressionable period of my life, I have mixed feelings when I drive by the place. In my lifetime, it went from a hardscrabble homestead where Dave and his wife depended on jackrabbits for part of their livelihood, to a beautiful lodge and cabins where a few nights lodging and dinner costs more than they spent on groceries in an entire year. The remembrance of how they must have felt when they couldn't get their sheep to the shelter of a shed during a storm–a mere 100 feet–and lost half their band comes to mind. It's called progress, but sometimes I wonder if maybe we've come too far too fast, to realize just how fortunate most of us really are.

§ § §

John Winchester was a man who owned a ranch about 15 miles southeast of Buffalo on Trabing Road. He was a person who could only be described as a character–none of it complimentary. I don't think he was ever married, at least as far as his connection with Johnson County was concerned. He was a loner who lived in an old house on top of a hill with a view that didn't include over three or four houses within thousands of acres of rangeland. My knowledge of him took place after the homestead era was over, and I would guess his ranch was enlarged by the addition of a few homesteads that were purchased after the original owners were starved and run out of the country by drought.

My first memory of him was when I was a freshman in high school. He had leased his place to a Basco named Martin Etchart, who was a character in his own right as far as I was concerned. My brother-in-law, Joe Bilbao, worked in Buffalo and hauled groceries and anything else that Martin needed on Sundays. He got me a job for a few weeks one spring, helping

Martin during the lambing season, and it was my first exposure to working around large herds of sheep–John Winchester and Martin, all at the same time. It was a very memorable period in my life. I'll concentrate on Winchester for this particular story because they are all intertwined. I'll leave the other two for later commentary.

I was sleeping in a tepee, thankfully, because Martin's sheep wagon was wall-to-wall bedbugs. Me and his other hand, Bob Smith, only went in at mealtime or to get a cup of coffee, which was always on the coal cookstove in a large granite coffee pot because lambing on the range was a 24-hour job, especially in bad weather.

Winchester had taken advantage of a federal government program that furnished trees and shrubs for shelterbelts to any rancher willing to plant them. He planted them in rows on top of the hill just north of his house and had a well, supplied by power from a gasoline pump. There was no electricity in the area at that time. That shelterbelt was a contention between him and Martin from day-one. It wasn't fenced, and when the sheep got anywhere near it, Winchester would boot them in another direction. That infuriated Martin, whose sheep were the one and only thing that mattered most in his life. I'm quite sure that a sheep free shelterbelt had been agreed upon when they signed the lease, but that wouldn't have made any difference to Martin, especially when he had too much wine to drink that Joe brought out every Sunday with the groceries.

Winchester had an old Model A Ford pickup, early '30s model, that he had put hasps on both doors and kept them locked with padlocks. I never saw him without a revolver strapped to his side, and though I never spoke personally with him, I was scared of him. I don't think he ever took a bath, and his body odor was nauseating. I was only up at his house once with my brother-in-law, but he met us at the door and never invited us in. In looking past him, I could see wall-to-wall newspapers piled up 4 or 5 feet high with just a narrow pathway in between the stacks.

One Sunday, as usual, Joe showed up with the groceries and wine, and by afternoon Martin was about half drunk. The four of us were sitting in the wagon, talking when Martin happened to look out the door up at Winchester's house and saw him chasing the sheep away from the trees, which were about a half mile away. We, Martin, Bob Smith and myself, had our horses tied on picket ropes a short distance from the wagon. Before anyone could stop him, Martin grabbed a rifle from a shelf and ran for his horse that was just an old gentle sheepherders animal. Martin was only a little over 5 feet tall, and his legs stuck out on both sides of the saddle because his horse was so fat. I don't know if he ever got his feet in the stirrups or not, but he was on a dead run. Every time he would over balance to one side, his horse would weave to that side and keep him in the saddle.

It would have been funny under different circumstances.

When Martin got to within about a hundred yards of Winchester, I could see him standing facing Martin with his hand on his revolver. They hated each other, and this was a perfect chance to kill him in self-defense, which he had a perfect right to do under the circumstances. About that time, Martin's horse stumbled, and Martin went flying over his head, rolling on the ground and losing his rifle. When he stopped rolling and got to his feet, he had a rock in each hand and was headed straight for his target when Bob caught up with him and held him down. Winchester never moved–just stood there with his hand on his gun, waiting for Martin to get close enough to use it. Joe showed up with his pickup a few minutes later, and he and Bob got Martin back to the wagon.

For some reason known only to himself, Winchester would advertise his ranch for sale every spring. The locals knew it was a farce and didn't pay any attention to it. I suppose maybe it was an ego trip and gave him the chance to feel important, talking to would-be buyers. He also was known to advertise for housemates in back East newspapers. The local gossip was that some of them ended up as hog food because hogs devour everything, including hides, bones, etc. and leave no trace. In that period of time, jobs were mostly nonexistent for single women except prostitution. Answering an ad in the paper from a man that had a big Wyoming ranch would sound plausible to many that were destitute. After she found out what she had gotten herself into, how would she ever get back or contact someone to help her? It was a 15 mile walk to town if she even knew which direction to go.

This was all gossip, but I keep thinking about an incident that I personally witnessed. One day, when I was at the wagon, Winchester drove up in his Model A pickup. He crawled out, and he and Martin started discussing something. A thin, sallow-faced woman and her daughter–I guessed her age at about 9 or 10–got out on the other side and stood by the pickup. They never said a word. When Winchester finished talking, they all got back in the pickup and left. I was only a teenager myself, but I can still picture those two women and have thought about it ever since. The one word that I can think of to describe the mother was hopeless. Her image is still floating around somewhere in my brain.

Winchester had the reputation for not trusting banks and burying his money somewhere on the ranch. I can think of an incident that kind of ties into that line of thought. Vern and Betty Rubottom lived catty-corner across the street from my house on Burritt Avenue. Vern, his son, Dave, and I worked together for the Wyoming Highway Department for a good many years. I only knew Betty slightly. We would wave at each other when we happened to see each other on our lawns. Several years after I retired, I was out on my lawn one day when I looked over at her house and impulsively walked over and knocked on the door. It was the beginning of a long friendship up to the day she died. What a wonderful interesting person. She had a memory that wouldn't quit and had even published a book, *Red Walls and Homesteads*, that I consider a classic and reread every four or five years. She was raised in the Mayoworth country and told me many, many stories about the area—even some about John Winchester, whom she and Vern knew very well.

Vern had inherited part of a homestead in the Sisters Hill area along the face of the mountain south of Buffalo. They sold it to John Winchester, and he paid them a down payment in cash. Sometime later, Betty was home when he showed up with the rest of the money. It was all in silver dollars inside a gunnysack covered with mud. Betty told me when Vern got home from work that evening, she had the silver dollars scattered out on the driveway and was washing them off with a garden hose.

When Winchester died, a guy I knew, Mickey Petrie, got the contract to clean up all the scrap iron, old farming implements, wagons, etc. from the ranch. I was collecting wooden wagon wheels at the time, so I bought what he had from Mickey. When I went out to pick them up, I asked him if I could look in Winchester's old house, which was in pretty dilapidated shape. What a mess! The piles of newspapers and trash that I had glimpsed through his open door many years before were still there, only more of them. The inside walls of the little rooms had been covered with some kind of wallboard, and someone had used a sledgehammer to break through the walls, looking for hidden money. It was the damndest mess I ever saw. I have always wondered if they found anything. After the silver dollar story that Betty told me, I always thought the perfect place to bury something would have been in the shelterbelt in back of the house that caused so much trouble between him and Martin. But I think someone else had gotten the same idea and used a metal detector because there were small holes dug up in various places.

The Winchester treasure hunt didn't end there. It ended up at his gravesite—literally. In his burial instructions, he had requested his body be interred on top of the highest point on the property he had purchased from Vern and Betty. I heard that some people looked the place over before he arrived, and he didn't quite make it up to the top of the mountain. I talked to one of the men, Ezra Jones, who volunteered to help cart the remains up to the designated spot. Ezra told me they had a hell of a time getting him to the top. It was solid rock when they got there, and they had to back down the mountain a little to find enough dirt to do the job.

Winchester started spending more time in Buffalo as he got older. He spent a lot of it in the 21 Club and the Occidental Bar, but I don't think he drank much–if any. It may have been for the social aspect of it because I don't recall anyone saying they ever saw him take a drink. He must have been very interested in boxing, which was quite popular at the time on television. All of the main events were broadcast nationwide, and the bars in Buffalo had large TV sets to entice their customers in for a couple of drinks. Winchester had a well-known habit of betting $100 or so on a match in the Occidental and walking down the street to the 21 Club and betting the same amount on the other boxer. It was sort of a town joke. He couldn't lose, but, of course, he couldn't win either.

He was still living at his ranch in this period of time, but I think he may have leased his place out. I used to see his old two-door early '50s Chevy coupe usually parked in front of the 21 Club with a 2x4 poking out from under the bottom of the trunk lid and tied to the trunk latch with baling wire so it wouldn't fall out. I had to ask the bartender why he did this, and it was because he was afraid carbon monoxide would collect inside the cab and not have a way out. I guess he hadn't thought that maybe the open trunk lid might suck the exhaust up through the trunk into the inside of the car, but evidently it didn't.

He used to eat his meals at the Lariat Cafe that was located where the First Interstate Bank is now. At the time, it was owned by Greta Daniels. It used to irritate her to the nth degree because when he sat down at the counter, he would use a napkin to wipe all the silverware off before he used them. His hands were so crusted with dirt that one day, a local livestock buyer, Everett Higgins, who was sitting next to him, asked Winchester if he had gloves on. I don't know if he took offence at the remark or not.

Whenever I drive by his old place on Trabing Road, I notice the tops of the 4-foot barbwire fence poking out of the dirt. Back in the drought years, he plowed up thousands of acres of native sod and planted dryland wheat. With nothing left to hold the topsoil, it blew until something stopped it, which was the barbwire fence plugged solid with tumbleweeds. It was part of Johnson County's federal government dust bowl project. It was a huge success if one wanted to bury his fence with tumbleweeds and topsoil.

I mentioned Greta Daniels a couple paragraphs back, and I thought of a story about her, so I'll slide it in here. She was a really nice hardworking lady. Besides the Lariat Cafe, she also owned the Buffalo Bakery at a later date, which was located across the street from the Occidental Hotel. My sister, Vi Duncan, worked for her at the bakery a couple of years before she got a job at the Courthouse.

Greta made a local bread that she marketed under the name of Buffalo Bread and also served pastries, coffee, etc. in her shop. She started having problems with someone who was smashing the loaves of bread after it had been delivered to the local groceries. One day, she hid in the storeroom of the local IGA store that was owned by a former classmate of mine, Bob Perry. When the distributor of her competitor's product, Sweetheart Bread made in Billings, came through the backdoor, he punched his hand through the wrappers of the Buffalo Bread to show his contempt for her product. Greta reported the incident to Bob Perry. I don't know what he did about it, but Greta didn't have any more problems with her bread being damaged.

§ § §

Betty Rubottom and her husband, Vern, lived catty-corner across the street from my house on Burritt Avenue. Betty was a wonderful storyteller and told me many things of interest about early day Buffalo. I've forgotten most of them but will repeat several that I remember.

Betty and Vern worked for the Soldiers' and Sailors' Home west of town at one time and became friends with a man who lived there–John "Posey" Ryan. Posey was an old frontiersman dating back to the Jim Bridger days, whom they knew very well and who had been stationed at Fort Phil Kearny on the Bozeman Trail during the Indian Wars.

One day, Betty had to drive to Buffalo for something and asked Posey to ride along with her and her infant son, David, who was only a few months old. She parked on Main Street in front of Gatchell's Drug Store and left Posey, holding the baby while she went inside to get something. When she came back out a few minutes later, Posey was dead and still holding the baby.

Another story I remember is about Mart Tisdale, Buffalo's sheriff for many years. Betty and Mart's wife, Dolly, were very good friends. One morning she was visiting Betty when they saw Mart pull up in front of the house, so his wife went out to the car to see what he wanted. She left the kitchen door open, and Betty could see them talking about something that Mart seemed to be very upset about. He finally jumped back into the car and roared off in a cloud of dust.

His wife was laughing when she came back into the kitchen. She told Betty a young girl who lived on a ranch on Clear Creek below town had gone to a dance on Saturday night with a young man and had come into Mart's office that morning and wanted him arrested because she was pregnant. Mart's wife finally convinced him that it was impossible for the young lady to know she was pregnant between a Saturday night dance and Monday morning. Mart was obviously embarrassed and retorted, "Well, how in the hell am I supposed to know that?" and jumped in his car and drove off.

One more story–Betty went to the Mayoworth School west of Kaycee while she was growing up. The students always put on a school play at

Christmas for their parents and neighbors. One year when she was in the fourth or fifth grade, she arrived before the other students and was in the process of changing her clothes for her costume when a young lady named Vivienne Hesse showed up. Vivienne had ridden horseback 20 or so miles from her father's ranch south of Buffalo for the dance that was to be held after the kids' program. Betty said that Vivienne was a very beautiful young lady and was changing her riding gear for dance clothes in the same room she was using. She remembered Vivienne telling her to be sure to pile her school clothes in a small bundle, tie her shoes by the laces, and put all of them in a corner under a bench. Vivienne told her that after the program, all the kids would be changing clothes at the same time in the same little room, and it would be a mess with scattered clothes all over the floor. Betty told me she never forgot the lesson.

It was also the first time Betty had seen a woman put on a corset. She said it was quite a process with tugging on the laces while sucking in the tummy, and it took a while for Vivienne to finish and get the desired wasp-waist look. Also, she made Betty promise never to tell anybody about her watching her struggle getting it on and laced up. Betty was in the nursing home when she told me this story. She drilled me with a five-second stare and said "YOU had better NOT EVER tell anybody either!" I haven't–until now!

§ § §

The Bailey ranch buildings were on Billy Creek about a half mile east of old Highway 87 where the road turns off to the Billy Creek gas field heading west. It is about 15 miles south of Buffalo. Paul and his wife had one daughter, Jean Claire, who was several years older than me.

In the summer of 1938 or '39, I was working for Paul in the hayfield and helping take care of his turkey herd. I was living with my father about a mile or so southeast of the ranch in a little log cabin on Crazy Woman Creek and walking back and forth to work. Paul paid me 50¢ a day when working with his turkeys and $1 a day for driving the team on the hay stacker. I wasn't big enough to do much of anything else. At the time, grown men were making $30 a month working seven days a week when they could find a job. In the winter they got room and board only. My summer wages paid for my school clothes when I moved back to Buffalo with the rest of the family in the fall.

Ranchers, like everyone else in the country, were trying to keep their head above water, so in addition to a few head of sheep and cattle, Paul decided to try raising turkeys, like a number of other farmers were doing. The summer I was there, he had about 1,600 head. The railroad between

Buffalo and Clearmont was in operation at the time and delivered the baby chicks to Buffalo in the spring and shipped the dressed turkeys out in the fall. The chicks were raised in brooder houses until they were big enough to roost in the cottonwood trees around the ranch house. Coyotes, bobcats, foxes, and other predators were pretty tough on them if they found them on the ground after dark.

There were uncountable millions of grasshoppers and Mormon crickets in the country during the drought years of the 1930s that ate every piece of vegetation in their path. They only had one desirable trait. They made good high protein turkey food that didn't cost anything extra for the rancher.

Each morning at daylight and again a couple hours before dark, an old man, Charlie Hamilton, and I would take them out through the hayfields to feed on the hoppers and crickets. He would take the lead like the Pied Piper of Hamelin calling out, "Turk-turk," and they would follow him. I would be about a quarter to a half mile in the rear, keeping the stragglers in the herd. The bunch would be about 100 yards wide moving along like a herd of cattle or sheep and was quite a sight. After a couple hours in the morning, it would start to get hot, so we would trail them back to the ranch buildings for water, and they would roost in the big cottonwood trees until it started to cool down, and we would take them out for their evening meal.

Rattlesnakes and bull snakes were pretty numerous on the ranch, and it was funny watching how the turkeys handled them. There would be 50 or so that would gather around the snake in a circle and start gobbling. Rattlesnakes would just coil up and buzz and strike at them if they got too close although I never saw one get bitten. If I could find a rock or old fence post, I'd kill it, and the turkeys would move on.

Bull snakes were a different story because they were so short tempered. The turkeys would circle them, gobbling like a bunch of maniacs, and the snake would coil up and put up with it for a short time, but after a while it would get mad and puff up and hiss and charge. The turkeys would jump back just out of reach until the snake charged in a different direction. Then they would crowd back in and increase the intensity of their gobbling. This would attract more turkeys, which meant more noise, and the sound was deafening. Some of the ones in the front of the herd would wonder what all the commotion was and head back for the rear. I didn't kill bull snakes, and sometimes it was a hell of a job to get the turkeys away from the poor thing. He was outclassed from the word go and outnumbered by a hundred to one.

I remember once they had a rattler cornered–circled is probably a better term. I was watching the show when Paul, who was irrigating in a hayfield a short distance away, came over to see what was going on. He had left his shovel in his pickup that was several hundred feet away, so he just stomped the rattler to death with the rubber boots he was wearing. I have to admit that I was quite impressed because I had never heard of anybody doing that.

It brought to mind a story my uncle, Karl Hepp, told me a few years before. Some guy was out irrigating one day, and a rattler struck, and the fang went through the boot into his leg. It broke off, and the fang stayed in the boot. After that, every time he put on the boot, they got bit. Uncle Karl didn't exactly say so, but I got the impression that some of the guys may have even died. At the time, I didn't think to ask him why they just didn't take the fang out or get some different boots even though that would have ruined a good story. Anyway, I know for sure Paul stayed alive for the rest of the summer, and he didn't throw his boots away either.

§ § §

One day, Paul didn't have too much for me to do, so he sent me down to the barn where two of his summer hired hands were putting up a temporary panel corral to dock some lambs. On one side, the wood panels came up about 6 feet short, so the two guys, Arlan Sand and Gene Snider, spent several minutes discussing the situation. They made sure I heard them, and I wondered why they didn't just use a long panel to bridge the gap because we had plenty of them. I had just graduated out of the eighth grade, and they were both in their late teens, so I knew better than to suggest that and get laughed at.

They finally decided to send me up to the house to ask Thelma Bailey, the boss's wife, where the panel stretcher was. She had never seen one before, so she wasn't quite sure what one would even look like. We went through several sheds and the garage looking for it but couldn't find it, so I went back and reported to the guys and told them Paul had gone to town, so we couldn't ask him. It was several miles to the next ranch, and they were going to have me walk over there to borrow one when Paul showed up. They used a long panel to bridge the gap and didn't mention the stretcher to him, which I thought was odd. It took me awhile to figure out I'd been fooled. I never told anyone about it–except for now–because I always hoped to be able to pass the experience on to someone else. I never brought the subject up to Mrs. Bailey either.

§ § §

Besides Arlan and Gene, there were three older men who worked there, Harve Pratt, Lew Jones and Charlie Hamilton. They had a routine of putting on new overalls and wearing them until they wore out without ever washing them. They would get stiff and shiny from dirt and perspiration. I suppose with such a hard surface it would wear longer. Being young and impressionable, I wanted to emulate them, but I knew my mother wouldn't even consider the idea, so I didn't mention it to her.

Most of the men would go to Buffalo on Saturday nights, and I would hitch a ride in with them and take a bath and change clothes. Mother would do my wash during the week. I took an extra set of pants out to the ranch and used them to work in. On Saturday night I'd change into my clean ones to go to town in and change into the dirty ones when I got back to the ranch. I'm quite certain she figured out what I was doing but never brought the subject up. She probably figured if I wanted to wear the same overalls to work in every day, it was no big deal and maybe someday I'd see the light, which I finally did.

The bunkhouse at the ranch was full of bedbugs just like every other bunkhouse in Johnson County. I hated to even go in and sit down with the other hired men while waiting for the dinner bell to ring. Maybe they were so used to them it was considered just an inconvenient nuisance. I remember some of the ranches at times would put some kind of chemical in a tin can, light it so it would smolder, and then leave the doors and windows shut for a few days. But in those days, men would quit one ranch and go to work for another, so even if one bunkhouse had been fumigated and cleaned up, the bugs would be back a short time later when the new help moved in.

The log cabin at Bill Potts' homestead I lived in that summer was no exception. The cracks in the logs were like a four-star hotel to the varmints. When you tried to fumigate them, they just went deeper into the logs, and a few always survived. We had our bedrolls on iron cots with a jar full of kerosene under each leg to keep them from crawling up the legs. They had to swim the kerosene moat before they could get to the bed. It worked great unless your bed tarp happened to touch the floor during the night and gave them a ladder up to the restaurant.

I remember one night just as clearly as when it happened 75 years ago, and I can't help shuddering, thinking about it even now. I had a nightmare and dreamed I was out in some tall sagebrush that was on fire and I was being burned alive. It was pitch dark in the cabin when I woke up in the middle of the night, and my body felt like it was on fire. I lit a kerosene lamp and found out why. The cabin was actually just a log shell with one window, a door and no ceiling–just an open beam structure with two log crossbeams to hold it together. My bed was directly under one of those crossbeams, and it was black with a long column of bedbugs, stretching across the full length of that beam. They had zeroed in and were dropping from the beam into my bed. My whole body was chewed up and looked like I had measles or a rash all over it. My skin crawls while sitting here writing about it. Of course, we fumigated the cabin and, thankfully, didn't have any more problems the rest of the summer.

Bedbugs were not only problems in bunkhouses. They were just worse than the houses in town. No woman would ever admit it, but they all had to deal with the things at one time or another. It was just easier to control them with plenty of water, soap and a few disinfectants if you lived in town.

It's kind of funny to think that what goes around usually comes around. Even with all of our modern day miracle contraptions, the dang things are still a problem in the twenty-first century multi-thousand dollar a night hotels because they haven't figured out a way to delouse their guests when they check in any more than the nineteenth century bunkhouses did.

§ § §

I don't know why, but I always called Paul by his first name but not his wife. She was always Mrs. Bailey without anything ever being suggested or discussed. She was always very nice and would tease me about things as she got to know me better. Her primary interest in things unrelated to the ranch was entering contests that were very popular with farm and ranch women during the Depression years of the 1930s. The vast majority of them worked from "kin see to kan't see" with little hope that things were going to improve in the foreseeable future, and the women's magazines they traded back and forth with each other were a form of escapism that could be enjoyed inside the walls of their homes at minimal cost.

Mrs. Bailey entered each and every contest she saw. I remember she won a few of them too–things like dishes, silverware, books, lotions, gadgets, and even small amounts of cash. Their mailbox was on the main Highway 87, gravel at that time, about a half mile west of the ranch house. The mail was delivered daily from Buffalo at about 11:30 a.m. Quite often she would send me on horseback with a packet of contest entries to wait for the mailman to show up. They all had contest deadlines, and she always wanted to be sure he received them personally. Every so often, I'd have a prize to deliver on the return trip that would put her on top of the world. If I remember correctly, I think first class postage at the time was 2¢.

In some ways, I think the Depression years were harder on the women than the men. At least the men were outside and had some freedom of movement. A woman was trapped in the house with kids to look after, and her trips to the outside were usually limited to the outhouse or small chores like feeding the chickens. They not only had to cook for their own family members but also for all of the hired help which could increase the regular crew of three or four to a dozen or more through the haying and threshing operations. This was all done without the benefit of refrigerators or electric

127

stoves or electric lights or water heaters.

The dishwater was heated in a reservoir attached to the wood cookstove, and the dishes were washed by hand in a dishpan and dried with a tea towel. The dishwater was then pitched out the back door because there was no septic tank system. Water for the kitchen and bath was carried into the house in buckets, heated on the stove, and dumped into a washtub. Depending on the household, several people took baths in the same water, so the whole operation wasn't repeated any oftener than necessary. The hired men always waited until they made the trip to Buffalo on Saturday night, weather permitting.

Without the means of keeping meat from spoiling for most of the year, chickens were the only source of fresh meat. They could be killed, dressed, and on the stove in a couple of hours, and a breakfast without eggs was very unusual. A steer could be butchered in cold weather and hung up in an outside shed as long as the temperature stayed below freezing. Steaks and roasts were cut off with a saw and used after they had thawed out. Hogs were butchered in the fall, and the meat was pickled or smoked. The milk from the milk cows was run through a hand-operated separator, and the cream was saved for butter and household use. The skim milk was fed to the hogs along with all the other table scraps. Nothing was wasted.

All ranches had large gardens that began with early ripening things like radishes and ending with the late maturing crops like melons and corn that were served through the summer. Fall started the canning season with the jars stored in the root cellar along with barrels of apples, each wrapped individually in pieces of newspapers. Carrots and potatoes were covered up with sand on the dirt floors of the cellar and would last throughout the winter as long as the ones that started to turn soft were removed periodically. The individual apples would have to be checked every week or so to remove the ones that had started to rot. Most of them had to be used just as soon as they were removed from the barrel.

Writing about the process used to prolong the life of the stored apples reminds me of a story my brother, Larry, told me many years ago. He had a friend who had been raised on a ranch north of town that had a particularly large apple orchard in one corner of it. There were several children in the family, and one of their weekly duties was to check all the apples in the barrels and pick out the ones that had started to spoil. They thoroughly disliked the job because, among other things, their parents didn't believe in wasting food, so all the bad ones had to be utilized in one way or another. He was describing the whole process to my brother when he hesitated for a moment, laughed and said, "You know, I was 22 years old and had left the ranch before I ever ate a good apple." Then he added, "My dad always told us boys that one bad apple spoils the whole barrel," so I guess there's a moral in there somewhere.

§ § §

Paul was over 6 feet tall and drove a big car, a Hudson Terraplane. It was heavy and handled the rough roads really well, but he drove it way too fast for the types of highways we had in Johnson County before the days of asphalt pavement. One of its features was called freewheeling. I think it was promoted as a gas saver. What I remember most about it was how quiet it ran when he would kick it into that mode. It was operated by pulling a knob on the dashboard and then using the accelerator to control it. It was just like coasting at 80 miles an hour with the engine turning over at idling speed. You were completely dependent on the brakes to slow down or stop because there wasn't any engine compression to help out. The only sound was the wind rushing by the car like present-day electric cars.

I was only a kid and didn't know anything about cars. Our family never even had one. Paul really scared me when I had to ride back and forth to town with him. I never did it if there was any way out. The Hudson was a four-door with a big, wide front seat. Mrs. Bailey sat right next to the passenger side door because Paul steered with his left hand and his right draped along the top of the seat. He talked all the time when he was driving and would turn around and face me while I was staring out the windshield at the oncoming curve. I don't think Mrs. Bailey even knew how to drive.

Highway 87 was gravel, sharp corners, no shoulders. Most people drove in the center of the road until they met someone and had to pull over to their side. Cresting the top of a hill was always a thrill. There weren't very many cars on the road, but when Paul would overtake one, he would tailgate until he found a place to get around it. I would be holding my breath the whole time. There wasn't a single straight place to pass without taking a chance between Buffalo and the ranch. Speeding was just pushing the odds to a higher probability of an accident.

On August 30, 1966, he and his wife were headed for town. Just a short distance from the ranch, he attempted to overtake and pass a truck and collided head on with a highway patrolman headed in the other direction. Paul was killed instantly, and Mrs. Bailey and the patrolman were seriously injured. Reading the newspaper account brought back a lot of memories.

§ § §

I think it may have been as a high school sophomore in 1940 when I first became acquainted with a somewhat reclusive man named Steve Muschel. He lived in a dugout on the Klondike Mesa at the foot of the

Bighorns just south of Crazy Woman Creek. A sheep man, Earl Henderson, hired me to help trail his herd off the mountain. He had been pasturing them with another rancher, Dave Elsom, who owned some land between Billy and Poison Creeks, and the grass was getting too short for both herds. Dave and I trailed the sheep, and Earl pulled camp. Both of them owned adjoining ranches on Trabing Road, and in later years Earl sold out to the McBride family.

I saw Steve again the following spring after quitting school a month early to help Dave Elsom through lambing and trailing his herd to the mountain camp. His son, J.D., and I stayed with the sheep all summer, and we repeated the routine the following year. I was also a month late getting back to school that fall. In the buildup to World War II, the draft had taken practically all of the able-bodied men in the County and put them in the Army, so agricultural workers were pretty scarce. The high school was cooperating by not enforcing compulsory attendance rules.

Steve Muschel had purchased some acreage along the livestock trail on the Klondike Mesa. At that period of time, it was wide open with no fences or cross fences or structures along its entire length. The tens of thousands head of sheep that trailed by on their way to and from their summer camps would spread out over the whole area. He built his dugout alongside the trail with a pick and shovel, and it was as primitive as any I have ever seen. As I recall, it was only 12 or 14 feet square with one narrow door and four windows. It was about 6 or 7 feet high with approximately 4 feet below ground level. As anyone who has ever driven up the mesa knows, it would be hard to find a rockier piece of ground in Johnson County. Over a period of several years, he also built a rock fence by stacking rocks up to a height of about 4 feet. He scrounged up enough dirt between the rocks to put in a small garden, where he raised a few hardy items like onions. While in the process of building the rock fence, Steve would accompany the trail herds past his place to keep them out of his garden. His fence has long since collapsed.

Dave Elsom knew him quite well, and they would visit while we were trailing by with the herd. It would take an hour or so because of the young lambs in the rear of the herd that couldn't travel very fast while the rest of the herd was strung out the full length of the mesa. He was a very friendly person of medium height, quite thin, with well-patched clothes. He had a noticeable accent but was quite easy to understand and to the best of my recollection was an immigrant from one of the Balkan countries. Needless to say, he was a bachelor.

To water his garden and for household use, Steve hand dug a well with a pick and shovel in the most unlikely location that could be imagined. It was a short distance from a steep several hundred-foot drop-off. How he figured he could hit water is one thing I have never been able to understand. As he inched his way down and got deeper, he may have resorted to a crude windlass of some kind. As far as I know, he removed all the dirt and rocks by crawling down an old rickety ladder, filling a bucket with a long rope attached, and then going back up the ladder and hoisting it out. He started fairly wide on top, but as he went deeper, it narrowed down. I have no idea how deep it was when he finished because it was difficult to see the bottom. I would guess it to be between 15 and 25 feet. He encountered some huge boulders and was unable to move them, so he just went around and under and kept going. When he finished, the boulders jutted out on all sides all the way to the bottom while getting closer together on the way down. I have no idea how much water he ended up with, but it was evidently enough to drop a pail down and scoop up enough for his household use and garden.

One of the stories I remember hearing him tell Dave was that he paid for the property twice. He had given the cash to the wrong person without getting a receipt, and they denied receiving it. Being an immigrant in a strange country with little understanding of our property laws, he already had two strikes against him when he stepped up to bat.

In June of 1942 on our way to summer pasture in the Bighorns, Steve was wearing a sling over one shoulder made out of an old towel. He made his living by doing day work for some of the local ranchers and fell off a haystack and broke his arm. Because it wasn't in a cast, Dave asked him if a doctor was helping him out, and Steve said, "No," because he didn't need one. He had a guardian angel that came to his dugout every night and took care of it. I thought about it all summer and made dang sure to check it out when we came off the mountain that fall. As near as I could tell, his arm had healed perfectly straight and was just as healthy as the one he was born with. Score one for faith and a helluva lot cheaper too.

I spent almost three years in the Army and didn't see Steve again until 1953. I was taking a band of my own sheep to the mountains, and we visited on the way past. I'm pretty sure he didn't remember me, but he was very friendly, and he had his rock fence completed. As I previously mentioned, he had stacked them to begin with, but they have long since collapsed.

A few years later when I was working for the Highway Department engineers, someone got the bright idea of building a two-lane highway up through Crazy Woman Canyon, and the Highway Department took the job of doing the survey. Lyle "Ozzie" Osborn was our party chief. One late afternoon in the middle of February, we were headed down the mesa for home and looked over and saw Steve, digging in his garden. We swung over to see what was going on, and I reintroduced myself. He was digging onions with a crowbar. The ground was frozen solid, but he told us the onions would last till May if the ground didn't thaw. He gave us a sackful to take home, and they were of excellent quality. Not too long after that, a local rancher was checking on him and found him, lying in the bottom of his well. He had been there for some time.

Evidently, he had been receiving some help from the County Welfare Department and had no heirs because they gathered his few belongings and hauled them to town to be auctioned off. Among them was an old .22 single shot rifle that looked like it had been used for a hammer and a collection of the crudest, dullest set of tools—some of them handmade—that I had ever seen. A couple of the items I considered were collectibles and was going to bid on them but suspected that they were trying to save a trip to the dump when the welfare secretary, Helen Clark, said it was all or nothing. I had to purchase the whole kit and caboodle.

The only two things of much value were a hand-operated copper tub wash machine that I traced back to a 1906 Speed Queen, and it was donated to the museum. The other item was a wooden octagon-shaped tin-lined cream can half full of sugar. After dumping the sugar out and cleaning it up, I added a couple coats of linseed oil to the outside, and it is presently sitting in my living room. It is a most memorable keepsake that brings Steve to mind whenever I look at it.

§ § §

Charlie Bishop had a ranch on Rock Creek in the late 1900s when I would stop by to visit him as his health began to fail. We had worked together on survey crews when the interstate system was being constructed in Johnson County from the late 1950s on. He was a super swell guy and one of the two best role models I ever met in my entire working career. He had originally filed on a homestead about 25 miles southeast of Buffalo in the early 1900s and told me many stories about the problems of making a living during the Great Depression and drought years. One of them was about proving up on his homestead that was still on his conscience some six or seven decades later. I thought it was ludicrous, but it was still on his mind that he had done something dishonest.

The Homestead Act had a number of requirements that had to be done before the government would issue a patent (deed) on it. One of them was living on the place for three years before filing final proof. He was in town one day and had made arrangements to ride home with the mail carrier, Bert Page. They were both in the Stevens Gas Station, which was located on the southeast corner of Benteen and Main Streets. There was a mix up in communications, and Charlie had to walk the 25 miles to get home. The final proof on his homestead was due in three days, and he would have had to walk back to town to sign the papers and then walk home, so he signed them three days early.

The issue was still bothering him some 60 or 70 years later, and he asked me if he had done wrong. I had to catch my breath for a few moments before I assured him I didn't think he had done anything dishonest. I didn't mention the thing that was uppermost in my mind–that I wished I had his problem instead of some of the hundreds that flashed through my head.

He told me when he first homesteaded, they could raise good gardens, and things like watermelons really did well. Very few homesteaders had the money to drill a water well, so they hauled the water from reservoirs in barrels, using teams and wagons.

Once, every fall after the crops had matured, they would have a fair, and people from all over Nine Mile would show up for the picnic that everybody contributed to. He said there would be at least 250 people show up. Nine Mile covered a lot of ground when you figured each family had at least 640 acres. He said they would have all sorts of games and races. For some or most of the families, it was their only entertainment for the entire year. Many of them, especially the women, spent most of their days trying to get their children through the year alive–little food, no doctors, and the closest neighbors a mile away if you had the time to walk over–plus the incessant wind drove them crazy. Trees were nonexistent but not rattlesnakes and assorted varmints that were attracted to the shade created by the house and the outbuildings. Even kindling for the kitchen stove had to be hauled with a team and wagon from miles away when the dried cow manure was used up–and this was in the good years.

I can still remember what he told me when I asked him what changed everything–three words–it quit raining. Some of the homesteaders hung on longer than others, but eventually the vast majority had to sell out to someone who was able to increase the holdings to the many thousands of acres that it eventually took to make a go of it. More often than not, it was a sheep man who grubbed along for many years before his outfit was able to support him. The situation hasn't changed since Charlie gave up and moved to where the water was over 80 years ago.

§ § §

Curly Galusha was a man I became acquainted with when I was in my early twenties. I think he was born sometime in the mid-1890s. I don't think any of my family knew much about his background even though he was good friends with my father and three older half-brothers. They said he was an excellent hand at everything he did on the ranches he worked for

133

and was one of those kind of guys that knew when you were going to be shorthanded and would show up to help close the gap. On the other side, they said it was difficult to return the favor because he never asked for any help when he was in a bind.

I remember him as a slow, deliberate type of person both in actions and speech who quite often tacked a one-liner on the end of his sentences. He was one of the most interesting and cleverest conversationalists I was ever around. He was kind of a loner and when given the choice, preferred working by himself. Good fences were a prime requirement on any ranch, and Curly built many miles of them. The most distinctive thing I recall about his dress code is that I don't ever remember seeing him without the heavy leather cuffs he wore around his wrists for protection when handling barbwire. I used to wonder if he even took them off before going to bed. Having experienced punctured wrists and torn shirt sleeves myself when building fence, I've often wondered why ranchers and commercial fencers don't use them, but I've never seen anybody wear a pair since I knew Curly.

He did me a big favor once, and I returned it by pulling a shabby trick on him that I always regretted, but he never once brought the subject up after it happened. The winter of 1948 and '49 was one for the books. Blizzard after blizzard blew in and closed roads all over the State, and the wind kept them closed for a long time after. Thousands of sheep and cattle either smothered or froze to death. The Johnson County Road and Bridge crew moved in with their equipment and bulldozed roads through the snow drifts so ranchers could get to their haystacks. When they ran out of hay, the State began dropping baled hay from airplanes to help out.

At the time, I was working at the Kostenbauer coal mine several miles northeast of Buffalo, delivering coal. We were just barely keeping up with town customers, and the roads were so bad it was impossible to make any ranch deliveries. Buffalo had only started the shift from coal to natural gas a few years earlier, and there were a lot of people still burning coal.

Like a few others in town, we had a milk cow for family use and ran out of anything to feed her. There were a couple feed stores in Buffalo, but a week or so after the first blizzard, they had sold all their hay, pellets and everything else cows eat and couldn't get any trucks into town to restock.

Up to this time, I had been buying hay from Curly who had leased the Cullen Watt Ranch a couple miles east of town on Highway 16. I asked him if he would sell me another load. I hauled and weighed it with the coal mine truck. He told me he wasn't sure if he had enough hay to get his own livestock through till spring if the weather didn't moderate, but he knew I was in a bind, so he told me I could have one more load.

The ranch house was only a few hundred yards off the highway, and I stopped at the house, and he told me which stack I could start pitching out of when I got to the hay field. From that point on, self-interest took center stage. By stomping it down and building the sides out, I put on half again as much as I usually did.

It took a lot longer than usual to load, but when I finished and tied it down, I drove into the yard at the house, went in, and got him so he could look the thing over. When he came out, he walked all around the truck, looking up at the top of the hay without saying a word. I could feel myself shrinking in size the whole time. Finally, he said out loud more or less to himself, "Well, I guess it's my own fault. I told him he could have one more load." Then he turned to me and said, "How much would you charge me to leave the truck load and take the rest of the stack?"

I have never felt more ashamed or put down in my entire life before or since. He lived for the next 35 plus years, and I visited with him a number of times, but he never brought the subject up again although I knew he never forgot it. Since then, when I think someone has taken unfair advantage of me, I think of Curly and try to keep it in perspective.

A few years after this unfortunate incident, he went to work as a seasonal ditch rider for a group of ranchers who lived along Piney Creek north of town. They got their irrigating water from Cloud Peak Reservoir in the Bighorns. Years later when Willow Park Reservoir was constructed, it was added to the system. His season lasted from early spring to late fall, and he was responsible for controlling the volume of water from the two reservoirs that entered Piney Ditch a short distance below Willow Park. The two reservoirs were about seven miles apart with Cloud Peak being at just about timberline. Cloud Peak water was contained at the reservoir site until it was needed and then released to flow down the creek to Willow Park.

There was an old cabin built by ranchers for the ditch rider to live in close to the headgate where Piney Creek was diverted. I can remember being in it and could see daylight showing through the shingles in several places, but the roof was so steep it could split a rain drop, and the water didn't have time to stick around long enough to leak into the cabin. The ranchers finally built a new cabin next to the old one that they intended to tear down, but Curly refused to move, so they had to wait for several years until he quit and they got a new ditch rider.

It was a really interesting old cabin that had mementos from previous forgotten ditch riders tacked to the walls. I remember the homemade kitchen cabinets had wooden hinges built by a long departed resident. It was possible to trace the history of the place back more than 60 years by the calendars nailed to the walls. They also served as an art gallery. I remember one of a nude Hawaiian hula girl doing a dance that some joker had fashioned a grass skirt to cover her up from the waist down. Anybody that was interested enough to see what was under the skirt would jab his finger in a fishhook nailed underneath.

The two reservoirs being so far apart, Curly would sometimes have to stay overnight at Cloud Peak. Somebody decades before had constructed the crudest log cabin I have ever seen. I don't think it was over 12 feet square with 6-foot walls. It had one small window and a homemade door that anybody much over 5½ feet tall had to stoop to get in. Fishermen, including me, who didn't have time to make it to their tent during a sudden rain or hail storm would crowd in three or four people deep. That was the limit, and everybody had to stand up.

It had an old stove and a crude bunk made out of poles to throw a bedroll on. Curly kept a cast iron skillet, a couple pans and some old silverware in a box for an overnight meal of trout from the creek. It also had a little rickety homemade table but no chair the last time I was up there. I suppose somebody had used it for firewood. It used to irritate him no end when someone would use up all his firewood and neglect to replace it. The door was never locked. There wouldn't have been any point in locking it anyway because someone would have kicked it in.

I have no idea what the issue was, but Curly didn't like a local man named Jack Meldrum. Jack spent a good share of his lifetime, fishing in the Bighorns, including Cloud Peak Reservoir.

My uncle, Karl Hepp, was a member of the Piney Creek Irrigators Association. One day, we were in the ditch camp cabin at Willow Park, visiting with Curly. He had just returned from Cloud Peak and was mad because someone had used the old cabin and left a mess. He told us no one was around when he got up there, but he damn sure knew who had used it. He said it was Jack Meldrum because everything was dirty except the washbasin. I guess that was the end result of eliminating all the unknowns to reach a circumstantial conclusion.

The headgates of both reservoirs were left open through the winter months, but along in early spring Curly would have to snowshoe in and close them so they could fill during the spring runoff. It would usually take several days by the time he walked in and out. One spring, he walked in and was gone for about a week. His wife, Myrtle, got worried and called my uncle, so he and I and Charlie Buell went in to check on him. We took snowshoes, but the trail was mostly clear, and we didn't have to use them. When we got to the cabin, Curly was doing fine. He said the fishing was good, so he had decided to stay an extra week.

Curly had a saddle horse he used to ride back and forth between the two reservoirs and to carry a few provisions for an overnight stay. There was a little corral close to the cabin with a few bales of hay, but most of the time he would picket him on a rope so he could eat grass. One cold foggy rainy day, he went out to get him and ran into a cow moose with a young calf. She put him up a tree for several hours. She finally wandered off, and he was able to crawl back down and get back to the cabin to warm up. He and my uncle were good friends but never missed the chance to jab each other if they had the opportunity. Karl passed the word around that Curly had gotten confused in the fog and tried to put a bridle on the moose.

Karl was a practical joker. You had to be careful when you were around him, but every once in a while he was on the receiving end. I remember one time in particular. His ranch was on Little Piney just below Fort Phil Kearny, and he also owned some land on up the creek at the foot of the mountains. It was a real pretty piece of property with lots of deer and other wildlife, including elk in the wintertime. A few wild turkeys showed up one year, and he started feeding them corn a couple times a week when he drove up from the ranch. A few years later, the flock had increased to several hundred. He was so proud of them you would have thought they were members of the family. He always kept the gate locked going into the place to keep anybody from disturbing them and to deter poachers.

A close friend of his, Wiley Burleson, and Duane Foss had permission to hunt whitetail deer on the place. They took along a gunnysack full of turkey feathers. They killed a couple whitetails and scattered the feathers with plenty of blood mixed in along with some empty shotgun shells so he would know it wasn't a stray bobcat.

When Uncle Karl found the feathers and shotgun casings, he went ballistic and got the game warden, Bill Morris, up to investigate. Of course, Bill wasn't in on the joke and didn't have any luck solving the crime. My uncle was so furious he was ready to take it up to the governor level if necessary.

I saw him quite frequently while the whole scenario was playing out but didn't have any idea it was all a farce. If I had known, I'd have driven out and scattered some more feathers myself. All I was aware of was that he was boiling mad, and it was difficult to get him off the subject.

As things escalated, the two "poachers" realized the joke had backfired. They were directly in the line of fire and could be the next two turkeys in the roasting pan. They figured the only way out was to admit it was all a practical joke, so they flipped a coin to see who would tell my uncle and who would tell the game warden. Wiley got the warden. I don't know exactly how Uncle Karl reacted, but Wiley said the game warden alternated between two extremes–cussing him out and laughing·

Uncle Karl and I got along very well with each other. I worked several years for him in the summertime, stacking hay both before and after I was married. We had to watch each other pretty closely because we both liked playing practical jokes. I got my share in, but it was neck and neck most of the time.

I picked up my mail one day–this was several years before I was married–and had six or eight letters from some Lonely Hearts Club ladies looking for a rich rancher to move in with. This was the first batch of 18 or 20 I received over the next couple months. When there was no response, some of them wrote a second time and the diehards three. I even got to wondering if the photos they sent were real or borrowed because there wasn't a dud in the bunch.

I didn't have the faintest idea who my benefactor was. Besides my uncle, I could think of several friends who would have jumped at the opportunity if they had thought of it. This was a brand-new twist, and my only shot of zeroing in on who was responsible was to keep my mouth shut until their curiosity got the better of them, and it worked. It was Uncle Karl.

He constrained himself for several weeks, but one day, he very casually mentioned that he had heard I was getting a lot of mail lately, and I nailed him. He tried to feign innocence, but it was too late, and he finally burst out laughing. He had gotten hold of a Lonely Hearts magazine and sent my resume in. I never had the opportunity to see what he put in it, but judging by the comments of the young ladies who wrote me, it went something like this, "Tall, dark and handsome cowboy searching for a lovely lady helpmate to share the rest of their lives together on a huge cattle ranch nestled in the picturesque foothills of the Bighorn Mountains in Wyoming." Since he was as snug with his money as I was, he would have crammed everything in one sentence to cut the cost down. Even practical jokers have a dollar limit on their humor.

I have no idea whose photo he used. It dang sure wasn't mine. He got to me good and really sucked me in. However, my guardian angel was hovering overhead, and I lucked out. Evidently, she pulled some strings, and I was granted the opportunity to retaliate before taking up permanent residency in Willow Grove Cemetery.

First things first...

Fred Gray in the Army – July 11, 1944

PART III

Army Life

October 29, 1943 — Draft notice sent from local draft board.

November 16, 1943 — Left Buffalo on bus for Cheyenne for physical and written tests.

November 18, 1943 — Drafted at Fort Warren, Cheyenne. Sent home to await orders to report for duty.

December 11, 1943 — Back to Fort Logan, Colorado, reception center and issued clothes, etc.

December 1943 — On train to Amarillo, Texas, for basic training that lasted about six weeks.

Spring 1944 — On train to Laredo, Texas, for gunnery training about a six-week course.

Spring 1944 — To Casper, Wyoming Air Corps Base for training on B-24 Liberator bombers.

May 18, 1944 — Received Gunner's Wings and promoted to PFC (private first class).

July 8, 1944 — Washed out of Gunnery School (airsickness). Went AWOL. Got caught. Busted to Private.

July 31, 1944 — Shipped from Casper to Hamilton Field, California. Bus to Rawlins and train the rest of the way.

August 1944 — Shipped around to several bases in California and Washington.

September 8, 1944 — Shipped out of Fort Lawton, Washington, on the USS Grant.

September 16, 1944 — Arrived Honolulu, Territory of Hawaii. 1500th Army Airforce Base Unit, Air Transport Command, Army P.O. #953.

October 3, 1944 — Flew to Canton Island. 1531st Airforce Base Unit, Air Traffic Controller, Army Post Office #914. Promoted to PFC, Corporal, Sergeant over the next year.

October 31, 1945 — Flew to Hickam Field, Honolulu. Promoted to S/Sgt. (staff sergeant).

March 5, 1946 — To processing center (Hawaii) for stateside discharge.

March 13, 1946 — Permission to fly to States. Private carrier.

March 17, 1946 — St Patrick's Day arrived in San Francisco.

March 21, 1946 — Discharged at Fort Douglas (Salt Lake, Utah). Train to Rawlins. Hitchhiked home.

Prior to being inducted into the Armed Forces during World War II, all local men had to report to Cheyenne for physical and written tests. The bus depot was at the Occidental Hotel, and the group I was with left on November 16, 1943. There were 14 of us: Charles R. Kershner, Leonard L. Finley, M.K. "Mike" Mikkelson, August J. Chabot, John P. Camino, Lloyd W. Kinnison, Jean B. Petrau, Virgil M. Nelson, Arnaud Curutchet, Donald C. Watt, John C. Wages, William H. Cook, Darrell T. White, and myself. I don't remember how many made the cut. The ones that did were inducted two days later, and we all returned to Buffalo.

On December 11, 1943, I was at Fort Logan, the Colorado reception center, where I traded my civilian clothes for Army ones. It was the biggest adjustment in my life up to that date. I didn't have the faintest idea of what I was getting into, but it was a long, long way from where I had just left. If there had been any way to sneak back home, I'd have done it. Two things set me off from the rest of the group within 30 minutes after I had changed clothes.

There were over 400 of us milling around in our new too large uniforms complete with permanent creases created by being stacked 5 or 6 feet high. We were getting ready for our first ever inspection by an officer, and an obnoxious sergeant was issuing instructions. Along with the uniforms, we had also been issued neckties, and my problem was that I didn't know how to tie one. One of the guys offered to help, and he tried but couldn't do it standing in front of me, so he stood at my back and reached over my shoulders, which was pretty awkward for him because we were the same height. It didn't help that the rest of the assembled men were watching and making remarks about the hayseed from out in the sticks that couldn't even dress himself.

He finally got it tied, we lined up, and as luck would have it, I was in the front row. The mouthy sergeant singled me out and asked if I could be prevailed upon to rearrange my belt, or if I wanted everybody else to follow my lead. I didn't have the faintest idea what he was referring to, but when I glanced down the row of soldiers standing at attention, it didn't take long to figure it out.

We had been issued web belts with shiny brass buckles, and I was the only one with the brassy stub end pointing to my right hip. There was nothing I could have done that would have been more obvious. In the previous 19 years of my existence, I had been completely oblivious that I was doing something different because no one had ever brought it to my attention before, probably because they didn't even notice. Anyway, my reputation as a Wyoming redneck was firmly established.

Later, I finally figured out what happened. I was the first boy in my family born after the preceding five girls. They had helped through the years in teaching me to tie my shoes and other basics. They had never given it a thought that boys and girls threaded their belts in opposite directions. It took me 19 years to find out, but I eventually got my own way. I had to follow orders for the next three years, but when I got back home, my belt went back to the original location, which, in turn, created a new problem.

I had a friend, Bill Perschillo, who handcrafted leather items. He had made himself a new belt and asked me if I wanted his old one. I took it even though he had stamped his name, Bill, in big letters on the back. Invariably, someone would comment that I had my belt on upside down, so I just told them it was my brand–seven seven I reverse B.

§ § §

Our group didn't stay more than a few days in Fort Logan. We were loaded on a troop train and headed towards Amarillo, Texas, for our six-weeks basic training schedule. It took several days on the coal burner, and the cars were full of tiny particles of coal soot. It penetrated everything, and sometimes was difficult to breathe. Washing our uniforms and luggage was the order of the day when we arrived. We took the long way around to get there because I remember some real pretty country around Little Rock, Arkansas.

I wasn't impressed with Texas. In fact, we traveled the full length from north to south after we finished basic training on the way to Laredo for gunnery training, and I didn't like any part of it. Being used to the Bighorns, I never saw any part of Texas that wasn't flat from horizon to horizon. Amarillo was cold and windy and Laredo was hot and dry. We spent about six weeks in each location. I heard a guy say if he had a ranch in Texas and a home in Hell, he'd sell his ranch and go home.

I don't know how many men were stationed at Amarillo, but there were thousands of them. The barracks looked like they had been thrown together in a hurry when the war started, and they probably were. They were just boards nailed together over a 2x4 frame. When the wind blew, dust filtered in and covered everything. So did the snow. There weren't any stoves in them. They were surrounded by wood walkways elevated a couple feet off the ground, and after it rained or snowed, the mud was so bad that at times we had to line up four deep on the walkways to do calisthenics. Two days later, we would have dust storms.

We were responsible for keeping our barracks swept out, so anybody that came in with muddy shoes got screamed at. I suppose there were at least 250 men to a room. We had bunk beds two high. When I left Buffalo a month before, the temperature was in the low teens. It was 30 when we got to Amarillo and felt much colder. I never really got used to it the whole time I was stationed there. I guess it was just the difference in humidity.

The whole time I was away from home, I had tremendous support from family, friends and relatives with cards and letters they sent. So did my brother, Larry, who was 6 years younger and missed serving during World War II. He enlisted shortly after graduating from high school. During one Christmas season when he was stationed on Enewetak Atoll in the South Pacific, his sisters cut a spruce tree in the Bighorns, boxed it up, and shipped it to him a distance of almost 6,000 miles. It arrived on time still green and in good shape.

During my basic training period in Amarillo, I wrote a short poem about the experience and sent it to my uncle, Karl Hepp, who had a ranch on Piney Creek. I had completely forgotten about doing it. When he died, his stepdaughter found it in his belongings and kept it. More than 60 years after I wrote it, she rediscovered it and mailed it to me.

It is such a juvenile piece of literature I had to laugh, but it brought back a few memories. My high school English teacher, Bess Muir, was affectionately known as "Ma" to the countless students she supervised during her decades-long career. She had overseen several of my attempts at composing poems. I am reprinting my "Amarilla" masterpiece and am glad she isn't around to grade me on it. She would have been appalled.

"Amarilla"
Well here I am in Amarilla
Where there's not a single hilla
At night when sleeping in my villa
The snow seeps through my window silla

And comes to rest upon my pilla.

I'm here to learn how the Jap to killa
And the way they explain it's simple rilla
But I never thought of it untilla
They sent me here to Amarilla.

Now you can say this poem's silla
And tell it to some Jack or Jilla
Who may think Texas is a dilla
And talk about the rocks and rilla
But as for me I've got my filla
Amarilla.

§ § §

After finishing basic training, we were shipped about as far south as we could get and still be in Texas–Laredo. We received our initial aerial gunnery training there. They graduated a class of 500 every week. Total time per class was six weeks. The casualty rate in Europe was catastrophic, and B-17 and B-24 replacement crews were in great demand. The Army Air Corps was trying to keep up.

The first part of training was becoming familiar with firearms. We fired everything from BB guns to .50 caliber machine guns mounted on concrete pads. A lot of the guys had never fired a gun before, didn't like them, and used every opportunity to avoid them if possible. At one point in our training, we were separated into groups of 12 with individual instructors that concentrated on small arms fire. All of my group was from back East except for me. When we were using 12 gauge shotguns on skeet and trap ranges, we were each issued a certain number of shells and had to turn in the empties at the end of the practice session to prove that the student had fired them. Their shoulders would start hurting from the recoil, partly because they weren't holding the gun properly. To compensate for the pain, they would hold it more loosely, which in turn magnified the recoil and made it worse. Sometimes the whole side of their bodies would turn black from the punishment. They would slip me their live ammunition, so I could fire it and they would have empties to turn in at the end of the session. At times, it was possible to get an idea of what part of the country they came from simply by observing the way they handled firearms.

From the small arms fire classes, we moved on to the aerial gunnery part of our training. Like most of the other students, I had never flown in an airplane before, and I had been thinking about it ever since we had started basic training in Amarillo.

From as far back as I could remember, I had always had severe problems with motion sickness. I always got sick riding in the backseat of a car and couldn't even sit motionless in a swing at the city park if the wind was blowing due to the slight movement. It was like a disease, and I guess the only people that can understand it are ones that are afflicted themselves. Anyway, I'll never forget my first airplane ride that took place in Laredo, Texas.

It was in an AT-6, being used for training students at the beginning of their aerial gunnery education. It was a small single engine two-seater with the pilot and gunner sitting back-to-back a few feet apart. Both had plexiglass windshields to deflect the wind, the gunner's behind his head. The gunner had a .30 caliber machine gun mounted in front of him, pointed toward the tail of the plane. There weren't any automatic shutoffs once he started firing. If he wasn't paying attention, he could shoot holes in the tail. There wasn't any intercom, but the pilot had a rearview mirror so he could keep an eye on the gunner. Communication was a previously agreed upon system of rolling the plane back and forth to dip the wings.

The machine gun ammunition consisted of two cans of .30 caliber shells with 100 rounds per can. The gunner would use up one can, eject it onto the floor of the plane, and ram the other one in. You had to be fast because the pilot only wanted to make one run at the ground targets. If the gunner didn't get all his ammo used up on the first pass, the pilot would get irritated, turn the plane on its side, and head back giving you the ride of your life just to teach you a lesson. Thinking about it in later years, I could understand his viewpoint. He was taking a brand-new student up once every hour who could shoot the tail off his plane. He stuck his neck out every time he left the ground.

We had been told in class that the ground targets were simulations of airplanes parked on the ground. In my head, I had visualized actual wood mockups but found out after my first ride they were just outlines of airplanes on the ground using either white paint or lime.

The agreed upon signal from the pilot was that he would dip his wings twice when approaching the target, which meant get ready to fire. The next time was one dip and commence firing. The wind was screaming by my ears at 200 miles an hour, and I was leaning out of the cockpit, trying to see mockups of plywood planes that didn't exist. The pilot knew I wasn't firing because the plane would vibrate with every shot. He dipped his wings again to let me know I was an idiot and had better commence firing. If I didn't and he had to make another pass, I was in for the ride of my life.

We were supposed to fire in short bursts to keep the gun from overheating, but I knew I was late and spotted a barbwire fence down below. I sighted on it and held the trigger down until the can emptied–all 100 rounds of it. I ejected the can and grabbed the other one, but I was so rattled, I turned loose of the gun, the slipstream caught it, and started whipping it back and forth. It couldn't go anywhere. I was so disoriented I grabbed the red hot barrel, and it burned through the skin into the bone in a fraction of a second. The pain was so intense I couldn't possibly have gotten the other can in the gun, so I just threw the whole damn thing overboard to get rid of it.

The signal at the end of the run was a single dip of the wings to cease firing, and I was supposed to nod my head to let him know I was out of ammo. He was watching the back of my head in his rear view mirror, and I nodded okay. He knew what I had done with the second can, but when we landed and he got out, he didn't mention it. He also didn't know that I had burned my hand.

To this very day, I can remember sitting in that seat completely paralyzed, but my mind was operating like nothing unusual had happened. He glanced at me and asked if I was a little airsick. I couldn't speak or move my head sideways to look at him, so I just nodded my head up and down a fraction of an inch each way. He told me to sit there for a few minutes until I felt better and walked away. I don't know for sure, but I think it was a good half hour before I could move and crawl out of that plane. My hand took several months to heal.

Looking back from a distance of 70 years, it might be a good idea to rewrite how my World War II wound was acquired in case any double or triple great-grandchildren get ahold of this story. In the age of computers, my pilot's rear view mirror accessory sounds a little iffy.

One thing I picked up right fast in the service was never ever volunteer for anything. I got my first lesson early on when we were attending rollcall one morning. As usual, the sergeant was calling out names and assigning persons for various jobs that had to be done that day, for example, KP [work under the kitchen staff]. He ended the list by asking if anybody had a civilian driver's license they had brought from home and, if so, would they be interested in volunteering for something that was going on that day. A dozen or so guys held up their hands. I would have been one of them but for one thing. The State of Wyoming never started issuing driver's licenses until after I got back home, and I didn't have one. When the volunteers arrived back at the barracks that evening, we learned they had been pushing wheelbarrows all day on a concrete job.

Another thing that was evident to me from day-one was about the food served in the mess halls. There were seven or eight million men and women scattered on every corner of the earth for over four years, and the United States had to start from scratch learning how to feed them. With the

146

possible exception of combat crews on the front lines, nobody ever went hungry, but to listen to the average GI, they were convinced they were being served food slightly above the quality of rations delivered to the residents of a hog farm. I personally felt that I had the most and best choices of food at any time in my life. Many of the mess halls had signs over the door saying, "Through these doors walk the best fed soldier in the world," and I believed every word of it. Every single one of us had come up through the Depression years of the 1930s, and the vast majority had to cut a lot of corners to get through. That included the food that made it to the dinner table. Most of us are blessed with pretty short memories.

While I'm here discoursing about the mess halls, I'd like to throw in a little info about the orderly room, which was the hub of the wheel. All information about the base flowed into and out of it, which always included a paper trail. If you needed 20 copies of something, for example, you used four sheets of carbon paper under the top page to be typewritten to get a total of five and then repeated the operation three more times. The paper was of poor quality and had a soft surface that would not print letters with sharp edges, and the last page was usually pretty blurry. If you used three pages to say what could be said in two, a promotion was usually in your near future because all politicians have to start from scratch somewhere.

Most of the rumors which armies all over the world thrive on, whether fact or fiction, usually started in the orderly room, where all the brass had their offices, including the CO, commanding officer. Some peon on the lowest level either saw or heard something he wasn't supposed to and elaborated on it to a close buddy who promised to keep his mouth shut, who in turn etc., etc. It would travel the full length and width of the base with blinding speed with each passer-on adding his interpretation until the final version was so garbled it would have been unrecognizable to the person that started it. I think this may have been where the idea of the internet was first conceived several decades prior to the birth of Bill Gates and Microsoft, who put it together in his garage.

§ § §

One afternoon four or five of us got passes into town. We were ready to leave but had waited for mail call to see if we had any letters from home. The mailroom was located in a main building, and the mail was sorted out by dividing the base into separate sections and delivering it to each location. When it was ready to be handed out, the announcement came over an outside loudspeaker. Nobody ever wanted to miss it, and if they were unable to be there, would have a buddy pick it up. I had received a couple letters plus a package from home.

I didn't have time to read the letters but opened the package to see what was in it. It was a box full of powdered sugar-coated donuts that my mother had made. No one ever left any homemade treats, lying around loose by their bunk because if they left the barracks for very long, it was long gone by the time they got back. I put the box in my footlocker and snapped the padlock shut.

We were late getting back to the base, and the lights were out in the barracks. They were turned off every night at exactly 10:00, and anybody coming in late had better be quiet while preparing for bed, or he would have a couple hundred guys coming down on him. The only light left on all night was in the latrine at the far end of the barracks. It was off to one side and cast a dim light through the door into the rest of the room.

Just before we entered the barracks, I happened to remember the donuts and asked the guys if they wanted one, which was a dumb question. We were clustered around my bunk talking in whispers, and I held the box out to each guy so they could help themselves. When I reached in and got mine, I thought I felt something like tiny cobwebs on the back of my hand. I was putting the box away when all four of the guys started gagging and running for the latrine. I didn't have the faintest idea what was wrong, but I ran after them still holding the box. When I got under the light, I saw that the donuts were a living mass of tiny red ants that had been attracted by the sugar. The guys were coughing and trying to wash ants out of their mouth, face and hair.

It was the funniest unrehearsed thing I ever saw while in the Army, and I lucked out because I hadn't had a chance to bite into my donut. I didn't dare laugh out loud because of making too much noise, so I bit down hard on my shirt cuff to muffle the sound, but I know it wasn't 100%.

§ § §

Before we were drafted, very few of us had ever been out of the continental United States, so we were all looking forward to our first trip to Nuevo Laredo, which was just across the border. Even then, we had to wait a month into our training to be eligible for a pass. It wasn't the wide-open, drug infested town it has developed into at the present time, but the streets were crowded with people, and there weren't very many vehicles. The American GI money that flooded in after the war started was a huge boost to the local economy.

On my first trip, the thing that impressed me more than anything was the open-air meat markets lining the streets. There were rows of skinned goats hanging from the rafters and lots of flies. As a kid fresh off the farm, I'd never seen fresh meat handled that way, and I haven't at any time since.

You could buy any sort of souvenir your little heart desired from the countless shops and street vendors hawking the streets. The upscale shops all had tags on their merchandise priced in US dollars, but there was a catch. If you questioned them before plunking the money down, the Mexican rate was only a fraction of what showed on the tag. I bought a sterling silver gold-plated belt buckle that was priced at over $30 and ended up paying $7. The craftsmanship was superb, and I'm still using it.

Before being issued a pass to cross the border, each GI had to attend a mandatory course on how to conduct himself in a foreign country. The panel was composed of several officers who concentrated on different forms of behavior that had to be either observed or avoided. It lasted several hours, and I remember the medical doctor, a major who discoursed on the subject of food and drink–don't touch it under any circumstances. A number of the guys in our outfit disregarded his warning and ended up in the base hospital. I had never heard of Montezuma's revenge before and had spent a lot of time growing up on a ranch as a kid, where we ate and drank almost everything that walked, flew or swam. Little by little, even the greenest of us was entering the real world, but the tricky part was yet to come.

This same major told us that prostitution in Mexico was as commonplace as buying a loaf of bread. He said that of all the ladies of the night and day who had been examined for a venereal disease, 90% were found to be positive. They hadn't gotten around to checking the other 10% yet. They had their individual places of businesses all around the perimeter of the main drag and sat on a stool out front soliciting business in broken English and undercutting their neighbor. He recommended we walk the streets in groups of 10 or so because when business was slow, the lady in front of her office would grab a lone soldier and shout for the gendarme who was hiding behind the house. The GI had two choices–pay up or be arrested. The two entrepreneurs then split the fee. With that, the major concluded the indoctrination course and asked the assembled men–all 500 of us–if there were any questions. There were none, and he told us we were dismissed.

§ § §

The Laredo phase of our training came to an end in the latter part of July 1944. We were split up and sent to other air bases for the last part of our schooling, which was actually being a crew member of a heavy bomber group for either a B-17 Flying Fortress or B-24 Liberator. There were 10 men on each, four officers, and six enlisted men. We were loaded on a troop train and sent to Casper, Wyoming, which was an Army Air Corps B-24 base. At that time, the Air Corps was the aviation branch of the Army. The US Air Force didn't come into existence until after the war ended. The base was northwest of town. Casper hadn't spread out that far yet.

I was only 120 miles from home, but the only real difference that made was that it was easier for friends and family to visit during off-duty hours. There was a USO Service Club on the base, and classmates from Buffalo sometimes came down for the dances, but that was limited due to gas rationing and replacing blown out tires. Each required either a gas stamp or tire permit, and the only ones that could get them were people who could prove it was contributing to the overall goal of winning the war. Dances didn't fit that category.

It was during the time I was stationed in Casper that I got into the most ridiculous situation of my entire Army career–bar none. [Fred's inside joke–Bar Nunn is a part of Casper.] In later years, it was something to laugh about, but there wasn't anything humorous connected to it while it was taking place.

During basic training in Amarillo, I met a kid from Loveland, Colorado, named Tommy Henson. We became good friends, and as luck would have it, we stayed in the same group when it was sent to Laredo and then to Casper. He eventually ended up being a tail gunner because of his size. Neither the tail or the ball turret that hung down under the bomber's fuselage had room enough for anybody much over 5 feet 7 inches unless he was pretty skinny. Once you got situated in either, you were practically immobile, and both turrets were claustrophobic. Tommy was a perfect fit at being just a few inches over 5 feet tall.

We were quartered in separate barracks about 100 yards apart, and one day we were sitting on his bunk, visiting when we got into a disagreement over some trivial matter and made a bet that whoever lost had to carry the other one to his barracks on his back. We got the opinions of several other guys in the room, and Tommy finally admitted I had won.

A World War was going on, and we knew we had to keep out of sight of any officer in the neighborhood lest they get the idea we weren't taking it seriously. We planned a route out through the junkiest part of the base, which we'd never seen one before, including behind the mess hall, which was a disaster area because of a couple dozen barrels of kitchen refuse.

I was only 3 or 4 inches taller but outweighed him by 30 pounds and had to climb up on a bucket to get on his back and wrap my legs around his neck. He was over balanced and laughing so hard it was difficult for me to get set, but we finally made it, and he wobbled off with me clinging to his head. We made it through the area behind the kitchen, but when we turned the corner at the mess hall, we came face to face with the pilot of his plane, who had come looking for him to tell him about a change of schedule.

None of us knew what to do. He was a tall guy, and his and my head were at the same height. What he should have done was reprimand both of us, and I could have slid down Tommy's back and taken the chewing out, but he didn't.

Tommy and I were 19 years old, and he wasn't over 23 at the outside. He was a second lieutenant that had gone through OCS, Officer Candidate School, to get his commission–what enlisted men referred to as 90-day wonders because it took three months to take the course. His training hadn't prepared him for anything like this. He was looking down at Tommy, explaining the schedule change, and I was praying Tommy would turn loose of my legs so I could get off his back, but he didn't and I couldn't.

When he finished talking, he raised his eyes, and they were level with mine. I didn't know what the hell to do. Army regulations specifically state that enlisted men shall salute an officer at the termination of a conversation and the officer is required to return it, so I dug my left fingers in Tommy's eyeball to keep my balance and saluted him with my right hand, and he responded correctly. I suppose this was the first time since the war started when one salute covered two men on one set of feet.

When the lieutenant left, we beelined it back to the barracks. The whole thing was so ludicrous we didn't even think it was funny–just embarrassing. We were concerned he would write up a report on the incident and we could lose our stripes plus whatever else they could think of, but nothing ever came of it, and Tommy said his lieutenant never brought the subject up, at least while they were in Casper. After the training period ended, his crew headed for Europe, and I lost track of him. I tried to make contact in Loveland, his hometown, after the war ended but didn't have any success. I don't know if he made it back or not.

Later on, I got to thinking about the whole fiasco and wondered if maybe the lieutenant felt just as immature in the way he handled his end of it as we did. That's when I began to see the humor in the situation, and the more I thought about it, the funnier it got–like it was a scene from an old *Three Stooges* movie with Larry, Curly and Moe and we were the characters. It would have been fun to relive the comedy with Tommy when it was a few years down the road, especially if we could have had his lieutenant's side of the story.

Tommy could be a real clown when he wanted to. He was a sharp kid and could change his facial expressions and alter his voice to fit the occasion. He must have read a lot in high school and evidently liked poetry because at times he would spout off lines that must have come from his English Literature class. If they didn't quite fit the situation, he would change it to what he thought was necessary, and he always got his point across. He had one he used on me so many times I memorized it without even realizing it. When I was in a foul mood and griping about something, he would open his eyes wide like a hoot owl and very solemnly recite the following verse:

> Be still sad heart and cease repining
> Behind the cloud the sun's still shining
> Thy fate is the common fate of all
> Into each life some rain must fall
> Some days must be dark and dreary
> While others will be bright and cheery

It always made me laugh. About 30 years later, I found out he had made up the last line and also found out where he got the poem to begin with. One day, one of my high school kids was talking about a problem he was having with one of his teachers, and Tommy's little jingle popped into my head, so I used it on him, but, as usual, the laugh was on me because he knew where it came from. It was the last stanza in a poem written by Henry Wadsworth Longfellow, and the title was "The Rainy Day."

§ § §

I washed out of gunnery school, busted back to private, and was assigned to working on the flight line with staggered shifts. Like everybody else I'd come up from Laredo with, I knew I was slated for overseas duty in the immediate future. Casper was the last stop, and I wanted to get home before I left because that was going to be the last opportunity until the war ended.

One weekend everything lined up perfectly, and I put in for a two-day pass that was denied with no reason given. It was pretty discouraging to think about sitting in the barracks with nothing to do for two straight days, so I decided to take a chance and go anyway. Things worked out but not in the way I expected.

Of course, I didn't have a car, but it was easy to hitch rides for anyone wearing a uniform. I had a Class A pass to get in and out of the base gate at any time, but it was limited to a 20-mile radius. If a guy went past that, you were AWOL, away without leave. If the MPs, military police, caught you, it meant a trip to the guardhouse.

I hitchhiked home on Friday evening after the shift ended and lucked out because I was invited to a dance at Horton's Dude Ranch Saturday night by several classmates, all girls who were working there that summer. The dance was a blast, and I had a great time. I never saw a single young man there that I knew.

I got back to the base at 7:00 on Monday morning, and when I stepped into the barracks, I knew I was in trouble. The guys told me my name had been coming over the loudspeaker all weekend to report to the orderly room. When I got there, the OC, officer in charge, wanted to know where I'd been, and the only thing I could do was play dumb and lie. I told him I'd gone to Buffalo but didn't know about the 20-mile limit.

He didn't buy it and said if I hadn't been scheduled to leave the base on the 2:30 afternoon bus to Rawlins to catch the train to California, it was a straight shot to the guardhouse. He also told me if I hadn't cleared the base by the time the bus left, I'd be there anyway. Clearing the base was the term used for getting signed releases from each individual department and that all clothing, equipment and paper work had been taken care of. It was a time consuming process and mostly a matter of standing in line, hoping someone hadn't screwed the records up because everything would come to an abrupt halt if they did. In a case like that, it could take a day or more. But the gods of fate were on duty. Everything went along without a hitch, and I made it with 10 minutes to spare. As I sank down in that bus seat, I thought about the guy who claimed he'd rather be lucky than anything else he could think of. Amen.

§ § §

After leaving Casper, the next stop was Hamilton Field, California. There were numerous bases scattered up and down the West Coast, and I was shuffled around and in and out of several. I can recall being in at least 11 different bases during the nine months spent in the States before shipping overseas, and two of them were for six-week stays each. It was like a revolving door.

I shipped out of Fort Lawton in Seattle on September 8, 1944, headed for Hawaii, the same date as my mother's birthday. The ship, USS U.S. Grant, had a capacity of a little over 1,200 men. Ironically, it was the same name as the troop ship my grandfather, Chris Hepp, arrived in San Francisco on in 1898 when returning from the Spanish-American War. His was scrapped a few years later, and mine hit the water in Germany in 1907. It originally carried paying passengers, but the United States borrowed it in 1917 during World War I and converted it into a troop ship. They never gave it back.

We started loading in the evening, moving along single file, each of us carrying a heavy duffle bag and being directed by a sergeant who was stationed at the loading dock between the pier and ship. Every so often the line jammed up, and he would stop us until things got moving again. As luck would have it, I was at the front of the line when he stopped me, and I set the duffle bag down while waiting for the order to start moving again. Like all sergeants, he was loud, mouthy and insolent.

When he ordered me to start moving again, I threw the duffle bag over my shoulder, and the damned thing knocked my helmet off. It rolled across the pier like a football. I dropped the bag and chased it, and the idiot sergeant screamed at me to let it go, but I kept going till I caught up with it. He used some choice words concerning my ancestry but didn't dare hold up the line for one really stupid GI. I grabbed my bag and ran as fast as I could to catch up with the end of the line. I sure didn't like that guy.

We filed down innumerable iron stairs to what I figured had to be close to the bottom of the Pacific Ocean, then into cubicles holding about a dozen men each. Hammocks were stacked along the walls, taking up every square inch of available wall space. If a big man was directly above you, he would sag down so low it was difficult to crawl into bed. I was the last man in our cubicle and really lucked out. The others had all taken the lower bunks, so I had to use their beds like a ladder to get to the top one, which was crammed in between pipes that stretched in every direction and covered the ceiling. One of them was an air duct that brought in fresh air, and it was a godsend because the air was so stale and the place was so claustrophobic. It was like being in an iron coal mine.

It took us eight days to get to Honolulu mostly because we didn't have an escort and had to zigzag the whole way in case a submarine located us and tried to zero in on us. I was seasick the whole time but could move around a little. Some of the guys spent the entire time in their bunks. We brought back food from the mess hall for them, but they couldn't keep much of it down. Infrequently, some of us were allowed to spend time on the deck, and I was up there every chance I got just to get some fresh air.

Trying to feed that many men was a big problem all by itself. We ate in shifts due to the size of the mess hall and limited cooking facilities. It was impossible to keep it clean, and the cooks were serving meals around the clock. Feeling woozy all the time, I had to force myself to attempt to eat something. None of us were used to the rolling motion of the ship, and there was water on the floor of the mess hall an inch or so deep. It moved from one side of the ship to the other as the ship rolled. You had to lift your feet as it passed under the table. With men coming and going constantly, the long tables were littered with scraps of food and spilled drinks. That, combined with the seasickness, was the kicker for most of us. In later years while following a shearing crew, I ate at a lot of sheep camps that had some pretty crude eating arrangements, but that trip across the Pacific was the most memorable.

Arriving in Honolulu was the icing on the cake. When we docked, the super sweet sickly smell of pineapple was so pervasive it felt thick enough to cut with a knife. Dole moved to the top of my four-letter word list. We spent the next two weeks at Hickam Field Air Base, quartered in a two-story barracks with bullet holes still in the walls. I remember one jokester coming down the stairs saying they had hot and cold running malaria on the upper floor.

Not to be outdone, another guy told a story about his grandparents who lived in the far reaches of the Arkansas hills. A well-dressed stranger showed up in their front yard one morning. His grandfather grabbed his shotgun when he went out to see what was going on. When he came back in, he told his wife he still wasn't quite sure what the guy wanted, but as near as he could figure out, somebody had started a fight somewhere because this guy's Uncle Sam had gotten a girl named Pearl Harbor in trouble and he said I should buy her bond, so I shot him.

During the layover on Oahu, we were restricted to base and didn't even get a chance to take in Honolulu. About a dozen of us were loaded onto a C-47 cargo plane and flown to Canton Island on October 3, 1944, which was part of the Phoenix group. Actually it was an atoll, the difference being it had a lagoon in the center surrounded by coral. Canton had an opening in one end and was a British protectorate. The spelling was later changed to Kanton.

I think it was about midnight when we arrived, but that's a guess because I've never worn a watch. We hadn't been issued oxygen masks, so I assume we were flying below the mandatory 12,000-feet limit. It was cold on the plane, and when we landed and the cargo door was opened, we were blasted by the heat pouring in. It was quite a contrast.

The next morning the new arrivals were lined up in front of the dispensary for a fast physical examination. The building, like all the rest of the structures in the compound, were just boards nailed to studs up about 4 feet high and then screen from there to the ceiling. The screen took care of the few flies, and there weren't any mosquitoes. We called them shacks.

There were a lot of personnel gathered around the plane for unloading the cargo and others that were rotating to another base–ordinarily after a year. It was funny how they were all dressed–short sleeve shirts and short pants, the first time I had ever seen men wearing them. I got used to them in a hurry because the next day I was issued a set of my own, and my arrival clothes went into a footlocker. They weren't worn again until a year later after the war had ended and I was rotated back to Hawaii. Due to the temperature on Canton, the new uniform was a welcome addition but took some getting used to. Many years later after the war had ended, my sister, Juanita, who was living in Seattle sent me a newspaper clipping announcing a new meteorological low had been established on Canton Island–70°–that brings back a few memories whenever I run onto it.

Nobody was used to the heat, and it was the old standard army procedure–hurry up and wait–which we did for over an hour. I was one of the ones in front who had crowded into the building. We all stood up to begin with, then a few sat down, and eventually some of us stretched out taking up the whole hallway. I went to sleep, and I heard someone say, "What the hell is going on here, soldier?" Six feet above me was an angry face framed by two sets of silver captain bars. The owner was standing astraddle of my legs, looking down at me because I was blocking the way to his office. I got to my feet in a hurry. Such was my introduction to the war in the South Pacific.

Not that I had anything to say about it one way or the other, but I never even got close to the fighting part. The only thing anybody on Canton Island had to contend with was boredom. By this time, all the action had moved closer to Japan. I had been transferred from the Air Corps to the ATC, Air Transport Command. My cousin, Darrell White, who was in the Coast Guard, always insisted that it stood for Army of Terrified Civilians. The ATC's sole purpose of being on Canton was to facilitate the movement of aircraft from the States to down-under as the war got closer to Japan. The Army contracted civilian pilots to fly new planes from the States to the fighting front. The pilots were limited to daylight flying only and hopped from one island to another until they reached their destination. Then they would be flown back to the States to pick up another plane and start over.

It's odd how some little thing in the past will shape your future in the most unexpected way. Every service member had a MOS, military occupational specialty number. It was cast in stone and followed you through your entire Army career. Mine was #521-Clerk Typist, and it was the only reason I ended up on a flyspeck of an island in the South Pacific instead of slogging through the mud in Germany or hiking up through Africa to get to Italy. This was because I had enrolled in Miss Fae Baird's Typing I and II classes in 1941 and '42 at Johnson County High School in Buffalo. One of only three or four boys in two separate classes of about 40 girls, I would guess this proportion was fairly typical for most of the schools because I never met very many guys who knew how to type.

Our era predated spellcheck and copy machines by 60 years. On test days, legal documents several pages long had to be completed without a single error or erasure. One boy in our class became so frustrated he threw his typewriter out of a two-story window, and it landed on a concrete pad.

§ § §

I was assigned to the operations room that handled all the information pertaining to aircraft arrivals and departures. It got pretty hectic in late afternoon when fighter planes started arriving from the States for their overnight layover and again at daylight when they started taking off for the next leg of their journey.

For a while, some of them would say goodbye by buzzing our building about 50 feet above the roof. The noise was deafening, and dust would come sifting down from inside the room. That practice ended when one of the pilots pulled up too fast and his plane disintegrated. It sounded like a bomb exploding, and pieces of it scattered all over the whole compound. One of the wings or what was left of it was only 100 feet from our building. The pilot ended up in the lagoon, and it took a while to fish him out. He sank and the rescue crew had to wait until the tide went out.

Due to wartime security reasons, we didn't have radio contact with any of the planes. That was handled by a small select group of men in Communications several miles from our headquarters. We kept in touch with them with a teletype machine. We worked around the clock in shifts, but there were few nighttime arrivals. The airport runway lighting would be considered crude by today's standards, and the lights were only turned on when the plane landed.

The island only had one tree on it, a palm tree. I still have a picture of it. It was the highest point on the entire island. It was about 50 feet tall, and a platform had been built on it to use as a lookout tower for spotting submarines. In actuality, the whole atoll is just one big rock, and that was how we referred to it in conversations. It is composed of coral, tiny sea organisms, that took millions of years to build. It made an excellent natural runway without the need for any kind of surfacing. It is pure white and will knock your eyes out without sunglasses. Officers were the only ones that were issued sunglasses, so unless you knew the supply sergeant or someone else in the supply room, you just squinted.

The atoll itself is shaped like a horseshoe. It is 28 miles around it but quite narrow and has a huge lagoon in the center that opens up on one end. In places, it is only several hundred yards wide. There was no fresh water. All our water had to be distilled from the ocean. The whole island wasn't very far above sea level, and a tsunami could have leveled it in a few seconds.

There were three groups of Army personnel located several miles apart, ATC, Communications and an infantry detachment, plus the Navy. All supplies came in by boat. In all the time I was there, I never saw a mouse, lizard or snake. The one thing it had plenty of was gooney birds, frigate birds. There were thousands of them. They nested in low bushes and didn't have any natural enemies. You could walk up to one, pick it up, and all it

*Fred Gray &
Gooney Bird
1944*

would do was squawk and try to peck you. They were terribly clumsy on the ground but could soar very gracefully once they were airborne, which took a while. Their wingspan was about like a golden eagle's. It was funny watching them land. Sometimes their brakes didn't work very well, and they rolled head over heels.

We were quartered six men to a building. They were very simple structures built of boards, screen and a roof that I mentioned previously. Each man had a cot, but there was no room for a chair. Corners were coveted because of the extra space. You never sat down on someone else's bed unless you were invited to do so. We each had a footlocker for personal items. Showers and latrines were centrally located in one large building. Everything else was scattered out. They were all bare bones–mess hall, barbershop, dispensary, operations, orderly room, guardhouse, and distillation and power plants. My home for the next year was Shack #82.

*Fred Gray
Canton Island
1944*

There was a tiny mailroom that was open for a short time each day when any mail showed up. The PX, post exchange, was pretty small too and only had a few shelves in it. It mainly existed for basic personal items like razor blades, shaving cream, toothpaste, and a few off-brand stale candy bars at times, plus envelopes and paper. It also sold cigarettes that cost 50¢ for a 10-pack carton, 5¢ each, and I always half regretted not taking up the habit. The ones I saw had tiny holes peppering the paper on each individual cigarette that I assumed was some kind of weevil either coming in or going out.

There was an EM, enlisted men, clubhouse that served beer when it was available, but I wasn't a beer drinker and was never in the place. Some of the guys that were told me it was usually lukewarm. Whiskey was an absolute no-no for enlisted men and would be a one-way ticket to the guardhouse if you were caught with it. Officers had access to it in their clubhouse.

*PV-1 Lockheed Ventura
Bomber on Canton Island*

Our swimming hole was in the lagoon, where we rigged up an old plank for a diving board. I don't know how deep it was because even at low tide I couldn't hold my breath long enough to touch the bottom. The first ones in had to be on the lookout for stingrays and jelly fish that were sometimes washed in with the high tide. Octopuses were creepy looking but not

158

considered dangerous like the other two.

There were two outdoor theaters, simple board structures with planks nailed to short posts for seats. Why there were two I could never understand. We seldom had any movies to show, and outside of a traveling USO group that made an appearance once or twice a year, they were never used for anything but an occasional lecture on some required subject. Our CO didn't like being there any more than the rest of us did, so the lectures were few and far between. When it was working, the sound system had to compete with the rest of the Pacific Ocean. One thing we didn't have to contend with very often was rain during the performances because it didn't. The two theaters were named Valley #1 and Valley #2, and I can say for sure that the guy responsible took a lot of liberty with the names because that island was flat, flat, flat.

For most of my stay, I was the only representative from Wyoming. When pictures of sheep appeared on the screen, the air would be filled with catcalls, "Hey, Wyoming, make you homesick? Baa, baa, Gray." Those guys were all from back East, and the only part of Wyoming they had ever seen was through a train window passing through Rawlins, so I just chalked it up to a bunch of ignorant New Yorkers from Brooklyn who, judging by their accent, couldn't speak English and shouldn't have been part of the United States to begin with. I made sure they understood this.

The base atmosphere was about as relaxed as it could get between officers and enlisted men. Clothes were sloppy because there was no way or reason to iron them. We didn't salute unless it was a visiting dignitary, and they were few and far between. We addressed officers as Lieutenant or Captain So-and-so. We never had inspections, bed checks or roll calls. If you knew some of the regular flight personnel from Honolulu and they smuggled in whiskey and you got caught selling it, you were in deep trouble. Nobody but the men in the guardhouse had firearms.

I remember one guy who got ahold of some whiskey and got drunk. He stole an M1 rifle from the guardhouse, went off his rocker, and emptied his part of the base. I don't know if he did it for real or just to get a Section Eight (mental) discharge. I don't remember what eventually happened to him, but fortunately he didn't hurt anyone on his rampage.

§ § §

I arrived on Canton with another kid I had never met before, and we became very good friends. I called him Dave, but his name was Howard Davis, and he hailed from Rutland, Massachusetts. Also, we called him Potty Davis because he couldn't pronounce his "Rs" very well. He pronounced ranch as "wrench" and party as "potty." He was put in charge of the Officer's Club and, as such, was also in charge of their bar, a dream job if anybody had any aspirations of becoming an alcoholic.

Each officer was either issued or bought–I don't know which–hard liquor by the bottle, and it was lined up on the back bar with his name on it. When he wanted a drink, it came out of his bottle, and Dave would mix it for him. He was not a drinker, even beer, so when an officer rotated to some other base, he quite frequently left his partially-filled bottle behind, and Dave would dump it down the sink.

Sometimes when I was on night shift with several hours of nothing to do, I would wander over to their club about 100 yards and knock on the back door. We'd sit there where he could keep an eye on the inside of the club and talk about what we were going to do when we got home after the war was over. Committing Hitler and Hirohito to Hell was a given. Suggesting he come out to Wyoming and try sheepherding was a little off the track, but I worked on it.

After getting out of the service, we corresponded for the next 45 years. In 1993, his son, Glen, decided we should have a reunion, so he drove him out to Buffalo, and we spent several days reminiscing. He owned a little farm surrounded by wall-to-wall people and still hadn't made up his mind about the sheepherding job, so I took him out to the Nine Mile area and showed him where he would be living. He didn't say "yes" or "no," but I got the feeling he didn't seem to be real enthused about the idea. As it turned out, I was right.

Army buddy
Howard Davis
July 1993

§   §   §

One time, somebody brought in a big turtle, the 200 pound plus kind, and some of the guys decided to vary the menu with some turtle steaks. The island barber, Ed Alley, volunteered to butcher it. I don't know if he had any previous butchering experience or not, but if he did, it sure wasn't with a turtle. They had it strung between two posts, and he walked around that thing two or three times, sharpening his knife on a whetstone, stalling and trying to figure out where to start. I don't know how many steaks they got out of it, but I think most of it was turned into soup.

Sometime later on, this same guy that was working on the turtle dismemberment approached me about a business proposition. It was my first attempt at entrepreneurship. Working regular shift work, I had a lot of free time and spent many hours just walking along the seashore, picking up rocks and seashells. When the tide went out, a huge area was exposed in the lagoon, and there were thousands of small sea creatures clinging to the tops and bottoms of the rocks. I started collecting some of the unusual ones to send home and finally figured out a way to clean them. Bury them in the sand for several weeks, and the ants would polish them until they resembled marble.

The barber was rotating off the island to Hawaii and said he thought he could sell some of the seashells when he got there. I didn't know him very well but didn't have anything invested in them but time, so I sent him several boxes with a couple thousand per box. It took a while, but I had plenty of whiles. That sounds like a lot of shells, but they were small and the boxes weren't all that big. Plus the fact it was much easier to get them to Honolulu than the ones I sent back home.

I have no idea what he got out of them, but quite some time later he sent me a money order. I think it was around 3¢ apiece. There wasn't a single thing to spend the money on except a poker game, and I didn't play cards, so I just stuck the money in my footlocker and waited until I got to someplace I could spend it.

As I mentioned previously, practically all supplies came in by boat, the most important of which was food. The harbor was on the far end of the island, and, believe me, the Navy took care of their own. Sometimes several of us would check out a vehicle from the motor pool and drive around to the Navy end of the island for the sole purpose of dining out at a first-class eating establishment, the Navy mess hall. They were very generous about handing out passes to visitors, and we took full advantage of the situation. All we needed was an official reason to be there, and we didn't lack in ingenuity.

Our ATC section of the island's menu consisted of almost all food coming in the form of canned, powdered or dehydrated condition. Rationing was in progress back home, and nothing was too good for our boys in the service if you were in the Navy. They had thick steaks, real eggs, sometimes fresh vegetables, bread with no weevils baked in, butter, many kinds of jellies and jams, fresh baked cakes, pies, and cookies. Of course, we were envious and would have reversed the situation if given the opportunity.

While on the Navy subject, every once in a while they would pass the word to all the other outfits on the island to get ready for a fish fry. They would park a destroyer at the open end of the horseshoe and at the peak of the incoming tide, which was like a huge river at flood stage, and drop depth charges like the ones they used on submarines. It would kill thousands upon thousands of fish which would float into the lagoon and collect along the shoreline. There was every different kind, color, shape, and size of fish imaginable. We would walk the shore and pick out anything we figured was edible. By today's standards, it was a huge waste of resources, but the gooney birds cleaned up the leftovers and nothing was wasted. And at that period of time, dead fish was the least of anybody's concern.

Our potable water had to be distilled from the ocean, and the distiller broke down on a regular basis. Soap didn't work very well with salt water, but at those times if we needed a shower, we would grab a bar and head for our swimming hole in the lagoon.

One of the men quartered in our shack was the nightshift baker that worked in the mess hall. His last name was Arnold. I can't remember his first probably because we all called each other by their last name. He would get off shift before daylight and, being sweaty, would always take a shower before going to bed. When he came in the shack to get his towel and soap before heading for the showers, he never used a light to keep from waking the rest of us up, but I know all of us would hear him. We tried to return the favor by being quiet when getting out of bed in the morning.

One morning, he came in before daylight and fumbled around finding a towel and soap in the dark. A short time later, he was back getting another towel, and we could hear him cussing to himself. The next morning we found out what happened. Halfway through his shower, the water turned to diesel fuel. He had a flashlight and headed for the swimming hole to get cleaned up. He was mad and forgot what might be below the diving board before he jumped off. Halfway down he remembered and was trying to reach shore before he ever hit the water.

I don't know exactly why, but I never really cared much for the guy. Nothing was ever mentioned, but I had the feeling none of the other guys in our shack did either. Living in each other's pockets, we were all careful about what we said to each other. Since he worked nights and slept days, we never had any interaction with him.

He liked to play poker in his spare time and evidently was pretty good at it because he had built up quite a wad of cash that he kept in his footlocker. It was against Army regulations to gamble, but that didn't prevent anyone from finding a game if he wanted to play. It was one of the few sources of recreation, and the games got pretty big even though the winners didn't have anything to spend their winnings on unless they sent it home or lost it in the next game. And there was always an infusion of cash with each new arrival from Honolulu.

Arnold's rotation date came up, and the night before he flew out, he tried to make a killing, and the vultures gathered to pick his bones before he left. He was a real sharpie himself and surely knew they were ganging up on him, just as he had probably done with past suckers. I suppose he thought he was smart enough to outsmart them, but he wasn't and he didn't. All through the night, we could hear him coming back to his footlocker to get more cash, and by morning he was flat broke. Just before he boarded the plane, he asked me to loan him some money. I don't know why, but I did. I knew I'd never see him again, and I didn't. It was one of those things you do on the spur of the moment, and you think back and wonder why in the hell you did it.

Months later, he made it back to the States and was discharged while I was still in Hawaii. I knew a guy who worked in the orderly room who got me the guy's home address when he was drafted, so I took a chance and wrote to him. He had gotten married in the meantime and damned if his wife didn't send me the money.

On the subject of poker, crap shooting was also a no-no. Somewhere along the way, I picked up this poem written by some anonymous budding poet. I like to think, maybe even a descendant of Edgar Allen Poe?

"Ravin"
Once upon a midnight dreary
As I knelt there weak and weary
With my last and only dollar
Lying there upon the floor.
How I prayed aloud to heaven
That my eyes might see a seven
Or my wrist might twist eleven
Only that, and nothing more.

Filled with fearful apprehension
And with thoughts I dare not mention
I beheld those ivories rolling
Rolling boldly on the floor.
And as I heard their sprightly clinking
While my hopes were slowly sinking
I just couldn't help from thinking
To be with me, never more.

Then I whispered to those ivories
Whispered to them soft connivings
Asking them to end my strivings
Serve me seven on the floor.
I was thinking of my Alice
And the weekend trip to Dallas
I could take her to the Palace
For a seven, nothing more.

Suddenly we heard a rapping
As of someone boldly tapping
Banging with a nightstick
On our barracks door.
Then an MP big and bony
With a manner cold and stony
Shouted out "Now this baloney
It must cease, forevermore."

When the MP's wrath descended
All my chance to win was ended
And my heart will ne'er be mended
What's this life worth living for?
Gone now is my date with Alice
And the weekend trip to Dallas
Oh, MP with heart so callous
Blast your soul, forevermore.

§ § §

At various times, we all took our turn at KP. The only redeeming feature of the job was the opportunity to get seconds on a particularly good dessert because the KPs always ate before the mess hall was opened up for the rest of the personnel. We always had plenty of food brought in by the Navy as I previously mentioned. All the bread for the island was baked by the small infantry unit based several miles away from the area. (If memory serves me correctly, the base hospital was there also, but I never had occasion to use it.) With the constant high temperature and low humidity, weevils infested the flour, and there was no way to either get or keep them out, so they were just baked in with the bread. We got used to them, sort of. We would hold a slice of bread up to the light and pick them out–anywhere from two to six to a slice–and the bread was filled with holes when we finished. Of course, they were invisible in the crust or pancakes, so we got a little extra protein at those times.

Refrigeration was a huge problem, so most of the rations were canned, dehydrated or powdered. One thing we did have plenty of was cockroaches. They were the biggest I'd ever seen and probably arrived with the Army because I don't know what they would have lived on before then. The mess hall had a concrete floor, was difficult to clean, and always had a greasy film on it. I've seen some of the roaches take off at one end of the mess hall, land 20 feet short of the far wall, and skid the rest of the way home.

We were supposed to swallow salt pills at regular intervals, and there was some kind of orange-colored drink the cooks made from powdered whatever that was supposed to supply some kind of nutrient lacking in our diet. We called this stuff battery acid. They mixed this concoction in large 10-gallon stainless pots that you dipped your cup in to fill it, and they set it on the self-serve counter. I never touched it unless I was first in line because some of the guys would have half of their hand under water when they dipped their cup in. Sometimes things like that bother me. I remember one time I was at the tail end of the chow line and glanced down at the near empty tank when I walked by, and there was a mammoth cockroach floating around. He had been there long enough to drown, and cockroaches don't give up breathing without a fight even in battery acid.

When I was on Canton, as far as I remember, it was a British protectorate and part of the Phoenix group of islands. There was a stone monument on one end with the British flag engraved on it. I don't recall ever seeing any British representatives present with maybe the exception of a few native islanders, all men who had been imported from some other island. I don't have the foggiest notion what their purpose was. I never knew where their quarters were, but during the day they occupied a small building about 12x25 feet with a fake grass roof. All I ever saw them do was pose for pictures, and personal cameras were few and far between. Civilians were nonexistent, and the Navy personnel that got back to the States once in a while would have been the only ones that could have acquired a camera. The movie stars charged a buck or so for posing.

My main regret when thinking about those islanders, other than wondering where they came from, was not taking the time to learn how they attached that grass to the top of the roof. They didn't have any sod to work with because there wasn't any, and the guys that had done the work were real artists. I've often wondered if it was woven and just nailed down like shingles.

Our base photographer, Leslie Edwards, was a kid who arrived on the same plane that I did and gave me pictures of the men and their building plus a lot more of our compound. Otherwise, I wouldn't have had any photos at all of the year spent on Canton. He developed his film in a little makeshift lab. All the pictures he gave me had to be censored just like letters before they could leave the island. It was impossible for anyone else to acquire film even if they had a camera.

I've already mentioned the lone tree on the island that was used as a platform for spotting submarines. Being the highest point, it was a good idea, but in our particular case it pinpointed a rather hopeless situation. The entire ATC personnel were in the drills that were conducted from time to time in the event of an attack by the Japanese. I have no idea how many

165

firearms were available to our particular group by the time I arrived because the war had shifted closer to Japan and all firearms were stored at one location in the guardhouse.

I was one of three men assigned to a machine gun crew, and it was a ludicrous situation. The gun was a World War I .30 caliber, water-cooled model. The age would have been insignificant if it had been operable. Ordinarily, the barrel had a metal jacket around it filled with water to prevent the gun from overheating. Our problem was that the jacket had rusted out. A 30-second burst would have turned that barrel into a corkscrew. Fortunately, the situation never arose when we had to fire it.

I would have loved to have been able to get it home for a souvenir and show my future grandkids how their grandfather saved America in World War II, but the opportunity never presented itself. If I'd tried it and got caught, I never would have had any grandchildren–Catch 22.

On the lighter side of things, one of the guys, Dave Hubert, who was from Pennsylvania, had a girlfriend that wrote him regularly and sent the words of the new songs as they were introduced back in the States. We spent a considerable amount of time sitting around putting the words to music–our version. We were pretty inventive and had a lot of fun doing it. It was months later and after the war had ended before I got close to a radio and heard the words and lyrics together at the same time. We hadn't even been on the same planet.

§   §   §

The two major news items with the exception of Japan's surrender that came by word of mouth before our CO had time to officially announce it was in 1945 the death of President Roosevelt and the dropping of the atom bomb. Of the two, the one that had the most immediate impact with me and others of my age was the death of the President. None of us had any idea what an atom bomb was, and I just figured that somebody had come up with a bigger stick of dynamite.

Roosevelt was different. I was eight years old when he was elected to his first term, and he was the only President I ever remembered. The thought of someone else being President wasn't on my memory list. It was just something that existed without conscious thought, like the sun rising every morning.

I remember very clearly when and where I first heard about the attack on Pearl Harbor and our high school assembly the next morning. They had rigged up a speaker in the gymnasium for Roosevelt's "Day of Infamy" speech, and I am dead certain that none of us students sitting there had any inkling whatsoever how it would affect our lives. The thought that some of us listening would be dead in the near future because of it would have been ludicrous. Roosevelt's voice was calm and confident as it was programmed to be. It would be left to future generations to learn some of the things he had neglected to tell us.

Roosevelt told us that Japan had sneak attacked a righteous, God-fearing nation that had done nothing wrong and we were all fused together under the Stars and Stripes with nothing to fear but fear itself. All we had to do was join together, and the good guys with Lady Justice on our side would eventually triumph. We believed him until decades later when historians would prove he wasn't telling the truth because of the politics involved. Whether it was justified or not is for each individual American to decide.

In my lifetime to date, there have been six major wars: World War II, Korea, Vietnam, Iraq I and II, Afghanistan. The Constitution very specifically states that only Congress has the right to declare war. Just World War II was handled in this manner. All of the rest were rigged with excuses to fit the occasion and get around this requirement even though the Vietnam War alone cost 50,000 American soldiers their life plus uncountable numbers of innocent civilians. Whether these skirmishes were warranted or not boils down to each individual's personal opinion from the President and Congressman on down the line.

When I was in high school, I remember a popular phrase used when discussing the usual ways to finance a war, "guns or butter" or "guns and butter," meaning either going all out to win with civilians willing to accept getting along with less or fighting while keeping the status quo back home. World War II was an example of the first. The American people overwhelmingly accepted rationing of food and other essentials for four years to contribute to the overall goal of achieving victory. They considered the sacrifice well worth the effort.

Politicians and presidents knew there was a limit to the taxpayer's tolerance for this kind of policy, and the second option kicked in. Borrow the money, let future generations pay the bill, and keep the electorate happy. We've been doing it ever since because only a small fraction of Americans are actually sacrificing anything. Those are the ones that are doing the actual dying and getting their arms and legs blown off. Their families are also paying the price. If it weren't for newspapers and television, the rest of us wouldn't even know there was a war going on because it isn't costing us anything in either money or comfort. The trillions of dollars in debt that have piled up is somebody else's problem not ours, and the lawmakers responsible have long since departed, mostly to write books and attend to the pressing need of acquiring sufficient funds to pay for their presidential libraries. The next time you hear a politician

167

gravely speaking about our brave American soldiers, you might suggest a more appropriate term would be "cannon fodder."

§ § §

May 8, 1945, was V-E Day, Victory in Europe Day, and the war focused on Japan that surrendered three months later on August 15th. I flew from Canton Island to Hickam Field, Honolulu, on October 31st to wait my turn for transportation to the United States and my discharge. It didn't happen until four months later. I was kept busy by taking over the duties of men who had already been sent back to the States for their discharges.

Another thing I just thought of–when you noticed a man that had shed his short sleeve shirt and cutoff pants for the full length variety, you knew he was scheduled for a transfer to another base in the South Pacific. His old uniform had to be checked in and left at the supply sergeant's warehouse.

Transportation for the millions of returning GIs from Europe and the South Pacific was the main problem. The whole issue was regulated by a point system to determine eligibility. It was based mainly on two things, length of service and actual combat experience. A lot of men who had been drafted before the war started hadn't been home for five or six years and had been in combat for most of that time, so they were at the top of the list. I was almost in the bottom rung.

A huge separation center had been set up on the base with quad tents for quarters to house the returning veterans from the South Pacific region, and they were arriving by the hundreds every day. I arrived on March 5th and was there for over two weeks before my lucky streak kicked in. While there, I met the only local man I knew since leaving the States, Doc Taylor from Kaycee. I was his first for someone from Johnson County, and we had a great visit. He knew he would be leaving later than I would, so he gave me a few messages to pass on when I got home.

Nobody at the temporary camp had to pull any duties. There was roll call morning and evening, but nobody cared if you attended or not because if your name was called out for a ticket home and you didn't answer, you went to the bottom of the list. It was quite an incentive.

There were six of us to a tent, and we had never seen each other before. As usual, in most every group like that, there is one who is destined to be either a future politician or a con man. Ours was named Jim Ryan, who was from Chicago and had the gift of gab like a true professional.

One day, we were sitting around killing time when he announced that if one of us would answer roll call for him that evening, he would take the bus to the main base and see if he could find us a way home. The idea was so absurd nobody even laughed. After he left, we discussed the different modes of transportation he might find, including one with a long rope and six life preserver jackets so we could tie ourselves together and float to San Francisco. But the joke was on us.

When he got back that evening, he told us he had gone to John Rogers Airport and found a civilian pilot who had flown in some Army supplies and was going back to the States empty. He agreed we could hitch a ride back with him if we could get the Separation Center's CO permission. We were at his headquarters office the first thing in the morning, and Ryan explained the deal. The CO called the pilot to check out the story, and everything lined up. The only hitch was that the pilot told him he wouldn't know where he would be landing on the West Coast until he got there. The CO gave each of us our service records we would need for the discharge center and told us to report to the closest Army base so they could arrange transportation and route us to the appropriate center. Mine was Camp Douglas, Utah, and the other five guys were from back East.

We took the base bus to the airport and hit the first snag. The pilot told us the plane needed to be worked on, and we wouldn't be leaving until the next morning. This was a repeat story for the next four days. We checked the schedule out with the pilot two or three times every day. There was no way he was going to leave without us if we could possibly help it.

It put us in a real bind because we didn't dare go back and tell the CO what was going on because we would have been put back on the stateside list, and that meant eight days on a boat if our name came up. We couldn't disappear in Honolulu for two reasons, none of us had enough money for rooms and if the MPs caught us wandering around the streets with no valid passes, we would have been in deep trouble, so we stayed on base.

Hickam Field covered a lot of ground, and there were a lot of different units. Ryan was a smooth talker and talked enough supply sergeants into issuing us a bed and meal tickets for the next four days. We slept in a different barracks each night in case someone started checking up on us. His main story was that we had become separated from our unit, which in a way was true, except he didn't tell them it was voluntary. We always arrived in late afternoon when we figured the sergeant was about to go off duty and wouldn't be too interested in checking things out real closely. One thing that really helped us was that there were a lot of temporary personnel moving around on the base, and regulations had been relaxed since the war ended. We had plenty of ID with our service records but didn't dare use them, so we signed off with fake names and serial numbers. It would never have worked under ordinary circumstances.

Anyway, we finally got airborne and landed near San Francisco on March 17, 1946, Saint Patrick's Day. When we got into town, the streets were packed with people watching the parade, and we scattered like a bunch of quail. None of us had any intention of reporting in to any base like our CO had told us and spinning our wheels for several days while the paper work was completed for our trip to the Discharge Center. All we wanted to do was get home the fastest way possible.

I had enough money for a train ticket to Fort Douglas, Utah, outside of Salt Lake City, my discharge station. When I arrived, I handed my papers to a very bored-looking buck sergeant sitting at a desk. He glanced at them and asked me what base in the States I had come from, and I told him I'd come straight through from Hickam Field in Hawaii. He got one of the "oh no not another one" look on his face and asked me the same question, and he got the same answer, but I asked him if it would help him out any if I flew back to Honolulu and started over. Evidently, he got the message because he handed back my records, and I joined the line of GIs in the hallway. It only took one day to make it through, so I was only in the barracks one night.

I found out later what had pushed his button when I mentioned Honolulu. Hawaii was still a territory at the time, and all discharges had to originate from a base somewhere in the continental United States so the GI's service record could be brought up-to-date and forwarded to his individual discharge center. That was the reason our CO had told us to report to the closest base when we landed in California, but the six of us had short circuited the system. However, there were no regrets about my sarcastic remark about returning to Honolulu and starting over. It was a good feeling to have the parting shot on somebody wearing sergeant's stripes on their sleeves.

Each soldier was issued a new set of clothing with his discharge papers. Lots of the guys said they had all the mementos they ever wanted from the United States Army and threw them away. The dumpsters were full, and the barracks were littered with brand-new clothing. Charles and I knew we would need work clothes after getting back to civilian life, so we picked out things that would fit us and shipped them home from the Discharge Center. During the following years, I wished I'd picked out more of them. The next day I was on a train headed for Rawlins, but I want to back up a little here.

In high school I had a crush on a girl, Billie Hurst, who I considered the most beautiful thing in creation. After I graduated in 1942, she and her family moved to Amarillo, Texas, but, of course, we were still keeping in touch. After being inducted at Fort Logan, Colorado, they shipped me to Amarillo for six weeks of basic training. I wasn't allowed off base for the first few weeks, but we were allowed visitors.

I didn't see her again until after the war ended almost three years later. After my discharge in Salt Lake, I was headed home on the train and stopped off in Reno, Nevada, where she was living. She was happily married, and she and her sister, Peggy, took me on an unforgettable tour of the town's nightclubs and gambling joints. There was a bunch of them, and it took until after daylight to take them all in.

We got through just in time for them to pour me back on the train to Rawlins, and I hitchhiked home from there. I had the driver let me out a half mile south of town, and from the top of the hill the place looked much smaller than I had remembered. I hoped it would be a cold day in hell before anybody pried me away from the place again, but it was a lot sooner than I could have possibly imagined.

It didn't take long to get back into the routine of civilian life, and I worked at various jobs during the next few years. I also attempted getting into the livestock business as a sideline and bought a few cows that I pastured with a local rancher.

The Korean War was going on, and I got the shock of my life when I received a registered letter telling me to report for duty at the Francis E. Warren Air Force Base in Cheyenne on October 16, 1950. I drove down and figured things weren't going to improve in the near future when I went through Douglas, Wyoming. Highway 87 and their Main Street were the same road. When I passed a gas station in the middle of town, I glanced down at my gas gauge, did a U-turn, and pulled up to the pump. The town cop pulled up beside me and gave me a ticket. Not that I didn't deserve it, but it was the first time I'd been caught and given a traffic citation, and it was not a good omen.

When I stepped in the barracks in Cheyenne, there were a couple dozen Wyoming ex-service men who were there for the same reason I was. We all had one thing in common—we were mad and depressed at the same time and completely helpless to change anything.

We were there three days for physicals and paper work and were told if we had a good enough reason pertaining to business or family matters, we would be sent back home for two weeks to get things straightened out. I had to do something with my livestock, so I took the window and returned to Buffalo. I sold them the next week at the auction yard in Sheridan and two days after that received a telegram telling me to stay home until further notice. I'm still waiting but would suppose my age might further complicate things.

As I mentioned previously, it was one more time when I thought about the guy who said he'd rather be lucky than anything else he could think of.

Fred & Patricia Gray – Married April 15, 1953

Carrie Connor

Stephen Connor

Robin Gray

Anthony Gray

Randy Gray

PART IV

Back to Civilian Life

Long before Army service put a halt to personal choices, my main goal of making a living was to somehow become self-employed in the livestock industry. This dated back to the era of time spent on Uncle Tom's ranch on Rock Creek during my high school years. Thinking back, high school was something that was just endured without any conscious thought whatsoever. While never mentioning it, my mother expected all eight of us kids to graduate, so quitting school was an option that was never even remotely considered. Perhaps it had something to do with her own upbringing. She was the second child in a family of one boy and four girls–she was born in 1889–who had to quit school in the sixth grade to help keep the ranch on Piney Creek north of Buffalo solvent.

I never really liked school and after arriving home from the service, could have gotten a free ride through college by taking advantage of the GI Bill but never even gave it any consideration like a lot of my friends did. I had grown up in the days when most of the men in the old-school livestock industry considered a college education a waste of time if one wanted to learn anything about cows or sheep unless you were a veterinarian. All that was required was enough money to get started, experience, and a willingness to work. One out of three was pretty fair odds and a good place to start while working on the other two.

I batted around at several different jobs, saved a little money, and in 1947 started purchasing a few head of cattle which had to be sold several years later when my number came up for a trip to Korea after that war started. Squeaking by that one was about as close as a person could get as I mentioned in the previous chapter. Almost 40,000 other GIs weren't as lucky and came home in body bags–a sacrifice that accomplished absolutely nothing.

The market price of livestock had been steadily rising since the end of World War II and showed no signs of weakening, so I decided to take the plunge and couldn't have picked a worse time. Even though still on the hook for possible military service, on December 12, 1951, I borrowed the money and purchased 319 head of ewe lambs at the Gillette Auction Yards for 43¢ a pound. Several weeks later, the market tanked and dropped to half of that. Prices stayed steady for the next year, and on January 1, 1953, I borrowed more money and bought 345 ewe lambs from my employer, Dave Elsom, who was also pasturing the first bunch, which were now yearlings. The new lambs cost 22¢ a pound and two weeks later were worth

17¢. It wasn't too hard to figure out what kind of a hole I had dug for myself when the next year 265 head of feeder lambs only put 14¢ a pound into my bank account. After thinking things over, the next step seemed to be to stop digging, especially when that was the only choice because the source of funding had dried up and staying awake at night thinking about it was becoming habit forming.

Yet, even after all those years of a continually sinking market, it would have been possible to muddle through by cutting some corners except for two things that were completely beyond my control. There was the inability to get a long-term lease on range land because of the competition of established ranchers who could outbid all under-financed newcomers. This, in turn, eliminated the prospect of getting long-term financing–a Catch-22 situation.

Every rancher or farmer, without exception, will eventually experience periods of lean years in the form of disease, drought, storms, or low prices among other things. To keep his head above water, he has to have long-term financing to carry him over the low spots. Otherwise, the bank will demand partial repayment in the lean years, and if the borrower can't come up with the money, he will be forced to liquidate and take a beating. This lesson was learned the hard way because the bank insisted on refinancing my note every six months.

§   §   §

At that period of time, there were hundreds of thousands of sheep in Wyoming, and a good share of those were in Johnson County. The larger herds were mostly owned by the Basque. A lot of the American second-generation ones were my classmates. Many of their fathers had gotten their start in the sheep business by striking a deal with an established sheep man and running a few sheep with his herd in return for herding the entire flock. This was advantageous to both parties. The employee didn't have to be concerned with anything at all in relation to his sheep–it was all furnished–and the employer would be guaranteed a worker who was on the job every day and all day with the same concern for his sheep as his own. The only problem was that the employee was limited to the number of sheep he could own because if he expanded, the herd would become too large to manage on the available rangeland. At this time, the worker's only choices were to stay small, sell out, or move to a place of his own. A lot of them–quite often with his boss's help–would buy more sheep and become independent or go into partnership with someone in the same circumstances as himself. That is exactly what I planned on doing.

After purchasing the first bunch of lambs in 1951, I put them in a herd owned by a livestock buyer named Fred Davison and his son-in-law, Charles Lawrence, and couldn't have picked two nicer men. I herded the entire band on a large tract of land that Fred was leasing southwest of Gillette at the head of the Belle Fourche River. It consisted of some 25 sections, was in good grass country, and had several reservoirs. The only drawback was that it didn't have a decent bed ground on the whole ranch. The wind blew constantly and would blow the sheep off the bed ground almost every single night unless they were in a corral. Sometimes when it was snowing and blowing, it would happen several times a night. I dreaded hearing the bell ewes take off on a steady walk at 2:00 or 3:00 in the morning, which meant crawling out of bed, dressing, and taking my dog, Snicker, to the head of the bunch and turning them back to the bed ground.

Ordinarily, a sheep wagon would face toward the southeast for best results, but in that country it was northeast because of the wind. Some of the corrals in that area were built in a circle with solid 6-foot board fences to provide shelter for the herd no matter what direction the wind was the coming from. It was the most miserable winter I ever spent working outside with the possible exception of one in Linch on an oil rig. It was a relief to get away from the place the following spring with the yearlings. I hired trucks and took them to the Dave Elsom Ranch 12 miles south of Buffalo. He was one of the most honest and admirable men I ever knew. Working for Dave the rest of the year, I ended up with the purchase of several hundred head of his ewe lambs, and since the ranch couldn't support both herds, looking for grass moved to the top of the priority list.

I finally found a place containing several sections in the Red Hills four or five miles northeast of Buffalo belonging to Mrs. Martin Pelloux. At the time, I tried to get a commitment for a specified length of time, the most common arrangement, but she refused. I later found out why. Part of the land she was leasing was owned by the state of Wyoming, and she had obtained a long-term lease of 10 years or so for her personal use only. This was and is a common practice in Wyoming where livestock operations require a long-term commitment to be at all feasible. These leases from the State are very desirable because of their minimal cost and usually stay with the same leaseholder for decades at a time. If the ranch is sold, the State land lease is almost always transferred to the new owner.

Mrs. Pelloux insisted on charging by the head—40¢ a month in my case—because if state officials had questioned our arrangement, she could claim she was only renting her private property and not the State land. This was a valid reason because the State and her private property weren't even divided by a fence. With a herd of sheep scattered out over a large area, it would have been impossible to tell if you were on State or private land.

After relocating the sheep from the Elsom Ranch, I spent the winter and spring there, lambed them out, and got a decent lamb crop but had problems with bobcats. There were a lot of coyotes in the area too, but I was lucky, and they didn't kill any sheep. Cats always killed by biting the lambs on the top of their head and eating it first. Coyotes usually killed by going for the chest cavity under the neck. Sometimes a coyote would kill a lamb, and the only outwardly visible sign would be two tiny spots of blood under their necks. When a pack of coyotes got into a herd at night, they would kill up to a dozen or so sheep at a time if they weren't driven off.

§ § §

Long before spring, the hunt was on for summer pasture. Mrs. Pelloux had said June 1st would be the last day but, surprisingly, had agreed to rent the pasture the following fall under the same terms. It was strictly word of mouth and the best she was willing to agree to.

Hearing of some land in the Hazleton area of the Bighorn Mountains belonging to the local sheriff, Harry Eschrich, that might be available, I stopped by his office in the courthouse to talk to him. He had one son, Jack, about my age, and we had spent some time together at their cabin on Poison Creek during our grade school years, and I was familiar with the property. He had around 800 acres of deeded land, and there was an adjoining 400 acres belonging to Bill Long that was included in the lease. He said he hadn't made up his mind about what he was going to do with his property the following summer–this was in December–but to keep in touch. In a small town news travels at the speed of light, and he was well aware of the bind I was in.

Stopping by his office on a regular basis trying to get an answer, he was always thinking it over but in mid-April finally said it was available. The price was $1,625 for the 1,200 acres for the summer months. Adjoining property was leasing for $1 an acre, but there I had no choice. Sheep aren't something that can be put on a shelf or hung on a hook while looking for something better. Now there was only one other hurdle to crawl over. There wasn't any money and no place to borrow any to pay Harry because my credit at the First National Bank was maxed out to the limit and beyond.

I went directly from Harry's office in the courthouse to the bank and into Wilbur Holt's office and sat down. He was the President of the First National Bank at the time. In the following years at various times, I sat down at different desks and discussed financial problems with his son, Bob, grandson, Ray, and great-grandson, Tom. Hopefully, Tom's the last one.

After I explained the problem, Wilbur looked down at the top of his desk for a long time and started drumming the fingers of his left hand, one at a time, on his desktop. It was easy to visualize the wheels turning in his head as he considered his options. Watching him, an old story came to mind about the sheep man who went bankrupt. He drove his herd to the bank, walked through the front door, and handed his sheep hook to the president. Whether it was true or not, I don't know, but it was a great story and fit the occasion perfectly. All that was missing was the sheep hook.

Wilbur finally looked up and told me to go back to Harry, give him a check, and bring the lease agreement back to him. I told him there wasn't enough money in my account to cover it, and he said to do it anyway. After getting back, he had me reassign the lease to the bank and wrote a deposit slip for the same amount to my bank account. I was still broke, but at least the woolies had something to eat that summer.

§ § §

Knowing extra help was going to be needed in the spring through shearing season and trailing to the mountain summer camp, I hired a herder, Manuel Cuevas, and went to work for the Highway Maintenance Department in Buffalo at the same time. The going wage for herders was $1,510 a month and the Highway paid $1.25 an hour, which was a little more and help was there when needed.

We finished shearing in late May and knew there was no chance of having much feed on the mountain before the middle of June at the earliest. The rent on the Pelloux place expired on June 1st, and she refused to extend the lease for two more weeks, so there was no choice but to get on the stock trail and head for the summer camp in the Bighorns. There was hardly any grass at all on the stock drive left over from the previous fall, but green grass was just starting to show up. Each trail herd was supposed to move each half day to a new bed ground and water, but we were the first one, so we slowed down as much as possible. Harriet's, a big sheep outfit, had several bands they took to the mountain each year, and they got behind us with their first herd, so we had to speed up to keep from mixing with theirs, which would have been a mess because there were no corrals nearby to separate them.

At the same time we were trailing sheep, I was hauling oil from Casper for the Highway Department that they used for laying down asphalt paving. It had to be hot when they fired up the paver in the mornings, so it had to be hauled at night.

I'd leave town about 6:00 p.m., drive to the Casper refinery, load, and get back to Buffalo about daylight The previous afternoon, I'd pull the sheep wagon to where Manuel would be spending the night with the herd, then unhitch, and drive back to Buffalo to start for Casper with the tanker truck, getting back about daylight. Then I'd drive to where the wagon had been parked the afternoon before. Manuel would already be on the trail, so I'd hitch up the wagon and catch up with him at the noon rest stop where we'd have dinner. Then I'd pull the wagon to the evening rest stop, unhitch, and head for Buffalo and the Casper trip while snatching a few hours of sleep whenever the opportunity presented itself. It got to be quite a drag.

It was raining the afternoon I left the wagon for him on the trail at the bottom of Crazy Woman Canyon. Returning the next morning, he was already on top of the mountain with the sheep. Crazy Woman Canyon Road was closed due to the washed out road, so the wagon had to be pulled to Buffalo and then head back for Poison Creek on the highway. There was 6 inches of snow on the ground when I got there. After unhitching and heading back down the stock trail to the Muddy Creek rest stop to meet Manuel, the pickup bogged down in the mud clear to the axles. Unable to dig it out, I lost my temper, slammed the door shut, and the window shattered. A couple hours later, another sheep man, Gaston Irigaray, came by with an old army surplus Dodge Power Wagon and pulled the pickup out. Manuel finally showed up with the sheep, and we went the rest of the way to camp. It was on a weekend and an opportunity to catch up on some sleep.

§ § §

Due to the inescapable fact of always being short of money, to help pay for the lease that summer, I took in several hundred head of yearlings belonging to another sheep man, Harry Jones, who paid $1 a head per month for their care. The weather was extra hot all summer with no rain, and by the middle of July it was evident we were going to run out of grass and have to move off the mountain a lot earlier than expected.

Knowing the winter months would require more pasture than just the Pelloux place because of Harry's yearlings, I had previously leased an additional 2,800 acres several months before belonging to an adjoining rancher, Jeff Bolinger, for the period from October 15th through February of the following year. The Pelloux place covered the gap until it was available, and I paid Jeff $300 down in mid-August with the balance due, $700, when we moved in. The grass on it was pretty short due to the lack of moisture, but it was the only alternative, and I felt fortunate to have been able to lease it.

We trailed off the mountain in mid-August, and when we arrived at the fall pasture, there was a surprise waiting for us in the form of some cows and calves which had been there all summer, judging by the amount of grass still remaining. I was devastated and immediately drove down to Mrs. Pelloux's house to find out who they belonged to. She said the owner was Everett Higgins, a local livestock buyer and seller, whom I had known for a long time. She also said he had been looking for a place to move them to for some time but hadn't had any luck so far. Under the circumstances, I felt it was useless to ask why he was there in the first place because the grass was already gone and I only had a verbal agreement with her to pay by the head per month, which, I suppose, is what Everett was doing. Double rent was probably being collected in the meantime. After driving to town and talking to Everett, who repeated the same thing she had said about not being able to find a place to move them to, it was evident the problem was all mine.

I didn't have the faintest idea what to do except that it had to be something. After mulling it over for several days and knowing I had rented the pasture first plus paying the agreed upon rent in advance, only one thing came to mind. That evening I rounded up the cows, took them through two gates to get to the county road, and left them in the right-of-way. A couple days later, Everett sent a young teenager, Pete Straight, out on horseback, and he put them back into the Pelloux pasture. The next day they were back on the county road. Evidently, he got the message because that's the last I saw of them.

He owned the Big Horn Motel and also had a little ranch east of town a short distance. I had been wondering what was going to happen after the cattle incident. A month or so later, we happened to meet on the sidewalk in downtown Buffalo. We visited a few minutes, and he never mentioned our previous encounter either then or in any of the following years that I dealt with him. I guess he figured in the livestock business, you'll always lose some but try to make up for it at a later date. At least that is what I had experienced, and he had been in the game a long time before I entered.

The lease on the Bolinger Ranch would expire at the end of February, and Jeff needed the place for his own use and couldn't renew it, so I spent the entire winter looking for a place to move to with no success. The only choice left was to sell out, but the first problem was to find a buyer. Passing the word around brought a few contacts but none with any credibility unless it ended up in a fire sale that wasn't even enough to satisfy the First National Bank.

There were only two viable prospects. One of them was a rancher from the Barnum area west of Kaycee, Harry Roberts, and the other was Grant Dickerson, who was the foreman for the 28 Ranch south of Buffalo that was owned by Calvin Case.

Grant spent a lot of time in the 21 Club, which like the Occidental Bar, was where a lot of livestock deals were made involving cattle, sheep, wool, lambs, and land. They were always concluded in a bank or lawyer's office, but they started in the bars. Most of the sheep men would stop by for a drink before supper and share any information they had about their industry. This was a guaranteed place to catch up with Grant, and, of course, he was well aware of the bind I was in.

The 28 Ranch was well established, and the owner had the funds to purchase the sheep, so I kept in contact with Grant, and one evening he made a reasonable offer with one stipulation. He wanted to tie up the lease on the Eschrich mountain camp that I had used the previous summer. Of course, I had no say over that, but he may have thought so, and after contacting Harry Eschrich and telling him what Grant had said, he agreed to it. Grant signed the purchase agreement for the sheep with a $625 earnest money check attached on February 24, 1954, and said he would take delivery on the 26th at the Pradere Ranch on Trabing Road south of Buffalo with the balance due then. Two days before the lease on the Bolinger Ranch expired, it would have been impossible to describe my emotions.

Manuel and I were on the stock trail with the sheep the next morning for the two-day trip, but on the second day when we were about a mile from the Pradere place, a blizzard hit just as we reached the Earl Henderson ranch at the intersection of the stock trail and Trabing Road. His lambing sheds and corrals were adjacent to the trail, so he let us put the sheep in there for shelter. The roads were bad, but after making it to town, I located Grant, and he volunteered to take delivery at Henderson's. He loaded up some hay and finally made it through the drifts to the corrals.

We counted the sheep the next day, and he handed me a check for the balance due, $12,500. The wife and I were out of the sheep business. What a stretch it had been! We paid off the loan at the bank, Manuel's wages, a lot of smaller bills, and still had a little left over.

Hiring Manuel had proved to be a wise decision. He was 100% reliable and kept his wagon absolutely spotless, which was a lot different from most of the herders I'd ever been around, including myself. He didn't drink or smoke, couldn't read or write, and had to sign his payroll checks with an "X" when he cashed them. He retired several years after working for me and rented a room in the Occidental Hotel, where he stayed until he died in 1977 at the age of 83. During his lifetime of herding sheep, herder wages never got above $150, but when he passed away, he left an estate worth over $20,000. He dedicated it to the City of Buffalo to further recreation facilities in the community. I never knew whether he had any relatives still living in Mexico or not.

I suppose anybody reading these stories may question the use of specific dates, money, names, etc., and chalk it up to a daily diary or questionable memory. That isn't the case. Having been a collector of junk my entire life, among the stuff is a complete collection of income tax records and cancelled checks–70 years and counting and dating back to

1945 the first time I remember filing taxes. This is the only time I can remember giving the IRS credit for anything and sure hope it's the last.

§ § §

In the summer of 1947, I went to work for Dick Greene, the State Senator from Johnson County. The Forest Service was building a road to the Sheep Mountain fire lookout station, and Dick had the contract to clear the timber from the right-of-way. We cut the trees down and stacked the limbs and underbrush in piles so they could be burned the following winter. The stumps were left about 2 feet high, so the bulldozers could uproot them easier, and the logs were skidded with horses and stacked in bunks. Shrum Lumber Company then hauled the logs to their sawmill in Buffalo.

We had several tents set up along Merle Creek. One was for the kitchen-dining room and another for the cook and her husband, Mr. and Mrs. Ross Wilson, to sleep in. A couple more were for the hired help. The men working there besides the Wilsons were the foreman, Dick Smith, Jack Garrett, Ray Canterbury, and Gene White, my cousin.

We always walked back to camp for dinner. On my first morning on the job, the foreman sent me back a half hour early with one of the skid horses. We were working in a heavily wooded area with steep hillsides, and I lost my sense of direction and got turned around. It took the rest of the crew two hours to find me, and they never let me forget it.

After finishing the Forest Service contract, our boss made a deal with Carl Shrum, the owner of the lumber company, to take over the logging operations, and we moved a few miles away to Camp #1 and spent the next couple of years at that location. At that time, his headquarters was in Buffalo at the present location of Buckingham Lumber Company.

If anybody wanted private living quarters at the camp, Shrum Lumber would furnish the materials for free. It was just native lumber and roll roofing for the roof but provided privacy for anyone that wanted to spend the time building one, and several married couples took advantage of the offer. Most of the single men slept in the bunkhouse, which was a long rambling building sitting on a little knoll overlooking the camp. It had a porch, running along the front of it where we used to gather after supper and discuss the day's events. All of the restrooms in camp were, of course, outdoor privies, and most of them had been built by one man.

His last name was Jelly–can't remember his first. If there was any opportunity to screw something up, he would find it. He was a tall, heavy set man, and all the privies he built were with him in mind–one size fits all. Anybody of lesser height had problems reaching the floor with his feet, and the seats had holes cut in them large enough to accommodate anyone up to

300 pounds.

One of the cabins below the bunkhouse was occupied by a man named Spears, whom we called Doc. His girlfriend lived with him, and they had a little boy about 5 years old named Arnie, who was the only child in camp and everybody's favorite. The whole area was surrounded by dense trees, and he was always running off, so his mother tied a bell on his bib overalls to keep track of him. It didn't take very long for him to figure out how to hold it to keep it from ringing, so she tied it in the middle of his back where he couldn't reach it.

One evening after supper, we were sitting on the bunkhouse deck, watching Arnie playing in front of his cabin several hundred feet away. All at once, he jumped up and made a run for the privy while trying to get his bib overalls unbuttoned on the way. We were laughing and making bets on whether he was going to make it in time or not. He got his pants down just as he reached the door, and when he flung it open, it stayed open, and we had a front row seat. The privy was one of Jelly's creations, and when Arnie finally made it to the top of the seat and got situated, he disappeared.

The comedy came to an abrupt halt, and all dozen or so of us made a run for the toilet. He would have smothered in the sewage in a minute or so even if we could have gotten him out in time, but he never made it that far. The hole was just the right size to catch him by the back of his head and his heels, and he was jammed in tight. He was scared to death and crying, and we had a helluva time prying him loose without hurting or dropping him.

§ § §

The cookhouse and dining room floor was wood and covered with linoleum. We all had spikes in our logger boots that would disintegrate a floor in a short period of time, so when we went in to eat, we took them off and slipped on a pair of slippers. All of us, that is, except Jelly. He had huge feet and would strap a board under each foot. It was like walking on a concrete floor with skis on and sounded the same.

His habits and ideas were a perfect match for his table manners. The cook, Mrs. Wilson, was cooking for a crew of 15 or 20 men on an old woodstove, and she always had pancakes, eggs and bacon for breakfast. To get a head start, she would start making hotcakes before she rang the breakfast bell and put them in the oven to keep them warm while she had more on the griddle. The plates were passed around the table from man to man, and everybody would take one cake and one egg while she caught up for everyone to have seconds–everybody, that is, except Jelly. When the plate reached him, the entire contents was scraped off onto his plate. Remarks by the rest of the crew passed completely over his head. I think

Mrs. Wilson was the one that got him off by himself and put it to him pointblank. Nobody in a logging camp ever wanted to get crosswise of the cook. Even the owners tiptoed around them. Loggers could be replaced on a moment's notice, but good cooks were hard to find, and nobody wanted to see Mrs. Wilson leave.

One day, when the wood's boss, Ray Canterbury, and I were scaling logs and working our way through the downed timber, we heard Jelly hollering at us. We finally located him in a thick patch of trees where he was trying to fall a huge spruce tree. He had cut completely around it with a crosscut saw, but it was perfectly balanced and wouldn't drop. When we reached him, he said, "Hey, Ray, which way do you think she's gonna go?" Ray replied, "I don't have the faintest idea, but I'm getting the hell out of here." Jelly took off with us, and the tree fell sometime during the night.

Loggers called the most dangerous trees widow makers, which were well-named. They were the ones that lodged in the top of surrounding trees when they fell. If a logger went underneath to cut it loose, it could collapse on him. Even experienced loggers sometimes took the chance and never lived long enough to take another one.

For wages, the loggers received $5 per 1,000 board-feet. The logs were scaled and measured to determine the pay. Forest Service personnel blazed each tree that had to be cut. Each logger had a strip several hundred feet wide that he worked in, and it ran from top to bottom of the mountain. They were side by side and eliminated a lot of the danger of somebody getting killed by a falling tree from one of his fellow loggers. Before the advent of chainsaws, we had a peak work force of over 30 men falling trees and cutting them into log lengths.

When Dick Greene's crew arrived, we were the only hourly help. He purchased a 4-foot two-man chainsaw–the first I had ever seen–and offered to drop the loggers' trees for them if they would take a 50¢ cut in their board-foot pay. They all agreed, and Ray Canterbury and I were the ones that cut the trees down. The saw really helped to increase production, but it was a miserable piece of equipment, and we spent a lot of time cranking on it to keep it running. We moved along the top of the strips knocking down trees as we went.

One early morning, we were dropping some trees for Wes Straight. It was on a steep hillside, and Ray and I had ahold of each end of the saw about 5 feet apart. Wes was standing directly behind us. We cut a big lodge pole pine, and when it started to fall, we stepped back from the stump and watched it go. It slid down the hill into the base of a tall, standing dead tree and flipped right back at us. We were looking directly into the rising sun and didn't see it coming.

It landed in the middle of the saw between Ray and me and slammed it to the ground. Wes was standing sideways, and it ripped the back of his jacket and tore off one of his logger boots without even breaking his leg. That was the closest any of us had ever come to getting killed, and it was a miracle it didn't happen to all three of us at the same moment. The saw blade was bent pretty badly, but we laid it on a flat stump and hammered it back into working order until we got a replacement.

Wes had a brother, Tom. They both had been working for Carl Shrum in the Hulett area. When he moved his operations to Buffalo in the 1940s, they came with him like most of his help did. They were both teamsters and skidded logs out of the woods with horses and stacked them in bunks. They were quiet hard-bitten men who had come up the hard way, minded their own business, and expected everyone else to do the same. They both had families living in Buffalo but had built a small cabin at the camp where they stayed and batched through the week.

At that period of time, poaching a deer or elk was a fairly common practice in the logging camps or anywhere else in the county for that matter. In the mindset of the loggers, it wasn't even considered a crime. They worked very hard to make a living. The meat cut the family's grocery bill in half, and the only consideration was don't get caught. Even that was a very unlikely proposition because there was only one game warden for the entire county.

One Saturday afternoon when everyone else had gone to town for their weekly shopping trips, Tom and Wes shot a deer. It was summertime, and they knew the meat would spoil quickly, so they dressed it out and hung it up in an adjoining shed to cool out overnight. Early the next morning, Sunday, they hauled it to Buffalo. On Monday, a game warden showed up in camp, but, of course, he didn't find anything. It was a first as far as anyone could remember.

Tom and Wes had been having some problems with the wife of a couple that also lived in a private cabin at the camp. They considered her a busybody who was always poking her nose into things that were none of her concern and figured the game warden's visit was too much of a coincidence to overlook. They thought she was the one that had turned them in.

One evening, the couple drove to Buffalo for groceries. The next morning when they fired up the cookstove, it smoked up their whole house. The guy got a ladder and crawled up on the roof to see what was wrong and found a deer hide stuffed in the chimney. I think his wife got the message.

§ § §

Ben Woods was one of the camp mechanics, and he and his wife lived in one of the private cabins. He had an old '36 or '37 Chevy pickup and overhauled the motor in his spare time on weekends and evenings. He finished the overhaul, and his wife took it to Ten Sleep the first time out of the shop. He told her to be sure and hold it under 35 miles an hour for the whole trip so the motor would be broken in properly, and she followed his instructions to the letter. When she left Ten Sleep and started for home, it was first gear all the way to Meadowlark, but she didn't quite get that far. To get to 35 in first gear, she had to wrap it up to top RPM, and it came apart halfway up the canyon.

He was one unhappy husband. I overheard part of the conversation between him and his wife. They were quite a ways apart. She was insisting she did exactly as he told her and held it under 35, and he was trying to point out that she should have had sense enough to know he didn't mean in first gear. I don't know if they ever got it settled or not.

§ § §

When Carl Shrum started Shrum Lumber Company in Buffalo, he bought several brand-new International trucks to haul logs off the mountain from his two camps in the Bighorns. Camp #1 was several miles east of Powder River Pass, and the #2 Bull Creek Camp was on the west side.

The trucks were all the same model and would leave Buffalo about daylight when they started up the mountain. Each of the drivers wanted to be first in line for loading logs when they got to our camp, so they raced on the way up. Since the trucks were all geared the same, the winner was usually the one that gained an advantage by shifting gears at the right time and forcing his competitor to eat the dust behind him. The mountain road was pretty narrow at that time period with no shoulders to help out if a driver goofed, and traffic was also light. Sometimes in the early morning, they wouldn't meet another car the whole way.

One morning, two of them were racing side by side when they rounded a curve and met their boss, Carl Shrum, headed for Buffalo. There wasn't any room left for him on the highway, so he had to leave the road to get out of the way. He bounced out through the trees before he got stopped and fortunately didn't do any major damage to his pickup. I don't remember anybody getting fired, but it cancelled the racing season for quite a while. Some of the drivers I remember were Wild Bill Holcomb, Red Wilson, Don Caywood, Cliff Slaybaugh, George Shrum, and Harold Mauck.

Harold had an experience with his truck one day when headed for the Bull Creek camp to pick up a load that neither he nor I ever forgot. He had lost the cap on the fuel tank and had shoved a rag in the opening to keep the diesel from splashing out. The truck exhaust stack was vented up the outside of the cab on the passenger side, and it passed by the fuel tank on the way up. The rag siphoned diesel fuel out of the tank, and the exhaust pipe set it on fire.

Fortunately, he was headed up a hill at the time and wasn't moving very fast, but when he leaned across the seat to open the door and try to smother the flames, he lost control, and the truck drifted off the road and landed on its passenger side. The fuel tank opening jammed into the dirt and put the fire out, but Harold didn't know that and thought he was going to be burned alive. He was standing on the inside of the passenger side door with the driver's door above his head, but it was so heavy he couldn't push it up far enough to get out of the truck. He finally got the window rolled down far enough so he could squeeze through the opening.

Since the truck was almost stopped when it landed on its side, damage was minimal, and the Bull Creek crew winched it and the trailer back on its feet. Harold was supposed to haul a load of lumber back to Buffalo from Bull Creek, but he was so shook up he knew it was a bad idea and headed for town with the empty trailer. When he passed our camp, he decided to piggyback the duallies for the trip home, so he pulled in for some help.

It was just past noon on a Saturday, and Doc Spears and I were the only ones left in camp. Our workweek ended at noon on Saturdays, the weekly paychecks were handed out, and everybody headed for Buffalo to get them cashed at the bars or grocery stores. It was the only time for the families to buy groceries for the coming week, and the single men were ready for their Saturday night party.

Harold was still shaking from the rollover and was as jittery as a cat on a hot tin roof. He asked me to ride to town with him to provide some moral support. I didn't want to, but said I would. I would have offered to drive but had never driven a truck that big before.

He needed a slight hill to back the duallies up to get them piggybacked, and there was one directly in front of the cook shack, so he backed up and set his brakes. Then he crawled out of the cab to the back of the truck platform to transfer the air hoses from the trailer brakes to the truck. I was standing at the rear of the trailer to break the connections when he said he was ready. He said go ahead, and I broke them, but he was so shook up, he hadn't turned all the valves, and the truck started rolling forward in slow motion like a Sherman tank out of gear. The motor wasn't even running, and it was dead quiet. Harold tried to get inside the cab before it hit the building, but it only had about 25 feet to go, and he didn't make it.

The entryway to the kitchen-dining room was three-sided with an opening in the center. It was 6 feet wide, the truck about eight, and the truck drilled it dead center and didn't stop until it hit the kitchen wall. The sides widened out, and broken boards came raining down and covered the hood.

All that was sticking out was the cab.

Doc Spears was in the dining room when it hit, and the vibration knocked him to his knees. He had no idea what had happened. The door was hinged to open to the inside, and when he finally got it open, the front of the truck was only inches in front of his face. I could see the International hood emblem poking out of the mess just level with the top of his head.

Harold was still standing on the running board, the door open, and one foot inside the cab. He was in shock, completely motionless, and resembled something carved out of marble. It was about the funniest thing I ever witnessed in my entire life, but because of Harold, I couldn't laugh. We finally got the trailer wheels piggybacked and headed for Buffalo. I faked it and kept up a chatter all the way to town, about 30 miles. I don't know who was more relieved when we got there.

The entryway was constructed of native lumber, and Doc cobbled it back together that weekend before anybody else showed up. The rollover provided an excuse for a few extra dings in the hood and cab, and nobody noticed some of them were on the wrong side. Harold knew he was in enough trouble already with the diesel tank fire and asked Doc and me not to mention the cook shack fiasco. I know I didn't–until now–and I don't think Doc did either.

There were literally hundreds of men that worked for Shrum in the Bighorns during the years he was in operation. A lot of them were drifters who were only interested in a few days' work to make a few dollars and then disappear. Just for the record, I can think of a few locals besides the ones already mentioned: Ray Phoenix, Lee Van Auken, John Steigleman, Jim Beydler, John Kovaleski, and Maurice and Cecil Huffman.

§ § §

Before conversion to natural gas in the 1940s and '50s, there were a number of coal mines in the Buffalo area, and a half dozen or so come to mind. All of them were slope mines except for the Wyoming Railroad Company mine just north of present-day Heritage Park on the stockyard road. It had a vertical shaft 12x16 feet and was a 150 feet deep. A steam-powered cage hoisted the men, mine mules, and one-ton cars of coal to the top, where it was dumped into a tipple.

Slope mines by contrast were much cheaper and easier to construct and maintain. The hand dug shaft began at the base of a hill and dropped on a steep grade until the seam of coal was reached. All of them could be walked up and down by the miners. The steeper ones had to be negotiated by hanging onto the roof supports. In the winter they collected ice and snow, and it was a problem just staying upright. Steam power was used to pull the loaded coal cars up the slope where it was dumped into the tipple.

When the Railroad Company mine flooded out and had to be abandoned, they purchased their coal from Jim Wertz, who had a mine four miles east of town on Highway 16. A sculptor, Mike Thomas, purchased the land in later years and built his studio directly over the mine slope. He had some problems after that when part of it caved in.

The Washut family had a mine in the Red Hills a mile or so northeast of this one that was purchased by Fred and Willie Kostenbauer in the early 1940s. I worked for them several years after getting out of the Army. There was also a mine on Kumor Road before reaching the Kumor ranch house. Another, owned by the Hotchkiss brothers, Tom and Dick, was a short distance northeast of the county fairgrounds. A rock house nearby was the first home of the Paul Goryl family when Paul moved to Buffalo from one of the Sheridan coal mines. He worked for the Hotchkiss brothers in the 1920s.

I doubt there are very many people who are aware there was a coal mine inside the city limits. It was at the east end of Foote Street and south of Clear Creek directly under the future home of John Buckingham. Rudy Pichlmaier dug the shaft but was flooded out shortly after reaching the coal vein and was never able to realize much income for his efforts. As a side note, he raised good crops of potatoes every year and allowed the neighbors to pick up the small ones when he finished harvesting. It was no small favor during the Depression years of the 1930s. At the time, he had the only house on the block.

Several years before I was born, my father opened the Gray coal mine and operated it through the team and wagon era. It was on TW Road several miles east of Buffalo. Coincidentally, some 40 years later, I was involved with the same mine only several hundred feet above it after it caught fire and smoldered for many years. I was working for the Highway Department engineers when Interstate 90 was constructed, and the new highway went directly over the top of it. We had to haul in tens of thousands of yards of material to smother the fire before the road could be built. I'm writing this almost 100 years after the mine was opened and sure hope the statute of limitations have expired for the Gray family as far as liability is concerned.

Writing about the old abandoned Railroad Company mine on the stockyards road brings back a lot of memories. It was one of my favorite haunts along with a number of other grade school boys who didn't let a 4-barbwire fence interfere with the best place in town to go exploring or play cops and robbers. Our parents had no idea of the hazards involved.

The buildings had deteriorated through the years, which increased their value as far as we boys were concerned except we had to be careful on the third-story floor tipple because some of the floorboards were missing. The vertical mine shaft was 150 feet deep and a favorite place to toss rocks in and count the seconds until they hit water. The mine was abandoned in the 1930s, but I know the shaft wasn't filled in until sometime after 1946 because when I got home from World War II, I went over and checked it out, and it still took several seconds for the rock to hit the water.

In later years, I worked for a surveyor, Bob Stuckert, who told me he and another kid were playing over there one day, and he decided to crawl down the ladder inside the shaft that had originally been placed there for the miners to get out in case of an emergency. He got down about 40 feet, the light was getting dim, and he ran out of rungs. It didn't take him long to get back up on solid ground.

They also found a box of dynamite caps but had no idea what they were or what they were used for. They heard the train coming up the tracks from Clearmont and lined several up on the tracks to see what would happen when the train flattened them out. Then they hid behind some sagebrush. Bob said there was a helluva explosion, the train came to a screeching halt, and the crew came piling out to find the problem. The boys knew they were in trouble if they were caught and worked their way through the brush until they were out of sight of the train and then hightailed it for home.

I used the term stockyard road previously and think it may need an explanation. Just a short distance past the Railroad Company's coal mine, it also had corrals for loading livestock and a concrete dipping vat that was filled with disinfectant for controlling scab and other livestock diseases. The concrete remnants are still in existence.

Prior to the arrival of the train in Buffalo in 1918, this road was the only one in town going to Clearmont and Gillette and is presently designated as County Road 8. It branched off from South Main Street at East Parmalee Street, turned left at the Heritage Park entrance, and intersected TW Road in the vicinity of the present-day Buffalo sewage plant. From there it continued down Clear Creek to Clearmont. This route eliminated the need for bridges over French Creek and Clear Creek.

East Parmalee Street was originally a narrow wagon road when it left South Main on an angle, and houses sprang up close to the road on both sides. It was too late to straighten and widen it when the Highway Department built present-day Highway 16, Hart Street, in the 1920s because the adjoining streets and houses were already along it.

§ § §

I hauled coal for Fred and Willie Kostenbauer's mine for three winters after getting out of the Army. Customers were charged $1.60 a ton for delivery, and I received half of what the truck made. More was charged for out-of-town loads. The daily average was approximately 15 tons, which amounted to about $12. All of it had to be shoveled off the truck with a scoop shovel. The hourly day was determined by how long it took to make the deliveries. The truck capacity was about five tons, and most of the customers only ordered a ton or a ton and a half at a time, so dividers had to be put in between the three loads. Each one was weighed separately, which used up a lot of time. To load the coal, there were sliding metal doors to pull open after driving under the tipple, where the different sizes of coal had been separated.

Each coal house in town was a different experience. Some of them were difficult to get to, and no two doors were the same distance off the ground, so unloading in some cases was very difficult to say the least. The one I disliked the most was on Carrington Avenue where Ray Canterbury lived. It had to be piled in the basement after maneuvering down two flights of stairs, carrying the coal in a peach basket. They were made of wood, had wire handles, and it took at least two, sometimes three, to outlast the load. We had offered to hammer a hole in his basement wall directly over the coal bin for nothing, but he was considering switching over to natural gas and wouldn't let us do it. His coal bin held about three tons, and we charged him $3.50 a ton for delivery. I sure hated to see him order.

When the bins in the tipple got too full, sometimes the extra weight would force the loading gate open and dump 10 tons of coal on the ground, which had to be moved with a scoop shovel. A customer, Dave Elsom, was loading his half-ton Chevy pickup once when the door blasted open and buried it with fine stoker coal clear to the top of the cab. It took a couple hours to get the gate shut and uncover his pickup. The rear tires were mashed to the rims, but we were lucky they didn't blow out. He was one unhappy customer and bought his coal in Sheridan after that, if I remember correctly, even though it was a lot higher price and farther to haul it.

§ § §

If I had to make a list of undesirable occupations, a coal miner would be at or near the top. The first two trips inside a coal mine were memorable with the first taking place when I was 14 years old. My brother-in-law, Willie "Bill" Kostenbauer, quit school before he finished the eighth grade when he went to work in a coal mine and stayed in the same line of work until natural gas closed all the mines around the Buffalo area in the 1950s. In 1938, he was working in a mine owned by Jim Wertz four miles northeast of Buffalo on Highway 16. He, my sister, Beulah, and their son,

Lynn, were living in a house trailer at the mine site.

I was visiting them one evening when he said he had to go back down into the mine to mate a shot and asked me if I wanted to tag along. A shot was when the miners would blow the coal seam apart with dynamite so it could be loaded in small cars and pulled to the surface.

It was prepared by drilling a 6 foot long 2 inch in diameter hole into the coal vein with a handheld auger. A stick of dynamite with a long fuse attached was then pushed into the hole with a wood ramrod–a metal one could produce sparks if it hit a rock–and the rest of the hole was plugged with cylinders of dirt so the full force of the explosion would be contained back in the coal seam. The cylinders were formed by wrapping old newspapers around the ramrod to mold them and then filling them with dirt. There was a tremendous amount of coal dust generated by the explosion, so the shots were set off the night before to give dust a chance to settle. None of the miners wore respirators at that period of time, and some of them died from black lung disease as a result.

At the entrance to the mine, he could only find one carbide lamp that was working, so I had to walk close by his side to keep from stumbling over something in the dark. The lamp was attached to his miner's helmet. When we reached the shot hole location, I watched him drill the hole, push the dynamite in with the fuse attached, and plug the rest of the hole with the dirt cylinders. The fuse had about 4 or 5 feet extending out from under the mine debris. When he reached down to light the fuse with his lamp, it ignited and also blew the light out. We were instantly immersed in darkness so thick it felt like it could be cut with a knife and is difficult to describe. I heard him cuss and a couple sparks flickered for an instant as he tried to restart his lamp, but it wouldn't relight, and the glowing end of the fuse disappeared under the mine tailings.

I was standing within 6 feet of him when the light went out and heard him say, "Grab hold of my belt," but I was so scared and disoriented I couldn't tell which direction his voice was coming from. I said, "Where are you?" The next instant he grabbed my arm and put my hand in the middle of his back on his belt. I hung on. He bent over and grabbed one of the little coal car rails and piggybacked us out the way we had come in. Nothing I can think of could have torn me loose from that belt.

It seemed like an eternity when he said, "I think we're far enough." We stopped, and a few seconds later there was a muffled thump, and the ground vibrated. It took me several minutes to stop shaking. He finally got the lamp working, and we walked back out to daylight. I vowed it would be the last time I ever went underground, but 10 years later when he and his brother had a mine of their own, I did it again.

It happened the winter after getting out of the Army, and they offered me a job hauling coal. Under no circumstances would I have agreed to work underground. Willie worked as a miner and his brother, Fred, who was my boss, was in charge of the business on the outside of the mine, including waiting on customers and hoisting the loaded cars up the slope to the tipple.

One day, I drove into the yard and had to talk with him about something, but he was nowhere to be found, so I knew he was down in the mine. No carbide lamp was available, so I had to settle for a flashlight with weak batteries, figuring they would last long enough to find him.

To save the batteries, I walked down the slope into the tunnel before using the flashlight. After turning it on, it was so dim I had to get between the coal car rails about 4 feet and bend over just a couple of feet above the ground. I knew I had to hurry and was walking so fast I was almost running when I rammed my head into something soft and came to an abrupt halt. I was enveloped in something that felt like thick cobwebs and had a horrible smell. My heart stopped and blood turned to ice. The odor came from reprocessed hay. The cobwebs were a tail because I had rammed my head into the hind end of a horse that was standing in the middle of the tracks.

His name was Joe, and he pulled the loaded cars to the foot of the slope, where Fred hoisted them up out of the mine. He was almost blind and probably at least 25 years old and had spent his entire life working underground. He heard me coming long before I ever reached him. If he hadn't been dead gentle, he would have kicked me clear out of the mine. That was the second time I vowed never again to go underground, and this time was for real.

§ § §

When my brother-in-law, Willie Kostenbauer, still worked at the Wertz mine, Jim's son, Oscar, worked on the outside waiting on customers and dumping the coal cars in the tipple after he had hoisted them up the slope. The cars carried about a ton of coal apiece. and their end gates were hinged on top. When they reached the end of the track on the tipple, a curved piece of rail would tip them up at a steep angle, and the bottom of the door would flip open to let the coal slide out.

If a chunk was too big, it would hang up on the top of the end gate and jam up the whole load. The only way to clear it was to sledgehammer the chunk to bits and pry the rest of the load out with a crowbar. This was a lot of hard work, and Oscar griped about it continually to the miners.

One day, when they dynamited a section of the coal seam, a huge piece was loosened but stayed attached to the ceiling. Just for a joke, they built tracks under it, backed a car in, pried it off the ceiling, and sent it up to

Oscar. It was a full load. He was furious, of course, because it took him several hours to break it up and get it out of the car. But he didn't blow up at the miners because he wanted to find out how they loaded it, but they never did tell him.

§ § §

The Wyoming Railroad Company that operated between Buffalo and Clearmont from 1918 through the 1940s was one of our customers at the Kostenbauer mine before the train went bankrupt and was abandoned. All of their locomotives burned coal. Their tipple was located about a block north of the depot near the west end of the footbridge on present-day Centennial Trail on Lobban Avenue. I hauled the last two loads it used before it went broke.

They had barely enough money to operate from week to week during their last few years and had accumulated a lot of debts. When I hauled their last loads, my boss, Fred Kostenbauer, told me to go to the their office at the depot and collect the money before unloading. C.C. Palmer was behind the counter when I walked in, and he emptied the till to pay me. A full load at the time was less than $25, and he paid me off in coins, none of which were larger than a 50¢ piece. Unlike the present, this was in the days when a silver dollar was a lot more common than paper ones.

Several times prior to this, they ran out of steam between the two towns and would walk to the closest ranch and phone for a load. If they were stalled at a place where we couldn't back the truck up to the engine, we would get as close as we could, and the engineer and fireman would help us pack sacks of coal to get enough steam built up to get to the parked truck.

The railroad was a big part of our family's life for the almost 30 years that it existed. We lived directly across Clear Creek to the northeast of the depot, which was the end of the line. We had moved there in 1929, the year before I started first grade. Our family, eight children, walked across the tracks all through grade and high school. Mother put the fear of the Lord in all of us as far as the train was concerned. We were never allowed to cross the tracks, all two of them, by ourselves until reaching the fourth or fifth grade. She had read somewhere, sometime, somehow, someone caught a foot in the rails when the train arrived. Our imaginations finished the story. The fact that it made only one trip a day was immaterial.

The track passed within a few feet of the end of the footbridge over Clear Creek. Our written in stone instructions were to stop and check both directions before leaving the bridge even though the end of the tracks at the depot was only a stone's throw to the south. The footbridge at that time was several hundred feet upstream from the present one. The old abutments are still in place, which brings to mind her admonitions whenever I pass by.

Incidentally, the footbridge was a great viewing point in the spring flood days when the railroad ties were being floated down the creek from the Bighorn Mountains. Tie hacks with long poles had to clear the log jams by jumping from one tie to another, and it required a lot of skill with no room for error. The ties were collected and loaded on the train at the tie boom, where the present south bypass bridge is located.

One of the engineers on the train was Ray Canterbury, whom I worked with many years later in a logging camp in the Bighorns. We were talking over old-times one day, and I mentioned how us kids would be standing on the edge of the footbridge, waiting for the train to pass so we could cross the tracks when steam would come blasting out of the engine right in front of us. It wasn't dangerous, but we didn't know that, and it was a scary experience. Ray laughed and said he did it on purpose just to see us back up.

He also mentioned something else. He said if a silver dollar had been placed in front of the engine driver wheels, the train couldn't get over it without backing up a few inches and taking a run at it. I don't know what a silver dollar would have resembled because I didn't have one, but do remember what a copper penny looked like after several wheels had passed over Mr. Lincoln's portrait because us kids did it.

Vern Rubottom worked for the Railroad Company probably longer than anyone else. We were both employed by the Highway Department many years later, and he told me a number of stories about it. He said many times the train would stop to deliver a package to a local farmer or rancher waiting along the tracks. One time, a rancher had to send a tire to Buffalo for repair. It was off an old Model T Ford that had the iron ring still attached to the inside rim and was very heavy. The conductor was standing on the steps of the last car so he could step off and pick it up when the train stopped. The train slowed down, but the rancher could see it wasn't going to get stopped in time, so he held the tire up shoulder high, and the conductor hooked his arm through it as they passed. He dang near got his arm torn off. Vern said when he first went to work for the outfit, there were 16 gates to open between Clearmont and Buffalo.

Another time, one of the train financiers had his car stuck in the mud alongside of the tracks when the train went by. When they saw who it was, they backed up, hooked a rope around the bumper, and eased him out of the mud.

One man, Charles Fieldgrove, was a school bus driver and put flanged wheels on his Dodge truck so he could run it up and down the tracks. He left it parked on the tracks all night and picked up the school kids early in the morning before the train started running. He made the same arrangements for the afternoon run. Then he drove it onto some kind of swiveled sled to get it turned around for the morning pickup. He must have been a really inventive guy, plus having the political pull, to talk the Railroad brass into cooperating.

John Miller told me his dad, Lige, had a dragline and did a lot of dirt work for the Railroad. Onetime, he took John with him to pick up rocks while he was working. He was parked in the middle of the tracks with the dragline, scooping up dirt and swinging the bucket back and forth to dump it. With the motor being on one side and blocking his view, he could only see one way. John said the train came up on his dad's blind side and coasted to a stop a couple hundred feet behind him. It sat there for a couple of minutes before the engineer blew the whistle to get his attention. John said his dad almost had a stroke.

Lige was one of many that the Railroad owed money to in its last days. It amounted to several thousand dollars, and he was the first to file a claim against it. It declared bankruptcy, and he finally got his money, but he told John the lawyer fees amounted to more than he received.

The railroad had a lot of critics through the years, but it served the community in many ways until changing times and bad management put it to rest. It had quite a few nicknames, and I remember a few: Galloping Ghost, Duffy's Bluff, CB&Q (Clearmont Buffalo and Quit) CB&BM (Clearmont Buffalo and Back Maybe).

§ § §

Writing about tie hacks and the footbridge brings another story to mind but not a very pleasant one. As I mentioned previously, we moved to Bozeman Avenue south of Clear Creek in 1929 and had to cross the old swinging footbridge to get to town or school. I was 5 years old.

The bridge was suspended by two cables stretched across the creek with the deck planks hanging down from them. It was pretty tricky to walk across because the whole thing swayed from side to side, and you had to keep ahold of the cables just to stay upright. The deck was narrow with nothing on the sides.

In May of that year, the creek was bank high with flood waters, and two eight-year-old boys, Arthur "Babe" Stevenson and Kenneth McHenry, started across the bridge on their scooters. Babe fell off, and Kenny was so frightened and in shock that he ran home, huddled in a chair, but didn't tell anyone what had happened. That night someone knocked on our backdoor. When Mother answered it, there were three men standing outside wanting to know if she had seen Babe. It was raining, and I can still remember seeing the drops of water dripping off their hat brims. It's odd how something so insignificant can be imprinted on a person's brain for the rest of their life.

After Kenny was finally able to tell what happened, the men in town searched the banks of the creek for the rest of the night. Babe's father, John Stevenson, was the one who finally found his son's body sometime after midnight, where it had been caught in the log jam at the tie boom.

It seemed to be kind of a hard-luck family. In 1950, Babe's uncle, Jesse Stevenson, was working for the Wyoming Highway Department. Less than a week after he was hired, Troy Pate, Paul Goryl and Jesse were working in the Bighorns in late April, clearing snowdrifts with a big rotary plow near Powder River Pass. Troy was operating the rotary. The shoulder of the road was marked with 6-foot poles, and the vertical banks of snow had frozen into ice. The plow was having trouble cutting the bank, so Paul and Jesse were breaking off the ice in front of it.

Anybody that has ever worked around a rotary plow knows that it creates a blizzard of snow with visibility reduced to zero at times, plus it has the earsplitting noise of a freight train. Troy was operating the plow and saw Jesse walk to the rear of the machine but didn't see him walk back in front to work on the ice bank and remove the pole markers ahead of the plow. No one knew exactly what happened next. The motor lugged down, and Troy thought it had picked up one of the poles, but instead it had pulled Jesse halfway up into the augers, and he was killed almost instantly.

In those days, they didn't have radios in the equipment, so Troy ran towards an old party line telephone at a sawmill a couple miles away to call for help. Part way there, a local man, Jay Coates, picked him up and hauled him the rest of the way. The patrolman, Jim Ward, who investigated the accident, told me Troy sat in the backseat of the patrol car all the way to Buffalo without saying a single word. He was in total shock. I went to work for the Highway Department shortly after this, and Troy was my boss for several years, but he never mentioned the accident to me or any other member of the crew that I was aware of.

§ § §

In the fall of 1949, I got a job with the U.S. Bureau of Reclamation, and it didn't take very long to figure out it was another government agency that didn't expect an employee to overexert himself. It was an era when both the Bureau and the Corps of Engineers got into the dam building routine at the same time and built many dams that should never have been constructed. Future years would prove just how unnecessary some of them were, but politics overruled common sense as usual. I think it's ironic that at the present time some of these structures are being torn down by the same government agencies that built them.

The crew I went to work for was surveying a dam site on the Middle Fork of Powder River above Kaycee, one of a number that had the preliminary survey completed but was never built. We were quartered at the Harlan Ranch, and the owners, Jim and Joann Harlan, had a contract with the Bureau to furnish our meals. There were over a dozen of us. I'll try to list the ones I remember just for the record. We were all under the Billings, Montana, office jurisdiction, but about half of us lived in Wyoming.

Earl Wick (Billings supervisor), Dodd Walker (party chief), Walt Hushbeck, Tony Mauro, Tito Padilla, Bryce Rumph, Kenny Tate and his buddy Speed, John Hoback, Willie Perschillo, Frank Bretzel, and three Weischedel brothers, Ted, Tudie and Jake. This list does not include the drilling crew that was there prior to the surveyors.

Jim and Jo Harlan were a young couple fresh out of college back East and brand-new to the West and ranching industry. Jim died some years ago, but Jo still resides at the ranch although her three sons have taken over its management. I see her infrequently, and we share a laugh over some of the incidents that took place while the survey crew was staying there–mainly over her role as cook for over a dozen men when she had absolutely no previous experience in even cooking for herself. She said she took the job for one reason only. She and Jim were flat broke and needed the money to pay ranch expenses. During the late winter, we moved to Kaycee and stayed there long enough to finish the Middle Fork project.

The next summer was spent surveying a reservoir site at Willow Park in the Bighorn Mountains. There wasn't anything but a horse trail into the area at the time, so a couple of the higher paid personnel in Billings figured they could find a better route and drove a vehicle in. They put cat heads on the front wheels of a little Jeep, which were nothing more than foot-long drums to snub ropes around when it got too steep. The idea may have sounded great, sitting at a coffee table in Billings, but in actual practice it was a complete washout. Another guy and I were picked to handle the ropes, mainly because I had been on several horseback fishing trips into Willow Park when I was a kid and knew what to expect when we got there.

When we came to a place too steep to climb, we would tie one end of the rope to a tree as far uphill as the rope would reach and holding on to the loose end, wrap the rope around the cat head while the driver tried to pull the hill. With one of us on each side of the Jeep, theoretically, we would have enough mechanical advantage to help boost the Jeep to the top of the hill, but theory and practicality weren't on the same page. It was supposed to work like a winch. Why they didn't just put a winch on the Jeep before we left Sheridan, I never figured out. It took us all day to get to Willow Park and back to the foot of the mountain, and they called for a tow truck. The Jeep was badly damaged. I don't know if they even bothered to get it repaired because we never saw it again.

§ § §

Jimmy Huggins from Story had a pack string of horses and contracted with the Bureau to pack our gear into Willow Park for the reservoir survey. Jerry Johns was his helper. They packed several large quad tents, stoves, cots, sleeping bags, groceries, and surveying equipment while the crew walked along behind the procession. It turned into quite an operation.

We were there all summer. Since our workweek ended at noon on Saturday, we would walk and run to the closest road which was at Horton's Dude Ranch and have somebody pick us up and haul us into Buffalo. Then we had to walk back to Willow Park on Sunday afternoon. Some of the guys lived in Billings. To stretch the weekend out, they would drive to the Buffalo airport early Monday morning and hire a plane to drop them off at Penrose Park. Even then, they still had a four-mile hike before breakfast to get to our camp at Willow Park.

The outfitter ordinarily brought supplies in about once a week. Several of the guys liked to have a drink before supper, so they would sometimes order a bottle of liquor. Invariably on those days, the pack train was always late, and the packers would come riding into camp about midnight under the influence and report that one of the pack horses had blown up at the forks and broken a bottle. It was always just one and at the forks, which was a place where two trails intersected and riders would stop and rest their horses for a short time and adjust the packs on the pack string. If two of our guys had ordered the same brand of liquor, it was a problem figuring out whose bottle got broken.

Because we were batching all summer, at times it was difficult getting clothes repaired. We always took our repairable along with our laundry when we took off for Horton's on Saturday afternoon and packed clean ones back in. We instituted a rule that stated if we got a hole or rip in any of our clothes, the guy had 24 hours to either change clothes or repair the hole. The penalty for not doing so granted all other members of the crew the right to stick his finger in the hole and rip it wide open if they so desired.

One day, I noticed a small hole had appeared in my pants leg right at the knee. I bunched it up, tied a string around it, and called it repaired. There was quite a discussion over my interpretation of the word, but I insisted the hole wasn't showing and that's all that counted. Actually, I felt pretty smug about thinking up the technicality, but I could tell some of the others weren't too convinced and would be watching the knee hole very closely for the next few days and with good reason. The hole kept fraying out, and I had to keep bunching it up and tying it until the bottom of the pant leg was level with my knee cap.

One afternoon, we were working about a half mile from camp when the string caught in a branch and the whole pant leg came apart. Somebody noticed it right away, and even though I screamed the rules guaranteed a 24-hour grace period, they ripped my pants off the belt loops and tore my shorts, shirt and hat off for good measure. I was stark naked except for a belt and shoes and had a half mile to go to get back to camp for more clothes. Horton's had a summer dude cabin along the way, and there was always a dozen or so people fishing or just wandering around, so I had to sneak through the timber like a coyote looking for a rabbit. Nobody reported seeing a naked idiot wandering around, and I never tried patching a hole with string again–rules or no rules.

§ § §

The three Weischedel brothers were good friends of mine, and we ribbed each other about everything and all things. They had been raised on a ranch out in the boonies near Recluse, which was about as far as you could get from civilization in all of Campbell County. They worked hard and played hard at everything they did. We had six-man squad tents set up to sleep in, and they all bunked in the same one.

One evening, they were over in our tent shooting the bull, and one of them said something smartass, and I told him if he didn't shut up, I'd throw all three of them out. He lipped back and said there weren't enough men in all of Johnson County to throw one Weischedel out of our tent much less three. All six of us jumped him, and his two brothers entered the scuffle to help him out–what a mess!

It was a big revolving body of nine men, and our only goal was to get them out of our tent. We weaved over one cot and smashed it flat with one of our group on the bottom. He decided he had enough right then, but it was still five against three in our favor. Our tent floor was about 4 feet above ground level with steep steps to go down. We got them pushed to the front of the tent and rolled through the tent flap and down the stairs in one mass, but one of them grabbed the leg of the stove and took it with us. The chimney came apart, and the stove turned upside down. It was full of ashes and completely covered all of us and the inside of the tent. They helped us clean up the mess, and we had quite a debate over who won, but I'm still not quite sure.

We didn't finish the survey that summer, so we were told to pile all the stoves, kitchen equipment and other junk in one quad tent and put the others over the top of it for use the next summer. The snow collapsed the tents that winter and ruined most of the contents. There were a couple of cabins nearby, and the owners received permission to take what they could use. The rest of the contents eventually rusted and rotted away because we never went back to finish the survey.

We were all transferred to the Sheridan office, but a couple months after we got there, I quit the outfit. Shortly after that, the Eisenhower administration went on a cost cutting binge, slashing the Bureau's budget, and every single one of our survey crew was fired. It was the end of the dam building era.

Our summer work at Willow Park wasn't entirely wasted. A few years later, a group of local ranchers got together with the Forest Service and received the financing to build the reservoir themselves. Their surveyors made good use of the work we had already done.

§ § §

Sundown (John) Taffner was Chief of Police in Buffalo for a number of years, and he told me several stories about his tenure. He was a big, easy-going man with a great sense of humor and was generally well-liked in the community. He was extremely strong, and most people that broke the law knew better than to argue with him, and the ones that didn't soon learned. He was always relied upon at the local Fair and Rodeo for his expertise in the wild horse and relay races, where brute strength and guts were the main requirements for getting a rider away from the starting point in the fastest possible time. His specialty was earing the horse by the head to hold him immobile until the rider was on board and headed in the right direction around the racetrack while in the midst of another dozen horses and riders doing the same thing. It was a great place to be if one was considering a one-way trip to the county hospital.

At that period of time, Buffalo didn't have the funds to maintain a large police force around the clock, so Sundown had to work his share of regular and off-duty hours like the rest of the men. The jail was small, and the cells only had a few bunks, so a couple of cots were set up in the hall to handle the extra drunks on Saturday nights. They were seldom fined and were turned loose on Sunday morning after they had sobered up unless they had been in a fight and barroom fixtures had been destroyed.

There was a little Mexican sheepherder called Shorty, Refugio Aliquin, who came to town at times to spend his money in the local bars. He never caused any problems, but one Saturday night he got drunk and started pestering the other customers by butting into their individual groups and making a nuisance of himself. The bartender told him several times to back off and leave them alone, but a short time later Shorty would be back.

Along in the wee hours of the morning, the bartender called Sundown and got him out of bed to come down and get Shorty to take him to jail for the rest of the night to sleep it off. The cell bunks were full, so Sundown handcuffed him to a cot to hold him until morning, and then he went home and back to bed. About an hour later, the bartender woke him up again and said that Shorty was back still chained to a piece of his cot.

Another time, Sundown was called to the 21 Club to handle a disturbance involving Merle Dunham, a local cowboy. Sundown was about 5 feet 10 but built like a lead brick and weighed over 200 pounds–all of it muscle. Merle was built the same way but about a head taller and 50 pounds heavier. He was pretty drunk, and Sundown had quite a time getting him to the jailhouse, cajoling and half carrying him, but he finally made it. He got the jail door open and was trying to back Merle through it when Merle grabbed ahold of the bars at both sides of the door and hung on. Sundown couldn't pry his hands loose, so he backed up a few feet, lowered his head, and hit Merle head-on just above the belt buckle. Merle was flattened out against the far wall, and by the time he got to his feet, Sundown had the jail door closed and locked. Understandably, Merle was quite upset.

Sundown hadn't been on the police force very long and later told Edie, his wife, that it was touch and go all the way from the bar to the jail, but he had an incentive to finish the job by himself without waiting for backup. Buffalo had a lot of rough and tumble cowboys, oilfield workers and lumber jacks, who liked to mix it up at the slightest provocation. Sundown figured if he could handle a man like Merle by himself, it would hopefully send a message to the rest of the Saturday night partiers to think twice before they challenged him–kind of like an insurance policy–and from what I remember, it must have worked.

I remember another herder who had a few problems when he got to town. His first name was Walt. I can't remember his last. He was bald as a jaybird on top of his head, but had real dark hair around the fringes and above his ears. He made a toupee out of a piece of bear hide to cover the bald spot on top, but it hadn't been tanned too well and wasn't very flexible, so it didn't stick like it was supposed to. He was very careful about it when he was sober, but when he got drunk, the thing would slide sideways over one ear. I don't imagine his fair-weather friends ever called his attention to it because he probably paid for all the drinks until his money ran out.

Skimmy Horn and Mons Kartvedt were a couple more characters I remember. Skimmy's real name was Vernon Schermerhorn, but I never knew it until after he died. He had worked for most of the sheep men in the county at one time or another and was usually available if a rancher needed help on a short-term basis. He and Mons became good friends as they grew older and spent a lot of time together. Mons had a herd of sheep at one time and had rented various places to pasture them through the years. I'm not sure if he ever owned a place of his own. He was very vocal when he and Skimmy were having a beer together. Skimmy seldom did much talking and just grinned as Mons was elaborating on a subject. Mons always had a pipe gripped between his teeth and preceded everything he said by holding his clenched fist above his head and starting the sentence with "We the people." He would talk as long as anybody would listen to him, who was usually Skimmy. When he quit the sheep business, he moved his sheep wagon to the city park and lived there for several years before he died.

§ § §

Most of the sheepherders in the County were young Basque men from Spain and France. Usually, a friend or relative in Johnson County would sponsor their entry into the United States by agreeing to provide employment for a specified length of time, which, I think, was usually three years. None of them could speak English. After arriving they would spend practically all their time in a sheep wagon miles from town in an environment they were completely unfamiliar with. With the exception of their employer and his family plus neighboring Basque sheep men, usually the only interaction they had with other people was a two or three week vacation in Buffalo after the fall work was completed. It was a very lonely existence for a young man in his early 20s.

Some of my classmates in the second American generation couldn't speak English when we started first grade together but were fully Americanized by the time we graduated from high school. With a few exceptions, this was when they started marrying outside of their own culture. One of my brothers-in-law, Joe Bilbao, was bilingual and helped many of my schoolmate's parents by translating between the two languages and explaining incomprehensible day-to-day interactions.

Quite a number of young Basque herders took their pay out in sheep and after a few years would partner with another in getting their own outfit put together quite often with the help of their former employer, and the cycle would start over. Several times in these cases, I witnessed the fulfillment of the old prophecy–shirtsleeves to shirtsleeves–in three generations. The first generation makes it, the second generation spends it, and the third generation starts over. It happened in the sheep industry in

Johnson County. Some of the first immigrants built up huge land holdings containing tens of thousands of acres by starting out herding sheep and sacrificing comfort for hard work A couple of decades later, their children had squandered it all and were broke.

I herded sheep myself for several years for the sole purpose of trying to get a start in the business but never once considered making it a lifetime occupation. I remember some that did. Their personalities fit the loneliness and lack of social activity that was required. They would spend the entire year by themselves and blow all of their income on a two- or three-week spending binge in town and be glad to get back to the only life they were comfortable with. It was difficult for others, including myself, to understand.

The bar owners in town were always glad to see them walk through the door. Some of the herders knew they would be broke when they left town two or three weeks later, so they would cash their check, a full year's wages, at the bar and have the bartender put the cash in their safe to be drawn out as they needed it. Some of them would be drunk the whole time, and a dishonest bartender would speed things up by telling them they had bought a lot of drinks on the house and subtract it from the cash in the safe. The herder either couldn't remember or prove anything different, so he was stuck. The odd thing about it is that he would repeat the same routine the following year.

I always thought it was odd that as a profession, a sheepherder was looked upon as occupying the lowest rung on the ladder, yet he was entrusted with the task of managing his employer's assets worth tens of thousands of dollars. He was further required to accomplish this by being on duty 24 hours a day on a minimal salary collected once a year. It was kind of a puzzler and about as hard to figure out as the bumper sticker on my pickup–"Be a Sheepherder 2nd Oldest Profession."

§ § §

City Hall was originally located where the city parking lot on north Main Street is at the present time. The Idlewild Cafe was connected to it on the south. In the 1980s, the City demolished the hall and purchased the cafe building for the present-day City Hall. The old building was two stories with a dance floor taking up the entire second story. It was accessed by stairs coming up from Main Street, but on dance nights the main entrance was on the north which was level with the outside yard over to the Courthouse. The City Jail was on the west end against the bank, and the Firehall was sandwiched in between.

Civil rights lawsuits were unheard of in those days, and sometimes the local police got pretty rough with some of the inmates who were mostly drunks. I knew one chief of police who had the reputation of dealing with uncooperative prisoners by shoving their heads down into a toilet. I didn't doubt the story because I was well-acquainted with the man and his personality.

A good friend of mine, John Miller, told me his dad, Lige, would temporarily take over the police duties when one of the regulars was sick or on vacation. On his first stint, he noticed something peculiar about how the hinges had been installed on the cell doors. They were pins that turned inside iron brackets. The proper way was to reverse the top pin, but these were both placed with the pin pointing up. If a prisoner had wanted to escape from the locked cell door, all he had to do was lift it up a couple inches and swing it open. Evidently, they never had any prisoners bright enough to figure it out because nobody had ever escaped from it that I remember.

After World War II in the latter half of the 1940s, the City Hall dances were well-attended. One reason was because automobile manufacturers hadn't caught up with the post war demand yet, and very few returning GIs owned an automobile that would have enabled them to attend an out-of-town dance. Alcohol wasn't allowed inside the hall, but it was only a couple minutes' walk to one of the local bars. The orchestra always took an hour break at midnight, and sometimes lunches were served. Usually, a couple of cafes stayed open until 1:00 or 2:00 in the morning also.

One Saturday night, a group of my friends and their dates had gathered at one end of the dancehall after the supper break and were waiting for the music to start the second half. One of my closest, lifelong friends, Walt Hushbeck, had a date with a local girl, Marilyn Francis. They had left the dancehall shortly before, and during the interval he had proposed to her.

When they came back in, she was flashing a large diamond engagement ring for any and all to see. We all crowded around the pair and were noisily offering our congratulations when an acquaintance of Walt's walked over to our group with his date to see what was going on. We didn't know them, and neither did Marilyn. When Walt introduced them to his new fiancée, he was so flustered he forgot her name. The whole group erupted with laughter. Under different circumstances I might have felt sorry for him but not then. Marrying someone when you can't even remember their name is something your best friends never let you forget.

§ § §

The first brand-new car I ever purchased was a 1949 Buick. It was also the first new vehicle I had seen sitting in a dealer's showroom since the

Japanese had bombed Pearl Harbor eight years before. When that happened, all factories in the United States immediately ceased production of civilian automobiles and trucks and converted their facilities into producing products directly connected to the war effort. When World War II ended and civilian production started again, the federal government put price controls on all new vehicles, and dealers were prohibited by law from pricing their vehicles above that amount. Buying and selling on the black market began immediately, and it took several years for the automobile manufacturers to catch up with demand.

All dealers had a buyer's list of customers that supposedly took turns in purchasing a new vehicle as they became available. Many people had their name added to the list of every car dealer in town regardless of make or model of car. The only way to get to the top of the list was paying the dealer in cash above the government mandated price. That amount was dictated by how badly you wanted the car. I had been waiting for three years and was driving a 1947 Ford coupe, purchased from a brother-in-law, Lee Duncan, who had bought a new Ford a year earlier. He was a good friend of the local Ford dealer, Charlie Hankins, who had elevated him to the top of the new car list.

Driving by the Buick garage, Riley Motor Company in Sheridan, one day, I spotted a new car sitting in their showroom and swung in to take a closer look. It was a real beauty. A jet black, two-door Super torpedo body with lots of chrome and the new automatic transmission called Dynaflow drive. I think it was the first model year when the round holes appeared on each side just below the hood. It had three, and its big brother, the Roadmaster, had four. This one cost $2,900, and I drove it home.

In those days, a new motor had to be broken in gradually to get it properly seated. The car manual spelled it all out–35 miles per hour for the first 500 miles with short 10 second bursts of speed up to 50. The next 500 was a little faster and so on until the motor was ready for high sustained speeds. Any deviation from this procedure could mean a blown up motor or an oil burner for the rest of the life of the car. With the biggest investment of my life, I sure wasn't going to do anything that might void the warranty. George Uroszek was the salesman handling the sale, and he was very explicit in explaining the break-in period. By following his instructions to the letter, there were never any problems.

I drove it to a dance at Lodore in Story that night and was so upbeat about the new car, I helped them close the place up about daylight. The highway at that time was very narrow with no shoulders whatsoever, and the sweet clover grew right to the edge of the asphalt. It was at least 5 feet high and all headed out. Air conditioning didn't exist at the time, and I had all the windows rolled down because it had been a hot day. Having 35 miles per hour welded to my brain, I hugged the lane and clipped off sweet clover seeds all the way home. The next morning it took a vacuum cleaner to get them off the rear seats. The first day of new car ownership turned out to be quite an experience, and it didn't end there.

About a week later, I called a girl, Jean Brug, who I had been trying to make points with and got a date to the drive-in theater in Sheridan, hoping the new Buick would be a plus in making a lasting impression. It did but not in the way I could have possibly imagined.

When we got to the drive-in, it was a chilly evening, so I hung the speaker on the inside of my window and rolled it up. When the movie was over, wanting to show her what a cool dude she was dating by being the first car through the exit gate, I slammed it in drive and blasted forward. Only, I had forgotten to unhook the speaker, and it rolled out the window to the outside of the car, where the danged thing flopped on the ground without even breaking the cord. The window was a new type of laminated safety glass, and it showered us with a million pieces of tiny glass particles.

Cars were big in those days, and being a two-door, it had a huge bucket seat on her side, but she wasn't sitting in it. We were both on my side, and I could feel her shoulder shaking and thought she had been hurt by flying glass and was crying. It finally sunk in that she was trying to muffle her laughter. Shock, humiliation and embarrassment are tough pills to swallow, especially when they're all hooked together. It was a long ride home at 35 miles per hour with the window flopping against the outside of the door. I think it would have been a great topic for conversation if we had tried it.

A few days later, the car had to be returned to Sheridan to have the window replaced, and I dreaded the thought of facing the salesman who had handled the sale. I couldn't think of a logical reason for how it had happened and sure wasn't going to tell him the truth. As it turned out, it wasn't necessary. After driving it into the garage with the window hanging down on the outside of the door, he said, "What in the hell did you do to that window? Throw a beer bottle through it without bothering to open it?" I said, "Yeah."

It was a little different situation a few months later when a friend, Carl Johnson, asked if he could borrow the car to double date with a guy named Vernon Hunter. Carl was taking Helen Gibson, a girl he eventually married. The Lodore in Story and a nearby nightclub, Pop Kelly's, were the popular dancehalls at the time. I had planned on driving out there myself that Saturday and knew of other guys that would be going, so it wouldn't be difficult to hitch a ride.

The next Saturday afternoon, he walked down to the house to pick up the car. We were discussing the dance when I asked him who Vernon was taking. He didn't really seem to want to answer, so I put it to him pointblank. It was Jean Brug, the gal I was trying to impress at the drive-in a few months earlier that had ended in disaster, but we had been on several dates since, and things were looking a little better. I had called her a few days earlier, but she said she was already committed for the coming Saturday night.

The irony of the situation was hard to miss. I had trapped myself in the ludicrous position of providing free transportation to a guy cutting in on my territory who didn't have a car of his own. Carl admitted it was a bad situation but claimed he didn't know who Vernon's date was until a few days before and it was too late to change anything now, which was true. I wanted to keep a close eye on Vernon and could think of only one way to do it, so I told him, "Okay, you can have the car, but I'm going with you," and I did.

The evening was an episode straight out of the old TV sitcom *Happy Days*. It was the weirdest most bizarre double date plus one that I was ever uninvited to and would take a week to describe in detail. When we got back to Buffalo in the wee hours on Sunday morning, Carl delivered everyone to their respective homes, and I got behind the wheel when he reached his. On the way home, the whole evening replayed over and over in my mind. It had been a night to remember and no part of it was ever forgotten.

§ § §

The Buick was a dream to drive. It was so big and heavy it floated over the rough spots in the road, but the gas mileage was terrible–something like less than 10 miles to the gallon. The Dynaflow drive was the first car I'd ever driven that had an automatic transmission, and it was okay in moderate weather, but below zero brought it to a standstill. Living five or six blocks from Main Street, on very cold days the motor would be revved up to the maximum RPM, and the car would be creeping along at three or four miles per hour. Not having a garage, it was impossible to start in very cold weather without jumper cables.

Once, I did something really stupid and took it deer hunting. I had just purchased a new gun, and it had a telescopic sight–the first I'd ever owned with a scope on it. After driving out in the Red Hills and sighting it in, common sense was overruled by poor judgment, and I went hunting. It was late afternoon and having hunted the area many times before, I parked the car on a dirt road and took off on a fast walk to a draw less than a mile away. It had a spring coming out of a side hill and was a good hangout for mule deer.

I shot a 3 point buck and after dressing it out, started dragging it towards the car. It was tough going, and daylight was fading fast, but there was also something else to think about. The area had a well-deserved reputation for rattlesnakes, and the thought of stepping on one in the dark wasn't very comforting. The September day had been unseasonably warm, and the buck wouldn't have cooled out properly if left overnight, so I took off on a run to get the car. The sagebrush was high, and the headlights didn't show up the rocks very well. After hitting some of them with the under carriage, that buck deer turned out to be the most expensive piece of venison I ever ate after paying for the car repairs.

That hunting episode brings to mind another one that was just as dumb if not dumber. I was walking up a draw and jumped a bunch of deer with a small buck in the group. They ran around the base of a hill without stopping long enough to get a shot at. The top of the hill resembled a big anthill, cone shaped, and came to a point on top.

Running up to the top and flopping down on my stomach just before cresting the peak and being skylighted, I laid the gun flat on the ground and pushed

Fred Gray hunting

the barrel over the top by holding onto the stock. Rising up very slowly, I could see the deer standing a short distance ahead looking back expecting to see something come barreling around the bottom of the hill after them.

There was no way to hold the gun properly and get the stock supported in the crook of my shoulder without exposing myself, so I curled my head over the top of the scope, sighted on the buck, and pulled the trigger. The recoil slammed the eyepiece back into my eye and knocked me unconscious. I have no idea for how long.

It was a miracle the eye wasn't permanently damaged because it took several weeks to heal. It was small consolation to find the buck lying where he had fallen. I sure regretted ever getting mixed up with that bunch of deer, but I suppose all the anti-hunting groups in the country would have been ecstatic if they had heard about it–perhaps even to the point of making me their poster child of the year.

§ § §

Our kids from oldest to youngest were Carrie, Stephen, Robin, Anthony, and Randy. We lived on Bozeman Avenue, the part south of Clear Creek, from 1954 to 1960 before buying Trailside in the Bighorn Mountains eight miles west of Buffalo, where they finished growing up. Our neighborhood was pretty isolated from the rest of town due to Clear Creek on the west side, a large steep hill on the east, and only one road entering it from Main Street on the south which dead ended on the north.

There were few organized recreational facilities for children in those days besides the swimming pool and playground in the city park, so their activities were pretty well limited to the neighborhood and the kids living there. Clear Creek was the main attraction and was safe to play in after the high water had receded in late June. They spent endless days building dams to catch fish, only going home when they got hungry and then back to the creek. The steep hill to the east was perfect for sledding in the winter.

Buffalo Flour Mill
1973

Directly west of our house across the creek was the old Buffalo Flour Mill, which had been built in the 1880s. After it ceased operations, a number of other businesses had moved in and out. At one time, it furnished all of the electricity and water for the entire town and was a magnet for a lot of kids to explore due to its conglomeration of old decrepit buildings. In the 1950s, it was being rented by the Claude Isenberger family that owned the John Deere Implement Company. They had a shop on the ground floor building at the south end, and their equipment filled the rest of the property, which extended a block and a half north to Foote Street.

I was working for the Wyoming Highway Department at the time and one day received a phone call from Mr. Isenberger, who told me he had been visited by our two youngest boys, Anthony & Randy. They had removed all the valve cores from the rubber-tired equipment because they had been fascinated by the sound of air rushing out of the tires.

My brain froze while trying to think of some kind of apology, but all that was on my mind was pumping up 30 or 40 large implement tires with a hand pump. Claude was real nice over the phone and ended the conversation by saying he had a large compressor and would take care of airing the tires back up but would appreciate it if we kept a little closer eye on the two boys. I assured him we sure would.

On the north end of the John Deere lot was an old two-story house that Buffalo Federal Savings & Loan had foreclosed on but couldn't find a buyer, so it sat deserted for several years. They hadn't even bothered to lock the doors, and kids in the area used it for a playhouse more or less. It had steep narrow stairs going to the upper floor with a sharp turn at the top and bottom.

Coming up with the idea of maybe fixing it up and reselling it, I got permission from the bank and looked it over. They didn't want much money for it and probably would have dropped the price even further, but after seeing it, I wasn't interested at any price. After starting up the stairs, I had a heck of a time crawling over a sofa that someone had tried to move from one of the upstairs rooms and had it stuck in the stairwell. Many years later, I was visiting with Anthony, my son, and found out who that someone was, but he insisted that as near as he could remember, it was all his younger brother's idea.

§ § §

One spring, someone gave my wife several bum lambs that she raised in a little pasture along the creek in back of the house. We had a little shed she locked them in at night because the dogs that roamed around town would have killed them. There were also a few bales of hay and some grain stored in it. One day, when Robin was about 5 or 6 years old, he took some matches out of the house and was experimenting with them in the lamb barn. The hay really burned well until the fire department arrived and put it out. The barn was damaged but still useable. The one good thing that came out of it was that it scared him so bad he never forgot or tried it again.

This kind of thing seemed like it was turning into a family tradition. Carrie and Stephen had some neighborhood kids, the Sturdevants, they were friends with that lived in the same block. Directly in back of their house across the alley, a man named Charlie Lusher had an old shed he used at various times for his horses. One day, the kids were in the barn with the two Sturdevants and got to arguing about just how flammable the hay was, and it didn't take them very long to find out. A neighbor, Bob Stuckert, and I were visiting on our lawn when a fire engine came screaming down the road. We saw the smoke and thought it was coming from Bob's house, so we made a run for it, but it was too late to do any good, and the barn was a total loss.

I was devastated because even though it wasn't much of a structure, it had a value and would have to be paid for. Carrie and Stephen hadn't gotten over the shock of the fire and could barely speak. When they were told they were going to have a face-to-face talk with Mr. Lusher that evening, I don't remember them speaking for the rest of the day just thinking about it. Dreading to see him was almost as bad as the fire.

I took them up to his house that evening, and they were like two statues as he very gently gave them a little lecture about the danger of playing with matches. When he finished, they apologized, and I told them to go out and wait in the car. It sure didn't have to be said twice. I asked Charlie about the damages, and he said it was just an old shed he hardly ever used, so there was no point in replacing it. I was just as eager to get out of that room as the kids were.

§ § §

Charlie had a brother, John, who had some vacant acreage along Clear Creek just southwest of the bypass bridge. He was in the dirt moving business and used it for storing his equipment. Among the items was an old army surplus Jeep, and he always left the key in the ignition. Many years later, I found out that is where Carrie and Stephen first started driving along with all the rest of the kids in that part of town even though it was around and around in a big circle. As they became more proficient, they even used reverse and backed around in the opposite direction.

One day, two of them, Lane Vanderhoef and Lyle Niswender, took a canoe belonging to John on a trip down Clear Creek when it was in flood stage. They hadn't thought far enough ahead about how they were going to get it back, but as it turned out, it didn't make any difference. On the way down, they hit a tree that was leaning out over the water and capsized. The water temperature wasn't much above freezing, and it was a miracle they both survived. Their parents never heard about the incident until 20 years later.

They weren't the only ones left in the dark about some of the things their kids were involved in during the growing up years. I found out about one after reading about it in the "Fifty Years Ago" column in the *Buffalo Bulletin*.

The article was about two children playing along Clear Creek who had found a case of dynamite, but it didn't mention their names. I thought the story was interesting and showed it to Robin, who said he remembered it well because he and a friend, Alan Hubbell, were the ones that found it and for some reason had neglected to mention it to me or his mother. He wasn't quite 10 years old at the time.

He said they didn't know what it was but had a little past experience with firecrackers. The sticks resembled big ones with no fuse, so they figured it would make a heck of a noise when it exploded. Just to be on the safe side, they threw several of the sticks across the creek that landed on some rocks, but nothing happened.

Alan's father, Charles, found out about it and reported it to the police, so the sheriff, Lawrence Francis, came down and picked it up. He hauled it outside of town and split the case up into several separate parcels. Then he backed off a considerable distance and detonated them with a rifle. The boys were right. It did make a heck of a noise.

I remember another shooting incident concerning the Sheriff's Department that happened about the same time. One of the deputies was in a room demonstrating a quickdraw with his revolver when he shot himself in the foot. Luckily, it was only a minor injury, and the main damage was to his self-esteem. The official version was somewhat different than the one that made the rounds of the coffee shops, but nobody believed it anyway.

§ § §

In 1953, we were renting an apartment on High Street in south Buffalo. It had originally been the Freeman Hospital and was owned and operated by Nora Freeman, but when she and Dr. W.J. Knebel married, they converted it into rental apartments, two apartments upstairs and two down. My wife and I were renting the one on the south ground floor, and a young couple with no children, Glen and Kathleen Means, were renting the north one. Their kitchen window looked out upon the backyard of the local game warden, Bob Frison, who had the reputation of being a tough, by-the-book law enforcement officer.

We were in the sheep business at the time and had leased a summer pasture in the Bighorns that was owned by the local sheriff, Harry Eschrich. His property was located on Poison Creek between Highway 16 and Hazleton. The county road ran through the middle of it. I was working for the Wyoming Highway Department at the time and had hired a sheepherder, Manuel Cuevas, to herd, and I tended camp on weekends to deliver groceries and whatever else he needed.

We had two children at the time. Carrie was 5, and Stephen was a year younger. He would usually accompany me on the trips to sheep camp. He was always ready to go on a moment's notice and asked innumerable questions about everything under the sun, which he remembered down to the last detail. This gift was responsible for one of the most heart-stopping moments of my life and is imprinted on my brain till death do us part.

I was having some serious financial difficulties at the time. The sheep industry had hit rock bottom during the preceding few years, and we were trying to muddle through having borrowed a lot of money trying to keep our heads above water. I spent every waking moment worrying about it.

It was in early June, and we had the first band of sheep to arrive on the mountain for the summer grazing season, so there was hardly any traffic on the county road. Stephen and I had just dropped off the supplies for the herder and started back to town when we caught sight of a small herd of elk grazing on the north end of the range. To me, it was several hundred dollars' worth of meat on the hoof. I always kept a rifle in the pickup in case we saw any coyotes, so I asked Stephen if he would like to go hunting Indians. To this very day, I don't know why I said Indian instead of elk but will be forever thankful for doing it.

He was very excited at the prospect. We had to go off the road in a roundabout way to get to some timber that would cover our approach to the herd. Then we threaded our way through the trees before getting close enough to get a shot at one of the yearlings. It sounded like a cannon going off, and I regretted it the instant the trigger was pulled because if there had been a game warden within five miles of us, he would have heard it.

I'd never dressed out an elk as fast as that one and cut off the head and feet to reduce the weight. Loading a whole elk, even a yearling, into the back of a pickup alone would have been nearly impossible under normal circumstances, but the adrenalin kicked in, and I horsed it in. Through it all, Stephen kept up an incessant line of chatter because he was so excited.

My brother-in-law, Willie Kostenbauer, and his brother, Fred, operated a coal mine four miles northeast of Buffalo in the Red Hills. When we hunted deer out there, we always dragged the carcass several hundred feet down from the mine's entrance to where the coal seam started and hung it up. We called it the slope. The bottom was a perfect place to hang wild game because it was dark and cool, devoid of flies in hot weather, and never got below freezing when it was cold. So that's where we headed with the elk.

Since the adrenalin was still on high, there was no problem dragging it down the slope, hanging it up, and skinning it before heading back to town. I was feeling a lot more relaxed, but the thought of living next door to a game warden had never left my mind. There were already enough problems trying to pay the grocery bill, and a fine for killing an elk out of season would have been the kicker at the bottom of the list.

After getting home from work the next evening, Kathleen and Glen invited us over for a drink before supper. As I mentioned before, her kitchen sink window overlooked the warden's, Bob Frison's, backyard and flower garden, which he worked in constantly during his off-duty hours. Carrie and Stephen were usually standing along the fence watching and pestering him with questions.

I was settled back on the couch relaxing with a beer in my hand, when Kathleen mentioned she had been washing dishes that afternoon with the window open and heard Stephen telling the game warden about his dad shooting an Indian, cutting his head and feet off, skinning him, and hanging the body down in a coal mine.

I froze and couldn't even speak for a few moments. I tried to smile and as casually as possible under the circumstances asked her what Frison did. She just laughed and said he went on clipping his hedge saying, "Yeah, yeah," not paying any attention to Stephen's fantastic story.

The rest of that beer was forced down in tiny sips to keep from choking, and I made up an excuse to get out of the apartment. Driving straight down to the mine, I hauled the elk to a garage at a friend's house and cut it up, wrapped it, and put it in the freezer. It took until long after midnight to finish the job, and I sure slept sound after that.

§ § §

That same year while we were still renting the apartment from Dr. Knebel, I applied for a civil service job with the Post Office. The regulations at the time specified that the applicant had undergone a physical by one of their certified doctors. Dr. W.J. Knebel was retired at the time, and his son, Dr. John Knebel, had taken over his dad's practice. The clinic was on South Main Street across the street from the present-day American National Bank.

Even though he was retired at the time, Dr. W.J. Knebel was still the only physician in town that the Postal Department recognized for giving the examination, so I phoned him and got an appointment. He said the clinic closed during the noon hour and to meet him there because we would have the whole place to ourselves. At the time, there were only two doctors, his son and Dr. Tom Nicholas, a nurse, and receptionist. My wife had worked there as the receptionist before we were married, and the nurse, Isabelle Samakee, was a good friend of hers. Isabelle was a super nice person to be around and had a great personality. A few years later she married a young man, Vernon Hunter, but it did not turn out well.

Dr. W.J. Knebel was a good doctor with an excellent reputation and had been practicing in Buffalo many years before I was even born. In fact, he was the first person to lay eyes on me when I first saw the light of day. He had a good bedside manner, talked in sort of a gruff voice, and carried on a constant one-sided conversation unless he asked a patient a direct question. He was a very comfortable person to be around who joked a lot in a dry humor sort of way.

He started the exam at noon but spent so much time telling stories the physical took a lot longer than it should have, and it was getting close to the time when the office personnel would be showing up. The examination room wasn't locked, and this was one patient who didn't want to be half dressed if someone came barging in. When we finished, he said he hadn't had a blood pressure test in a long time, and since he had just given me one, it was only fair that I should return the favor.

I tried to stammer my way out of it, but he didn't pay any attention and sat down in the same chair I had just vacated. Then he rolled up his sleeve and started giving instructions on how to use the cuff. It was terribly embarrassing, and I was all thumbs trying to get the damned thing on right when the door opened and Isabelle walked in. He never missed a beat and told her we were busy, not through with the office yet, and didn't want to be disturbed.

Noticing the doctor-patient scenario, she tried to muffle her laughter but didn't do a very good job–just smiled with gritted teeth, backed out of the room, and closed the door while Dr. Knebel started over again with the instructions.

His son, Dr. John, was cut from the same material as his dad as far as a sense of humor was concerned. One time, I had gone to the hospital to visit a friend but didn't know what room he was in. I was walking very slowly along the hallway, looking in the open doors trying to spot him when somebody came up from behind and said, "If you don't get out of here, I'm gonna give you an enema." It was Dr. John.

§ § §

We started building our first house at 196 Bozeman Avenue in Buffalo in 1954, and it was a rather unusual situation the way we acquired the lots. Actually, the property was a full half block bordered on the west by Clear Creek. It was empty in the 1940s and hadn't had a legal owner since the town was laid out in the late 1880s, I suppose because of its location next to the creek and vulnerability to flooding plus the availability of a lot more desirable building locations in the rest of town.

Since the block didn't belong to anyone, and nobody was paying taxes on it, we had to establish squatter's rights by utilizing it. Not having enough money to build anything on it, the cheapest way was to put a fence all the way around the perimeter. While we couldn't stop anyone else from using it like we were, they would have to gain access without using our fence or gate, which was considered private property.

I went out to the city dump and picked up some old woven wire and built the fence with a gate in it. Then I bought a milk cow, named her Sally, and started the process of gaining title to the parcel. Anybody else could have done the same thing with a horse or cow if they could have figured out a way to get it over the top of the fence without opening the gate. That would probably have been a little tricky. After that, we paid the back taxes for the past five years, about $2 a year, and advertised in the *Buffalo Bulletin* that we were applying for a deed from the City. If anybody had contested the application, we would have had to go to court. If that had come to pass, we were one up on anybody else because we could prove we were using it, but nobody did, and the City issued a title. It was quite a learning experience.

It didn't take long to find out the learning experience was in its infancy. In the preceding years, I had spent almost three years in the Army, worked at a variety of jobs after getting discharged, gotten married, started a family, and had just gone broke in the sheep business. I'd heard it said many times before, "Cheer up. Things could be worse," so I cheered up, and sure enough, things got worse. Now, all that was left was build a house to cover the family and not much money to do it with.

I was working for the State Highway Department at the time, earning a $1.25 an hour, hauling tanker loads of hot oil from Casper during the night. I'd leave Buffalo about 6:00 p.m., drive to Casper and load, get back home about 2:00 a.m., catch a few hours of sleep, and start pounding nails. A lot of coffee and NoDoz pills were swallowed on the way home.

The house was 24x34 feet with a full basement, and half of that was a garage. Eight hundred and sixteen square feet for five kids, a wife and myself about the size of some kitchens by today's standards. A couple years later, the garage was remodeled into bedrooms for the kids.

Plywood wasn't in common use because of the expense, so do-it-yourselfers used native lumber that came from local sawmills. It didn't have the quality of shipped-in West Coast lumber and took more time to work with, so it was a tradeoff–less money for more time spent using it. I formed the basement walls with 1x8 inch boards. It took a while, but whiles were a lot cheaper than cash at that period of time.

For gravel to pour the concrete basement walls, I borrowed a truck and hauled pit run gravel from the bottom of Bull Creek six miles south of town. It was clean, and a lot of people used it. The site was owned by the Shambaugh family that allowed local people to haul what they needed with no charge. Any holes left from digging would be filled back in by a flood or spring runoff, so the supply was inexhaustible.

The borrowed truck didn't have a dump box, so the gravel had to be shoveled on by hand and unloaded the same way, then handled a third time when it was pitched into the cement mixer. I think some of it was worn out just handling it.

One of my brothers-in-law, Lee Duncan, had a little tractor with a bucket on it, so I mixed the mud in a rented mixer, dumped it in the bucket, and he worked his way around the forms. My oldest sister, Beulah, tapped the forms with a hammer to settle the mix. It took us all day, but we did a good job. We poured the floor later, and I got to practice the art of finishing concrete that came in handy for the next umpteen decades.

Needing a stringer to span the full 34-foot length of the basement to set the subfloor on, I came up with sort of a weird idea that fluctuated between a brainstorm and stupidity from start to finish, but after starting there was no choice but to keep going.

The old Wyoming Railroad that operated between Buffalo and Clearmont for so long had gone bust a few years before, and the rails had been sold for scrap and hauled out of the country. During that time, the railroad right-of-way had been returned to the various ranches it had passed through, and the owners had leveled the berm and started farming it again. The Bolinger Ranch five miles northeast of Buffalo, originally Redman's, had built an irrigation ditch over the tracks in the meantime. The berm was about 8 feet high, and there were two 30-foot connected sections of rail that the salvage crew had to leave because they couldn't tear the ditch out. I traded the landowner, Jeff Bolinger, some short pieces of rail he needed for a cattleguard and got a friend who had a cutting torch to help me get what I wanted. We tunneled under the ditch embankment, measured off 34 feet, and cut it with the torch. Then we slid it on a two-wheeled pole trailer and hauled it to town.

Getting the thing across the full length of the basement and supported was a whole new ballgame, and it took some doing. Several come-a-longs, some 4-inch pipe for support, and a lot of careful sliding got it in place, but it was a little difficult to pound nails in. I never did get that one figured out. Thirty years later, I did the same thing to my house on North Burritt during a remodeling job. I suppose these may be the only two homes in Buffalo that used part of our old railroad in their construction that are guaranteed termite proof.

We had planned on building with native logs, so before getting the subfloor finished, I contacted Andy Hanson, who sold house logs from his sawmill in the Bighorns. I wasn't acquainted with him at the time, but have never met anyone any nicer or more dependable. He furnished us with logs, credit and good advice. It took most of the summer to get the log walls up, and we had mostly run out of building funds, so I had a visit with Bob Holt at First National Bank.

Bob said the bank's rules required a roof before they could loan any money. He didn't have any choice or leeway about that. Then, he very casually mentioned he didn't interpret the rules to mean the house had to have windows, doors or anything else in place–just the roof. He said if we could get that done, to come back and see him. We already had the log walls up, so with some help from Andy with the rafters and sheathing, we got the roof on, and Bob loaned us the money to finish the house.

However, money wasn't the only problem we encountered. Since this was the first house I had ever attempted to build, there were constant goof-ups, and the first major one was the ductwork for the furnace.

Ray Wallace had a sheet metal shop on Lobban Avenue directly west and across the street from the old Railroad Depot. Before the sub-floor was built and when the basement was still wide open, he had taken some measurements to give us some cost estimates for what the furnace installation might be. He had drawn up a rough sketch of what the interior rooms would ultimately be because the only plans I had were in my head. We lucked out twice in a row because he was just as helpful as Andy Hanson had been.

The standard distance between floor joists was 16 inches, but wanting to be sure the floor was good and solid, I put them on 12. The fact that the joists were native lumber and extra thick decreased the distance even more.

Instead of a 14-inch space between the joists, there was only nine, and the floor would have supported a bulldozer. In all the weeks it took to build it, the thought that something just might not fit had never entered my mind. When Ray showed up with a pickup load of tin ductwork he had already fabricated, it was fortunate he possessed a good steady heartbeat.

Anyway, he hauled it all back to his shop and made something that fit and never brought the subject up again. He did a lot of work for us in succeeding years, but I noticed he always made sure he saw exactly what he getting into before he did any measuring or fabricating.

§ § §

Another man I became well acquainted with while building the house was Art Greenleaf. He had an aggressive personality and a rather abrasive manner of speaking but was willing to try almost anything to make a living. I don't remember anything about his family, but he must have had several children because of something he said about his housebuilding experiences.

In those days, it was difficult to get financing to build a home, and lots of guys like Art and myself had no choice but to try it themselves if they had a family to support. Small homes were the only option and almost always involved adding on rooms as their family expanded. This often ended up being a hodgepodge of a house with problems that could have been avoided if it had been constructed all in one piece at the same time.

Art and I were discussing this drawback one day when he said if he had it to do over again, he would buy a big lot and start building bedrooms at the front and keep adding more as his family expanded. He said it as sort of a halfway joke, but it had a lot of truth wrapped up in it.

At the time I became acquainted with him, he owned a large piece of property on Fetterman Street a block west of present-day DJ's grocery store. Fetterman, as a street, may have existed on paper at the time, but it was only a dirt road that wasn't even connected all the way through. The whole area from the city shop (at that time it was the Wyoming Highway Department) to the west was mostly alkali and greasewood with pockets of solid rocks that had once been the bottom of Clear Creek. There were a few ramshackle buildings scattered out in a haphazard manner throughout the whole area. I remember one house that belonged to the family of a junk dealer who bought hides and metal. I sold him some deer hides, and when I followed him into the house to get paid, there were chickens standing on the kitchen table.

Art had a sawmill on his property and a few years later added a Redi-mix concrete batch plant. I bought some 2x8-inch planks from him, but the box on my pickup was too short to haul them, so he said I could use his 30-year-old Model T Ford truck. I was a little leery about using it and asked him if he was sure I could make it to the house with them, and he said he could but didn't know about me. That was a lot to swallow, but for once I kept my mouth shut because there weren't any other options. Since I was afraid someone I knew might see me driving the thing, I used it one early morning before the town traffic picked up.

The Model T had an 8-foot bed, and when we finally got the planks loaded, they extended 8 feet over the end of the truck bed. After starting for the highway, the front end didn't have enough weight on it and was hard to steer because the front wheels were mostly riding on air. Even Art could see there was going to be a problem when I started up the rise to get on the highway, so he walked alongside until we got there. When I started up, the front wheels came clear up off the ground, so he jumped on the front bumper, and it added just enough weight to get on the road. If there had been any possible way to back out of the deal, it would have been right then, but it was too late.

To get to the house, I had to go all the way down Fort Street to Main, turn right at the stop sign, then drive to the south side of Clear Creek bridge, then turn left, and follow the creek for six or seven blocks. At two miles an hour it took a while. If that load had shifted a few inches to the rear, I would have been stalled on the road with the end of the planks resting on the ground and the front wheels 3 feet off the gravel because the road hadn't even been surfaced yet. After unloading the truck and returning it to Art, it was several years before we had any more business transactions, and that involved his concrete operation.

He had purchased an old concrete batch truck and was the first one in Buffalo to do so. A few years later when the interstate highway construction got in gear, Al Reeves bought him out and built a new batch plant on the east edge of Buffalo that is still operating under different owners. I have often wondered why Reeves Concrete even bothered to purchase Art's equipment because it was mostly junk, and they had to have state-of-the-art equipment to keep up with the demand that happened almost overnight. The 70 mile stretch of I-90 between Buffalo and Gillette was a top priority in the State with multiple contracts and hundreds of workers on the job all at the same time.

When we built our house, we put a double garage underneath the main floor, which required driving down an incline to get into. It was probably one of the most stupid ideas I ever had. As our family expanded, we had to have more room, and the most logical thing to do was plug the garage doors and remodel it into living quarters. After tearing out the doors and getting forms built, I went up to talk to Art about the delivery of the concrete.

I was working five days a week with Saturday off and losing a day's wages through the week was something I couldn't hack, and he didn't like to work Saturdays. Plus the Johnson County Fair and Rodeo parade was being held at 10:00 a.m. the next Saturday morning when I wanted to pour. He said under no circumstances was he going to miss that. Finally convincing him it would be a simple pour and he could get the load off in less than an hour, he agreed to show up with the truckload of mix at 7:00 a.m., but he didn't bother to drive down to look at the forms, and that was a huge mistake.

During our conversation, I asked–or thought I'd asked–how far up he could reach with his chute, and he heard–or thought he'd heard–how far out, so when he showed up with the concrete, the top of the forms were at about 7 feet, and the truck was on an incline which made matters worse. There was no way we could unload the concrete, and he went ballistic.

In the initial seconds it took for the shock to wear off, I realized there were eight cubic yards of concrete that was going to be dumped over a bank somewhere, and I was going to pay for it. My mind was racing while he was raving. He finally shut up long enough for me to say something.

The forms were built with 1x8-inch boards. We could take one of them out on our side as far up as he could reach with the chute and fill the forms with concrete, then dump the rest of the load in my old pickup. After replacing the form board, I could shovel it over the top of the forms by hand, so that's what we did.

When he emptied the last of the concrete in the pickup, it flattened the rear tires clear to the rims, but by some kind of miracle they didn't blow out. Standing up in the middle of the concrete, I shoveled as fast as I could because it was a hot day and it was starting to set up. My legs were covered with the wet mixture clear up to my knees, and I found out later just how toxic it was when my legs swelled up and the skin peeled off. Infection set in, and it took several months for them to heal. All in all, it was another lesson learned the hard way and one that was never forgotten.

§ § §

Another building experience that stuck with me was when we installed the sewer, water and gas lines. Basically, the entire neighborhood had been the old Clear Creek channel many hundreds of years before and was almost all rock with boulders ranging up to 4 feet in diameter. There was barely enough dirt to backfill over the pipes to protect them after they were installed. To make matters worse, when the road was surfaced with asphalt in later years, they had to fill in more dirt over the main lines to make it level. We hired John Terry to do all the plumbing in the house. He brought his backhoe for the outside work. He had to dig 12 feet or more before he finally found the sewer line, and it was solid rock the whole way.

About 10 years later, we sold the house to Steve Nuckolls. Whenever he ran into something that was boxed in or underground, he would give me a call. In the summer of 2010, he started having trouble with tree roots plugging up his sewer line, so I went down and showed him where it was.

One day, I received a call from Ron's Plumbing, owned by Ron Hepker, saying they had something they thought I might be interested in seeing. When I walked in, Ron handed me a memo and a page torn out of a notebook that looked like it had been buried at one time or another. The memo, dated September 1, 2010, stated that Steve Nuckolls had called and said tree roots were plugging up his sewer line, so Ron sent Mike Betz down to dig it out with a backhoe.

Later, Mike said when he got down a couple of feet, he uncovered an old drive shaft that someone had placed over the line to mark its location. When he lifted it up, a bottle fell out with the following note inside:

Sewer line laid on June 1, 1954, by John Terry.
Gas line laid on June 2, 1954.
Sewer line lies directly below this old drive shaft 10 feet down.
I hope to hell I never have to dig this damn thing out ever again.
Fred K. Gray, June 2, 1954

Mike was later overheard making a statement to the effect that the job took twice as long as expected because some idiot had stacked the pipes on top of each other in the same trench.

Leon Rich (left) & Fred Gray (right) – 1972

Highway Crew – Fred Gray, Henry Bauer, Bob Herzog, Charlie Kershner, Lyle "Ozzie" Osborn

PART V

Highway Department Work

Beginning in the early 1950s, I was employed by the Wyoming Highway Department in Buffalo for the following 33 years before retiring in the mid-1980s. I worked for the Maintenance Department for the first few years before transferring over to the Engineering Division. During that time, we either built or rebuilt every single foot of State and Federal highways in Johnson County, plus helping crews in Crook, Campbell, Sheridan, Big Horn, and Washakie Counties. We also participated in the construction or updating of county roads and the rebuilding of State secondary highways, for example, the Kaycee-Sussex and Kaycee-Barnum roads. During the peak years of Interstates 25 and 90 construction, there were literally dozens of separate contracts being worked on at the same time. Our engineering personnel numbered about 80 people. Hundreds of workers employed by the contractors were a huge boost to the local economy.

President Eisenhower was in office and responsible for kickstarting the interstate highway system. When I first heard about a divided highway, I didn't have the faintest idea what one looked like but soon found out. If memory serves me correctly, our governor at the time was Joe Hickey, who was a stout opponent of the idea and wasn't bashful about saying so. He maintained they were overkill for states like Wyoming and promoted a two-lane system with a passing lane in the middle. Subsequent events, like head-on collisions, proved they were about as close to being a guaranteed route to suicide as one could get.

Our survey parties consisted of six persons and our equipment, such as transits, measuring chains, etc. Strange as it may seem, with basically minor improvements it was probably about the same that George Washington used when he started his surveying career. When I retired, we were still using drafting tables, hand-cranked calculators, typewriters, and hand signals because the walkie-talkies of that era were just making their appearance and weren't very effective. With the introduction of computers, satellites and other modern equipment, the vast majority of surveyors today have no more idea how to use a transit or slide rule than I do a smartphone, and by the time anyone reads this, they will probably be relics too.

Before I retired, one of my crew members was a young man named Larry Herzog. He stayed and made a career with the Highway Department and as of this writing is still there. They rebuilt Hart Street on Highway 16 in Buffalo in 2009 and 2010. It was a congested mess for the entire two years due to rebuilding the road while maintaining traffic at the same time to keep all the businesses going, mainly motels and fast foods places. He told me at times when his crew was working in amongst all the contractor's equipment and tourist traffic, the noise was so bad their radios were worthless. For communication he had to teach his crew hand signals that we and surveyors 100 years before us had used–sort of a back to the future situation.

After the battle between Buffalo and Sheridan over the location of I-90 from Gillette had been decided, the State Highway Department and Bureau of Public Roads poured all the money available into finishing it because none of the road could be utilized until it was completed. Most of the Wyoming interstates were built in eight or 10 mile segments, if possible, and then tied into the old existing roadway until the next section was constructed.

In the construction of I-90, we built both dirt roadways, including bridges and overpasses, on east and westbound lanes and then surfaced the eastbound lane and used it for two-way traffic. It was several years later before the westbound lane was paved. The eastbound lane ribbon cutting ceremony was held at Powder River in October 1962. The very first project in Johnson County for the construction of I-90 was the bridge over Clear Creek a mile northeast of town. I think the contract was let in 1958.

Like the vast majority of State highway employees, our survey crew was just a bunch of peons when it came to knowing what was taking place in the top echelons of the department. Like all large organizations, it was impossible to keep 100% of what was going on from sifting down through the ranks. We were well aware of some of the political deals that were made among people at the top. The interstate system was so huge, and so much money was involved it must have wasted billions of dollars on a national scale due to politics. In our area, the millions thrown away were just a miniscule part of the program.

I wonder how many people are aware that from an engineering standpoint, the intersection of I-25 and I-90 at the tri-level north of Buffalo should have been built southeast of town. This was because it was the best and cheapest place to put it. To start with, it would have eliminated the need for the two bridge overpasses by the City landfill on TW Road. The ones over Highway 16 to Clearmont, the pair over Clear Creek, and the three-level structure north of town would have been a much simpler and cheaper cloverleaf design. This was the original idea that was discussed before Buffalo and Sheridan got into the battle over the location of I-90.

Sheridan was fighting for a route from Gillette that would have passed near Clearmont and on to Sheridan, giving them a straight shot for all the east and west bound traffic. Buffalo would have been bypassed completely by I-90, and Sheridan would have become the only location in Wyoming besides Cheyenne with the intersection of two interstate highways. Even though the final route was a major victory for Buffalo, Sheridan hung on long enough to insist I-90 had to pass north of town. It did but came at a cost and a big one.

The next instance of interstate politics that I remember was at Lake DeSmet. It was a classic example of the number one rule when trying to figure out what's going on–just follow the money.

We had surveyed a preliminary route for I-90 from Buffalo to the Johnson-Sheridan County line just north of Piney Hill. This was in the days when all the houses and subdivisions along Rock Creek Road and Lake DeSmet did not exist. The majority of the property we crossed over was owned by Reynolds Metals Company, including Lake DeSmet.

From Buffalo, we had generally followed the ridge west of Lake DeSmet that Highway 87 was located on and had crossed back and forth over it several times. It was a good route with no major engineering problems that we were aware of. When we reached the Father DeSmet Monument, our line was just east of it but far enough away from the lake to not create any problems. From there, we continued northwest and crossed the Lower Piney Creek road less than half a mile east of present-day Exit 44 (Story interchange), then across Piney Creek and up and over Piney Hill to the county line.

After completing the survey, we plotted it up by hand, and a short time later, Reynolds and the highway brass from Cheyenne, Sheridan and Buffalo had a meeting in the Buffalo office to discuss the pros and cons from Reynold's point of view. They were a huge company that was considering a major investment in Johnson County, and nobody in the State of Wyoming, Governor included, was interested in squabbling over something as insignificant as an interstate highway location. Evidently, they only had one major objection to our survey because a few days later, we were back at the Father DeSmet Monument.

It's completely irrelevant, but I'll throw a little history in here about the property at that location. Joe Potts and Teeny Mikesell purchased the acreage from my uncle, Tom White, in 1944 and a year later sold part of it, 53 acres, to the Johnson County Sportsman Association for $568.18. They, in turn, gave it to Johnson County with the stipulation it was to be used for recreation purposes only. In later years, it was exchanged for the present recreation area on the south end of the lake. Reynolds Metals Company arrived in 1954 and began drilling for coal and purchasing property and water rights.

Before the lake was raised and they covered it up, there was a cove several hundred yards north of the monument with a steep bank on the west side. There were three privately owned lots along the shoreline with old house trailers that I think were used mostly for weekend fishing trips. Our survey was on top of the ridge west of them.

None of it made sense to us at the time, but after the Reynolds meeting, we altered the line, dropped off the hill, and ran our stakes through all three lots even though we had to move out into the lake to do it. We couldn't even finish that part of the survey until the lake froze over, and we went back and drilled holes in the ice to find out where the top of the ground was.

I can only imagine what the property owners thought when they showed up and found out an interstate highway was going to be built over the top of their trailers. The Highway Department has the right of eminent domain when building roads, which gives them the legal authority to take possession of your property whether you like it or not. They appraise it, make an offer, and if you don't like it, you hire a lawyer and go to court. It's not very comforting to know that as a taxpayer you're also footing the bill for their legal costs as well. Thankfully, multibillion dollar firms like Reynolds Metals Company didn't have that option even as large as they were. In that case, I suppose if you had a property owner who was reluctant about selling, it might help to get somebody else to use a little pressure to help him change his mind. But that's just speculation because eventually the three property owners sold out to Reynolds.

Anyway, all I know for sure was how things finally turned out later on. The Highway Department headquarters in Cheyenne contacted our office and informed us Reynolds Metals had changed its mind about the location of the road at the monument and all the rest of our survey as well because they were going to build a new dam and raise the lake level. They had no objections to moving it a mile or so to the west, so that's where we built it. I don't think anyone realized it at the time, but that put the law of unintended consequences in gear for the rest of I-90 in Johnson County.

By moving the highway so far west, we ran into two unforeseen problems. The first was that we entered the adjoining property to the north owned by Karl Hepp differently than he had been led to believe and destroyed the winter feeding grounds he used for his livestock. He refused to accept the damages offered in payment by the Highway Department and took them to court. The jury agreed with him, awarded the money he claimed for damages, and ordered the State to pay his legal costs. It was the first time any of us had heard of a landowner winning a lawsuit on an eminent domain basis in this area.

The second problem was much more serious because of the human cost involved. The change in the location that moved us into the high ridge of the Hepp Ranch on the south side of Piney Creek increased the grade (steepness) to the point where the Bureau of Public Roads had to grant us special permission. I think their specifications called for a maximum grade of 5% on interstates, and we were over 6%. They were the 800-pound gorilla that had to approve all interstate locations because they were paying about 93% of the cost.

All local drivers know what has taken place since–the dozens of accidents, some with fatalities, that have occurred in bad weather when crossing the overpass bridge going to Story on the way down the hill to Piney Creek. It was a huge engineering error, and there is no way to permanently correct it.

The next fiasco, all political, was at the county line just after topping the ridge north of Piney Creek. We slanted the road to the northwest when it should have been to the northeast. A rancher friend of mine, Charlie Kershner, had a saying, "If you ain't got water, you ain't got nuthin." The same thought can be applied to the material lying under a highway. If the soil is unstable, the road can't handle the traffic after it's built. That was the reason the Geology Department in Cheyenne had a drilling crew that drilled holes to determine what the soils were like under all of the proposed locations in the interstate system. Anybody traveling from Buffalo to Sheridan on I-90 can see what's happening north of Piney Hill in Sheridan County. The dirt slides are constantly moving and taking the highway with them. In the years since I-90 was completed, the Highway Department has awarded contracts totaling millions of dollars repairing the sections of road that have slid off the embankments, and the future will see many more.

In that particular area, there were four separate routes considered for the new interstate, and the drilling crew drilled all four of them. At the time, the head geologist in Cheyenne was a man named Bill Sherman. Because of the two new interstates in Johnson County, he spent a lot of time in Buffalo, and our crew became well-acquainted with him.

He told us the four routes they drilled were evaluated from a geologic standpoint on a one to four scale with number one the best. It was located about a mile or so east of the present I-90 in some scoria hills and can be seen in the distance when driving between Buffalo and Sheridan. It was the one they recommended, but number four was chosen by the powers that be and, of course, is the present route.

Scoria rock, also known as scoria cinders, is the byproduct of ancient coal fires and the material of choice for highways in this area because of its lightweight and porous qualities. It's ironic to think the roadway could have been built over existing deposits to begin with instead of excavating tens of thousands of cubic yards of unstable material and hauling in scoria to fill the hole–a very expensive process and never ending because Nature doesn't give up very easily. Some of the cut sections visible from the present roadway, show seams of low grade coal more than 50 feet deep, which are worthless and detrimental as far as a suitable road base is concerned.

Bill was understandably upset about the choice of routes. When we asked him why it was chosen, he said as far as he knew it was all politics. Some of the Sheridan businessmen and local politicians wanted a view of the valley and mountains like the one at the turnout south of Sheridan and had enough influence to get it done. I'll have to admit it's very impressive, but it came with a pretty hefty price tag.

§   §   §

As has always been the case, towns are either made or unmade, specifically determined by their location or politics. In our particular area, it was some of each and dates back to the wagon trains and later railroads of the 1800s. In that era, towns grew up at locations most advantageous to the traveling public. Clearmont and to a lesser extent Ucross was a classic example of politics. It was a thriving little town and would have continued growing if I-90 had followed the old Highway 14-16 route from Gillette even though an interstate cutting up through the irrigated Clear Creek and Piney Creek valleys would have been a disaster. Buffalo and Sheridan went eyeball to eyeball over the location, and Buffalo came out on top.

Kaycee was in a somewhat different situation with the location of I-25. Considered from a strictly engineering standpoint, the most logical and cheapest location for the new highway was several miles east of town, but I only remember it being very briefly mentioned by people at the top who were responsible for deciding the location. The topic was avoided as if it were the plague and for good reason. Anything different than what presently exists would have led to the Johnson County War sequel.

Kaycee would have dried up like Midwest and Edgerton have since they were bypassed. Even though the bentonite deposits under I-25 south of town and on past Powder River is an engineering headache that has no solution except to tear it up and resurface it every few years when the ground heaves enough to present a safety hazard, it's still much better than the alternative would have been.

Thinking about Kaycee and bad roads reminds me of an incident my sister, Edith, had long before the interstate system ever came into being. She was 3 years older than me and was married to Martin Hibbard, Jr., whose parents had a ranch west of Kaycee on the Mayoworth road. They were living on the place at the time. I think Stuart Cellars bought the ranch in later years.

One time, Edith was visiting in Buffalo, and it started snowing as she left town and headed for Kaycee. By the time she got there, it had turned into a blizzard, and she knew she didn't dare start for the ranch. The road hadn't even been graveled yet and was all gumbo mud in the 1940s. She had three small children at the time, and the oldest was only 5 years old.

There was a small motel on the north end of town called Log Cabin Camp that consisted of a half dozen or so one-room cabins. They were pretty primitive and had outdoor privies for toilets. When she went in to register, she asked the owner the price of the room, and he said, "Four dollars fifty cents with and four dollars without." Edith said, "Without what?" and he replied, "Wood and coal."

§ § §

In the late 1940s, maintenance and engineer crews for the Highway Department shared the same building where the city shop is now located on Fort Street. At that time, there were five permanent maintenance employees that I remember, Troy Pate, Ray Clark, Paul Price, Earl Hughes, and John Thorburn, who was the foreman. Bob Evans was the mechanic. On the engineer's payroll were Grover Powers (resident engineer), Darrel White, Lyle Osborn, John Mueller, Harry Washut, and Walter Patch. The list changed quite frequently due to temporary help being hired in the summertime. As the highway system expanded, a new building was constructed to the west with separate spaces for the two groups, plus a radio operator's office and a large drafting room for the Engineering Department. A large shop building was also included so more snowplow trucks could be housed inside during the winter months.

At that time, the highways were never officially closed because of bad weather. Travelers were allowed to use their own judgment as to whether to continue on during blizzards. Weather forecasts were notoriously inaccurate, and most drivers made up their minds as to whether to continue or not simply by looking out of their car windows. This caused huge problems for the plow drivers because an abandoned car completely covered with snowdrifts was invisible to someone trying to clear the road. Worse yet were the ones that had just stalled and had people in them.

The snowplow drivers worked around the clock as long as the blizzard lasted. I can remember seeing the strain on the drivers' faces increase as the hours went past the first day into the second and beyond. Their stubby whiskers were more prominent, and their eyes sunk back into their foreheads due to lack of sleep and trying to see through the windshields while worrying about crashing into an invisible stalled motorist. Quite often visibility would be so bad they were trapped themselves on their way back to the shop to gas up.

The Highway Department brass knew that something had to give because the traffic count was increasing all the time, so they began sending out Engineering Department personnel in separate vehicles, most of them without radios, with flashing lights at each entrance into town on eight-hour shifts. We stopped all vehicles and told them they would have to return to Buffalo until the weather cleared.

This created some unusual circumstances. If a driver got mad and continued on, the only thing we could do was record their license plate numbers if they were visible, and turn it into the Highway Patrol at the end of our shift. I doubt that anybody with out-of-state plates was ever fined if they got across the State line before the patrol located them. Sometimes the whole State was shut down, and Highway Patrol had more important things to do. I don't think the fine was over $25 to begin with.

The Legislature tried to stay on top of things by raising the fine for running a roadblock to $100, and that didn't work very well either. A highway employee on a road closure detail between Gillette and Buffalo on the old Highway 14-16 who did have a radio in his vehicle, stopped a group of snowmobilers from Wisconsin on their way to Jackson. They asked what the fine was, and since there were five of them, they figured it was only 20 bucks apiece, so they drove around the guy and continued on.

Sometime after that incident, the present system of actually lowering a barrier across the highway and officially closing the road took hold, and the fine was raised to $750. Some people still take a chance and go around it, but if they get caught, their wallet takes a hit.

Thinking about the snowplows reminds me of something funny that happened to me one day. The Maintenance Department plow drivers had been working overtime to clear I-90 towards Gillette after a three-day blizzard and had gone home to get some sleep. There were still patches of snow along the shoulders of the road that needed to be cleared off, so our boss, Gail Money, told me and John Miller to take a plow out and make a pass to Powder River and back. Both of us knew how to drive a truck, but neither of us knew much about plowing snow. It was only a few degrees above zero, the wind was blowing, and it was still spitting snow. I had already put on all the winter clothes I had, so I told John I would gas up the truck while he put on his winter gear.

All of the plow trucks had outside saddle gas tanks mounted on the frame, plus one inside the cab behind the seat that spanned the full width of the truck. It was filled from the spout outside of the truck. I pulled up to the pumps, took the cap off the spout, and put the nozzle on high automatic shut off. I had my back to the wind, waiting for it to click off when I heard something gurgling out from underneath the door. I shut the gas off in a hurry. When I opened the door to see what was going on, I looked behind the seat, and there wasn't any gas tank. I found out later, the mechanics had removed it to make room for a new radio system they were going to install behind the seat, but they had neglected to remove the outside filler tube and gas cap, which dead ended behind the seat.

I had already pumped in at least 10 gallons of gas and had to roll the windows down because of the fumes. When John came out and got in the passenger side, the first thing he did was complain about the gassy smell. He started to roll his window up, and I had to tell him what happened.

It was the only truck available, so we headed out of town with both windows open and snow blowing in. We couldn't even use the heater because it had an electric switch. The spark could have ignited the fumes and blown the truck up with us in it. It was a long cold trip to Powder River and back. I told John if he ever told anyone that I had tried to fill the truck cab up with gasoline, I'd run over his lunchbox with the rear duallies. As far as I know, he believed me.

§ § §

In the 1940s, there was a gun shop located where North Main Street and the bypass road intersect. It was owned by the Baldwin brothers, Homer and Gomer, who were twins. The Highway Department purchased the property when it constructed the bypass road in the 1950s, and the Baldwins built a new gun shop just across the road to the west. It has since closed.

I bought several guns from them when they were at the old location and got to know them quite well. They were raised in the back country hills in Missouri under very primitive conditions and told me a number of stories about their upbringing. I remember one in particular.

Their country schoolhouse was located several miles from their home, and they walked to it every day. There were several other boys that lived along the route who joined them. Along the way, they had to cross a deep gully with an iron bridge spanning the gap.

Most people know what happens if the top of the tongue is touched to an iron structure in very cold weather. If no water is available to pour on it to take out the frost, the part of the tongue touching the iron stays on it when you pull free–a very painful experience. Country kids are taught to dip a bridle bit in water in very cold weather before putting it in the horse's mouth to prevent this from happening.

One bitterly cold morning when they were crossing the bridge, one of the boys on a dare put the flat of his tongue on the bridge and was stuck fast. It was a very serious situation because his tongue would have been frozen by the time they ran for help and he would have lost the whole top of it if they had pulled him loose.

They asked me what I would have done under the circumstances, and I admitted I didn't have the faintest idea. They both broke up with laughter when they told me they urinated on the tongue to get it loose.

§ § §

Chris Johnson was a retired farmer who had previously owned a dairy farm on the east edge of Buffalo. Over a period of years, his property had been completely destroyed by highways. Highway 16 split it on the north, the truck bypass on the west, and I-25 on the east. In addition, Clear Creek cut through it on the south. His home was on the present site of the Bozeman Trail Steak House. The original Bozeman Trail was in the same location. He told me when he started his dairy farm in the 1920s, the ruts made by the wagon trains were still visible.

When I was going to grade school, I used to fish, trap muskrats, and shoot ducks, pheasants and grouse on his property like a number of boys my age did before I ever met him–without permission, of course. In later years, he used to kid me about shooting some of his chickens that ran loose on the place. In actuality, I really never did, but probably the only reason was because I never ran into one when it was on my side of the creek. He had a narrow plank bridge suspended on cables to get across the creek, and we would try to get it swinging back and forth sideways far enough to knock someone off into the water. Years later, my brother and I bought the isolated parcel from him that was lying directly across Highway 16 and built Indian Campground.

After he retired, the Wyoming Highway Department purchased part of his property to construct the overpass on I-25 and Highway 16. One summer they hired him to keep track of the dirt being moved. I was on the survey party at the time. That's when I became acquainted with him, and we became good friends even though there was a big difference in our ages and backgrounds. My personality was a hundred eighty degrees in the opposite direction from his. He was very quiet and unassuming, but I started kidding him about any and everything, and it didn't take long for him to respond in kind. He was a quick thinker, and his one liners would cover me up at times. He played a joke on me once that I was never able to top.

The Highway Department purchased the right-of-way for I-25 from him a year or so before they actually awarded the contract to build it. It wasn't fenced from the rest of his field, so they told him he could keep using it until the road contractor moved in. He figured if he was lucky, he could get another crop of oats off it, so he took a chance and seeded and irrigated it. He raised a nice crop of oats, and while it was growing, I never let him forget that I, as a taxpayer, resented the fact he was using my land for personal gain, and I dang sure wanted my share when it was harvested.

One day, just before he combined the oats that fall, we had our survey suburban parked in that area, and I reminded him once more of my contribution to his oat crop and expected my share of the proceeds. We were working out of sight of the survey vehicle for several hours. When we showed up for lunch, I found my lunch bucket crammed full of loose oats he had stripped from the heads of the grain. My sandwiches and dessert became unwrapped along with a peeled hardboiled egg, and it was impossible to get all the chaff removed, so part of my dinner was raw oats with the outside hull still attached. While sorting through the mess, I uncovered an unsigned, three-word note written on a scrap of paper, "Here's your share."

A couple weeks later, I got a chance to flip to the other side of the coin with a member of the survey crew. There were six of us, and I didn't care which one took the hit. There were two old sheds on the right-of-way that had to be demolished before we could put in stakes, so the contractor burned them. We were working back and forth through the debris when I picked up an old pocketknife that had gone through the fire. The bone handle was a big glob, and it only had one blade left. I started to pitch it to one side when I had an idea.

Bill Sand was one of the crew members that was usually whittling on something in his spare time and used a real expensive pocketknife. The whole crew had seen it many times. I got him off to one side and explained what I had in mind. He was all for it and pulled off a performance worthy of an Oscar at the Academy Awards ceremony.

When we stopped for lunch, he finished eating and took out his knife and started whittling. He made sure everyone in the crew got a good look at it. We went back to work, and a couple hours later I steered the conversation back to pocketknives and asked if anyone had an extra one they would sell. Nobody did, but Bill said he wasn't willing to sell his but might consider trading it for another knife sight unseen. A guy named Roy Gilbert jumped in with both feet and swallowed the bait.

Bill asked me to set the rules, so I had them face each other with their knives covered up in their fists and the other hand outstretched with palm up. I counted to three and said, "Drop it."

When that old burned up relic hit Roy's palm, his jaw would have hit the ground if it hadn't been hooked to his face. None of the rest of the crew knew he had been set up and broke out laughing. Bill handed Roy's knife back to him and told him he could keep the black smoky colored one for a souvenir. I don't know what he ever did with it, but I'll bet that's the last time he ever traded for something sight unseen.

§ § §

Our survey crew actually spent more waking hours with each other than we did with our own families. The suburban was like a second home. We usually knew what was in each other's lunchbox before they were even opened and traded items back and forth like first and second graders do. I remember one maintenance worker, Paul Price, who brought an apple for dessert every single working day of the year. It was a ritual watching him peel it around and around with his pocketknife in one operation, and I never remember him breaking the peel at any time. It came off in one strip, and I have wondered if his wife ever watched him peel one.

Lyle "Ozzie" Osborn was our crew chief on the survey party, and we worked together about 15 years. Usually, I could guess what his wife packed in his lunchbox before he even opened it and what he liked the best. His favorite was a sandwich made of leftover meatloaf with tomato sauce topping. His wife always saved enough from the previous evening meal for his next day lunch.

One time he had it packed in his lunch for several days in a row and couldn't believe his good fortune. Neither could we. A few days later, quite by accident, he found out why. Their cat had jumped up on the counter and licked the tomato sauce off the top of the meat, and his wife and kids wouldn't eat it. She hated to throw it away, figuring what he didn't know wouldn't hurt him, and I guess it didn't.

He had a hardboiled egg for lunch every day. His wife always cooked a dozen or so at a time and put them in the refrigerator. He would grab one every morning and put it in his lunchbox as he headed out the door. When we were eating lunch at the office in the wintertime, he always cracked it by tapping it on the underside of his desk. I happened to be watching him one day when he did it, and he got the oddest look on his face. He had picked it out of the wrong basket, and it hadn't been cooked yet.

We had five children, and my wife had six lunches to make every day for work and school. No cafeteria existed in those days, and we lived eight miles from town. We had pancakes for breakfast some mornings, and she always made extras because all of us preferred the leftover pancakes for sandwiches instead of bread except in hot weather when she used grape jelly for the spread. It would soak through by lunchtime and resembled something a group of kindergartners would mix up with a wide choice of powdered colors. One good way to eat it was with the eyes pointed skyward and the mind on something else.

§ § §

235

To the people that know me best, I have the reputation of being a nitpicker and will have to admit it is with some justification. Changing things that may or may not need changing is a hangup that may have been inherited from a long departed ancestor, but it's hard to shake. A case in point is the elevation sign on Powder River Pass in the Bighorns that hits me head-on when topping the pass.

It touts 9,666 feet above sea level, and its wrong although it's been listed that way at that location and on countless maps for longer than I can recall. The nine and several sixes are easy to remember and a pleasing mix of numbers for anyone bent in that direction, but it still bugs me.

I didn't know it was in error until our survey crew discovered it during a four-year seasonal reconstruction period of Highway 16 in the Bighorns. It was duly recorded in our survey data, but the powers that be probably didn't notice it or if they did, considered it of no importance.

The contractor placed the new sign, as per his contract, with the wrong data, and the universe continued on its daily run like nothing important had happened even though the elevation was actually several feet lower than the sign indicated. I considered taking the issue up with my immediate supervisor but figured the odds of accomplishing anything were from zero to none, so I just avert my eyes when passing it on the way to Ten Sleep. But it doesn't help all that much.

§ § §

In all the years our survey crew spent tromping over Johnson County, I suppose the two main hazards–live ones anyway–were wood ticks and rattlesnakes. Certain brushy draws seemed to be tick hatcheries, and we were extra careful about checking our clothes when working in them. Unless it was an extra wet spring, the tick season dried up with the weather by the first part of July.

Rattlers had a longer season that lasted from early spring until they started denning for the winter in September and even into early November if the weather stayed hot and dry. Every one of our crew, sooner or later, had close calls with snakes, but we lucked out, and nobody ever got bit. We ran into them in every part of the county, mountains excepted. The Red Hills east of Buffalo was the worst. The scoria rocks were a magnet for them and provided uncountable places for dens and a great variety of dinner items like rodents and rabbits. It was the first place we started surveying the I-90 route on the long road to Gillette.

During one fall day in September, we ran onto a big one that had an extra-large midsection, and we assumed it had just finished a meal of rabbit, but we were wrong. She had six stillborn baby rattlers in her stomach. Our party chief's son, Jerry Osborn, was in a biology class dissecting frogs and fish, so we thought they might like a different specimens to practice on. We put them in a tin can and went back to work. It was lucky it had a lid because when we got back to the suburban a couple hours later, the stillborns were alive and well.

We donated four of them to Jerry's biology class after making sure they couldn't bite anybody and took the other two back to the office, where we put them in a gallon jar and placed it on top of a file cabinet. They were about 8 inches long and had a single black button on the end of their tails that turned into a blur when somebody got too close to the jar. From day-one, they would coil and strike the glass when anybody got near it. We made bets with the other guys in the office, that they couldn't hold their hand against the glass without flinching the first time they tried it. Nobody ever did, and it took several tries to keep your hand in place.

Our boss was on vacation at the time, and when he showed up, he wasn't amused with what we had done. The order of the day was get rid of those damned snakes and don't waste any time doing it. Several days before he showed up, I got to thinking about what a wonderful opportunity it was to play a practical joke. All it would cost me was my job if I goofed it up.

I could go back to the office after hours when no one was around, remove the two rattlers from their glass cage, and then drop it on the concrete floor in front of the file cabinet. We had eight or 10 desks in the room plus file cabinets and other equipment. There would have been a dozen or so employees searching for a pair of snakes that didn't exist, and they didn't dare sit down and go to work. If I never told anyone what I'd done, it would have been impossible to pinpoint the guilty party. It would have been a perfect practical crime, and it wouldn't make any difference what they did or how long it took them to do it. The broken glass on the floor said accident. From that time forward, any time anyone slid out a desk drawer or opened a file cabinet, they couldn't help but think, "What if?"

The word rattlesnake on a printed page brings to mind a lot of creepy thoughts even to someone who's never seen anything but a picture of one. The story would have been on the front page of every newspaper in Wyoming and beyond. The free publicity would have extended to the Governor's office, who, incidentally, was the boss of the Highway Department, and he might have had a little difficulty convincing the voting public we were all hardworking, conscientious employees. The more I thought about it, the more ingenious it seemed.

But the one downside to the whole idea was insurmountable, and I had to give it up. They would have fired the whole survey crew for bringing the rattlers into the office in the first place, and I was the only one responsible for the follow up. Besides, I got to thinking about it and wondered what was the point in conceiving the best joke in the history of the town when I couldn't even tell anybody what it was. But I still think it was a great idea.

§   §   §

Chick Osborn, Ozzie's brother, was a member of our survey crew for a couple years before he quit and took over his father's honeybee business. Wyoming Bee Maid Honey was its moniker. He was a tall, quiet, skinny guy and universally liked by everyone in our department.

One day, we were scattered out in the Red Hills area, searching for a section corner in a heavy sagebrush patch when he stepped on a coiled rattlesnake. He wasn't aware of it at the moment, but its head was under his boot. It couldn't strike, but the tail and rattles were pounding on his pants leg. We heard him squawk like a chicken with a rubber band around its neck. When I turned around to see what was wrong, he was balanced on one foot with his 6 foot 3 inch frame stretched toward heaven.

There was no way to move sideways without putting his other foot on the ground to get leverage. He was so shook he thought if he did, the snake would hammer it. Everything happened so fast, and I don't know exactly how he did it, but he finally moved off dead center and got away from the thing. The crowning irony was that the snake disappeared in a nearby hole because we didn't have anything to hit it with.

The whole episode didn't get funny until we were headed back to town at quitting time. We told him his one-legged position on top of the snake was a good indication he might have a career in ballet dancing, but I don't think he ever even considered it.

I remember another time when we were working down on Powder River, it was in the middle of the summer and terribly hot. When we stopped for lunch, we were parked in the middle of a sheeped out area without a single blade of grass or sagebrush poking out of the ground. We opened the side and rear doors of the suburban while we were eating to get some air flowing through, but it didn't do much good.

We had one girl on the crew at the time, and she had this thing about snakes. While we were eating, the subject turned to rattlesnakes because we had encountered a number of them in the years we were locating the route for I-90.

This gal went into some detail about how she hated the things, and she had a lot of support from the rest of the crew who contributed stories of their own. It was quite a coincidence, but when we finished eating, she was the first one to step out of the vehicle and spotted one about 20 feet away headed for the rear of the suburban. I have no idea where it came from unless it was out of a hole in the ground. She screamed, "There's one of the damned things now," and started backing up like she was the target, but she wasn't.

Snakes are coldblooded creatures, and their temperature is regulated by the outside air. They have to get in the shade when it's overly hot, and the suburban was the only thing sticking above ground. When it's dry and hot in snake country, it's always prudent to give a rock and sagebrush plenty of clearance when walking by.

Through the years, I had heard stories about how they lunge forward when they strike. Others say they coil up like a folded ribbon and just straighten out to about half their length. One day, I ran onto one in the middle of a dirt road and decided to check it out. I estimated him to be about 3 feet long. I got a long stick. When I poked it at him, he struck, and I guessed the distance to be about 18 inches. This was kind of an average distance because I tested him three or four times, but he was so fast his head was just a blur when he hit the stick, so it was hard to tell. I wasn't interested in checking it out with a tape measure to find out for sure, so don't take my word for it. I am dead certain about one thing. If someone who has never seen a rattlesnake before and gets close enough to hear the buzzer go off, they don't have to see it to know what it is.

We had an interesting situation with rattlers when we were placing hot asphalt road surfacing on I-90 in the Red Hills east of town. It was in the fall when the days were hot, but the nights cooled down quite rapidly. During the night, the snakes would crawl up on the asphalt because it was warm, and were stuck fast by morning when it cooled off. It was also the time of year when they were headed for their winter dens, so a lot of them were on the move.

A few years before I went to work for the Highway Department, I was working for the Kostenbauer brothers at their coal mine in the Red Hills four or five miles northeast of town. There were plenty of snakes, and in hot weather they would crawl down the slope (tunnel) going into the mine to cool off. The slope roof was supported by posts with planks on top to keep the dirt from caving in. It was about 6 feet high. Snakes would coil up on the crossbeams about head high, and you had to be extra careful when walking up or down because your face or neck would have taken the hit.

Another time I remember quite vividly was when a group of us were hunting antelope on the Iberlin Ranch down by the Pumpkin Buttes. We were driving down a dirt road and spotted a rattler coiled up in the middle of it. I jumped out and used the last of a roll of film in my camera to take a few pictures. I was sitting in the backseat with the door open, putting in another roll of film and hunched over the camera to keep as much light out as possible. One of my best friends, Leon Rich, walked up to the open door, and I heard him say, "Are you finished with this yet?" When I straightened up, my nose was level and an inch away from a writhing rattler with the rattles still attached. Leon had cut the head off, and it was harmless, but in the millisecond before my eyes got the information to my brain, I had enough time to turn to stone.

I think one of the oddest stories I ever heard about rattlesnakes came from a young man on my crew, Brett Condit. His mother and I had been classmates, but I had never met Brett until he began working for the Highway Department. He hadn't had any previous experience with survey work, but he was a fast learner and became the best instrument man I was ever around. It was a lucky day when he went to work and was assigned to my crew.

He was very quiet and never initiated a conversation. It took a while to find out two of his main interests were music and rattlesnakes. I was very surprised to learn he had formed a rock band and played at various functions. His friends told me his personality would do a flip flop when he was performing in front of a live audience, and he was very good at it. I was more comfortable with Frank Sinatra, and rock music was out of my league, so we stayed with snakes.

His best friend was a boy named Dave Money, who just happened to be my boss's son. Brett told me they snared rattlesnakes with some kind of stick and wire contraption. I don't know why, but it had never occurred to me to ask him what they did with them. I guess I just assumed they killed them.

We were working in the Bighorn Mountains one summer. When we stopped for lunch one Monday at noon, he happened to mention that he and his buddy, Dave, had spent the weekend on the John Marton Ranch outside of Casper, hunting snakes and had caught two or three rattlers. I asked him what they had done with them, and he said they had put them in the cage with the others. Others??? He said they had about 45 total, but they were kind of hard to count in one bunch, so he wasn't too sure. I asked him where the cage was located, and he said at his house.

I knew he was renting a home in the 700 block on North Carrington, and I was living in the 700 block on North Burritt, so I did some rapid calculations in my head and figured I had a 15-foot alley and an empty weed grown lot between me and 45 rattlesnakes if somebody left their door open. In addition, I suppose the whole north end of town would have been on red alert until the two entrepreneurs had recaptured the escapees. The only thing that could have possibly made the situation worse was if one of my kids had been involved, and it was close because Dave had been a good friend of my youngest son, Randy, when they were in grade school.

Fortunately, Dave's father found out about the enterprise about the same time I did and told him the rattlers had to be disposed of–and now. Brett told me later that the only market for rattlesnakes was Reptile Gardens in Rapid City, South Dakota. They hauled them down there and sold them by the pound. I don't know how much they received, but Brett told me it wasn't quite enough to cover the cost of gas. I got to thinking about it and figured either the market was way down or they were pretty small snakes, but it wasn't either. Later that summer, I talked to some locals that had visited Reptile Gardens, and they told me our sagebrush variety crawling around in the Red Hills are pigmies compared to the ones they saw.

After going bankrupt in the snake business, Brett added a footnote that I thought was a fitting end to the whole operation. He had a friend, Wes Reisland, who also liked rattlesnakes, but, as far as I know, limited his likes to just one that he kept for a pet. He was working at the Irigaray Uranium mine southeast of town towards Powder River and was away at work from early morning to late evening. Brett told me when the guy left the house in the morning to go to work, the pet went into the refrigerator for the day. The temperature would only take a few minutes to put it in hibernation mode. I assume it was in some type of container, but the whole situation was so weird I never asked and can only imagine what would have happened if someone unaware of the situation had opened that door and reached in for a carton of milk.

Sometime later, I was discussing the trio's reptile operation with Randy Money, Dave's older brother, and he told me something Brett had neglected to mention. Their friend, Wes, was allergic to the antivenom used for rattlesnake bites and wouldn't have been able to get the shot even if he had been bitten. I guess he didn't figure it was a problem because all boys are bulletproof at that age. He also remembered the state of the art cage the boys had used. It was a wood box with a screen on top and securely latched with a couple bricks to hold it down in case something bumped it. He said the odor was horrific.

Trailside on Highway 16 in the Bighorn Mountains – 1939

PART VI

Trailside Living

I spent the best years of my life at Trailside after we purchased it in 1960. All five of our kids were raised there, and we met hundreds of special people, many of whom could only be described as characters. I've forgotten most of them, but sometimes with someone's offhand remark one of their images will come to mind and the story behind it. I've always regretted not keeping a diary through the years, but the thought never even entered my head.

One day, I got to thinking about the history of the place and how it even originated to begin with, so I started backtracking through the records at the courthouse and correlating it with what I could remember people telling me. It turned into quite a project, but some of the kids encouraged me. I was retired with nothing else to do anyway, so I kept at it. It turned into a fun learning experience, and I never regretted it.

Reaching back as far as recorded history is available and borrowing a biblical phrase–in the beginning–the original owners of Trailside were the Crow Indians. The United States government through a series of lies, deceit, broken treaties, and a better grade of ammo cheated them out of it and in 1878 started construction of Fort McKinney, which was three miles west of the future town of Buffalo, Wyoming. The Fort McKinney-Wood Reservation was attached to the fort on the west, and it extended into the Bighorn Mountains. Some of this area became private and City property after the military left, but the majority of it came into the possession of the State of Wyoming and a couple of federal agencies, the Forest Service and the Bureau of Land Management. Some of it was set aside as a stock drive for ranchers to get their livestock to and from their summer and winter ranges, and it is still being used for this purpose. The future Trailside was on the west end of the Wood Reservation eight miles west of Buffalo on present-day Highway 16.

The first recorded land transfer concerning it was a patent for 40 acres from the United States government to Carroll H. Parmelee on June 19, 1911, and was signed by President William H. Taft. It was granted according to "1820, April 24, 03 Stat. 566, Act Making Further Provision for Sale of Public Land," legalese and gobbledygook to justify the theft and disposition of someone else's property. This act made provisions for the sale of lands, public or private, in entire, half, quarter, or half quarter sections less than 160 acres after July 1, 1820.

I was not able to find what Mr. Parmelee paid for the 40-acre tract. The

244

price was not listed in the Patent Deed and simply stated, "Cash patent consideration: Full payment, dated June 19, 1911." However, I did find similar sales of property in this area for the same period of time. They ranged from $1 to $1.50 an acre.

From this point on, the parcel went through a number of owners, but it was always part of additional acreage. I was only interested in how and when the 14 acres that comprised Trailside were eventually carved out of the original 40 acres of Mr. Parmelee's tract, so I chased it when it was part of a larger acreage, and then dropped the rest of it.

Three months after he purchased it, Mr. Parmelee granted a 100-feet right-of-way easement width to Johnson County for a change and alteration of Road Survey #72 along Mosher Gulch. This spelling was used throughout the documents I saw, but I have seen it spelled Mosier on some later maps. I don't know where the name was derived from. This was before the State Highway Department became involved with Highway 16. On April 5, 1913, Mr. Parmelee gave a Warranty Deed to Charles N. Walters upon payment of $1,200 for the 40-acre tract plus additional considerations.

On November 1, 1917, Charles N. Walters and Margaret B. Walters, his wife, granted a Mortgage Deed to the American Bankers Insurance Company of Illinois for the sum of $15,000, payable in five years at 6% interest. This mortgage was paid in full on March 16, 1921, and five days later Walters Company gave a Mortgage Deed to The American Bankers Insurance Company for a consideration of $20,000 at 7% interest for five years. The interest increased to 10% if the loan went past the maturity date.

Walters Company was formed on June 27, 1918, by a Warranty Deed issued by Charles N. and Margaret B. Walters. Charles was the president, and Karl F. Walters was secretary. Eighteen hundred and two acres were mentioned at this time.

Two years after the 1921 mortgage on April 17, 1923, Walters Company gave a Mortgage Deed to the Nebraska National Bank of Omaha in consideration of $50,000. Interest wasn't mentioned on the document but was handled by a separate promissory note. This loan was paid in full three years later.

On September 27, 1924, Sheriff M.A. Woodside conducted a foreclosure sale on the 1921 Mortgage Deed and split the auction into tracts. The original 40 acres that Mr. Parmelee had purchased brought a bid of $13,547.32. The total amount auctioned brought $23,707.81 and was purchased by the American Bankers Insurance Company that were simply reclaiming the amount due from the money they had loaned the Walters Company, plus interest and expenses. This is the way foreclosure sales are handled when the property is worth less than is owed on it. Being underwater is the modern expression.

On October 2, 1929, the American Bankers Insurance Company in payment of $8,500 issued a Warranty Deed to Antonio Silva for the original 40-acre tract of Mr. Parmelee plus other acreage. Mr. Silva was a local sheep man, who was known locally as Black Antone and owned the French Creek Ranch. He, in turn, on July 1, 1932, issued a Mortgage Deed to Ned Quinn and Annie McDonough for $47,000 at 7% interest for a period of three years. Mr. Quinn passed away, and there were several documents related to the couple in clearing up the mortgage and land titles with Antone Silva.

On November 16, 1934, Mr. Silva issued a Warranty Deed to John F. and Golda F. Dodson, husband and wife, for 14 acres for a consideration of $126–$9 an acre. This is the split that became Trailside from Mr. Parmelee's original purchase of 40 acres on June 19, 1911.

The Dodson's later gave easements to the State of Wyoming in April 1938 for Highway 16 construction and another in April 1944 to the Forest Service for a telephone line. In 1953, the Dodson's sold their property to Grainger and Ruth McKenzie, who then sold it to Layton and Lucille Wilson in 1955. The Gray family purchased it from the Wilsons on April 15, 1960, and to date still own it.

I realize the preceding few pages concerning the history of Trailside are probably boring to most readers, but I thought they might be of interest to future owners. Maybe sometime in the next 100 years or so, the Crow Indians will get it back either by Warranty Deed or bow and arrow. Justice eventually will be served come hell or high water.

§ § §

I never knew Fred Dodson personally. After getting out of the Army, I worked for several years in logging camps in the Bighorns in the late 1940s and would see him outside on the driveway or lawn as we drove by Trailside. In hot weather, the driveway would be full of cars with their hoods up, letting their motors cool down. A lot of my information about Fred came from a local man named Harold Hook. Harold's father, Dick, was the sales manager at McKibbon's Motor Company, a Dodge dealership in the early '30s in Cedar Rapids, Iowa. Fred Dodson was the parts manager. Harold told me his dad had a boyhood friend, Jake Williston, who talked him into moving to Buffalo. His dad mentioned it to Fred, and he and his wife, Golda–no children–decided to move with him.

I thought it remarkable that both men quit good jobs during the Great Depression to move to a state they knew nothing about, much less find employment when they got there. I was raised during that period and remember what a tough time my family had getting by on a day-to-day basis. Grown men were working on ranches for $30 a month during the summer season when they could find a job. After the seasonal layoff, some of them had to work through the winter months for room and board only.

Harold Hook said that Dodson was a perfectionist and everything he did had to be planned to the last detail. He owned a 1927 or '28 four-cylinder Dodge car and bought a trailer to make the move. He marked a chalk line of the trailer's dimensions on his basement floor and built boxes for each separate item to fit in.

When they got to Wyoming in 1933, Fred and his wife stayed at Lucasta Camp. It was a log cabin tourist stopover on Highway 16 along Clear Creek about a dozen miles west of Buffalo. Then he started looking for a job.

He noticed tourists were having a lot of problems pulling the steep grade out of Buffalo–2,000 feet in 8 miles–so he and Golda decided to build a house, gift shop and gas station to accommodate them.

They purchased 14 acres with the highway running through it from a rancher for $9 an acre and started "wearing out shovels" as he phrased it in a letter he wrote me some 30 years later.

Harold told me Golda was a really nice person, and he liked her very much. She started serving meals and built up a large clientele from Buffalo, but it got to be too much for her, so she dropped back to pie and coffee only. Of course, the whole time they were in business they were also building the facilities, so it must have been quite a stretch. Harold was only a teenager, and Fred hired him to work on weekends and summers, and he slept in a tent.

As near as I can ascertain from some old photos, the Dodson's lived in an old homemade trailer and constructed the souvenir shop first and then a basement adjoining it to the north. Harold told me they lived in the basement dug with a pick and shovel before adding the house on top. I have no idea how long the process stretched out. One thing that took precedence over everything else–Fred smoked one cigar every evening at exactly the same time–5:00 p.m.

Another routine that never changed was the search for rocks. I have some early photos of the place. He must have spent countless hours placing rocks both inside and outside of the house. He built a beautiful fireplace in the living-dining room and also a rock wall 6 or 7 feet high on the patio. I always wondered how and where he found such a collection of rocks and figured some of them must have been imported, but Harold said they were all local. Every evening without fail, they drove the mountains pulling the trailer and looking for unusual rocks. When they found a likely candidate, Fred would measure it and discuss it's potential before they loaded it.

Unfortunately, when the building was demolished almost 70 years later, there was no way to clean the mortar from them, and they were all buried.

At some point after getting their house built, the Dodsons built a cabin a couple hundred feet in back of their home. It was constructed of slabs and was a pretty simple structure. We only used it for a local couple to live in during the summer months when we needed extra help. It extended over a cutbank, and Fred parked their car under the cabin in the winter. It provided excellent protection. Next to it and built into the same bank was a small building that housed their electric generator. REA, the Rural Electric Association, arrived in the late 1950s, so we had dependable electricity when we bought the place.

A draw directly behind their back door, Hay Gulch, had a small stream flowing down it that they used to irrigate their lawn. For house water, Fred built an underground cistern about 100 yards up the draw that tapped into a spring. He piped it to the house and had a trouble-free, gravity flow water system. When we built our new cabin, we tapped into it, but we had to add a pump.

Harold Hook had told me Fred was a perfectionist in everything he did, and I eventually came to realize what he was referring to. I ended up either digging up, tearing down, or remodeling everything he had done. In all of his construction projects, I never once stumbled on something he had cut corners on when building it. Many times when I was trying to pry something loose, I would notice he always went overboard to make something particularly strong when he could have taken an easier way out. I also noticed his ingenuity in overcoming a problem by substituting what he had on hand for something that was either too expensive or unavailable. One particular instance comes to mind.

After we had lived there several years, I found out one thing about the place that I had always wondered about. The front part of the log building that was built first and became their souvenir shop had a concrete floor on a monolithic slab. It was colored and scribed to look like tile. The logs were chinked with mortar like all log cabins at that time, and they all had the same problem. As the logs dried out after being cut or had absorbed moisture from a long wet period, they would shrink away from the mortar and allow all sorts of critters, like flies and spiders, to come and go as they pleased. Flies were especially bad in the mountains in the fall when the nights started cooling down and they were looking for a place to spend the winter. This room was never used for living quarters–just for displaying souvenirs in the summer months.

The adjoining living quarters that had been built at a later date was also logs but had been caulked with a product I've never heard of before or since. It adhered to the logs regardless of how much they shifted, and it used to irritate me no end when our kids would press their fingers in it or punch their initials into it with a screwdriver.

One day, a local businessman, Safford Fairlie, who owned a garage in Buffalo, happened to stop by for a beer, and as we were visiting, I happened to mention the pliable caulking. He knew exactly what it was and told me when he was in high school and Fred Dodson was building the place, Fred had hired him to make and mix it by hand. He used a washtub, and the ingredients were raw linseed oil, wheat flour and yellow ochre added for color. Fred used mice contaminated flour he bought from the local stores and bakery because it was cheaper. The raw linseed oil, which never hardens, kept the mice from eating the flour.

When we demolished that section of building almost 70 years after it was built, the caulking was as pliable as the day it was applied. I've often wondered if this was Fred Dodson's original idea. I asked a number of old-time builders about it, and none of them had ever heard of it before. It amuses me to see tubes of modern day caulking compound guaranteed to stay pliable for 50 years. All you need for a refund is the original sales slip and what's left in the tube.

Even though I never met the guy, I've done so much research on him, I feel like I know him personally. He was willing to tackle almost anything. He had the guts to quit a good job in the middle of the worst Depression the United States had ever known, drive a 1,000 miles to a state he had never been to before, didn't know a single person who lived there, and then figured out how to make a good living from something no local person had ever dreamed of–a classic case of not being able to see the woods because of the trees.

Photography was another of his talents. Harold Hook told me Fred took hundreds of photos of the Bighorns. He said it was nerve wracking to watch him set up his tripod because everything had to be exactly right. I know that some of his photos later appeared in *Arizona Highway* magazine. I was never able to confirm it, but a couple of things made me wonder if he was considering some kind of venture into the commercial photography field.

After he finished building the gift shop, he built a large attractive rustic sign out of logs and placed it just outside the entrance. It had "Trailside Studios" in big block letters cut into the center of the sign. I never could get the connection between studios and a souvenir shop. After the buildings were moved and torn down, we kept the sign for a keepsake and moved it up to our new cabin. The other thing I wondered about was a real puzzler.

When we purchased the property in 1960, the sale included all of the existing inventory. It was mostly current items with a few odds and ends dating back to the original owners, the Dodson's in the 1930s. Among this latter group were a large number of black and white postcards that Fred had a publishing firm print of some of the photos he had taken in the Bighorns. There were over 20,000 of them. That is not a misprint–20,000. I don't have the foggiest notion why he had so many of them printed. I don't know how many the previous owners sold, but we priced them at six for 25¢ and still had a dozen shoebox-size boxes full when we closed the business.

In my opinion, Fred Dodson was a very inventive guy who didn't make many mistakes that I was aware of. He was full of ideas the average person would never have thought of. I think he had an idea, and the postcards were part of some largescale commercial operation that never saw the light of day for some reason or other.

In the stack of cards was one that caught my attention. It was a sketch of the original Trailside building done by J.W. Winingar, a local rancher who had acquired quite a reputation in this area as an artist in 1946.

Just on a hunch, I got Fred's address from a local guy, Troy Pate, who had been good friends of the Dodsons and wrote Fred a letter in March 1973, asking if he knew what had happened to the original work. He lived in Kalona, Iowa, at the time. I lucked out because he wrote right back and sent me the original sketch which I have since donated to the Johnson County Library. He wrote a really

Fred Dodson interesting letter.

I wrote back and thanked him for the sketch, and that was the last contact I had with him. A few years later, some of his relatives stopped by Trailside on their way to Yellowstone and gave me some pictures of him and a few he had taken of the house when he owned it, but he had died by that point in time. The original letter is a little the worse for wear.

Kalona, Iowa
Mar 29, 1973

Dear Fred:

Received your letter today. Glad you wrote when you did as I am getting ready to leave for Arizona in a few days. Your letter stored up a lot of memories. My wife and I went to Wyoming in the winter of 1933-34. Stayed at Lucasta Camp. Good sausage was three pounds for 25¢. No jobs were available. When warm weather came we used to see the tourists stop to water their cars from what now is your front door. It was called a spring, but was just piped from the creek.

Anyway it gave us an idea. Ed Miller was the ranger then. We had made friends with the Millers and Ed was a friend of the ranchers. So Ed talked Antone Silva into selling us 14 acres in the corner next to the National Forest. Price was $9 per acre.

I started wearing out shovels in Sept. 1934. By hunting season we were cutting our logs. Shot my first deer up there too. The Gray boys had a pole camp up there and they snaked out our logs and I think hauled them down for us. They also had a little towheaded boy in camp with them. He must have been about two. One evening about sundown as my wife and I came past he fell in the creek. I guess he would not have drowned but we helped him out. He wasn't long getting to where his dad was. If you were born about 1932–well I wonder.

A Norwegian notched our logs. Can almost say his name but can't quite. Maybe I will later. He was an artist with an ax. I built the fireplace myself. Must have been about 1937. I took many pictures while there but am sorry to say most of them have been misplaced and the negatives lost. You are lucky on the etching. I have always saved it. I found it today and am mailing it to you with my compliments and you are entirely welcome. I remember the postcards you mentioned. They are good negatives but they did a rotten printing job. I don't know what they called the paper. It was the same kind the etching was printed on. It has kind of a linen finish.

Will be glad to answer any questions. We spent 20 interesting years there. Troy and Marjorie are wonderful people. Tell them hello for me. My wife died about three years ago. She loved it at Trailside and enjoyed meeting the tourists. I might get out that way again. I'm 83 now but am driving to Ariz. next week and maybe to Cal.

Was nice to hear from you.
Sincerely
(signed) Fred Dodson

Comments about his letter: In paragraph one, Lucasta Camp was about four miles on up the road from Trailside and directly above and south of Highway 16 from the High Country Estates subdivision. In paragraph three, the Gray boys were my two half-brothers, Claude and Harold, and the towheaded boy was Claude's son, Zane. In paragraph four, the Norwegian was either Whitey or Axel Mathison. I knew them both. The name was pronounced Muh-tee'-son at that time. In paragraph five, Mrs. Dodson named Trailside.

§ § §

We did not know the people we purchased Trailside from, Layton and Lucille Wilson, when we first bought the place but later became good friends. My wife and Layton's birthday were on the same day of the month. At times, we would meet them in Sheridan and have lunch together. They shared many stories about their time on the mountain. I recall a couple in particular.

One summer, they spent a lot of time trimming brush, raking leaves, and cleaning up in general. They had it all piled in one location and had rigged up a pump and hose next to a small stream in their backyard to control the fire in case it was needed. It had been a dry summer, and they weren't taking any chances, not only because of their home but because a 4-barbwire fence was the only thing that separated them from the Bighorn National Forest property about 300 feet away.

Layton said when they lit the pile, it went up like they had poured gasoline on it and was completely out of control. They didn't have a phone to report it, and it wouldn't have done them any good even if they did. The County Fire Department at that time only had two small tanker trucks eight miles away in Buffalo, and it would have taken them over an hour to pull the steep grade up the highway, and the steep terrain where the fire was burning would have made it impossible to get anywhere close to it.

Hunter Ranger Station was six or seven miles beyond their house, and the ranger saw the smoke and came barreling down the road to help. He was a good friend of the Wilsons. With the three of them, they finally got the fire under control but not before it jumped the boundary fence. Layton said it didn't burn a very big area, all grass, and didn't reach any trees, but he later got a bill from the Forest Service for damages. It was a little over $11.

The following winter it cost him several times that much to buy a new TV antenna when he opened his backdoor one night and startled two bull elk that were feeding on his lawn. They took off like racehorses and took the antenna and several hundred feet of wire with them.

At about that same time, he was doing some remodeling inside the house. It had two small windows facing the east, and he decided to enlarge the opening and replace them with a large picture window. It was a log building, and he had some big logs to saw through. He was on an 8-foot stepladder and using a chainsaw when he lost his balance. He was breathing heavily because of the altitude and exertion and had his mouth open when he fell. He released the trigger on the saw when he started down, but there was a millisecond before the chain stopped moving, and it caught him across the mouth. He had false teeth, and it chewed them up.

His wife told me there were pieces of teeth scattered over the whole room, but the chain never touched either side of his mouth.

The only reason they bought Trailside to begin with was kind of a fluke. They owned and operated Arrowhead Lodge above Sheridan at the time and saw an ad in the Sheridan paper that the place was going to be auctioned off along with all the furnishings, which included an organ. They had been looking for an organ, so they drove over and bought it and ended up buying the house too.

When we bought this tourist business from them, they already had a malt beverage permit. Since the whole operation was a complete flip on anything I had ever done, I wasn't sure that I wanted to get involved with selling beer. Layton said it was a big help in paying the bills, and we had a large mortgage to think about, so I renewed the license.

Shortly after getting geared up, I had a bunch of locals in the place one day when the county sheriff walked in. He knew everyone in the place personally and visited with them for several minutes, but when he started out the door, he caught my eye and motioned with his finger to come out on the lawn. I didn't have the faintest idea what he wanted when I caught up with him out of earshot of the others. He started talking real casually as if discussing the weather and said he had had a business like ours at one time further on up the mountain, Caribou Resort, and knew the problem of paying bills with such a short summer season. (At that time, selling beer or liquor on Sunday was against the law.) He told me that when some local person he knew would stop by on a Sunday morning going fishing and needed a six pack, the beer went out the door in a paper sack. Just one thing, he said, keep it away from the kids. Then he walked over, got in his car, and drove off. I can't remember saying a single word the whole time. Anyway, I kept it away from the kids or tried to, but it took some doing.

I got to dreading May and high school graduation. On average, it seemed like every three or four years a death occurred on the mountain due to underage kids, automobiles and liquor–mainly after or during a beer bust.

The kids knew partying on government land, like the Forest Service, was illegal and would be broken up by law enforcement if they were caught, so they devised some safeguards to improve their odds. Only one or two persons were entrusted to know the date, time and location of the party. They were responsible for collecting dues from their classmates, buying refreshments, and setting the time, date and place for the gathering. Any place selling beer or liquor was a target for buying what was needed for the celebration, and if the kids couldn't get it themselves, they could always find someone older to purchase what they needed for a small fee.

A short time before the party–sometimes only an hour or two–all of the participants were notified as to time and place and advised to leave town by different routes because any mass exodus would immediately be noticed by someone and reported to the cops. They were on high alert in the weeks preceding and shortly after the graduation ceremonies, but the kids won the war most of the time.

I don't know why, but at that period of time, cops were not allowed to bust up a party on private property without permission of the landowner, and I never knew a landowner who wanted to see his kid arrested for underage drinking. Through the years, I assisted in a number of drunk driving accidents that occurred in the vicinity of Trailside, but one of them stands out over all the rest.

One morning in 1971 at about 2:00, we were awakened by the sound of someone hammering on the front door of the lounge. Two of our bedrooms were on the second story just above it. A window looked directly out over the door and the highway. In a situation like that, I always tried to get a feel of what was going on before going downstairs and opening the door. It was a little unsettling to open a door at night to a complete stranger when we didn't even have a telephone to call for help if we needed it.

I went to the window, and the man's voice from below said he had had a wreck below Trailside and needed some help getting his girlfriend out of the car. Anthony, our son, was awake for the whole conversation, and when I asked the guy who he was, Anthony said he recognized the guy's name and voice, so I went downstairs.

I switched on a light, and when I opened the door, the kid practically fell on top of me. He was either stoned or dead drunk or both. He said he had wrecked below the house somewhere when he went over the bank and had left the headlights on. I loaded him up in my pickup and started down the mountain. It was pitch dark outside.

He was on the side that could see down the canyon wall for the headlights, so I drove very slowly along the edge of the roadway. He was so drunk I had to keep prodding him to look out the window. We went all the way to the bottom of Mosier Gulch at Dead Man's Curve, and he didn't see any lights, so I drove on into town and stopped at the sheriff's office. They had to radio for a highway patrolman, so I hauled the kid to the hospital to get rid of him even though I knew he wasn't hurt. He insisted on going back up the mountain with me and wouldn't get out of the pickup, so I had to go inside to get enough help to manhandle him. Then I started back up the mountain. Although I didn't know it, the patrolman and sheriff's deputy still hadn't left town.

When I got to the canyon, I drove on the left side of the highway, where I could see the bottom and finally saw two headlights a couple hundred feet below me right where the catch-net truck runaway is presently located.

254

Only the lights were vertical instead of horizontal.

I pulled over and stopped just as the highway patrolman, Bob Warne, and a deputy sheriff pulled up in their vehicles. It was a terribly steep bank to try to get down through the rocks in the dark. And would you believe it? I was the only one who had a flashlight.

When we finally got to the car, it was lying on its side with the lights still on, but the girl had been ejected and was lying some 50 feet from the vehicle. She was dead. There was nothing we could do but sit there in the dark and wait for the ambulance and a stretcher so we could pack her out. It took almost an hour before it arrived but seemed like a week.

We didn't do much talking because all three of us had children that age and were thinking, "What if?" I remember the patrolman, Bob Warne, telling us a couple nights before he had checked out a beer bust at the TW Ranch a few miles east of Buffalo. The kids had a bonfire going, and the owner's son was standing next to Bob's car when he opened the door and got out. The kid had been drinking and got pretty mouthy. He told Bob it was private property and he didn't have any authority on the place, which he didn't. He told Bob he and his friends were all old enough to know what they were doing. When Bob finished telling us the story, he was quiet for a moment and then added, "I wish I had that kid sitting here beside me at this very minute."

I found out the next day the two kids were returning from an all-night party in the Bighorns. My son, Robin and his future wife, Janice, were their classmates at school and heard the news the next morning at school class-day exercises. The girl was the daughter of Ed Long, one of my classmates when we graduated in 1942. Her name was Kathy, and she was 17 years old.

§ § §

In actuality, Trailside was a great place to raise kids when they were growing up. Outside of playing with matches and burning the mountain down, we didn't have to be very concerned about them getting involved and into trouble with a lot of other kids. They loved living there and had plenty of room to wander–no neighbors for miles in every direction. In nice weather, sometimes the only times they spent much time in the house was when they got hungry. They had friends in town that were welcome to come up and spend a few days when their parents gave the okay. They were generally bored when they were guests in town and usually came home before they had planned to. We had a couple of horses for the two older kids to ride, and the younger ones had their assorted pets to take care of– dogs, rabbits, chipmunks, rock chucks, assorted birds, and water snakes, even a peacock named Gregory Pecker. All of the kids were eased into waiting on the traveling public while they were still in grade school.

Everything got to be a hassle when they approached high school age and extra-curricular activities, learning to drive, motorcycles, and other town attractions kicked in. We made hundreds of extra trips up and down the mountain. It was even worse when they started getting summer jobs in town and getting their own cars. There were no gifts. If they wanted a personal vehicle of their own, they had to pay for it and maintain it themselves.

The mountain road was a dangerous place to travel. Lots of traffic in the summertime and steep icy roads in the winter. As a family, we had our share of close calls and car wrecks. I had a steady job in Buffalo and hauled the kids back and forth to school and to their summer jobs in town. During the short daylight hours in the winter, we left for work and school before daylight and got home after dark, in retrospect, just for the privilege of sleeping in the country. Since Buffalo has expanded into subdivisions outside of town, I see hundreds of family's doing what only a small minority of us did when our kids were growing up. I sure would never want to repeat the experience.

We raised five children there. The oldest, our daughter, was 12 years old when we bought it. There was no school bus, so there were daily trips up and down the mountain during the school year that I tried to coordinate with my job in Buffalo, but it didn't work out too well. During the summer, my wife and kids had to run the place until I got off work and could help out. We usually had one extra person hired during the months of June, July and August. Our season lasted from the latter part of April through hunting season in November.

Winters were a blessing. There was very little traffic in our early years, and the mountains were quiet. Some days in the middle of the winter, practically the only traffic was a half dozen or so logging trucks going down to the sawmill in Buffalo, and that ceased in March when the snow became soft and roads were too muddy to use. At that time, there were a couple of private sawmills that operated all winter. The loggers received board and room at the site and only came to town once a week.

In the early '60s, practically all of the truck traffic consisted of the logging trucks and the ones hauling livestock to and from the summer pastures on the Bighorns to their winter range east of Buffalo. The others went around by way of Casper to get into the Basin country. It was a lot longer but much easier on the trucks. The trucks at that time had to grind their way up the mountain in low gear all the way to Hospital Hill and most of the hills all the way to Powder River pass. Then it was low gear again from Meadowlark Resort all the way to the foot of Ten Sleep Canyon.

Brake systems and engines had a long way to go to reach present-day standards when big diesels can make the same trip almost as fast as a car.

Probably 90% of the tourist traffic drove from east to west to get to Yellowstone and then took another route home. Practically all of the cars came from back East through the Black Hills. The Bighorns were the first real mountains most of them had ever seen. Some of their questions would make you wonder. The most common was, "What is that white stuff up on the peaks?" On a 100° day in July, snow was out of the question. Ned Deloney, who owned the polka dot station and store called Alabams in Buffalo, always told them it was large deposits of salt. It took some convincing on our part to get them to believe he was only joking.

Another funny thing–when they were entering the canyon several miles below Trailside at Dead Man's Curve, some of them had the impression they were going downhill and were worried because their car was losing power. When they stopped at Trailside and started asking what was wrong with their car, we would just point back down the highway, and you could see the light come on.

The reason the Dodsons built Trailside in the first place was because they noticed so many cars were overheating and spewing steam out of the radiators. I don't think antifreeze had been invented yet. I know pressure radiator caps hadn't. Even though it isn't as hot, water boils faster at a higher altitude. Trailside was 7,000 feet, so pulling the canyon on a hot day with an early 1930 something Chevy or other vehicle spelled trouble.

Fred Dodson was a true entrepreneur, so he put an old stock water tank on a hill by the house about 40 feet above the roadway for pressure and pumped it full of water. Then he ran a pipe down to where he could park a few cars in a row, just like an old-time hitching rack, and put in individual faucets. He had a sign that said something like "Pure Rocky Mountain Spring Water." The overheated cars that were spewing steam would pull up to a faucet, and Fred would pull the plug on the bottom of the radiator to let the rest of the water drain out. It would take about a half hour for the motor to cool off before he could pour in cold water, so the tourists would usually wander into the gift shop and buy a few souvenirs or pop while they were waiting.

Fred charged $1 a car for this service, and it worked like a charm. The tourist didn't know he was almost to the top of the steep grade that was causing his overheating problem, and I don't suppose Fred felt he had any obligation to volunteer the information, so everyone was satisfied. Troy Pate, who worked for the Highway Maintenance Department, was a very good friend of the Dodsons. He told me that on a hot day Fred would change the water on 18 or 20 vehicles at a buck apiece. And this was during the Depression years when the going wage around Buffalo was $30 a month if you could find a job.

Another innovative idea that kind of grew with the business was canvas water bags. They were made by Sheridan Tent & Awning Company with their logo and printed with the words "Cools by Evaporation." This is basically true because the bag is a little porous and seeps water out through the canvas over a long period of time. As it evaporates, it cools the inside liquid. We used these bags on ranches and construction jobs before the invention of insulated coolers, but it was mainly because they wouldn't break if you dropped them. If the water was any cooler than a glass gallon jug sitting in the shade, it's news to me because I never could tell any difference.

I have no idea who started it–maybe Fred Dodson–but I first remember seeing water bags hung in front of radiators in the late '30s. Since it cools by evaporation, the idea was that it would help cool the motor as the engine water filtered down through the inside of the radiator exactly like modern cars still do. It was actually the worst thing a person could do because it shut off the air coming through the front of the radiator as the car was moving. But it didn't stop people from thinking it was a good idea because Fred Dodson and the next three owners, including us, sold a lot of them. The customer is always right–even when he's wrong.

Thinking about Fred and his water business is a good example of the free enterprise system at work. He took a product that was familiar to every single person on the face of the earth– water–and made a thriving business out of it without any sort of packaging whatsoever. He never advertised it for sale or asked anyone if they wanted to purchase it. It was a 100% customer voluntary action.

They willingly paid him a full day's Wyoming wages–$1–for something that never cost him a cent and thanked him for it when they pulled out of the driveway even though it was free for the taking if they wanted to walk less than 200 feet away to a small stream and fill a bucket like the locals did.

§ § §

The Dodson's granted an easement in April 1944 for a telephone line, and the Forest Service had it built to Hunter Ranger Station. It included Camp Comfort and several cabins along Clear Creek on the way to Hunter. It was a two-wire, 10-party line that was later extended to the Sheep Mountain Fire Lookout Station. From town to Hunter, the line was mostly on the south side of Highway 16 but then it crossed over to the other side all the way to the Lookout.

Shrum Lumber Co. started logging operations in the 1940s and had a camp on the north side of the highway several miles east of Powder River Pass. They extended the line to their operations, but it was usually out of order due to trees knocking the lines down. I worked there a couple of years.

The main line up Mosier Gulch to Hunter was built as cheaply as possible, and some of the poles weren't even treated. When one rotted off, it was wired to a fence post, which usually lowered the lines somewhat. In places the wire sagged low enough to catch a horseback rider at chin level. The line at Trailside was directly across the highway from the house, but we were never interested in hooking up to it. I don't know if any of the three previous owners did either.

In the early 1960s, the Forest Service sent out bids for anybody that was interested in purchasing the line as far as Hunter Ranger Station. The rest of the line had been abandoned. Nobody, including us, was interested, and they finally sold it to Camp Comfort for $1 with the stipulation the line would be maintained as far as Hunter. Radios were worthless in the mountains, and of course cell phones did not exist.

The line was constantly broken down, and the caretaker, Art Oliver, at Camp Comfort was responsible for fixing it. We became well-acquainted with him. When it quit working, he would start at Hunter and work his way down the mountain, looking for the break. If it wasn't something obvious like a tree falling across it, he would have to stop at intervals, climb the pole, and attach his mobile phone to the line and try to contact the Buffalo office. Ninety percent of the line was too rough to drive to, so he spent most of his time walking to the line, climbing the pole, attaching his mobile phone, and then returning to his vehicle. On a hot day, he was ready for a beer by the time he got to Trailside, which usually stretched into several more before he left.

One afternoon when I got home, my wife told me the repairman had dropped off a spare mobile line checker phone for her express use in an emergency. She now had the means to contact the outside world in the event of a catastrophe–if all the poles, wire, etc. were in working order. She had tried to explain several times she really didn't feel it was necessary, but he was insistent, so she finally agreed to accept it. She still didn't seem to be too enthused about the whole thing, so the kids and I tried to convince her what a great idea it was and she could practice climbing poles every evening after supper.

At that time, the TV show *Green Acres*, starring Eva Gabor and Eddie Albert as a citified couple moving to the country was quite popular. In the show, they hadn't gotten the telephone installed in the house yet and had to climb up the pole and hang on while they talked. There were numerous scenes of Eva, sometimes in evening gowns, clinging to the pole while carrying on a conversation seemingly with no effort at all. The kids insisted if Eva could do it, it would be a walk in the park for their mother. Unfortunately, she got rid of the portable line checker contraption before they had a chance to find out.

§ § §

The line from Hunter Ranger Station to Sheep Mountain Lookout was eventually abandoned, and in the summer of 1968, Bill Sand, Jr. and a couple of classmates, John Wilcynski and Carey Cummings, were hired by the Forest Service to disconnect what wires were still hanging on the poles and roll the wire up.

They figured out a very unique way of doing this. The whole line was on the west side of Highway 16, so they parked a Dodge Power Wagon with a heavy duty winch at Hunter and winched the wire all the way from the lookout station roughly eight miles. Bill told me it was a very strong copper-steel line, or it wouldn't have worked. It got hung up a few times, but they could estimate about where it happened and would drive back up the mountain and free the line. They finished the job without breaking the wire.

I was personally involved with the next phase of telephone service in the Bighorns. I was working for a local surveyor, Bob Stuckert, who had a contract with the telephone company–I think it was AT&T at the time–to survey a new buried line from the city water intake reservoir above Buffalo to Hunter Ranger Station and split it there with one line going to Paradise Guest Ranch and another to the highway maintenance camp on Pole Creek.

The telephone company had previously sent a questionnaire to all residents in the Bighorns, saying that they would consider installing a new line if they could get enough subscribers to pay for it. Business and cabin owners were all in favor of it, and it was over-subscribed by more than 50%.

We did the survey in February and March with deep snow the whole way and had to shovel a hole down through the snow every 100 feet to plant a stake. It was necessary to use a frost pin and sledgehammer to get through the frozen ground. We got it all surveyed, plotted and submitted it to the telephone company and two weeks later received notice the project had been cancelled.

It seems the telephone company was divided into sections–I think they called them exchanges–and everything on the west side of the invisible line above Camp Comfort was in the Worland Exchange. In other words, those people would have to receive their telephone service from a line beginning in Worland, then to Ten Sleep, then up and over the top of the Bighorn

260

Mountains, and then down to the spot just north of Camp Comfort, which encompassed about 95% of the subscribers.

Those people got their congressional delegation involved but to no avail. The feds said rules are rules–even the stupid ones. So they built the new buried line to Hospital Hill and tied onto the old overhead 10-party line built in 1944.

§ § §

One problem we hadn't foreseen when we bought Trailside was having five young children and a room full of pop, candy bars and potato chips for the tourist trade adjoining our living room. It didn't take long to draw up a short list of regulations–one treat per child per day. It worked really well, and we never had any problems to speak of with the treats. Sometimes one of the kids would forego their daily allotment for a few days in a row and save up for a really special one-person party, but we couldn't think of a logical reason why it wasn't technically allowed under the terms of the contract. It didn't happen very often, so it was kind of a nonissue.

To cut down on sugar and the associated dental bills, pre-sugared cereal of any kind was never purchased. Toast and oatmeal or Cream of Wheat were a standard breakfast along with milk and orange juice. Living 10 miles from the closest grocery store was a definite advantage when sitting down at the table and either eating what was placed in front of you or going hungry. Take your choice.

One incident comes to mind when thinking about the store. We also sold cigarettes. Needless to say, we hadn't even thought about emphasizing the fact that they were not considered treats. Their mother and I considered it a given.

The boys had built a playhouse halfway up the side of a steep bank several hundred feet in back of the house. They rigged up an old woodstove to cook with and ran the chimney out through the side of one wall. They even scrounged up some old carpet to cover the dirt floor. The house was strategically placed with a commanding view to prevent anyone from approaching the place without being seen by the occupants.

One day, they invited their mother up for tea. She had to stoop to get through the door, but they had some small chairs placed around a little table, so it was okay once she got seated. Sitting there sipping tea and making small talk, she noticed a suspicious looking bulge under the carpet in one corner. She never mentioned it, but a short time later, she went back for a closer look when the boys were out of sight. The bulge was an emergency survival kit, containing half a dozen full cartons of assorted brands of cigarettes. Just like the one in Boston, the aftermath of the tea party had far reaching consequences.

§ § §

I mentioned previously there were seven members in our family. Actually, there were eight. I forgot to count Spot. We always had two or three dogs as the kids were growing up that were all special, but Spot was extra special. He was a big white Samoyed with a half-dollar-size black spot over his left ear. We got him as a pup before we moved to Trailside. Some of the kids were just babies then, and he lived to see a couple of them graduate from high school. As with all of their pets, the kids picked out the names, and I never figured out whether they were innovative when choosing his or just practical, probably a little of both.

He had the disadvantage of having seven different bosses all at the same time and had to deal with the whims and personalities of each, but he never seemed to have any trouble–just went with the flow. He had a mild disposition, seldom barked, and never offered to bite anyone, which is saying something because we had hundreds of tourists running around the place in the summer, and a number of them had little rugrats who had never been around a dog before. They would run up to him, grab him, pet him, and he just took it in stride. After taking the roughhousing of our five through the years, he probably figured he had seen it all.

The two things he hated throughout his lifetime were rock chucks and porcupines. When he heard a rock chuck's high-pitched bark, he was off like a shot and would spend hours trying to get through the rocks to its den. He seldom succeeded, but it wasn't from the lack of trying. The one exception was one summer when Randy raised a baby rock chuck on a bottle, and it was running around loose. Somehow he knew it was off limits and never bothered it, but that was the only one.

He lost every battle he ever had with a porcupine, but it didn't stop him from tangling with the next one that showed up. It was terribly discouraging to have him show up with a face full of quills. Sometimes he would attack with his mouth wide open, and the quills would be lodged deep in his throat, and we would have to haul him to the vet to tranquilize him. Other times, I would have two or three of the kids sit on him to hold him down, so I could pull the quills with a pair of pliers. It was a very painful experience, but he never tried to bite. [Cutting the tip off the quill releases the vacuum, allowing it to be pulled out gently.]

Our daughter, Carrie, always took him with her when she was riding her horse, and they became quite attached to each other. She relied on him for protection in case something might happen, and one time something did.

There were some vertical rock cliffs a couple hundred yards behind our house that were 50 or 60 feet high. One day, I happened to glance up there and could see Spot running like crazy back and forth along the rim. I took off on a dead run and found Carrie stuck halfway up the wall. She had tried to climb it and couldn't go up or down. Her face was plastered against the rock so she couldn't cry for help, but Spot knew she was in deep trouble. I was able to climb up far enough to get her foot on one of my shoulders to support her, but I was balanced on one foot. It seemed like an eternity before the kids and their mother lowered a rope from the top that she was able to grab, and we worked our way back down.

A little different situation happened once when Robin, grade school age, got a new camping tent and set it up on the lawn to try it out. It was a really dark night, and he woke up about midnight to the sound of something walking around the tent sniffing and rubbing against the nylon. He was petrified because we had both mountain lions and black bears in the area. He said he heard it wander a short distance away from the tent, so he peeked out through the tent flap and saw Spot's white coat. Spot spent the rest of the night in the tent, but I don't think it was by his choice.

Another time, I got home from work one afternoon, and the kids met me at the door all excited. Somebody had put a spell on poor old Spot. We always had quite a number of Indians going by the place between the Crow Indian reservation just across the line in Montana and the Wind River Arapahoe-Shoshone reservation across the Bighorns near Riverton. Quite a few would stop and have a beer or a pop for the kids, and we got acquainted with a number of them.

One afternoon, my wife heard the shop doorbell ring and stepped out of our adjoining dining room to wait on a man who ordered a Coke. He was sitting on the other side of the counter, visiting when she felt Spot brush against her leg. She hadn't even known he was there. He growled in a really low tone, but the man heard him. She was terribly embarrassed and tried to apologize because it had never happened before. The guy spoke pretty broken English and told her it wasn't the dog growling but some evil spirit inside him. He asked her if he could put a spell on the dog so he would never growl again and waved his hands over Spot and spoke a few unintelligible words. The kids were really impressed. I don't know about Spot.

A couple weeks later on a Sunday morning, the family had all gone to church, and I was running the place by myself. A guy came in and asked me, "Where dog? Where dog?" I didn't have the faintest idea what he was talking about, but then he said something about a spell, and it sunk in. I called Spot, who was asleep in the living room. When he came out, the guy waved his hands over him and muttered a few words I'd never heard before and told me the spell had been lifted. Spot was free to go, and he did–back to the living room and back to sleep.

I relayed the message to the kids when they got home, and they remembered they hadn't heard Spot growl the whole time he was under. Of course, they didn't happen to think they hadn't heard him growl before or after either. As near as I could tell, it didn't make any difference to Spot one way or the other.

§   §   §

We didn't have any neighbors for several miles in every direction, so during the summer months the kids had to entertain themselves because their mother and I had our hands full taking care of the tourist trade. They had a lot of room to roam around in and on nice days spent their entire time outdoors, only coming in the house when they got hungry. As a consequence, they accumulated quite a few pets through the years.

We always had a couple of dogs that were part of the family but no cats. Living directly adjacent to the highway, it was a problem keeping them off the road because there was so much traffic. We lost one young German shepherd that was hit by a car and killed.

We also lost a peacock. The peacock was a birthday gift for Anthony, our second youngest. He was a beautiful bird, but he irritated me no end. He had half a million acres of trees to roost in but chose to use the top of the screen door on the back porch, and we never were able to break him of the habit. He always left a large pile of manure every night right in the middle of the step, and invariably I would be in a hurry coming out the door and forget it until it was too late.

Anthony named him Gregory Pecker for a very good reason because if he was in a bad mood and somebody got too close to him, he would hammer them with his beak. It felt like being stung by a wasp. He pretty much left me alone because when he tried it, he knew he was going to get whacked in return.

I can remember one really funny incident when he almost got somebody else. Early one morning before the family was up, I was out front by the gas station when a car with South Dakota license plates pulled up to the pumps. It was a young couple in their late teens who were trying to act nonchalant but weren't doing a very good job. I found out why when I opened the little door to get to the gas cap and found a note taped to the inside–just married.

Our gift shop was in a separate building about 50 feet from the station, and the girl spotted Gregory, roosting on the outside of the window sill about 5 feet off the ground. He wasn't moving and looked like he was carved out of stone. She was real self-conscious and giggly and said to her new husband, "What a beautiful bird." For some reason, I spoke up and said he wasn't a real bird, just one that had been mounted. About that time, Gregory moved his head slightly, and the girl exclaimed she saw him move. I told her my kids were on the inside and operating his body with wires. The girl giggled, ran up the steps, bent down over Gregory, and he missed her nose by about a quarter inch. She screamed and backed off, and her new husband and I broke up laughing. She was a really good sport and after she settled down joined in the laughter.

I finished fueling their car, he handed me some bills, and I went into the station to get his change. When I came out, they were sitting in the car with the motor running, and he had his window rolled down. I handed him his change through the window, thanked them, and said, "Enjoy your honeymoon." I had to grit my teeth to keep from laughing. Their eyes got real big and their jaws dropped open, but I just turned and walked away.

I have often wondered how many times a service station attendant said something similar before that couple figured out how everyone knew they were just married because they were trying so hard to act natural and failing. The guy that taped that note out of sight by the gas cap had the last laugh because self-service gas stations were 40 years in the future, and that kid would have had no reason to open that cover door.

As far as Gregory was concerned, he got a lot of attention from the tourists through the summer but got to be quite a pest. If he found a window open, he would come in the house, which was an absolute no-no. He got so big that when he tried to fly, he just couldn't hold any altitude and would come crashing back to earth. He finally figured out if he launched from the top of the house he could glide a long way before lowering his landing gears. I watched him take off one day, but by the time he crossed the highway, he was only 5 or 6 feet above the road, and he intersected a little red sports car on the way down the mountain. There was a helluva thump, and feathers flew in every direction. The guy never even slowed down, but I'll bet he was wondering what the hell kind of birds they were raising in Wyoming that were half as big as his car.

§ § §

Another family addition we had one summer was a black bum lamb that someone had given my wife, and she raised him on a bottle. We kept him in a cage for a couple weeks until he became acclimated and then turned him loose with our two dogs. I don't know if they appreciated him or not, but they didn't have any choice because he had forgotten what another sheep looked like. They were the only animals moving around the yard, so he adopted them. When they moved, he moved. In actuality, that was the only reason he survived. We had lots of coyotes, bobcats and a few foxes that prowled around the house, especially at night looking for an easy meal, but none of them got close to the two dogs.

We called him Blackie for obvious reasons. It was funny to see him try to copy everything his bodyguards did, including their dog food and kitchen scrap meals that were placed in individual dishes on the porch. They would growl at each other as a warning to backoff when one would intrude on their individual space, but I think they figured their constant pest was too dumb to get the message and tolerated him. I don't ever remember seeing any sign that they had bitten him.

When we had friends visit us, the dogs would be jumping around with excited yelps, and Blackie did his best to imitate them, but he was a dismal failure because he never lost his sheepish accent–pun intended. If it hadn't been for some extra strong DNA, he may never have even developed a taste for grass. That would have been one for the books.

Being a wether, his only option in life was to end up on somebody's dinner table. Being black was a double whammy because black wool was of inferior quality, and since the fibers would integrate with the other wool at shearing time and bring a lower price, sheep men were eliminating black sheep from their herds.

During the winter when deep snow and below zero weather were standard features, we always let the dogs stay in the house, but, of course, we couldn't extend the invitation to Blackie, who had grown into a large animal. Leaving him outside without the dogs for protection was out of the question because of coyotes.

We kept putting off the decision of what to do until after the kids had started back to school, but my wife and I talked it over and decided we had to get off dead center. One day, when everyone was gone, I locked the dogs in the house, picked up a .22 rifle, and he followed me some distance from the house. I wanted to make sure it was a clean kill, so I held the muzzle end of the gun against his head. Just before I pulled the trigger, he turned his head and started nibbling the end of the barrel, and I chickened out.

A good friend of mine, Charlie Bishop, had a little ranch on Rock Creek just north of town and butchered sheep, cattle and hogs for his family's use and also for sale. I told him I needed a favor and wanted to make a trade. Sheep for sheep. I hauled Blackie out to his ranch, and a couple weeks later, he brought us a box full of lamb chops and assorted cuts. I didn't ask him if it came from his herd, and he didn't volunteer any information. None of the kids ever brought the subject up either, and I still don't know.

The .22 rifle that Blackie nibbled on belonged to one of the boys and was involved in another incident that could have had some tragic consequences. Fortunately, everything turned out for the best before it had to be fired.

§ § §

For a couple of summers, I hired an older retired man, Wes Straight, to run the gas station till I returned home from my job in town in the evening. He and his wife lived in a cabin in back of our main house. Every morning just as I left for work, Wes would show up with a .45 pistol that he put under the counter directly under the cash drawer. I knew I was wasting my breath, but a couple of times I told him if someone came in with a gun and wanted the cash, to help them carry it out. He wouldn't say anything, just look at me and grin. I knew him pretty well because we had worked together a couple of years in a logging camp in the Bighorn Mountains. He was old-school, worked hard, tough as nails, and just wanted to be left alone. If someone had come in and demanded cash, Wes would have dropped him before he got out of the door.

It was really a problem being in such an isolated spot 10 miles from town and no phone and no way to get help in an emergency with every conceivable type of person driving by all day and night long. I always kept a gun handy, but the problem with that was having the opportunity to get to it when it was needed. By then it would be too late.

I remember one time in particular when I was in the gas station, and three young men with Nebraska license plates pulled in. They visited awhile, needed gas, but didn't have the money to pay for it, and really looked the situation over. They wanted to cash a personal check on a Nebraska bank, which, of course, I wouldn't accept, and things were getting a little tense.

My wife was looking out the window of the gift shop, a separate building about 50 feet away, and could see that things weren't looking too good. Unbeknownst to me, she had one of the boys, Robin, 10 years old at the time, get his .22 rifle and crack the door of the gift shop open so he could see out but they couldn't see in. She told him, "If they jump your father, shoot." It was only a single shot we had bought for him when he was 5 years old, and he knew how to handle it. Thankfully, he didn't have to. Another car pulled up to the pumps, and the boys left. They stole a couple cases of oil among other things and threw it out on the asphalt a quart at a time on their way back to town. I have often thought that was probably the best no sale I ever made.

§ § §

One day, Randy, our youngest, came running down to the house all excited, carrying about a half dozen baby rock chucks in a bucket. They weren't very old because they were hairless and still had their eyes closed. I don't have the faintest idea how or where he was able to dig them out because rock chucks usually go pretty far back in the rocks to have their young. He wanted to keep them, but I told him he would have to take them back to the nest because they would just die if he tried to feed them. As usual, I didn't know what I was talking about, and he finally talked me into keeping one of them and taking the others back. I didn't know if the mother would accept them or not, but our choices were pretty limited. I figured their odds of living, including the one he kept, weren't very good.

His mother found a little milk bottle that I think probably came from Carrie's dollhouse. They warmed up some milk, and the dang thing took right off sucking it. However, there was one problem. The kids were still in school, it was mid-May, and I was working for the Highway Department in Buffalo, so their mother inherited the job of feeding the new member of the family every 30 minutes or so. It only drank a few drops at each feeding, so she had to take the thing with her every time she went to town.

A week or so later, she had to go to town for the kids' end of school programs at the grade school on Fort Street. Of course, she had to take the welfare case with her to feed between the various class presentations. It was a warm afternoon, and she parked in front of the school and left the chuck on the front seat. She slipped out and fed him between programs, but the sun worked around and got to bearing down on him. When she came out after they were over, she had a few ounces of baked chuck. She was devastated, of course, and so was Randy.

A couple weeks later, Randy asked me if he could keep one of the ones he had returned to the nest if they were still there. Doing some rapid calculations in my head, I figured there was little chance of that being possible, and I really felt sorry about him losing the first one through no fault of his own, so I said, "Okay." He was out of the house and back in five minutes with another one, but this one had fur and its eyes open. I was about a 150% sure he had out gunned me and had been keeping a daily check on his herd from the time he lost his first one. So it was back to the bottle.

Randy Gray & DC, the Rock Chuck

This was about the same time as a movie or TV show came out with a cat or something similar as the star. I think it was called *That Darned Cat*, so Randy called his new pet That Darned Chuck, DC for short, and he really turned into a neat family pet. Randy kept him in a cage for a time but finally turned him loose outside during the day. He had to lock him back up at night because our dogs were death on rock chucks. I don't know how he survived to adulthood, but he did.

To feed him, the kids would just hand him his bottle of milk, and he would tip it up, hold it with his paws, and gulp it down. We catered to tourists at the time, and they would feed him peanuts and popcorn when he sat up and begged. I don't recall him ever biting anybody. The kids handled him like a pet cat and got a little rough with him at times, but they never had any problems catching him when he was running loose in the yard. Sometimes they got careless with him when he was in the house, and he would disappear under the fridge or inside of a cabinet. That was when he would do something that really irritated me.

One part of the house was a huge open beam room about 1,000 square feet that we used for a gift shop at the time. Later years, we turned it into a living room. We had a bar set up in one corner and sold pop, beer, snacks, etc., the usual tourist stuff. On the counter we had several racks that held about a dozen individual packages of potato chips, Cheetos, etc. The bar was about 4 feet high. DC would sneak in there at every opportunity, and by wedging himself between the bar and the log wall, he could climb up on top of the bar and help himself. If he had enough time, like five or 10 minutes, before somebody caught him, he would open up all his presents– chips, peanuts, candy, anything edible–and take a few bites out of each one. Tourists took a dim view of buying something to eat that looked like a rat had already started chewing on, so we had to throw away everything he had touched.

Another of his little quirks as he got older was with rugs. We tried to keep him outside, but he knew all about open windows and screen doors that weren't quite shut. I suppose it was nesting instincts, but we would come in from outside and find three or four throw rugs sticking out all around the refrigerator. He would pull one under as far as it would go and then go get another one. It was frustrating to get him out from under the fridge because he would squeeze clear to the back, and there was no way to yank him out. We would usually have to bribe him with something he liked to eat and then grab him before he could crawl back in. But he could be funny too.

The gift shop was a big room, and we had a number of old round oak tables to display merchandise on. They were old style. I had restored and refinished all of them, and they really looked nice in the log building.

One afternoon, a local, elderly couple was sitting at the bar, nursing a couple of beers. They had a little tiny dog they took with them wherever they went. They always carried him because at one time a large dog had attacked him and almost bitten him in two. He still carried large scars on each side of his body. I don't think he weighed over 4 or 5 pounds soaking wet.

He was lying at the foot of his owner's stool when DC came rushing into the room. I suppose it was the first time the tiny dog had ever seen what looked like a dog that was smaller than him, so he immediately charged the chuck. DC slammed on the brakes, reversed directions, and took off like the devil himself was after him. The floor was wood and pretty slick so both the chaser and chasee had trouble getting traction. Their feet were just a blur. DC finally made it to one of the pedestal tables, and when he felt his back against something solid, he got his courage back and started back at the bully who probably outweighed him by a couple of ounces. The dog went into retreat mode after he got himself turned around and headed for the safe zone under the barstool. History repeated itself, and it was DC's turn under the table. It was one of the funniest things I ever saw. They repeated the routine several times till they played out and went to their respective safehouses like professional boxers do between rounds. A large mouse could have bluffed both of them at the same time.

Another time, when DC was half grown, Pat, my wife, had some kind of meeting to go to in Buffalo. When she got to town, she pulled into Reimann's Service Station to get some gas. This was in the days when service stations actually provided services like gassing the car, checking the oil, and washing the windshield. There was no such thing as self-service.

She had gone inside the building to wait until the attendant was finished and was visiting with the owner. The door opened, and the guy who was servicing her car came in and spoke to his boss. He said, "You won't believe this, but there's a rock chuck running around out there on the driveway." Pat couldn't get out there fast enough to scoop up DC. He had evidently crawled up on the frame somewhere and rode the car to town until she stopped for gas. She didn't have time to take him back home, so she had to take him with her.

DC really got to be a big animal by fall when the kids started back to school. They still carted him around like a rabbit or cat, but I knew that sooner or later something was going to happen. He was a pet but also basically a wild animal and had sharp claws and big teeth. I figured the only way out was to transport him up the mountain someplace when the kids were in school. Rock chucks start hibernating in early September even in nice weather. They eat like crazy after the pups are grown and put on lots of fat to last them through the winter.

The situation took care of itself. We had an old cabin up in the back of the house, and DC crawled under the foundation and made a nest for himself. For several weeks after the kids started to school, he would come down to the house once a day, and Pat would feed him. I suppose he finally went into hibernation before winter set in, and I wondered what would take place in the spring. We had lots of rock chucks as usual, but it would have been impossible to recognize him unless one would have come up and greeted us. None did.

§ § §

Randy had a knack for catching unusual pets. We had lots of chipmunks around the house. He would livetrap them, put them in a cage for a day or two, and then turn them loose. I was pretty adamant about this. Once, he caught one with only three legs. The left front one was missing, either born that way or the result of an accident, but it certainly didn't hamper his movements any.

From day-one it was a really unusual critter. Randy carried him around on his shoulder, and the thing would take a nap in his shirt pocket. At no time did it ever exhibit the characteristics of a wild animal. Randy never even bothered to put him in a cage. When he got tired of playing with him, he just turned him loose. When he felt like renewing the relationship, he would bait his livetrap, and an hour later the chipmunk was running around on top of his shoulder and searching his pockets for hidden treats. I always thought every animal, like humans, has its own distinct personality, and I never was able to figure that one out.

Of all the pets that Randy acquired, a family of mice was the one that got to me the most. I hated the things and had traps and bait set out for them as standard procedure. The original house was constructed of natural logs, and there was no way to seal them 100% mouse proof unless we burned the house down. They destroyed a lot of our souvenirs, especially during the winter months when we were closed, unless things were packed away in glass display counters or metal trunks. Invariably, we would overlook something in the fall and find a mound of shredded paper or feathers in the spring.

The house was heated with a coal stoker with a coal bin in the basement. One day, Randy happened to walk by the door to the bin and heard something squeaking. He dug around in the coal and came up with a half dozen hairless, eyes closed, baby mice. I don't know how long he had them before I found out about it because he knew what I would have done with them. Anyway, he built a cage for them outside and spent some time feeding them with a baby bottle.

I gave the matter considerable thought and finally figured out the best course of action was to do nothing, so that's what I did. I never mentioned the danged things again and don't know what happened to them. I suppose if he succeeded in raising them to adulthood, and I caught them before they got back to their birthplace in the coal bin. Anyway, I sure hope so.

Our number four child, Anthony, spent his time with fish and rabbits. He was very meticulous in everything he did and would spend an entire day cleaning out his fish tank. I always figured it was safer to drink it when he finished than the spring water that came out of the mountain and was piped to the house.

His rabbit cage was almost as sanitary. He had quite a few. I don't remember what eventually happened to them. I suppose he gave them away because I know we didn't ever have any rabbit for lunch besides one or two snowshoe rabbits that Randy shot one winter. He fried them, and we tried to eat them, but they were so tough all we gained from the operation was a lot of exercise for the jaw muscles.

Anthony had an unusual thing happen with his rabbits. He went out to check them one day and found a large visitor inside the cage with them. It must have just gotten in because all his rabbits were still alive. He opened the cage door and swatted the thing with a stick to run it out the door. We had no idea how it got in because the cage wire was half inch mesh. If it had been a weasel, all the rabbits would have been dead. They were the most vicious thing for their size that were running around up there. He said the varmint was dark brown and a lot bigger than his largest rabbits. The only thing I could come up with was a pine marten. I would sometimes see one when fishing at the high lakes above timberline when they were scrounging along the shore looking for dead fish or the entrails from ones that had recently been cleaned. I never saw one at the lower elevations.

Carrie and Stephen, number one and two children respectively, both had horses to ride. Carrie's was an old retired cow pony named King that I bought from a friend of mine, Charlie Kershner, who didn't have a place to keep him. He guaranteed him not to kick, buck or bite, and he lived up to his reputation 100%. Carrie spent countless days riding around the mountains, mostly by herself, and visiting friends that lived in some of the lodges and cabins several miles from Trailside. It was an experience she never forgot and probably the happiest time of her whole life.

Stephen had a little pinto half-Shetland pony named Kola, which means friend. I was told it came from a reservation in South Dakota. He never lived up to his name. Like a lot of small horses, he was too smart for his own good and dumped Stephen a number of times. All the other kids were afraid to ride him, which was just what he wanted.

One day, when the family was gone, I happened to walk up in back of the house where he was standing with King. I was irritated with him because he was getting so ornery, so on an impulse I thought I'd teach him a lesson. I slipped a halter on his head, grabbed the halter rope, and swung up on his back. It was the last thing he had ever expected and for a few moments didn't know how to react. Then he put his head down and started hopping around like he did with Stephen. His nose was scraping the ground between hops, and from my vantage point, I couldn't see his head or neck. It was like sitting on a barrel at the edge of a cutbank and so funny that I started laughing and was relieved that nobody was around to witness the comedy. After a minute or so, I could see that neither of us was making any headway, and I thought, "What the hell am I doing up here?" so I slid over and down his neck to the ground just like the waterslide at the city pool. Neither one of us learned anything from the incident. His disposition didn't improve, so I finally sold him. None of the kids lamented the parting.

§ § §

Two miles directly north of Trailside on Forest Service property where French Creek comes out of the canyon was the remains of an old gold mining claim and a shack we called the Yarwood Cabin. In the 1960s, all that remained of the building were the walls and part of the roof. There was a lot of junk scattered around like tin cans, iron bed frames, a cookstove, and the remains of an old Model T Ford, frame, gas tank and part of the body. A guy I worked with, Jimmy Dawson, told me once when he was fishing, he blundered onto the remains of an old moonshine still hidden back in the brush, a remnant of the Depression days' Prohibition era. Many years later, someone hauled all the trash away, maybe the Forest Service, and about the only things left were a few small pieces of mortar that had held the rock chimney together. Even those were hard to locate the last time I was there a number of years ago.

The old mining shaft dug into the side of a hill had caved in, but there were still pieces of small iron tracks that had been used to haul the ore to the creek for processing. The creek was several hundred feet from the shaft. The owners had fashioned a small cart on wheels out of an old piece of galvanized metal to transport the diggings. It had a hinged lid on one end to dump the load and was pretty crude but evidently worked. This was in the days of make do or do without mentality.

In the 1930s, my uncle, Tom White, had a ranch on Rock Creek that joined a neighbor whose name was Yarwood. Many years later, I finally made the connection that it was the same family that had the gold mining claim on French Creek.

An old prospector refiled on the claim sometime before we moved to Trailside, and I got to meet him. He showed up the first two years after we bought the place, 1960 and 1961. I had some interesting conversations with him. He was quite a character. He was a small, sparse man, quite vocal, and looked like he had been using a pick and shovel since he was 2 years old.

I have no idea how old he was. Somewhere between 70 and 90 is as close as I would venture a guess.

Besides French Creek, he told me he had gold mining claims in Idaho and Utah that he worked at various times of the year and was absolutely certain that a truck load of gold was located just below the surface of each if he could just pinpoint the spot. He also told me he had found some good gold color flecks in the sandbars along French Creek. I would sure have like to know where they were because the smallest grains of sand I ever saw when fishing that stream were six or eight inches in diameter.

He lived in an old black Cadillac that he had completely gutted. He parked it in the city park when he was staying in Buffalo. He had cut a hole through the roof in back and ran a stovepipe up through it to get rid of the smoke when he fired the woodstove up. The driver's seat was a box that doubled for a storage cabinet.

The rest of his gear was in a little two-wheel trailer he towed behind the Caddy when he wanted to go somewhere. It also carried his little four-wheel go-kart that he used to get to French Creek when he parked his rig at the house. It was pretty simple, just a flat piece of plywood with four wheels attached. The steering wheel was a lever that moved back and forth to turn the front wheels. There was a little gas motor mounted on the back that had a chain drive attachment attached to the four wheels. The seat was just a flat board about two people wide. I would guess the top speed was about three or four miles an hour, but I think it would have climbed a wall if it could have gotten enough traction.

Our oldest boy, Stephen, was 11 or 12 at the time and rode the thing up and down the hills at the house. They were terribly steep but the cart would creep up and down like a caterpillar crawling over a log. I can't remember what it had for brakes. The guy never showed up after the first two summers, and I never found out what happened to him. I can't even remember his name if I ever knew it to begin with.

§   §   §

Our four boys all liked to play chess and spent countless hours hovered over their chessboards, but they had one problem that most players didn't have. Living in the mountains with no close neighbors, practically all of their games had to be played among themselves, and they got bored because they were so well-acquainted with each other's habits and playing abilities, so they tried to think up different schemes and innovations to make the games more interesting. I remember one in particular.

We had a grove of large aspen trees along a little creek across the highway from the house. Two of the boys, Randy and Robin, carried some lumber and tools several hundred yards up the creek and built a platform in the tallest tree they could find. They took two separate chess sets–kept one in the house and crawled up the tree and put the other one on the platform.

We had a CB radio hooked up to an antenna on top of the house, and they had a walkie-talkie that Robin took with him when he crawled up on the platform. When they made their separate plays, they would radio the move and position on the board for the other player. He, in turn, would duplicate the move on his board so they could stay even with each other. At least that was the idea.

What actually happened was that after the first hour or two, one would radio his move to the other, and he would call back and say, "You can't do that. I've got one of my men there," and the argument would begin. It always escalated past the point of no return, and they would both get mad and turn their radios off. Game over.

Some 50 years later, Robin and I were cutting firewood from the aspen grove and found the old tree he had used. It had rotted off and blown down, but the platform was still attached. We cut the trunk off on each side of the platform leaving about a 6-foot length and hauled it across the road to where we had built a new cabin. We set it up, and put a birdhouse on top of it. Robin told me, as far as he could remember, he and Randy never finished a single game.

§ § §

When we first moved to Trailside in 1960, there were no modern toilet facilities for the tourists. The house, of course, had indoor plumbing and a septic system, but for the tourist trade it was outdoor privies. We bought the place in the spring, and I didn't have the time or opportunity to modernize the restrooms for the next couple years. We also didn't have the money. The situation made for some interesting moments.

Originally, the privies at Trailside had been constructed by the WPA, Works Project Administration, prior to World War II. This was a job creation scheme dreamed up by President Roosevelt during the Great Depression era of the 1930s when the unemployment rate was so high. It put men to work on public projects building streets, installing pipelines, etc. Practically all of it was done with hand labor. It was discontinued when World War II started. One of their projects was pouring concrete pedestals for outdoor privies.

Fred Dodson had them installed sometime after he started building Trailside in 1934. His only problem with these was that the only place he could put them was across Highway 16 from the gas pumps and souvenir shop. Believe me that was responsible for some interesting situations.

Quite a number of our customers were from New York, and you didn't need a license plate to know where they came from. The women dressed differently than the rest of the country. Most of them dressed to the nines and wore 4-inch high heels. When her husband pulled up to the pumps, she would step out of the car and ask where the restrooms were. We would point and say, "They're across the highway. Be careful of traffic while crossing. Just follow the dirt path down that steep bank and go through the willows till you get to the little plank footbridge crossing the creek. Then turn left till you get to the one marked 'Ladies.' Don't pay any attention to the water snakes. They're harmless."

You can imagine the look on some of their faces. Invariably, they would ask how far back it was to that little town they had just passed through, Buffalo, and we would say, "Eight miles, but it's 70 to the next one, Ten Sleep." You could almost see the wheels turning in their heads as they tried to figure the odds. Could they make it?

Layton Wilson, the previous owner, told me he had one lady who was so incensed when he pointed across the highway, she demanded that she be allowed to use their private toilet in the house. He refused. Evidently, he had had a very trying day because when she started marching for the house, a separate building about 50 feet away, he was just two steps behind her. When she went through the door, she met Lucille, Layton's wife, face to face and made her demands. Layton told me if Lucille hadn't backed him up, there would have been a divorce in the Wilson family. Fortunately, she concurred with Layton.

Actually, though it seems funny now, at that period of time there weren't many modern toilet facilities in the Bighorns. All the private cabins and most of the tourist accommodations had outdoor privies, not inside outhouses as some joker called them.

As time passed, the Forest Service and State became more restrictive, and cabins and lodges had to either install septic fields with leach fields or in the situations where it wasn't possible, like next to a creek, put in closed systems with no outlets and pump them regularly when they filled up. These would be suitable for small cabins that weren't used year-round but were not practical for any business that catered to the public like lodges.

At one time, South Fork Inn installed a very expensive system, but the ground water was so close to the surface, it never worked properly. The Pines and Meadowlark had the same problem and ended up pumping their sewage out of the creek bottoms to a higher elevation, so it could be treated properly. Hunter Ranger Station built a large building to house their summer help and ended up using a swamp for their leach field, which solved the problem of it ever plugging up. Some of the rest of us didn't have that choice.

276

§ § §

Anybody who has ever lived outside of town for any length of time knows the feeling of hopelessness when the septic system fails. Invariably, it occurs at the worst possible moment, for example an hour before a large group of invited dinner guests are expected. It is an experience that few will ever forget right down to the last detail. Mine was over 50 years ago.

We were the fourth owners of Trailside. Of the previous three couples, only one had a child still living with them. There were seven of us, five kids, so you can probably guess where this is leading.

Fred Dodson had installed a septic tank when he built the place, and it worked great for the next 25 years because of so few people using it. Out of sight, out of mind. When we purchased the place from Layton Wilson, he took me to the general location of the tank. He didn't know exactly where it was and said the previous owner had gone through the same routine as he was giving me. He said he had never had any sewer problems and the owner before him hadn't either.

The sewer backed up two years after we moved in, and I had to do something fast and the hard way. When the Dodson's installed the septic tank some 25 years before, they had also planted some small spruce trees in the same location. They were now some 60 feet tall and there was absolutely no way to get a backhoe or septic tank pump close enough to the location even if I had known where it was. I got a shovel and started digging some exploratory holes. It took a while, but I finally located the septic tank almost directly under one of the spruce trees. It was made entirely of wood planks, and the top was constructed with a double layer of water soaked boards and a couple layers of old linoleum on top of that. It was so heavy I couldn't lift it but finally slid it sideways with a crowbar and uncovered the mess underneath.

After going over the list of options, I was left with one choice–a 5-gallon pail with a 4-foot rope tied to the bale to lower it down into the tank and dip it out one bucket at a time. It was the most memorable unpleasant job I ever got into. I would hoist a bucket full of the slop out and then have to carry it a ways to empty it. It took a lot of effort to hoist that bucket out, and at that altitude, 7,000 feet, I was soon puffing like a long distance runner. I pulled one bucketful out, and when I set it down to catch my breath, I lost my footing and dropped the bucket. Some of the damned stuff shot straight back up into my mouth as I was gasping for air. I didn't dare even breathe while I made a run for the creek to wash my mouth out. I had to go down over a steep bank and some big rocks to get there. I have never before or since appreciated clean water as much as I did then. As you can probably guess, a new septic system and leach field moved to the top of the emergency to do list.

I hired a local contractor, Bob Smith, to install it, and he did a good job. I helped do some of the grunt work. When we lowered the new concrete tank into place, we both had a good laugh over my previous experience with a buried wooden tank. That led to more stories about making do with whatever material was available. I remember one in particular he told me about.

He was born and raised in a rural area of Indiana before transplanting to Wyoming in the days when money was practically nonexistent. A neighboring farmer was trying to grind out a living on a small farm and needed to replace his outdoor privy with something inside the house for the wife and kids. The problem was that he didn't have the money to put in a tank and leach field, so he contacted Bob, and they improvised. An adjoining swamp was utilized for a leach field without the need for any alteration or expense of any kind, including pipe or gravel.

Bob borrowed a backhoe and dug a hole. The farmer had an old Ford station wagon that had quit running, so they took out the seats and opened up one of the vent windows and set it in the hole. Then they ran a pipe from the house through the window and covered it up. I asked Bob if the job had been approved by the county sanitarian. He said he didn't remember.

§ § §

Early attempts at getting television reception was another situation that provided our family with some laughs in later years although we didn't consider it very humorous at the time. Buffalo was on the fringe for receiving television in the 1950s with station K-2 in Casper the first and only choice. It was transmitted directly from their tower because satellites were years in the future and unheard of.

Frank Kirnig owned a local electronics store in Buffalo on the southeast corner of Fort and Main Streets and was the first to promote a tower to receive and transmit the Casper signal as near as I can remember. He placed it on Bald Mountain just west of town, and it was supported by voluntary contributions. But as in all ventures like that, there were a lot of people who took advantage of the situation and rode on the backs of others. A few years later, a tower was constructed on Windy Ridge that worked much better and also picked up the Rapid City transmission tower. Even though we could see this one from our house at Trailside about three miles to the east, it didn't do us any good because it was pointed in the other direction to service Buffalo. Our only option was an antenna of our own to pick up the signal from Casper, and the biggest obstacle was Grouse Mountain, looming above us about a mile to the south.

We went to the highest hill we could find on our property, which was over a 100 yards west of the house next to the Bighorn Forest fence, and planted a 25-foot 4-inch pipe in concrete. Then we mounted a 12-foot mast on top of that and ran a TV ladder wire from it to the house. It still wasn't high enough to clear Grouse Mountain, but we got a picture at times that bounced its way in. Then we placed a pair of rabbit ears on our 12-inch black and white TV set with a sheet of aluminum foil just behind them to help reflect the signal when and if we got one. The rabbit ears were two small antennas about 18 inches long that were manually rotated back and forth to try to pick up the picture. Even at the best of times–depending on the weather–it was like viewing the screen through a blizzard. Hence, the term snow that plagued all TV sets in our area at the time. The local outdoor movie theater, owned by Sam Rosenthal, located about a mile east of Main Street on Highway 16 advertised their multi-thousand square inch screen with "guaranteed no snow" due to the competition they were getting from the new-fangled source of entertainment. Television eventually put it out of business.

One other unavoidable problem we had at Trailside was that the ladder wire between the antenna and the house lost transmission power for every foot of line, and we had several hundred feet of it to contend with. All in all, the odds of getting any picture at all was next to nothing, but we spent a lot of time trying.

The antenna and pipe on top of the hill was so heavy I had to use a 3-foot pipe wrench to rotate it back and forth when trying to pinpoint the signal coming in from Casper. When the wind wasn't blowing, we used walkie-talkies for communication so the person in the house watching the screen could tell me which way to turn it. Most of the time the wind would cause too much static to hear each other. Then plan B would kick in, and we would station relays–our kids at intervals along the line to pass verbal instructions from house to hill. Needless to say, this did not work very well.

It took too long to pass from kid to kid to be relevant. Invariably, someone would say to reverse (rotate and backup) when they meant rotate and go ahead, and the rotator on top of the hill, me who was half frozen and mad enough to chew nails, would stomp back down the hill to the house and tell the screen watcher, my wife, to get her act in gear. She, in turn, let it be known to all interested parties that my high pitched voice was not at all appreciated, and if I could do a better job, have at it. Sometimes things were put on hold for several days. Anyone from outer space who was hovering over this operation taking notes would have gotten the idea they were watching a bunch of ants on CODE RED ALERT scrambling up and down the ant hill.

Through all the years the kids were growing up, we were never able to get a decent picture on a regular basis, but it wasn't for lack of trying. Ultimately, our efforts paid off in a way none of us could have possibly imagined. After the onset of cable and satellite TV with Texas-size screens and hundreds of channels available, the topic of our early attempts to get even one viewable picture would arise at family dinners, and our past efforts were paid a 100 times over with laughter.

§ § §

But along with the good came the bad, which were not funny, and I can remember a couple involving pickup campers, one of which could have burned me to death.

One day, a pickup with a camper on the back pulled up to the pumps with a couple inside. They were real friendly, and after I had gassed their vehicle up, the man and I visited for the next 10 minutes or so while his wife was in the gift shop. About 15 minutes after they had continued on their way to Yellowstone, a boy of about 10 or 11 came out of the restroom looking for his parents. They hadn't seen him get out of the camper, where he had been sleeping. He was devastated and thought he had been abandoned. He was from back East somewhere and wasn't used to so much empty country with no telephones, busses or crowded streets, and he started crying.

His parents had been gone too long to catch up with them, and we had no way to notify any law enforcement officers for help. Luckily, a couple of our boys were in the same age group and entertained him as best they could for the next couple of hours until his parents returned from Ten Sleep, where they had stopped for supper. I can imagine their shock when they entered the camper and no boy.

We had another incident involving a pickup camper that was probably the most stupid adult event I was ever involved in, and the closest I ever came to being burned alive. It still bothers me to think about it.

One afternoon, a pickup with a homemade camper on the back drove up to the gas pumps with two men in the cab. It was only a half ton model and had way too much load on it. The camper was longer than the truck bed and extended over the tailgate, which caused the front end to raise too far off the ground. Sometimes this caused problems when trying to fill the tank, and it would airlock.

The gas tank cap was on the left side between the fender and end of the pickup bed. Just as I started to fill the tank, one of the men opened the door of the camper in the center of the vehicle and went in to get something. When he came out, he left the door open. I put the nozzle in the tank and put the automatic shutoff on the low notch but kept hold of the handle in case it bubbled back and I had to shut it off manually. They were both standing about 8 or 10 feet away by the station door, and we were visiting back and forth.

All at once, flame was everywhere. It scared me so badly all I could think of was getting rid of the nozzle, so I jerked it out of the tank and threw it. The nozzle and hose hit the ground, and the automatic shutoff tripped and shut off the gas. There was a trail of fire all the way from the gas tank to the nozzle. I have no idea why none of the gas splashed on my clothes.

One of the men grabbed a small throw rug in front of the station and started beating the flames. I think the other guy was using a jacket or something, but everything happened so fast I don't know for sure. It was all over in a few seconds. I was shaking so hard I could barely speak. If the tank had been full when it caught fire, it would have exploded and killed all three of us or burned us so badly we would have wished we were. It would have also burned up the gas station, our house and part of the Bighorn Mountains because of the tall dry grass in back of the station.

I was so shook-up I started babbling like an idiot and apologizing for starting the fire even though I didn't know how I'd done it. The driver finally got a chance to break into my monologue to say something and said he knew how it had started. There was a propane refrigerator just inside the door directly over the gas tank. It was a hot day, and the gasoline fumes had reached the pilot light. Then he added something that just blew my mind. He said the same thing had happened once before.

It sounds funny to say so now, but everything seemed to slow to a crawl. My brain locked around what he had just said, and I couldn't shake it. I know it was just the reaction of coming back to earth after having the wits scared out of me and trying to comprehend why he had let it happen again. I vaguely remember going through the motions of taking the money he handed me to pay for the gas and making change, and I remember standing in the door of the gas station watching the tail end of the camper pulling off the driveway onto the highway. I thought, "There goes the most stupid person I have ever known, bar none."

§ § §

We had two gas pumps at Trailside, regular and ethyl. When one of them malfunctioned during the summer tourist months, we were in deep trouble. Paul Cook was the Standard Oil dealer for this area, and he was number one in my book. He had a number of stations to take care of and always went above and beyond for the little accounts like ours. The parent company could not have cared less. He always tried to keep a couple of extra pumps on hand at the bulk plant on Railroad Avenue for emergencies because getting one from the company during the busy season was a chore. Buffalo, Wyoming and little towns like it were just a nuisance in the overall scheme of things. We experienced this firsthand one summer.

Our two pumps were mounted on a concrete pedestal end-to-end. I was gassing up a tourist car one late Sunday afternoon and had just hung up the regular hose when a car pulled alongside and hit the other pump with his right front fender. It tore it off the pedestal and just missed me and the other driver. We were very lucky because the pumps weighed several hundred pounds apiece and would have put both of us in the hospital or graveyard.

The driver was a logger named Gus–his last name escapes me–and he was headed home for his cabin at a local sawmill in the Bighorns. He was somewhere between 60 and 70 years old, and I knew him very well and liked him. He had worked his entire life in the logging woods and was a good hand. He drove an old Chevy coupe with a few dings in it. I never saw him get past 45 miles an hour even after having a few beers on his weekly trips to Buffalo for groceries like this one.

He was terribly apologetic and told me he would pay for all the damages, which I knew he would. I also knew he didn't have any car insurance. The problem from my point of view was what I was going to use for an income from the ethyl pump until Paul could get another one. We had very short tourist seasons, especially on the mountain, and this was the middle of July. He was willing to do anything I suggested, and I wanted to be fair with him, so I came up with this suggestion.

Most of the tourists that gassed up at little out of the way places like ours knew they would be paying 3¢ or 4¢ a gallon more for gas than they would in town–ours was 4¢–32¢ a gallon–so the vast majority of the ones that stopped had forgotten to fill up in Buffalo. I got so I could guess pretty close to what a tank would hold when I saw their license plates because most of them filled their tank in South Dakota, and their next fill up was Buffalo. None of the out-of-staters were used to the open country between Gillette and Buffalo, and the first thing on their mind was to fill their tank in town before starting for Yellowstone.

I told Gus if a tourist pulled up and wanted ethyl gas, I would try to talk them into regular, which most of them took to keep from driving back to Buffalo. They knew from looking on their map they had a lot of driving to do to get to Worland, and Gillette to Buffalo with no towns was fresh on their minds. If they chose not to take the regular, I would guess how many gallons I lost on the sale, and Gus would pay for my markup, which at that time was about 10¢ a gallon. We would settle up when I got my ethyl gas pump replaced, so that's what we did. It took Paul five weeks to get another pump, and Gus kept his part of the bargain. It was kind of unorthodox, but it worked, and neither of us could think of a plan B.

§ § §

One of the most unusual things that happened at Trailside through the years was in September 1960, our first summer, when an airplane, being towed by a tractor, came slowly up the highway past the house. The highway was much narrower at that time, so it took up the whole roadway and extended out into the barrow ditch on both sides. Traffic was backed up for a considerable distance both up and down the mountain.

It seems the pilot and passenger in the Cessna 120 from Blackfoot, Idaho, had taken off from the Buffalo Airport that morning after failing to find someone to buy gas from. The pilot figured if he could fly low enough over the Bighorns, he could save enough gas to make it to Worland almost a 100 miles. He miscalculated. He followed the highway where Highway 16 intersects Mosier Gulch and flew up the canyon following the roadway. He realized he was in deep trouble when the road started rising faster than the plane could climb with no room to turn around and go back because the peaks on both sides were above the plane.

He made it almost to Bear Rock just below Trailside when the plane hit the road. Luckily, neither occupant was injured, but one wing clipped a highway sign post. The plane just cleared the hood of a station wagon headed in the same direction. The car was from South Dakota headed for Yellowstone with a man, wife and a couple of kids in it. I can imagine the guy's shock when he had to slam on his brakes to keep from rearending an airplane that appeared out of the blue. He was still shaking when he stopped at Trailside a few minutes later. I would guess it was the highlight of their trip–Old Faithful and the bears taking a distant second place.

The plane was towed to a wide spot off the highway just across from our house. The wings were removed, and everything was hauled back to the Buffalo Airport for repairs. Of the many dozens of wrecks we witnessed over the course of many years, which were all caused by out of control vehicles going down the mountain, this was the only one that was going up.

§ § §

There were many, many wrecks on the mountain while we were in business with lots of injuries and fatalities. One of the most miraculous ones happened right at the house. I was standing in front of the gas station, which was located less than 50 feet from the shoulder of Highway 16, just before dark on a Sunday afternoon. Local people were streaming off the mountain towards home, and tourists were headed for their motel rooms in town. It was just at dusk when visibility isn't too good, and some people had their lights on, plus a light rain had just started falling.

A local girl, Hope Mennell, was headed downhill with another girl in the front seat of a big four-door sedan. Two guys in a pickup had just turned around in front of the station and pulled out in front of her. Both drivers were at fault because she was driving too fast, especially with the light conditions and a wet road, and they evidently misjudged her speed or maybe didn't even see her.

She was directly across from me when she slammed on her brakes and swerved into the left downhill lane to miss rearending the pickup, which never even stopped. Just below the house she hit a rock wall with the left front of the car and bounced down the barrow ditch a couple hundred feet. Neither of the girls were wearing seatbelts, which in those days was just a belt around the waist. The girl on the passenger side was thrown out through the door when it flew open, and Hope went through the windshield on the passenger side. It took me less than a minute to run down to the wreck.

The girl that had been thrown through the door was on her feet and in shock but was stumbling around through the rocks that littered the ground. Hope was lying on her back in the barrow ditch with water running under her and was crying because her back was hurting. She was trying to get up, and I thought her back was probably broken, so I held her down. I recognized her because her mother had babysat some of our kids when we lived in town.

Several other people got there shortly after I did, and somebody produced a blanket that we covered Hope up with, but we couldn't do anything about the water running under her back. Her girlfriend didn't seem to be badly injured and was loaded up in somebody's car and sent to the hospital. We didn't have a phone to call for help and had already sent someone down the mountain to get an ambulance started back up. It took over an hour but seemed like a week.

Hope was conscious the whole time but crying because her back hurt. When the ambulance finally got there, they had a heck of a time sliding her on the stretcher because they didn't dare try to lift her. I'll never forget the feeling of relief I felt when I saw the taillights of that ambulance heading down the mountain with the siren going wide open. The miracle of the whole event was that neither girl was seriously injured. Neither of them had been drinking, and they never found out who the two men in the pickup were.

§ § §

Our four boys contributed their fair share of the wrecks on the mountain, especially with motorcycles, which I hated. I had known too many people who had serious head injuries when they crashed. Our youngest son, Randy, turned out to be the biggest worry with bikes and survived a number of crashes without serious injury. He led a charmed life.

I can't remember for sure, but I think the whole motorcycle era started with a guy named Emmett Wagoner. He was a government trapper and had been hired by the County to try to keep the predator population under control. Coyotes were the biggest problem, but sometimes mountain lions and black bears would start working on the livestock during the summer grazing season.

Emmett had a little trailer he towed behind his vehicle with a little 85cc Kawasaki motorcycle loaded on it. Quite often he would park his rig at Trailside and unload the bike so he could get to areas that weren't accessible to his pickup. He set a lot of traps and also dug out a number of dens of coyotes and shot quite a few. When he quit his job with the County, he sold the bike to our oldest son, Stephen. As Stephen moved up the line to bigger bikes and automobiles, he, in turn, passed it on to his younger brother and so on down the line. We lived next door to a large rancher who didn't mind the kids learning to drive running up and down the hills. They were too young to be riding on the highway. I think beginners permits started at 14 or 15 years of age.

At no time did we ever purchase a vehicle for any of the kids. They all had summer jobs and had to save up for what they wanted to buy, including vehicle repairs and insurance. It was a good lesson, and they all carried it throughout their adult careers.

As I mentioned, Randy was our biggest concern and went through a half dozen bikes, each one bigger than the last, up through his adult life. One day, two of his high school buddies showed up at Trailside on their bikes, and the three of them took off for town. A half hour later, Randy was back after hitching a ride with a local motorist. He was walking with stiff disjointed steps, and the back of his shirt was in tatters and covered with blood. He told me he was in the lead of the other two kids going around a curve when he looked back and lost control of the bike. He jumped just before it went over a steep bank and crashed into some big boulders. He landed on his back and skidded down the asphalt taking off all the skin in the process. He could barely walk, and the bike was totaled.

Some 30 years later, he was home on a vacation from his job in Seattle. We were driving to Buffalo when we passed the spot where his bike left the road, and he asked me if I remembered what he had told me about the wreck. I said I did–that he had lost control when he looked back at his two buddies. He said that was exactly what happened, but he had neglected to mention that he was standing up on the seat when he did it.

His worst ever bike wreck–even though there were no injuries–was after he graduated from high school. He had a big 1000cc Kawasaki and was coming down the mountain from Trailside after dark. He had a buddy on the seat behind him, Howdy Nimick, who had his head bowed down to protect his face from the wind. The speed limit in that area was 65 miles per hour, but Randy told me he was a little above that. Just before reaching the place where the present-day city water treatment plant is located, a deer ran across the road in front of them, and they intersected. It was over in a fraction of a second, but the bike stayed on the road until Randy got it stopped. The guy riding behind him didn't even know what had happened except that they were both covered with blood.

Randy told me he walked back up the road until he found the deer. It was in two pieces. He picked one up in each hand and started back for the bike. That's when the realization of what a close call it had been hit him, and he got sick–really sick. He had hit it exactly in the middle and hadn't even wrecked even though the bike was ruined because it sprung the frame.

After butchering the deer with his bike, I think he was a little short of funds to consider replacing it right away, so he thought it would be fun to learn how to fly an airplane. He got his pilot's license and invited some of the family to join him for a ride. I spoke up and said I was completely satisfied with staying connected to the ground. He didn't take any offense, having gotten use to some of my idiosyncrasies during the last couple of decades or so. The family members that went with him enjoyed the ride immensely and didn't have any deer problems whatsoever.

Flying the friendly skies was fun and lasted for some time, but to keep his license updated required a significant amount of rental time in the air at several hundred dollars an hour, so he bought another motorcycle just like the last one he wrecked.

He had driven it for some time without incident when he decided to move to Seattle for a change in occupations. He took his car and left the bike stored in my garage for the next couple of years, not realizing it should have been prepped for such a long period of storage. He found that out after hauling it home and sold it for a fraction of what he paid for it. I couldn't have been more thankful, and it was his last bike to date.

Looking for something different after selling the bike, he emptied his bank account and bought a 25-year-old classic 1967 Pontiac GTO. He told me it wouldn't run very well on the gas sold at regular service stations, so he purchased high octane special fuel from a man who sold it by pumping it out of 50-gallon barrels and didn't mind filling 5-gallon cans at over $5 a gallon, five times what the regular stuff was selling for. I've forgotten how many milliseconds it took to get airborne. The GTO also had another problem from day-one. Just like all owners of vintage cars, he was afraid to drive it very much or park it in any public parking lot for fear of someone damaging or vandalizing it, so he finally sold it and told me he was thinking about taking up scuba diving next. I don't remember if he followed through or not.

I remember a couple more incidents involving his vehicles, but I'll have to backup several decades. When Randy was in the first couple years of high school, he rode his bike to town every day that weather permitted. One day, when he got home, he was about half frozen, and it got him to thinking about something he had read involving electric heated vests, so he decided to make one. I think he may have taken an old electric blanket apart to salvage the wires, and he handstitched them on one of his old sweaters. It took him a long time, but he stuck with it until he ran out of wire and had to substitute some of a different size to finish the vest.

He finished and checked it out. Everything went as he had planned except the wires being different sizes heated up differently, and one side of his vest got hotter than the other. He didn't consider this a major problem, so he wired the thing to his bike battery and rode to school. I don't recall how long the thing lasted, but he used it for a considerable length of time.

He had a habit of doing things on the spur of the moment and thinking about the possible consequences at a later date. I think he may have inherited some of this quality from his father. I don't remember whether he was riding one of his bikes or in his first car, but one day, he decided to drive down to Clearmont and knew he wasn't supposed to be going. A patrolman snagged him about the time he got to Ucross and gave him a talking to. The cop knew him, and when he got through chewing him out, he told Randy he could give him a citation on five counts, but since it was his first offence, he was going to give him a break and only give him a ticket for one, and it was his choice. The patrolman, Pete Haler, told me later Randy thought about it for a moment and then asked him, "Which one's the cheapest?"

§ § §

When the Bighorn National Forest was established over 100 years ago, it was split into summer grazing units and leased to local ranchers who pastured sheep and cattle on it. The one surrounding Trailside was called the Clear Creek Unit. At the time we moved there in 1960, there were perhaps a half dozen permittees. All of them were for cattle except for one sheep outfit in the Elk Lake vicinity that I think was leased by the 41 Ranch south of Buffalo. We would see them trailing their herd past just north of the house on their way to and from their summer pasture. One year, they lost several head that roamed the country to the north and west of us.

I don't know how, but they survived the coyotes, lions and bears for the next two or three years, and we would see them at various times. They were wool blind the last time I saw them. Some breeds of sheep have open faces with no wool covering their eyes, but these were the fine wool Rambouillet type that needs to have the wool sheared from around their eyes periodically so they can see where they're going. A wet snow covering their faces can freeze solid and completely blind them. These were wearing several years' coats of wool and resembled large wooly dogs from a distance.

As the years went by, the smaller ranch owners gradually sold their permits to the larger ones, and at the present time there are only two left in the Clear Creek Unit, Christian's and Gregory's. All of the permittees originally trailed their livestock up and down Highway 16 above Buffalo, but today the two remaining use trucks at times because of the hassle of contending with so much tourist traffic.

The Forest Service was originally more lenient with rules and regulations but has gotten more restrictive like all bloated government bureaucracies eventually do. Depending on the moisture during the months of April, May and June, at the present time they are limited to bringing their livestock up in early July and have to move down in October. Even this schedule can be cut short in droughty years. They are charged by the month for each pair, cow and calf, with a formula that takes several things into consideration.

At Trailside we are joined on two sides by the Forest Service but have no contact with them except on the issue of fencing. Unlike the State Highway Department, which owns and maintains all of the right-of-way fences, the Forest Service exempts itself, and the landowner is legally responsible for keeping his livestock inside his fence and Forest Service livestock–whether owned or not–out. It's a classic case of heads I win, tails you lose, which I feel is basically unfair. At the very least, the cost and responsibility should be shared equally like private landowners are required to do. The Forest Service does require the permittee to participate in part of the fence upkeep, but since he only uses it for a few weeks or so in the summer months, he has no incentive other than to prop it up for the short time he is using it, which is exactly what I would do under the same circumstances. There would be no point in wasting money on permanent improvements.

He is already paying a monthly fee for the grass his livestock is eating. The fence should not be his responsibility any more than billing a tenant in an apartment rental for a new coat of paint. If the rent doesn't cover the upkeep, then raise the rent until it does. This is what the private sector does to keep its head above water and try to make a profit. Unfortunately, government agencies aren't even required to break even. If you need additional revenue, just raise everybody's taxes–even the ones that are not involved.

I hate to get started on the subject of Forest Service policy for fear of running out of paper before finishing a lengthy thesis on government mismanagement, so I'll back off the subject because I think I've already made my point. Most of the property in our vicinity was owned by some government agency or other, and I suppose the few private landowners may feel the same way we do.

§ § §

Camp Comfort was our closest neighbor about two miles to the southwest and was owned by the Thom family, New Yorkers who used it for summer vacations. It was completely surrounded by the Bighorn Forest, and so was a dude ranch about a dozen miles to the northwest, Paradise Ranch, which was owned and operated by Jack O'Brien. These properties were known as inholdings but still had to put up with the problems of getting along with the government like we did.

Jack had tacked the name Wyoming in front of his name for publicity purposes and would take a trip back East with his guitar each winter to promote his dude ranch business. He had built up quite a sizeable clientele through the years. He shuttled a lot of his guests back and forth from the Sheridan Airport, and they would stop at Trailside quite often on the way past to have a beer or pick up a souvenir in the gift shop.

In his younger days, he had cowboyed with a young Indian from the Crow reservation just across the Wyoming state line in Montana, and they became good friends. After Jack purchased Paradise, they kept in touch, and I became acquainted with him when he would stop and have a beer on his way back and forth from Paradise when visiting Jack. I have no idea how old he was.

I really enjoyed visiting with him because he had so many stories about the beliefs, customs and history of the Crow Indians. He talked in short broken sentences, wasting no words, and straight to the point but was easy to understand. Once, he told me that the ground below the stools we were sitting on and as far as we could see in every direction belonged to the Crows and someday they were going to get it back. I made the remark that if it happened, I hoped it would be before we wasted all our money getting the mortgage paid off, but the joke fell flat.

I had read a lot of history about the local wars between the Indians and Americans and knew what he was referring to. The Crows had been promised the land between the Bighorn Mountains and the Black Hills through a treaty with the United States government, which the government ignored when it came time to honor it. Our house was sitting in the middle of the disputed area.

I noticed a little bias in some of his stories about battles with other Indian tribes stretching back hundreds of years. The Crows usually won, but when they didn't, it was because they were outnumbered at least twenty to one. Even at those times, they fought till the last Crow was killed and took 10 or 15 apiece of the other side with them. But the stories were interesting to listen to and included a lot of details about the fights.

As a side note, I want to throw something in at this point. In all of the times I visited with that guy, for the life of me I can't remember his name or even if I ever knew it to begin with, so I'll just refer to him as "the Chief" because if he wasn't one, he certainly deserved the title.

Jack O'Brian provided the standard Western diet of entertainment for his Eastern guests at Paradise, and one of them was staging Indian powwows several times a summer complete with tepees, dancing, drums, war bonnets, and tomahawks–the whole ball of wax. His buddy, the Chief, did the legwork on the reservation, and we would see several carloads of men and women go by Trailside, headed for Paradise with long tepee poles tied on the tops of cars protruding out on each end.

Besides paying for the performance, I think Jack furnished plenty of drinks to keep the party going in the right direction. We experienced the last act on one such occasion.

Our bedroom was on the second floor directly above the lounge. The window just above the door looked out over the front of the building and the gas station. If somebody knocked on the door after we had closed, I would find out what they wanted by conversing from our upstairs window. It was usually someone broken down or needing gas. We also had a floodlight illuminating the whole area but never left it on after closing the place for the night, figuring it would just attract more people.

One Sunday morning in the wee hours before daylight, we were awakened by a lot of commotion on the driveway and somebody knocking on the lounge door. I went to the window, flipped on the floodlight, and saw a half dozen cars pointed in all different directions and a couple dozen Indians scattered all over the driveway and front of the gas station, laughing and talking. It was the powwow gang homeward bound.

I heard a voice below me say, "Need gas." I looked down and was staring at the Chief, who was looking up at me. I said, "We're closed," and he said, "Need gas." Since I was at a loss for words, I put on my pants, shirt and shoes and went downstairs. I opened up the door of the lounge and stepped out into the middle of happy hour plus four–what an experience at 3:00 in the morning! I was engulfed in a crowd of celebrants all talking and laughing at the same time in a language I'd never heard before. The back of my neck started tingling like a nervous bumblebee. They were all three sheets to the wind with the other one fluttering except for one person, the Chief, and he was stone cold sober.

I had read a lot of histories about wagon trains, Indian fights and scalping parties, and for the first time in my 40 plus years on the face of this good green earth, I mentally thanked my Creator for the oversight in not planting any hair on the top of my head.

The next 45 minutes were unreal. The Chief took over and told me exactly how many dollars' worth of gas to put in each car, and they were all different. At 28¢ a gallon, a couple bucks went a long way. We only had two pumps, regular and ethyl. They all took regular, and it was one hell of a job jockeying them up to the pump one at a time because the driveway was crammed with cars, and everybody was jabbering at me in Greek or whatever.

I finally got them gassed up and headed for the lounge, which I had locked when I went outside, with the Chief right on my tail and the rest of the group strung out behind. I opened the door, stepped in, and when the Chief cleared the opening, he slammed the door shut and said, "Lock it." "Yes, sir!!!"

The outsiders started hammering on the door and tapping the windows wanting in. The Chief handed me a check Jack had given him for putting on the powwow and said, "Small bills." It was for almost $300. We always kept the receipts from the business, mostly cash, thankfully hidden in the cupboard in another room. There was a face looking in from every outside window, and I didn't dare turn on a light, so I had to fumble in the dark with what little light was coming from the outside floodlight to get the cash. The Chief didn't even count it. He backed up against the lounge door where the window watchers couldn't see him and started stuffing bills, which were mostly ones, fives and tens into separate pockets–different amounts in each pocket. I have no idea how he kept the pockets straight, but I did notice the biggest wad of bills went inside his shirt.

When he finished, he stepped back from the door, and said, "Open." I was so used to taking orders, I never hesitated. When the rest of the herd crowded into the room, he emptied each pocket to the right recipient, I guess, and they all pulled out for home. It was still dark outside.

My wife and a couple of the kids had been watching the proceedings from the upstairs window, so I filled them in on the details they had missed. We all went back to bed, and I had time to run the whole scenario through my mind a dozen times before it got daylight and was time to get up. The next time the Chief stopped for a beer, he didn't bring the subject up and neither did I.

§ § §

One time in the mid-1960s, I was standing on the lawn when a new black Caddy pulled up in front of the gift shop, and two portly couples crawled out of it. They were on their way to Yellowstone. The men were wearing suits that even I could tell hadn't been purchased at JCPenney's, and both were wearing expensive wristwatches and large rings. The two women were decked out in earrings and several diamond rings apiece that I figured would pay off the mortgage on our house with room to spare.

The women went into the gift shop to look at some souvenirs. The two men stayed outside, and we struck up a conversation. After a few minutes, one of them kind of introduced himself by asking me if I had ever heard of a firm named B. Gross and Company that used to have junkyards in Sheridan and Buffalo. They purchased all kinds of metals, hides, furs, and every other imaginable thing laying around that a person might want to get rid of. I told him I certainly did remember it because it was located in the old Buffalo Flour Mill, which was directly across Clear Creek from where we lived when I was growing up. He then told me I was looking at the original B. Gross in person. In a fraction of a millisecond my mind raced back 30 years to when I was still in grade school.

Two employees, Emil Nelson and Sam Rubin, were running the Buffalo end of the business, and I had dealt with them many times when I was selling brass, aluminum, zinc jar lids, and muskrats that I had trapped. I had scrounged the metals from the city dump when it was located at the north end of DeSmet Street, where French Creek Road begins, and had trapped the rats along Clear Creek. I hauled the metal items in a little wagon that I pulled from our house to the dump about a dozen blocks to the northwest.

They paid for these things on a sliding scale. It was all based on the size and age of the selling person. I, as a 10 year old, would get 25¢ for a muskrat hide that a person two or three times my age and size would receive 85¢ for. I accepted this payment plan because B. Gross and Company was the only place in town that would buy things I had to sell even though I didn't think it was exactly fair.

One particular instance comes to mind, and since I am now past 90 years of age and still remember it, you can probably get an idea of just how particular it was. Clear Creek was only a couple hundred yards from where we lived, so I had a little trapline for muskrats that I would check before and after school and on weekends. I had one muskrat that had outsmarted me several times by circling around my trap instead of over it, so I changed tactics and sneaked up from behind and blasted him with a .410 shotgun. I hadn't thought too far ahead when I did this because I knew the pellets would destroy the value of the pelt, but I had already pulled the trigger, and it was too late.

My mother always let me skin and case (mount) the skins in the kitchen sink, and I was devastated when I saw all the holes. I worked on it for a long time and finally patched them with membrane and bits of muskrat meat until it looked like a number one pelt. Mr. Nelson gave me 25¢ for it, and I was home free. All of this played out in my mind as I was looking at the gold capped teeth in Mr. B. Gross's mouth as he talked endlessly about his successful business venture in buying and selling hides and furs.

After he and his party pulled out of the driveway and headed for Yellowstone, I got to thinking about that shotgun riddled muskrat pelt I had sold to Mr. Nelson. I knew it was so well camouflaged that he just passed it on up the line to the firm he did business with and so on and on until it got to the guy who was making a fur coat or scarf for retail sale with the finished product. He couldn't use it, of course, so he just raised the price to cover his loss.

I think a person eventually gets credit or pays for everything he's done, right or wrong, throughout his lifetime. It all ends up on the spreadsheet, and things have to balance out either in this life or the next one. It doesn't make any difference if it's me, the Pope, the President, or Mr. B. Gross or if it's trivial or life threatening, or whether it's a trillion dollars or a riddled 25¢ muskrat pelt.

It's small consolation and one shot in a million, but I like to think Mr. B. Gross may have ended up paying for the replacement hide when he purchased his wife's new fur coat even though it was 20 or 30 years later. The whole thing seems to have become a little complicated, and I'm not sure what to think about the guy that sold him a worthless rat hide to begin with.

Which reminds me of another story about my trapping career. In those days, muskrats were considered pests, and a person didn't need a license to catch them. It was different with mink, and a guy had to have a permit. One night, a mink wandered into one of my muskrat traps, and I didn't know what to do about it, but I sure wasn't going to waste a stroke of luck and throw it away. It was a terrible experience skinning it. Mother made me do it outside because they smell worse than a skunk due to some kind of musk gland.

When I finally got it skinned, cased and cured out, I took it over to B. Gross's and asked Mr. Nelson what he would give me for it. I had already checked in a fur magazine and knew it was worth about six bucks, which was more money than I had ever had at one time in my entire life. He told me he could get in real trouble if he bought it from someone without a permit, but since I was such a good customer and he liked me, he would take a chance and hope the sheriff would never hear about what I had done. He gave me $1.50. If he hadn't done me such a big favor and they had caught me, I have often wondered if my mother could have talked Sheriff Mart Tisdale into putting me on probation before he locked me up until after I had graduated from the fourth grade.

§   §   §

As I mentioned previously, I was in the sheep business in the early 1950s. When I sold out, I also sold my sheep wagon. I later regretted it and started looking for another one strictly for nostalgia's sake. They became harder to find in later years because people were looking for them for the same reason I was.

I passed the word out, and sometime in about 1970, the local sheriff, Bo Turk, came up to Trailside and told me he knew of one for sale for $150, which was in the ballpark for price. He described it, and I bought it sight unseen. However, he said there was a process we would have to go through before the sale. As near as I remember, here was the process.

The State of Wyoming owned strips of land throughout the County and State that were used by ranchers, trailing sheep and cattle from one range to another. In the Johnson County area, it was primarily from their winter range to summer camps in the Bighorn Mountains. Every half day of trailing, morning and afternoon, ended up with a rest stop with enough range, grass and water for the herds. Some stockmen took advantage of the situation and spent extra days on the trail to get the free grass, so range riders were hired to patrol the stock drives and keep all the trail herds moving at half-day intervals.

The one hired for the Kaycee area was an old-timer from the Sussex country named Mike Streeter. At times, he had to have a place to sleep when he was too far from home, so he had an old wagon running gear with a small house on it that was big enough to sleep overnight in, but that was about all. He parked this thing on the stock trail on Bear Trap at the south end of the Bighorns. A number of years later, he used the Pheasant cabin on Bear Trap to stay in and left his old wagon on the trail where it sat abandoned for many years.

The sheriff, Bo Turk, was the guy to go see if one wanted to find out anything historical about the south end of the County. I think that may have been where he was born. Bo knew the history of the old running gear Mike used for overnight stays. It was the original running gear from the Cheyenne Territorial Prison and had been used to transport prisoners to Cheyenne from all over the State. He never told me how it ended up at Bear Trap in the Bighorns, but I'm pretty sure he knew.

Bo wanted to get those running gears to the Jim Gatchell Museum in Buffalo before it fell apart or someone hauled it off. As sheriff, he had the authority to dispose of abandoned vehicles on State of Wyoming property. I don't know if wooden wheel running gears qualified as a vehicle or not, and I don't suppose it was important enough for anyone to waste any time trying to find out. I hadn't laid eyes on those running gears on Bear Trap for 30 years, but a few days after I wrote the check, it was sitting on the museum lawn. I also learned that I had donated it to the Jim Gatchell Museum, and shortly after that, I pulled my sheep wagon to Trailside.

§ § §

When I see a half million dollar motorhome rolling down the road, towing a $30,000 car with a couple bicycles strapped on the back and a TV antenna sticking out of the roof, I think of my introduction to the modern campground industry over a half century ago. Before that time, camping consisted of a canvas tent, some blankets and a portable woodstove made out of tin. A few cooking utensils always included a cast iron skillet. Canned fruit, pork and beans, along with a few staples like potatoes, eggs and bacon, were basic items in the food line because of the lack of refrigeration. You parked in the most convenient place available outside of town where you hoped no one would object–quite often on a deserted area owned by absent landowners.

If it was a long journey across several states. At least two spare tires were a must because towns were a long ways apart and cellphones and AAA were nonexistent. In case of a breakdown, you were mostly on your own, and showers and laundry were put on hold until you arrived at your destination. Times have certainly changed.

When we moved to Trailside in 1960 and I was commuting to work in Buffalo, I began to notice a few tents set up in the grass on the property just west of the Soldiers' and Sailors' Home, currently renamed Veteran's Home of Wyoming. The land belonged to a man named Vic Suhr, and he charged $1 a night for the privilege. Practically all were tourists headed for Yellowstone National Park. A few were also staying overnight in the city park, which was free.

At about the same time, my brother, Larry, was building a trailer court in town just south of Hogerson Street between Adams Avenue and Main Street called the Boll Weevil Court, which is still in operation under a different name. Because some of the house trailers of that era didn't have indoor toilet facilities, he built a separate building for them that also included showers and washer-drier hookups. Noticing what was happening at Suhr's and the city park, he also started renting overnight spaces on the lawn.

My wife and I decided to get into the act at Trailside, so we hired John Lusher, a local contractor. He sent George Hibler up with a dozer to level off a few hills in back of the house. We were in the process of installing modern restrooms at the time, so we added showers and washer-drier facilities to handle the campers. They were practically all using tents with the exception of a few old school buses that had the seats removed. I still remember the first popup camper I ever saw. I thought it had been built to cut down wind resistance when towing, which it did, but it was an eye-opener when the guy started raising up the top half with a hand crank.

My brother and I got to wondering if maybe the camping industry was on the verge of an upward trend when we started noticing little items pertaining to it in the newspapers. I remember reading one in particular that said General Motors would install a trailer hitch on any new vehicle if the customer ordered it. At that point in time, customers ordered exactly what accessories they wanted when purchasing a new car or pickup and could even pick it up at the factory in Detroit and drive it home to save on transportation costs if they wished. Choices are a little more limited now— no more plain Jane's, and all the vehicles are loaded with add-ons plus the prices to go with it.

Anyway, since we both had our feet wet, Larry and I decided to take the plunge and built Indian Campground on Hart Street just east of Main Street. Most of the locals thought we had lost our minds, but history proved otherwise, and it is still a thriving business over 50 years later.

Our campground at Trailside provided the opportunity to meet a lot of interesting people through the years. With nothing to do after supper, most of them would wander down to the lounge and gift shop to browse and visit. As a general rule, they didn't have the faintest idea about the customs and thoughts of anybody living west of the Missouri River. Some of their questions would make you wonder if they were serious or just joking. One instance in particular comes to mind.

One evening, a young couple checked into the campground, and an hour or so later, the man wandered down to the lounge, and we got to visiting. I would have guessed his age to be in the late 20s. He was exceedingly pleasant to talk to, quiet, well-mannered, intelligent. When I asked him what he did for a living, he said he was a mathematician and worked for the United States Space Agency. At that time, they were playing catchup with the Russian Sputnik coup by putting a man on the moon before anyone else did. I was pretty impressed and a little awed because math had been my toughest subject all through grade and high school when it was called arithmetic, and things hadn't improved since I'd memorized the multiplication tables in the fourth grade.

I asked him many questions about the program. I'm sure a lot of them bordered on stupidity from his viewpoint, but he answered all of them without a hint of condescension or superior-like attitude. While we were talking, he was wandering around the room looking at various Western items that we had hung on the log walls to create a Western atmosphere, like spurs, traps, deer antlers, and a couple of old rifles. He began asking many questions about their origin and purpose but was especially intrigued by a petrified buffalo skull that had been dug up on Crazy Woman Creek during the construction of I-90 between Buffalo and Gillette. It was in excellent condition, and he asked several questions about the teeth, horns, etc. and then pointed to two holes in the top of the skull and asked me what they had been used for. I said, "Just about everything the critter did because those are eye sockets." His face turned a dull red, and he laughed self-consciously while he made a funny remark about his goof up. It was kind of odd, but despite coming from polar opposite backgrounds, I think we both realized at that moment, we were still on the same page.

§ § §

Another time, an old family joke got its start when an ancient school bus that had been converted into a motorhome pulled up and the occupants got out to look our camping facilities over. There were 10 or 12 of them. The old bus had Arkansas license plates, and most of the seats had been removed to make room for extra tents and other gear. A hole had been cut through the roof at the back, and a stovepipe extended a short distance above the top of the bus. There was a small woodstove inside. It was evident they had been on the road for some time and were on a barebones trip to Yellowstone. I figured they had spent most of their nights camped along the highway and only stopped at a commercial campground when they needed a bath.

I was busy working on a car at the gas station, so I told our oldest boy, Stephen, to take the group up to the campground in back of the house and show them what we had to offer. He was about 12 years old at the time.

We were tied into the REA, Rural Electric Association, for our electricity needs and used electric water heaters to provide hot water for the campers' use in the shower rooms and automatic clothes washers. The rates were pretty high, but it was dependable and a lot more convenient than operating our own generators or switching over to propane gas.

When Stephen came back to where I was working, he said the people had decided to stay overnight and he had already collected the money. When I asked him what he had charged them, he said, "A dollar." "Apiece?" "No, the whole bus load."

Our family has discussed his business transaction a number of times through the years and have always wondered if the geysers and grizzly bears in Yellowstone were the highlight of their trip, or were they overshadowed by the 10¢ showers they took before they got there.

§ § §

One time a guy I knew pretty well stopped by and wanted to charge a tank of gas or something. He was a likeable person but the type that made it from one paycheck to another. I didn't see him too often, but he would sometimes spend a couple hours nursing a beer and swapping stories with someone he knew in the lounge. I told him we didn't do any charging, but I would loan him a few bucks personally to tide him over. This was a mistake because it became a habit. I liked the guy, but I didn't know how to break the routine. Sometimes I wouldn't see him for several months at a time, so I told him he would have to write a check for the amount and I would return it when he paid it off. That way there wouldn't be any misunderstanding about what he had borrowed or when it was paid. We both knew he didn't have a checking account. This agreement stretched out over several years and worked great, but I never let him get in very deep.

At this period of time, there were only two banks in Buffalo. The First National issued yellow check blanks, and the Wyoming Bank & Trust printed white ones. Personalized checkbooks were few and far between, so all businesses kept a stack of the blanks on their counters. When you purchased something and wanted to write a check to pay for it, they would just ask you, "White or yellow?" and hand you a blank.

One time, when I was visiting with this guy in the lounge, a few of his buddies showed up, and they got to trading stories over a couple of beers. He hollered at me and told me to set up a round for his friends. I served them, and not having any idea whether he had any money or not and not wanting to embarrass him by asking, I just looked at him. He never missed a beat. He said, "Give me a check." I said, "White or yellow?" and he said, "Doesn't make any difference. Either one will do." Anyone with an account in both banks put a guy at the head of the class according to his beer drinking buddies. I had to grit my teeth to keep from laughing.

§ § §

After we bought the place from the Wilsons, Layton and his wife would drive over from Sheridan every so often to see how we were doing, and I told him about this incident. He laughed and shared a couple of stories about the beer business he had been involved in.

One very early Sunday morning just as he was getting out of bed, a man knocked on the front door. When Layton let him in, he could see that the guy was pretty wasted. He told Layton he needed a six pack pretty bad. Layton wasn't at all interested because he had never seen the guy before. Then the guy introduced himself and said he knew it was against the law to sell beer on Sunday, but he was the county attorney and had had a bad night and needed a six pack in the worst way. Layton looked straight at him for several seconds and then said, "Well, if you've got guts enough to come in here and ask for it, I've got guts enough to sell it," and he did.

The other incident was when a young lady came in and wanted to buy a case of beer. She had a valid driver's license, but in those days there was no picture on it, and descriptions were pretty sketchy, so you never knew whether it was valid or not. If a person was underage, they just borrowed one from a friend or relative with the same general description. Anyway, Layton said this lady was really sincere and made a believer out of him, so he sold her the beer. The next day he had a visit from the sheriff. The lady was indeed underage, and there were some problems.

A prominent local banker's son in Buffalo had gone into his bedroom pretending sleep. When his folks had gone to bed, he crawled out through the bedroom window, took his father's car, and picked up a few friends. They chose the oldest looking one–and a great actress–to buy the beer and went onto a party. In the wee hours, the driver delivered all his friends to their respective homes and started for his in south Buffalo.

A couple of blocks from his house, he ran off the road and through a fence into someone's garden. The wire fence got twisted around the driveshaft, and the car came to an abrupt halt. The kid left, walked home, crawled back through the window, and went back to bed. When the law got everything straightened out, they absolved Layton from any wrongdoing, as he had done what could have reasonably been expected of him to make sure the lady was of legal age. I don't think I ever told him that the beer-buying lady was my niece.

§ § §

Since bartending was a completely new experience, I had a lot of learning to do. A bartender gets into the personal lives of some of their regular customers simply because at times his duties require him to stand there behind the bar and listen to the mostly sad details of their lives from their point of view anyway. There are two main requirements from the bartender's side of the bar. Number one is listen sympathetically with only a nod of the head or say something like, "Really?" or "Why?" or "I don't blame you," for whatever reason as long as it is in agreement with the teller.

Don't ever offer any advice or a personal opinion. The number two requirement is don't tell anybody what you heard. It's exactly like being a doctor only a lot cheaper for the patient. You'd really be surprised at some of the revelations shared over a couple beers.

As I mentioned, I was new to this profession, and it took a little time to catch on to the program. Lumberjacks in the Bighorns at that time were handed their weekly paychecks at noon on Saturday and were off to Buffalo to cash them at the local bars and do what shopping needed to be done. The vast majority were unmarried men who lived in slab shacks at the sawmill or logging camp. I had previously worked in the timber camps in the Bighorns and knew most of them. Late Saturday evening, they would head back to camp to spend Sunday resting for the Monday morning workday.

Mostly, they were an independent group who worked very hard in a dangerous occupation for only moderate wages. Their lack of income was made up by having no rent to pay, and their board was provided by the company they worked for that ran a cook shack. The cook put out good food and a lot of it. If they didn't, they couldn't keep help–just like all the ranches in the country.

This one particular group always came down together in separate cars and quite often would stop at Trailside on their way to town or back on Saturday evenings. Only one of the group was married recently and had no children yet. Of course, the wife always accompanied her husband.

Somewhere along the line, she became pregnant, and all through the spring, summer and fall months, I was kind of kept up-to-date through confidential comments that the individual loggers would make when they happened to stop for a beer by themselves that there was a connection between the husband and his best friend that seemed a little odd–to me anyway–but no one else seemed to think so, as far as I could tell. When the whole group stopped by at the same time, everything was just as natural as blue sky and green grass–no friction of any kind.

One day, one of the group stopped by and told me a new baby boy had just arrived at the hospital the night before and both the husband and best friend passed out cigars to celebrate the event. In the ensuing years as the boy grew up, I noticed he was usually riding in the best friend's car when the group stopped for pop and beer–just one of the things I think about every once in a while.

§ § §

I've mentioned Andy Hanson once before when we were building our home in Buffalo in the 1950s and he furnished the house logs. When we decided to build a new gift shop at Trailside, he was the first one I contacted. He was a super swell guy. and I really liked and respected him. He married a woman named, Ruth Kershner, but with his Swedish accent, he couldn't pronounce the "th" and it came out "Root."

In the 1930s while the local railroad was in operation, he worked as a tie hack in the Bighorns getting out railroad ties and mine props and eventually started his own sawmill. His logging camp was located a mile or so west of Highway 16 on Sourdough Creek, and he used horses to get the timber to the sawmill. The area had suffered a major forest fire in the 1940s, the Duck Creek Burn, which the Forest Service was unable to contain. It finally burned itself out late in the year when snow started falling. The trees were killed and branches and bark burned off, but most of them remained standing and made excellent house logs. Due to the high altitude, rocky terrain, long cold winters, and little summer moisture, the roots lasted for decades, and even today uncountable thousands of them are still standing. They resemble giant toothpicks standing on edge when viewed from a distance.

One time, when Andy was at Trailside, he noticed a horseshoe we had nailed up over a door for good luck. I didn't know what he was getting at when he asked me if we actually considered it a horseshoe, but I found out. The next time he stopped by, he handed me one like he used on his big skid horses. It measured 7x9½ inches and was twice as big as any I had ever seen. I still have it in my collection of junk.

In all the years I knew him, I don't remember him ever even once ordering a beer. He always had a Coke or ice cream sandwich. Once, when we were visiting, he told me about falling off the wagon and getting in deep trouble. One evening, he went into the Central Bar on Main Street to discuss the details with a guy that wanted to buy some logs from him. He said the place was jammed, and he had to crowd up to the bar to see the guy who was sitting on one of the stools. He glanced down and saw a $5 bill lying on the floor. This was in the days when it bought four or five times as much as it does now.

He had no idea who had dropped it but knew every man in the place would claim it as theirs if he opened his mouth. He needed some time to think about it, so he covered it up with his foot. After mulling it over, he figured that the most honest thing to do was spend it where he found it. When he got the chance, he reached down and picked it up. Five dollars bought a lot of drinks in those days, and he didn't get it used up till closing time.

His wife had been expecting him home for supper from the sawmill. When he didn't show up, she got worried and drove up the mountain, looking for him. When Andy finally made it home, she was gone, so he drove up to the sawmill trying to find her. She was just ready to head back down and get some help because she thought he had been hurt or killed back in the timber someplace. When "Root" found out what had happened, she hit the roof. Andy told me he was relegated to the doghouse for the foreseeable future.

I remember a little witticism that reminds me of what happens sometimes when things get started on the wrong track and keep going– cheer up, things could be worse, so I cheered up and sure enough, things got worse. That's exactly what happened to Andy, and part of it was my fault.

The $5 bill episode hadn't leveled out yet when I looked him up about a week later. Our new gift shop had an open beam ceiling, and I needed five cross-logs to tie it together. They had to be good ones because they would be exposed. They had to be perfectly straight, 34 feet long, no more than 10 inches in diameter with as little taper as possible and cut from standing timber to eliminate any danger of rot. Little did I realize what I was setting him up for, but he filled me in on the details when he dropped them off a few days later.

He said he had stood on the ground and looked up the trunks of half the trees in the Bighorn Mountains to find five that were straight enough to meet my specifications. By the time he finished, his eyes were so bloodshot he could hardly see. As luck would have it, "Root" drove up to the sawmill just as he skidded the last one into the mill. She took one look at his bloodshot eyes, thought he had been on a weekend drunk, and headed back to town without waiting to hear Andy's side of the story. Convicted on circumstantial evidence, his period of isolation was extended indefinitely.

I knew I was the one that had started hammering nails in his coffin to begin with. It took a while to get to all's well that ends well, but he finally made it, and I was glad to see the whole thing die a natural death.

§ § §

Bill Forsha, pronounced Forshay, lived several miles up past Trailside on Highway 16 West where the road drops down off the hill along Clear Creek. Part of his property had a pretty little pond on it along the highway on the south side. The road cut his 40-acre parcel in half, and he eventually subdivided the whole north side into small acreages called High Country Estates. He also sold off a couple small pieces of property along the creek on the south side of the highway where his house was located. During the construction of I-90, he came to work for the Highway Department engineers in Buffalo, where I was employed, and we became friends.

His dad, Bill Sr., was a good friend of Layton and Lucille Wilson, who owned Trailside at the time, which in a roundabout way was how we came to buy the place. Bill's dad happened to mention to his son that Layton was thinking about selling the place, and Bill mentioned it to me, so a few days later I drove up to the place, introduced myself, and eventually bought it a little over a year later.

Bill and I were the same age. Since we both lived in the Bighorns and commuted to work, we had a lot in common. During the fall and spring, especially fall, we had to put up with seasonal weather changes which included fog. He always called me Foggy at these times because he lived at a higher elevation. A lot of times he would leave for work in clear cloudless sunshine, and by the time he reached Trailside, it was 15 miles per hour soup. I always dreaded these times. The highway was on a steep 7% grade in front of the house, and I would have to cross traffic to get in the righthand downhill lane. At times, the fog was so thick visibility would be limited to less than 100 feet. Cars creeping up and down the mountain were almost noiseless, and the fog muffled what little sound there was. I would pull up to the edge of the road, open the door, and step out with my left foot on the ground and listen for the sound of motors. Then I'd jump back in and gun it to get across the uphill lane and into my downhill side. I always held my breath for that one second ride. Coming home, it wasn't so bad because I only had a fast right turn to get on our driveway.

Bill had some health problems relating to his service in World War II and lots of times just felt miserable. He told me his outfit was bivouacked someplace in Europe one night, and the sentries fell asleep. He was awakened when a German soldier poked him in the stomach with the front end of his rifle. One of the sentries woke up and started shooting, and the German pulled the trigger. Bill woke up in a field hospital. The medics gave him a blood transfusion that was contaminated, and he ended up contracting jaundice. That was the end of his combat experience, but he never got over the effects of the transfusion, which at times turned his skin a yellowish color because of the medicine he was taking.

Bill was a good hand, and we worked together for the next 10 or 12 years. He also had a very short temper. The old party telephone line ran right by his house. It serviced three or four cabins below him, including Camp Comfort and several cabins along Clear Creek above, and terminated at Hunter Ranger Station a couple miles farther up the creek. The line was originally owned by the Forest Service, but they had sold it to Camp Comfort for $1 a few years before while still retaining the right to stay on the line. Camp Comfort was located on private property and completely surrounded by the Forest Service. It was owned by a family back East who had constructed several cabins for use during the summer months. Bill wanted to tie onto the line, so he called the owners and asked their permission, but they refused. He checked the Courthouse records and found out the Forest Service had neglected to obtain an easement through his property when they built the line in the 1920s. He called the Camp Comfort owners and asked them where they wanted their telephone poles piled when he got through cutting them down with a chainsaw. There was no way to route the line around his place, so he had a telephone installed in his house a short time later.

Bill and his wife Marilyn had two children, Janie and Johnny. As they got older, they started driving to school in Buffalo. Janie had a little Volkswagen Bug, and one morning coming down the road, she ran off the highway a short distance below Trailside and down a very steep bank, where she ended up in the top of a group of aspens–literally. The vehicle was so light the trees kept it from hitting the ground. Janie wasn't hurt, and as I remember, the Bug didn't have much damage either.

The year they bought the place, they decided to make it a year-round residence, but that only lasted one winter. Their waterline that was tapped into the creek froze up, and they finished the winter by keeping a hole chopped in the ice and hauling water to the house in a bucket. From that time on, they spent the winter months in town.

When he and I were working together, I remember a funny story he told me about his dad. Bill, Sr. lived in Gillette. One morning he walked into the garage, got into his car, pressed the garage door opener, and backed out of his garage. Unfortunately, the garage door hadn't received the signal from the door opener.

Bill took early retirement from the Highway Department, and he and Marilyn tried to be snowbirds during the winter months. They rented an apartment in Lake Havasu, Arizona, intending to stay till spring, but boredom got the best of them, and they moved back to Buffalo a few months later. Both of them had been raised in Wyoming, and they couldn't adjust to wall-to-wall people and heavy traffic.

He told me about a situation he had with a traffic jam. He was first in line coming up on a side road to a T-shaped intersection with no traffic light, just a stop sign. He said the main highway was solid cars driving bumper to bumper. When he looked in his rearview mirror, he could see cars stacked up behind him for as far as he could see. He said it was impossible to make a U-turn and head back the other way, so he and everybody behind him were trapped because nobody on the main line would allow anybody to cut in front of them.

He sat there for an hour with absolutely no way to move when a car on the main line came creeping along at 10 miles an hour. The people noticed his Wyoming license plate, and the driver rolled down his window and hollered, "Hey, Wyoming, I'll let you in here," and he slowed down just enough to let Bill slip in the line ahead of him. The car just behind Bill was right on his bumper and tried to follow, but the Arizona driver closed the gap immediately and cut him off. Bill heard him holler, "Not you, you California son-of-a-bitch."

Bill and Marilyn did quite a bit of traveling after that until Marilyn died unexpectedly of a heart attack. He bought an apartment in Buffalo and lived there while doing some traveling, fishing, etc. He was either loading or unloading his boat at Tie Hack Reservoir in the Bighorns when something happened, and he was found sometime later floating in the water.

When he was living on the mountain, Hunter Ranger Station was on the north fork of Clear Creek several miles above him with several cabins scattered along the creek between them. They were all privately owned, but the land they were sitting on was owned by the Forest Service, and the cabin owners paid a yearly rental fee. Bill's 40 acres was private property, and the Forest Service had no jurisdiction over it.

He had a neighbor a short distance up the creek, Joe Bejino, who owned a bar in Buffalo and had a cabin on one of the Forest Service plots that he used during the summer months. After he passed away, his son, Jack, came into possession of it. Like the majority of cabin owners, he had an outdoor privy. Through the years, many of them converted them into more modern bathrooms with either septic tanks, enclosed vaults, waterless compacts, or electric toilets that incinerated the waste at extremely high temperatures.

Jack installed a new indoor electric type and shortly thereafter had a large group up for Sunday dinner. It operated perfectly, but with so many people using it, it got an awful lot of use in a short period of time. His mother-in-law went in to use it, but the bowl was so hot, it was just like pouring water on a red hot stove. It hissed, and a cloud of steam came blasting up from below. She started screaming at the top of her lungs, and a dozen people tried to get through the door at the same time, but it was locked from the inside. When he told me this story, I got the impression the new toilet didn't improve relations with his mother-in-law even one tiny bit. She refused to enter the room ever again.

§ § §

Between the Forsha's and Bejino's cabins on Clear Creek was the Lucasta Camp. It consisted of a few small rental cabins catering to the tourist trade and had been constructed sometime in the 1920s. When we moved to Trailside in 1960, it was owned by an elderly woman named Anne Baker, who paid a yearly rental fee to the Forest Service for use of the property even though she owned all the improvements. It had long since stopped being used for rental to overnight guests due to lack of modern plumbing facilities. She still rented the cabins, but it was only to people living in Gillette or other Wyoming towns, and they paid a yearly fee. Most of the renters had been there for many years. It still had outdoor privies, and cabin renters packed water from an outdoor pump for cooking and washing dishes.

We became well acquainted with Anne after we bought Trailside and visited her many times. I have never known a nicer lady in my entire life. She had been through some terrible family issues during her life but never let them get the best of her. I never saw her when she didn't have a smile on her face, and I knew she must be crying inside. She was a small, gentle lady but tough as a boot.

I don't remember what year Anne told me she and her husband moved to Lucasta, but I do remember talking to him when I delivered a load of coal to them in 1947. I also remember when she finally reached the age when she had no choice as to leaving the place and asked the Forest Service personnel for permission to sell her holdings. Packing water and stacking enough wood to last the winter was too much.

The buildings had deteriorated almost to the point of no return, and the higherups had been wanting to burn the buildings, restore the grounds, and eliminate the lease for some time. They refused her request but told her she could keep the place as long as she wanted, which they all knew wouldn't be too far in the future because of her age.

To the best of my knowledge, her only income besides rentals from the few cabins was a very small amount from Social Security. When her cabin was demolished, she moved to a small rental unit in back of where the present-day Kum & Go Convenience store is located on North Main Street. I used to visit her at times. She hadn't lost any of her upbeat personality or humor. Sometime after that as she required more care, she moved in with her only close relative, a grandson, and his wife until she passed away.

I thought I could salvage a couple of the old cabins, but it was a bad decision. I hired a local house mover, Mickey Petrie, and in 1976 we moved them down to our property in back of Trailside. They were 8x12 feet each, and we butted them together end-to-end to make a summer cabin for guests and the kids to sleep in. I spent a lot of time trying to make the old round logs mouse proof but never succeeded. I finally gave up, and a guy who was building a cabin in the Hazelton area in the south Bighorns picked out the best of the logs, and we burned the rest.

That was the end of another interesting chapter in the history of the Bighorn Mountains that I was involved in. The only thing I kept for a remembrance of Lucasta Camp was the original key to number five cabin that was connected to a replica of a 1937 Indianhead nickel. It had been distributed as an advertising token by "Security West, Billings, Montana, member F.D.I.C." I'm fairly confident that the key preceded the bank by several years.

§ § §

Charlie Brown was another friend who lived on the mountain and also worked at the Highway Department with Bill Forsha and me. When Bill subdivided his property, Charlie bought one of the acreages and built a nice log home on it. The only reason he did it was because of Forest Service regulations. He had previously owned a cabin on the North Fork of Clear Creek above the ranger station and was paying a yearly lease to the Forest Service for the ground it was sitting on.

The last couple of years, he and his wife had spent all their time up there. One day, he got a letter telling him that was not permissible. According to the Forest Service rules and regulations, he would have to move off the premises for a specified time each year because he could only use it for a vacation home. The fact that his presence was a deterrent to vandals who broke into cabins above and below him every few years was not considered relevant, so he bought some property from Bill and sold his cabin.

Charlie had spent his childhood growing up in a dirt roof shanty in the Nine Mile area with several brothers and sisters. A homestead in Johnson County was a good place to starve to death. His dad, Wilbur, stayed in Buffalo part of the time and worked as an electrician to earn enough money for the family to live on. I remember where their homestead was and would guess the distance at about 30 miles from Buffalo. I also knew his dad.

Charlie told me once when he was a preschooler, his dad was working in Buffalo doing electrical work, and the rest of the family was on the homestead. A three-day blizzard blew in, and they spent all three days in the dugout. They had a milk cow, and to keep her from freezing to death, they brought her into the house. They didn't have any barn or shed outside.

His dad had no way of getting to his family during the storm, but when it finally quit, he loaded up what he could carry and started walking home. The drifts were so bad he couldn't get a horse through. He had to thread his way along the tops of the hills and flounder through the snow until he got to the Earl Henderson Ranch along Trabing Road, where he spent the night. I would judge he was about half way. He made it home the next day. I have often wondered what he carried in the way of food. He was a short, powerful, muscular man and under the circumstances was probably carrying at least a 100-pound load. I suppose beans were one of the main items. Charlie said it was a mess in the dugout, but they kept the milk cow alive.

§ § §

Bob Warne was one of the highway patrolmen during the years when we were building Interstates 90 and 25. The patrol office was in the same building as the Highway Department at that time, and the two groups cooperated on a regular basis in things related to automobile accidents. At times, there was only one patrolman on duty available for all of Johnson County, so we would help control traffic while he was busy with other things. Bob was easy to work with and a favorite with our crew because of his sense of humor. He had a joke or funny story for each and every occasion. I remember a couple in particular.

Dead Man's Curve in the Bighorn Mountains at the bottom of Mosier Gulch was a 30 miles per hour curve at that time and the site of numerous runaway truck accidents. Losing its brakes before reaching it, an out of control vehicle would leave the roadway and plunge over the steep bank at a speed of up to a 100 miles per hour. Not that it would have made any difference because the guardrail at that time consisted of a single cable strung between posts. There was even a steep four-wheel drive, two-track road from Clear Creek, entering the highway in the center of the sharp curve. Survival rate for truck drivers going over the bank was always zero.

One early morning, a truckload of very hot asphalt road oil from Cody went over the bank and exploded on impact. It drenched the entire area in black. One lone spruce tree about 60 feet tall about half way down the hill was in the line of fire and took the full brunt of the load but was undamaged otherwise. The driver was killed.

I was coming down the mountain from Trailside on my way to work and saw the patrolman, Bob Warne, standing on the shoulder of the road where the truck had left the highway. I parked down below 100 yards or so and walked back up to see what had happened. A few minutes later, a car with a couple inside drove slowly past and parked behind me. They walked up to where Bob and I were visiting and watching the cleanup crew way down below by the creek.

The couple that joined us were Black. The oil-covered spruce tree became the topic of conversation, and the man remarked how pretty it was. Bob said, "I think so too, and I believe there should be at least one black tree in every forest." The guy laughed and said, "Right on, man! Right on!"

Another time, on a late Sunday afternoon, a guy came rushing into the lounge, looking for a phone to report an accident that had happened on a sharp curve below Trailside. Of course, we didn't have one so he ran back out the door and drove off to I don't know where because the next lodge several miles up the road didn't have one either. Since it was Sunday, there was a lot of traffic streaming down the road towards town, and I knew they would be jammed up down at the accident site a half mile below us, so I and my son, Robin, took off on a dead run down the highway. The road was jammed with cars, and we threaded our way through and down over a steep bank to the wrecked vehicle. Three or four men were clustered around a man lying on his back in some rocks. They told me several other passengers who had been in the car had been loaded into private vehicles and were headed for the hospital. They thought this guy, the driver, might have a broken back and were afraid to move him until an ambulance got there. This guy was conscious, swearing profusely, and very drunk.

The patrolman, Bob Warne, arrived a few minutes later, grabbed a blanket out of his patrol car, and spread it over the drunk, leaving his face exposed. The drunk swore at him and insisted on getting up. We had to forcibly hold him down, which just made him madder and increased his profanity to a higher level. It started to sprinkle, and Bob pulled the blanket up over the guy's face to protect it from the rain, and the drunk went ballistic. He called Bob every name in the book pertaining to dirty pig cops and what he thought of them. Bob uncovered the guy's head and said, "I apologize, Mister. I thought you were dead." The drunk went into orbit.

There were six or eight of us clustered around the guy, and we exploded with laughter. By that time, any sympathy we felt for him had evaporated. He launched into a new profanity tirade, and we laughed through the whole performance, but it didn't slow him down any.

It took another half hour for the ambulance to arrive, and it kept raining and got colder. We were all soaked. The medics strapped him on a stretcher to immobilize him, and it was one heck of a job to carry him over the slick rocks to the ambulance. He never stopped swearing. None of the group in the wreck was seriously injured, including the drunk driver, and I think all the penalty he received was a fine.

I remember hearing about another incident Bob was involved with. Highway Patrol had set up a sort of sting operation on I-90 between Buffalo and Sheridan. There were two sets of patrolmen stationed eight or 10 miles apart. When they stopped a motorist for speeding, they would radio the other group all the information about the car and driver after they turned him loose. The idea was to see how many motorists would resume speeding after getting out of sight of the one that arrested them. Each patrolman had a lot of miles to cover, and the odds of seeing another one in the same area were pretty slim.

Bob got a call involving a guy that had just received a ticket for speeding, and a few minutes later, the car came cruising over the hill above the speed limit, so he turned on his blinkers and ran the guy down. He parked behind him. When he walked up to the guy's side window, the man already had his wallet out and was digging for his driver's license. Bob never even asked him for it. He put on his best smile and said very pleasantly, "Hi, there. You're kind of a slow learner aren't you?" Welcome to Wyoming and smartass cops.

§ § §

In the early 1970s, our youngest children were getting close to graduating from high school, and we were tired of catering to the traveling public, so in 1972 we closed the business down and used it for a residence only. Traffic had increased tremendously and the noise with it, especially with trucks and their engine brakes. Thirty years later, we started building a cabin behind the existing building as far from the highway as we could get, a couple hundred yards or so. After its completion, the highway was under reconstruction, and we decided to get rid of the old house. This was in 2003.

The original buildings the Dodsons had built could not be moved and were torn down. The new addition we had built was sold to David and Jackie Stewart, who had it moved to a location along Clear Creek about a mile east of Main Street on Highway 16 in Buffalo. They added an addition and made it into a beautiful home.

The mountain road was under reconstruction at the time and nearly impassable for the building, which was 32 feet wide, to get through. The contractor, Ames Construction, was very cooperative and shut down all of their equipment while we were coming down the mountain. I was flagging and holding up traffic behind the building.

When we reached the traffic light at Fort Street and Burritt Avenue, the house mover couldn't go down Main Street and had to jostle the building around to head north on Burritt. I hurried and got ahead of him to my house on the corner of Burritt and Hogerson Street just in time to get my picture

Trailside moving day

taken of both houses and myself as he passed by – one of the most unusual coincidences I have ever experienced.

The house was too high to get under the I-25 and Highway 16 overpass, so Highway Patrol stopped the interstate traffic and let the mover go up the offramp on the south bound lane towards the fairgrounds, cross the median, and go down the onramp on the north bound lane–one more advantage of living in a place like Wyoming with cooperative patrolmen.

In the summer of 2016, the big 92 was dead ahead, and I figured maybe it was about time to think about changing directions, so I put Trailside on the market and sold it to John and Cydney Long. It had been a seesaw ride from day-one when I first stepped foot on the place. I don't see how the next trip could be any more interesting than the first, but with the luck of the draw, a person never knows for sure. There might even be enough material in there to write another book about it. We'll just have to wait and see.

Incidentally, John just happened to be the son of the girl I had a crush on in the third grade, Mary Dixon, which sort of proves that what goes around comes around. Sometimes it just takes a while.

INDEX